a design for news

a design for news

A newspaper design manual including/

- ☐ The design concept/
- ☐ The design revolution/
- ☐ One newspaper's redesign/
- ☐ American newspaper design/1980/

**Principles of design and layout rules
of the Minneapolis Tribune/**

Text/Wallace Allen
Associate Editor

Design/Michael Carroll
Design Director

Published by the Minneapolis Tribune
Minneapolis Star and Tribune Company
425 Portland Av. Minneapolis/Minn./55488

First printing/

Library of Congress Cataloging in Publication Data

Allen, Wallace, 1919-
A design for news.

Subtitle: A newspaper design manual including the design concept, the design revolution, one newspaper's redesign, American newspaper design, 1980, and principles of the design and layout rules of the Minneapolis Tribune

1. Newspaper layout and typography—handbook, manuals etc.I. Carroll, Michael, 1946-
II. Title.

Z253.5.A44	686.2'252	81-2022
		AACR2

ISBN/0-932272-04-5

Acknowledgments/

The author thanks the following publishers who granted permission for use of excerpts from their books:

The MIT Press: Chermayeff, Ivan, and others, **The Design Necessity**. Cambridge, Mass., Copyright 1973 by the Massachusetts Institute of Technology.

Dover Publications, Inc.: Grillo, Paul Jacques, **Form, Function and Design**. New York, N.Y., 1975, c. 1960. Copyright 1960 by Paul Theobold and Company.

Oxford University Press, Inc.: Neutra, Richard Joseph, **Survival Through Design**. New York, N.Y., Copyright 1954.

Gius. Laterza & Figli: Munari, Bruno, **Design as Art**, Bari, Italy. Translated by Patrick Creagh. Copyright Bruno Munari, 1966. Translation copyright Patrick Creagh, 1971. Penguin Books, London, 1971.

Studio Vista: Rand, Paul, **Thoughts on Design, London**. A Studio Vista Van Nostrand Reinhold art paperback, New York, 1970.

An excerpt is used from The Shape of Things, Noel Carrington, Nicholson & Watson, London, 1939.

Thanks also to the editors and publishers of the following publications for granting permission for use of quotations in this manual:

The Bulletin, American Society of Newspaper Editors, 1350 Sullivan Trail, Box 551, Easton, Pa. 18042.

Editor & Publisher, 575 Lexington Av., New York, N.Y. 10022.

DESIGN, the journal of the Society of Newspaper Designers, c/o Richard Curtis, The News American, P.O. Box 1795, 301 East Lombard St., Baltimore, Md. 21203.

Print, 355 Lexington Av., New York, N.Y. 10017.

Byline, a journalism quarterly produced by students at Northwestern University's Medill School of Journalism, 1845 Sheridan Rd., Evanston, Ill. 60201.

newspaper design notebook, Source Publications, Inc., 426 Fairoaks Circle, Chapel Hill, N.C. 27514.

Washington Journalism Review, 2233 Wisconsin Av. N.W., Washington, D. C. 20007.

Thanks also to these persons or firms who granted permission for use of materials or helped in other ways:

Mrs. W. L. White, The Emporia Gazette, 517 Merchant St., Emporia, Kan. 66801, for permission to use parts of W. L. White's **Redesigning for Readability**, published in Seminar Quarterly, September 1969.

Arthur W. Schultz, chairman, Foote, Cone & Belding, 401 North Michigan Av., Chicago, Ill. 60611, for use of newspaper front-page designs created under supervision of Dan Kelly.

Donald M. Anderson, author of **Elements of Design**, copyright 1980 by Donald M. Anderson. Holt, Rinehart & Winston, 383 Madison Av., New York, N.Y. 10017, 1961.

Jack Z. Sissors, The Medill School of Journalism, Northwestern University, Evanston, Ill. 60201, for excerpts from the Inland Bulletin and from correspondence with him.

Muriel Underwood, Chicago Society of Typographical Arts archivist and historian, for her thorough and patient research on James T. Mangan.

Peter Palazzo, Palazzo & Associates, 155 East 55th St., New York, N.Y. 10022, for furnishing page photocopies of the New York Herald Tribune.

Gladys W. Allen, who spent hours on library research.

The Pillsbury Company, for permission to reproduce four advertisements.

The Associated Press for use of two AP news graphics.

Material for the chapter on American newspapers in the 1980s was furnished by editors and design directors of those newspapers. For this we thank:

Paul Janensch and **Johnny Maupin**, The Courier-Journal, The Louisville Times, 525 West Broadway, Louisville, Ky. 40202.

James A. Geladas, Telegraph Herald, P.O. Box 688, Dubuque, Iowa 52001.

George Beveridge, The Washington Star, 225 Virginia Av. S.E., Washington, D.C. 20061.

J. Ford Huffman, Times-Union, 55 Exchange St., Rochester, N.Y. 14614.

Robert J. Haiman, St. Petersburg Times, P.O. Box 1121, St. Petersburg, Fla. 33731.

David B. Gray, The Providence Journal-Bulletin, 75 Fountain St., Providence, R.I. 02902.

Louis Silverstein, The New York Times, 229 West 43rd St., New York, N.Y. 10036.

Marty Petty, The Kansas City Star, The Kansas City Times, 1729 Grand Av., Kansas City, Mo. 64108.

Robert Lockwood, The Morning Call, Sixth and Linden Sts., Box 1260, Allentown, Pa. 18105.

Ed Orloff, San Francisco Examiner, 110 Fifth St., San Francisco, Calif. 94103.

Acknowledgments would not be complete without mention of Minneapolis Tribune colleagues who have given help and advice along the way:

Among them are Bruce Adomeit, Charles W. Bailey, Mary Joan Berg, Charlotte Koski, Richard Parker, Larry Pearson, Richard C. Reid, Steven Ronald and James Whalen.

Special thanks must go to Frank Ariss, originator of the Tribune's design, who read the copy and offered encouragement and helpful suggestions.

Contents/

Design/
Why this book
was produced

This book was planned as a manual for the people who design and lay out the pages of the Minneapolis Tribune.

It soon became much more than that.

The Tribune was redesigned in 1971, a pioneer among the many newspapers that have taken on a new and modern look over the last dozen years. But not until now have the principles of Tribune design and layout been gathered in one volume.

That is the practical purpose of this book. But we soon realized that a manual in itself was not enough. We had questions about the nature of design.

What, really, does design mean? What is its function, its place in everyday life, its meaning for a newspaper?

We decided to explore the design concept briefly, look at the newspaper design revolution of the 1970s and tell the story of the Tribune's redesign — all important and interesting subjects in themselves, and, we thought, relevant background to statement of Tribune design principles and rules of layout.

We thought, too, that it would be interesting to show how some American newspapers looked at the start of the 1970s, and to tell how they got that way. So an editor who was much involved in the redesign of the Tribune in 1971 and a designer who played a part in that redesign searched the files for the memos, scratched their heads, talked, read, did research and put it all on the record.

Basic to all of this is our conviction that some understanding of the process and purpose of design is helpful to the journalist who lays out newspaper pages.

The editor and the layout person can't hope to acquire all the knowledge and understanding of the trained designer, nor is it often easy for the designer to poke into the editorial mind. But the more each knows of the other's field, the better they will work together and the more they will achieve.

This book is dedicated to the concept that news in printed form is vital to the people's welfare. It is offered with the thought that, while content is certainly a newspaper's major concern, design is a vital factor in making news available to and acceptable by the public.

Wallace Allen
Michael Carroll

February / 1981

Chapter

1/

Design/

Does anyone know what it really is?

Design/
Does anyone know what it really is?

Design, the act of putting constructs in an order, or disorder, seems to be human destiny. It seems to be the way into trouble and it may be the way out.

Richard Neutra
Survival through design

What is design?

It's human destiny. A technique. A science. Truth. Everybody's business. A union of beauty and utility. A means of communication. An attitude. A necessity of life. A way to unite form and performance.

Writers have used words like these to describe design. Architects, graphics experts, advertising designers, they have written about it in eloquent and even reverential terms.

Ask some designers what design is and they look puzzled at first, and then disbelieving. Why is a definition needed? They have absorbed design theory without needing to put it into words.

Design — as a concept — is not easily defined. It is elusive and illusory, difficult and confusing. And the literature of design, to the layman, may be both baffling and enlightening.

Baffling — because you find dozens of differing definitions of design and hundreds of tantalizing hints of its essence. You react like the designer to whom you put the question. You wonder if design can be — or even should be — defined.

Enlightening — because you learn how pervasive a natural and artificial factor design has been in men's lives since the beginning of time. Design is, in a word, essential.

Design is easily defined by some who

practice and write about it; they see practicality as its basic element. For them, design is a matter of arranging elements or components — whatever their nature — so they work well together or convey a clear message.

For others, design is a philosophical concept, a state of mind, an approach to life, something that is felt, not taught. It is not so easily defined.

There are many questions and considerations: The relation of form to function, the importance of the esthetic component, the role of truth and beauty, the moral dilemma posed by the fine design of objects with destructive functions, the difference between good and bad design, the question of taste, the social preferences of an era and their influence on design.

Designers dwell on these questions which, with hints of the answers, should be part of the background and thinking of anyone having to do with design. Newspaper editors and those who lay out news pages are among these people.

Designer Paul Rand gives us the message:

An erroneous conception of the graphic designer's function is to imagine that in order to produce a 'good layout' all he need do is make a pleasing arrangement of miscellaneous elements. At best, this procedure involves the time-consuming uncertainties of trial and error, and at worst, an indifference to plan, order or discipline.

For the news editor who lays out pages, design must be more than "a pleasing arrangement of miscellaneous elements" on a page. To do the job well, the editor must take both the practical and the philosophical approach.

Design involves principles and

rules, to be sure, but it can't be reduced to them because it demands original thought, the essential element no matter what the form.

At its best, design helps to establish clarity, order, efficiency and beauty. Used carelessly and without thought, it may produce opaqueness, disorder and ugliness. As Richard Neutra noted, design may mean order or disorder. Either may be deliberately or accidentally designed.

Newspaper design is affected by all these considerations. To design well — to lay out pages well — the journalist should have at least an inkling of the concept of design and some knowledge of its historical and social importance.

The conceptual and historical clues are found in the writings and thoughts of designers from Plato to Walter Gropius, who said it is up to the designer "to breathe a soul into the dead product of the machine."

In 1938 James T. Mangan, a Chicago advertising executive, distributed a statement about design to members and friends of the Society of Typographic Arts of Chicago. This is part of what he wrote:

A new word has lately crept into our business language — the word is DESIGN.

Design is neither your idea, my idea, nor anyone else's idea. Like the weather, it is nobody's property and yet everybody's property. Design would exist today, even if you or I didn't, for it doesn't depend on either of us for its meaning.

Design is a technique for accomplishing an end. If the work is true design, a jury of twenty competent designers can get together and, without a single dissenting vote, decide that the specimen examined is design.

The ability to recognize and pronounce on design is a proven fact. Yet if you asked the twenty designers on the jury just how they went about deciding on design, their answers wouldn't help you much. If you asked them to state the rules for producing design, they would be unable to answer you.

But don't condemn design because designers are not articulate. A poet, an artist, a mechanic, a good ball player, even, cannot tell you how he "does it."

The general purpose of design: to get the point of the whole thing — the message, the idea, the propaganda — across to the largest number of people in the shortest space of time. In effect — "design works."

Design is a technique, a science, and as such is artificial; but its essence is TRUTH and in appearance and content all design must be natural. Design doesn't seek to be beautiful for beauty's sake, but becomes beautiful when correctly executed. Such beauty is natural beauty, pleasing and holding a whole world of readers. Good design, therefore, can house no affectation, no phoniness, no unnecessary trappings or unnatural impedimenta. It must always ring true.

Design is the creation of a designer. A designer is an artist, engineer, craftsman, or scientist who is acquainted with the basic formality of design and can command its elements to work for him.

Mangan's statement — remember that it was made more than forty years ago — is comprehensive and thoughtful. It expresses some basic concepts of the nature of design and offers some practical hints for its use.

Mangan wrote, of course, about man-

A designer is a planner with an esthetic sense. Certain industrial products depend . . . on him for their success. Nearly always the shape of a thing, be it a typewriter, a pair of binoculars, an armchair, a ventilator, a saucepan or a refrigerator, will have an important effect on sales: the better designed it is, the more it will sell.

Bruno Munari
Design as art

made design. But before man's designs there were nature's — some of them illustrated in this chapter — from the varying forms of snowflakes to the natural patterns of land eroded by wind and water.

Design is, first of all, a natural phenomenon that determines the shape and order of animate things in a way that aids or makes possible their natural functions. In the case of inanimate objects, design leaves a trail that has a recognizable form.

Whether form or function comes first could be long debated, but form and function cannot be separated. It's sufficient to say here that natural design either springs from or serves function. And nature's designs, like man's, may be either beautiful or ugly.

Nature provides the design for the tree that sends roots into the earth to gather water and branches with leaves high into the sky to catch sunlight. Nature's processes produce the concentric rings of age that appear in the cross section of the tree trunk.

Nature designed the anteater with its long snout to help it scoop up insects for food.

In each case, form allows function and function is aided by form.

Design is produced, too, through nature's continuing processes. There's design in the rocks that carry strata of minerals gathered during their lifetime. And there's design in man, seen by some as the ultimate in form and function.

. . .drawing may be taught by tutors; but design only by heaven.

John Ruskin

From the very beginning man went to nature for design inspiration — as man still does.

Paul Jacques Grillo tells how the Greeks derived the curve of the Doric capital from the curve of the common sea urchin; that's what makes it different from the true curve. Note, too, the design similarity between the Ionic capital and the swirls of the seashell.

Grillo tells, too, how designers of airplanes watched butterflies and dragonflies in flight, and designers looking for speed in vehicles noted the fast movements of the sharks, rays and squid in the ocean depths.

Compare the designs of the airplane and the butterfly, and the ray and the delta-wing bomber, and note the dramatic similarities.

The patterns and textures of nature as well as nature's forms appear in man's designs. Mangan saw in nature the wellspring of design and in design the reflected truth and beauty of nature.

The design plans of man may, of course, not all be good, or may go askew. Donald M. Anderson wrote in "The Elements of Design":

"Now it is clear that design and the public good may not be in perfect alignment . . . The process of design is . . . pragmatic; methods effective in achieving the preconceived end are used. Occasionally design stems

---

Always design a thing considering it in its larger context — a chair in a room, a room in a house, a house in an environment, an environment in a city plan.

Eliel Saarinen
Finnish architect

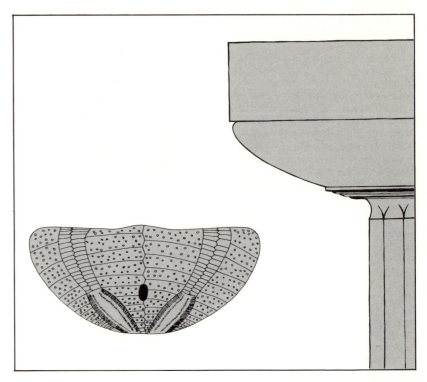

from potentially harmful practices.''

Consider, for instance, says Anderson, the political campaign whose design may be based on false premises. Or the tattooed man, whose skin displays colorful designs but who may develop blood poisoning from the needle. Or, newspaper designers might add, the newspaper designed to sensationalize the news.

As contemporary writers see it, design is necessary because things must be sorted out, organized and made understandable in an age of increasing complexity. Design can make order out of chaos. Or design, if it is bad, can create chaos.

''Design is necessary because it serves human needs,'' say the authors of ''The Design Necessity.'' ''That is its only excuse for being. As human needs have become more complicated, and human beings more numerous, the design necessity has become more intense.''

And, they say, ''design is an urgent requirement, not a cosmetic addition . . . design can save money . . . design can save time . . . design enhances communication between people . . . design simplifies use, simplifies manufacture, simplifies maintenance.''

Carrying the theory of practicality further, the authors say that ''everything that is made by men to serve human needs has to be designed. When we refer to the architect of a foreign policy program or the designer of a scientific experiment, we acknowledge that

A chair is a very difficult object (to design). A skyscraper is almost easier. That is why Chippendale is famous.

Ludwig Mies van der Rohe

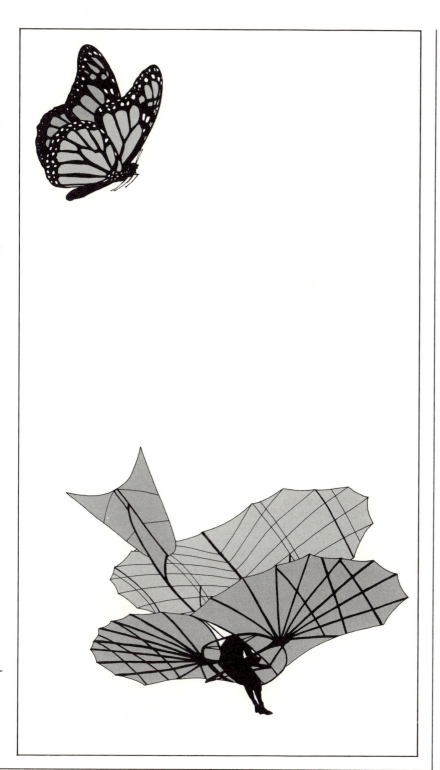

programs and experiments are as designed as buildings, posters, and traffic circles."

Anderson writes: "The idea — the definition of the problem — the thinking — the planning — the rejections — the correlation of parts: this is the process of creation called design. A political campaign is designed to elect a candidate as a knife is designed to cut bread."

Frank Ariss, who redesigned the Minneapolis Tribune, says that although there may be no rules, there is an order to producing design. Start with questions, he suggests: What are you trying to say and to whom? If enough questions are asked, he says, the design will occur as the answers are sorted out. In other words, design is more a **process** than a plan.

In nature, design has a purpose, open for everyone to see if not explain. Man's designs usually are purposeful — the means carefully planned to bring about the desired effect, whether commercial or esthetic. Man's designs may be used to sell a product — or to satisfy the human longing for beauty.

They are most successful if they are esthetically pleasing and have a basis in truth. If they are deceptive, they deny nature's imperative and court disaster.

Paul Rand sees form and function as inseparable and essential to the production of esthetic worth — and

---

Knowledge of the shape of words and the possibilities those offer for communication can be very useful to the graphic designer.

Bruno Munari
Design as Art

incidentally offers good advice to editors who deal with design and designers:

"That the separation of form and function, of concept and execution, is not likely to produce objects of esthetic value has been repeatedly demonstrated . . . Similarly, it has been shown that the system which regards esthetics as irrelevant, which separates the artist from his product, which fragments the work of the individual, which creates by committee, and which makes mincemeat of the creative process will, in the long run, diminish not only the product but the maker as well."

"Ideally," wrote Rand, "beauty and utility are mutually generative" — another idea for editors to think about.

But some see the dark side of design. Not only may it be used to create disorder, if that is the designer's purpose, but to create objects of

destruction whose efficiency is dependent upon meticulous design.

Noel Carrington makes the point:

Some have contended that any object which fulfills its function to perfection will necessarily be beautiful to look at. I do not think that this will bear very close examination, and it is one of those rather dangerous cliches that can do quite a lot of harm. For instance, there are machines that are masterpieces of their kind; but I do not think anyone but their makers finds them very beautiful.

Beauty, it seems, is in the eye of the beholder. To some the death-dealing army tank or the high-flying swept-wing bomber may have the same terrible beauty as the man-eating shark. Form and function for the tank, the bomber and the shark are inseparable; their design may be perfect for serving their function.

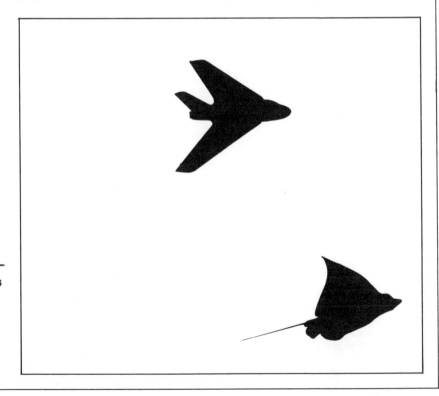

As design changes from year to year and age to age, it leaves a record of man's customs, living habits, thoughts and achievements. Design writes and reflects social history.

Form may change, but seldom does function. The Gothic cathedral and the Cape Cod church have different forms but their function is similar. The robes of the Renaissance prince are far different from the modern businessman's gray flannel suit, but their function is the same.

The first edition of the Minneapolis Tribune bears little resemblance to the Tribune of today, but the purpose and function of each are the same.

Grillo brings design down to earth:

Design is everybody's business: We live in it, we eat in it, we pray and play in it . . . Design is not the product of an intelligentsia. It is everybody's business, and whenever design loses contact with the public it is on the losing end . . . Design is an end in itself. It is the achievement of man's logic in adapting his creations to his natural environment and way of life.

And so it goes — and could go on and on — as designers talk about their craft. There are no easy answers to the questions about design. But the would-be designer — or the person who lays out newspaper pages — can benefit from thinking and learning

about design, what it means and how it may be used.

The last word here goes back a long way in history. Keep in mind what today's design experts have said about form and function and compare what Plato wrote in the fourth century B.C.:

Are not the excellence, beauty and correctness of every manufactured article, or living creature, or action, to be tried only by reference to the purpose intended in their construction, or in their natural constitution?

The aim of design is to bring form and performance into correspondence, not to substitute one for the other . . . Everything has to have some look. All other things being equal, beauty and ugliness carry the same price tag.

The Design Necessity

Chapter

2/

Design/

What does it mean to newspapers?

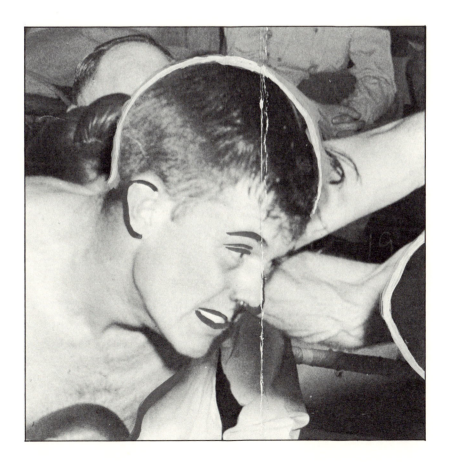

Design/
What does it mean to newspapers?

American newspapers are atrocities in their presentation of news. Other industries have moved forward to meet the times but our newspapers here, as well as those in other countries, are a hundred years behind.

Frank Ariss
Designer, 1974

For decades the design of most American newspapers was no design. The product of many minds, the typical American newspaper was a hodgepodge of conflicting typographic styles.

Newspaper artists — not designers — concocted headings for columns, all of them in different styles. They abused photos with airbrushes, mutilated them with mortises and desecrated them with overprinted type.

With beautifully designed type at hand, editors sent capital letters screaming across busy pages on which contrasting typefaces went to war. Seeking variety, editors set type in innumerable measures, adding to the nightmare of unreadability.

A profusion of rules — black, Benday, decorative — contributed to the confusion. Nameplates clung to Old English type, because that was the time-honored style.

Public taste was not offended by such typographical chaos; there was little sign of revolt. It is hard to see today why the virtues of order and simplicity did not dawn sooner in the editorial mind. After all, designers in other fields were setting the example.

The magazines of the 1950s

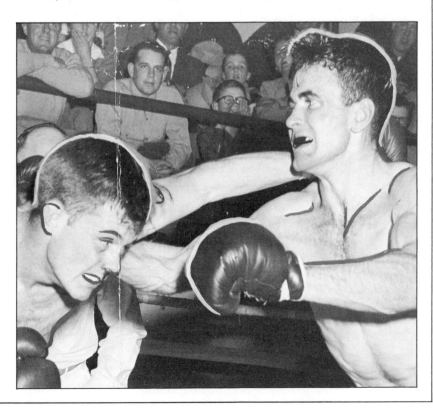

reflected a revolution in design. Posters, many of them beautifully designed, were a popular art form in the 1960s. Advertising design changed drastically to accomplish its end — the selling of a product.

The objective of this concentration on design was effective communication of information and messages. The guiding principle was presentation of information in its simplest, clearest, most dramatic form.

Newspapers were surrounded by the evidence. Truly astonishing changes were occurring in graphic design, and the changes were being embraced by the public. In products used every day, form and packaging persuasive to buying were becoming more and more important — and form was more and more closely related to function.

We were living in designed houses, driving designed cars, wearing designed clothes, playing designed games, flying in designed planes, reading designed books, wearing designed eyeglasses, buying

Much of what's new in newspaper design has to do with opening our minds to what used to be exclusively magazine ideas. It starts with more aggressive ideas about editing. We don't sit back so much, waiting for whatever happens to come across our desks. Even in business and sports we don't do this. Instead, we do a lot more creative thinking in advance and plan ahead what we want to cover and how we want to package it.

Louis Silverstein
Assistant managing editor,
The New York Times,
in **The Bulletin**, American Society
of Newspaper Editors, November
1979

1950

1960

1970

1980

Advertising styles changed over the years.

groceries in designed packages, flocking to get designed hair styles.

Design was used as a major selling device, its importance drilled into us. Design was, as Grillo said, everybody's business.

But newspapers — the major purveyors of information — retained their archaic forms, and few editors thought about their appearance, even in the midst of a rapidly changing society.

Light began to dawn in the 1960s. Change was in the air and its breath began to touch newspapers, pushed by societal ferment and the economic facts of publishers' lives.

Challenged by falling circulations and realizing finally that their newspapers were not communicating well, editors and publishers discovered design.

A pioneer was the New York Herald Tribune, which sought economic revival through redesign. In the early 1960s the Herald Tribune adopted a design that would be striking today.

Peter Palazzo, the Herald Tribune's designer, called it "a simple format . . . a framework for illustration . . . When I came in, they were in such bad shape, they said, 'What the hell; what have we got to lose?' There was absolutely nothing at stake."

The Herald Tribune gained readership and ad linage after the redesign, Palazzo said, but it could not survive New York's jungle of journalism.

Here and there newspapers began to hire design firms to transform the image of the front page. Designers began to appear in newsrooms. The face of the American newspaper began to change.

Proponents of design were spreading the word.

Jack Z. Sissors, graphic arts consultant and associate professor

Front page followed Peter Palazzo design, 1963.

of journalism at the Medill School of Journalism at Northwestern University, told a conference of the Inland Newspaper Association in 1969:

"This new concept (total design) is needed because American newspapers do not reflect the contemporary scene. Their designs tend to be a hindrance rather than an aid to communication.

"As I study newspapers today, all that I see are fundamentally the same basic designs that were used years ago. Most newspaper designs have not changed very much, even though everything around the newspaper is changing.

" . . . if you look at other aspects of modern life, such as architecture, furniture, automobiles, appliances, you see products which have been redesigned to reflect the contemporary scene. They not only function better than they did before, but they are designed to reflect modern life."

And Phillip Ritzenberg, design editor of the New York News, wrote in the September / October 1971 issue of Print:

" . . . virtually the entire industry clings to archaic graphic forms. While newspaper journalism continues to change and grow, the average newspaper itself still resembles a bulletin board hung with shreds of

Design is not merely a cosmetic gimmick. It's a means of reflecting a newspaper's personality. It's also a way to market a newspaper.

Paul Back
Director of design, Newsday,
in **DESIGN**, NO. 1, March, 1980

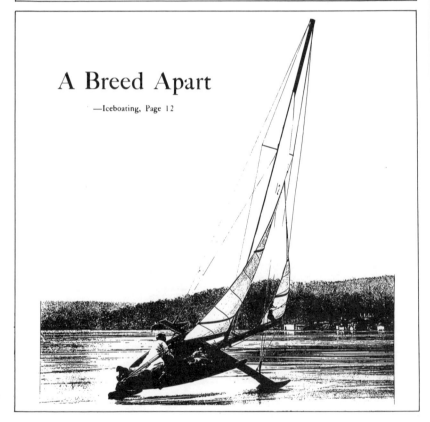

1965

information, disorder passing for spontaneity, stridency passing for immediacy.

"Newspapermen — and designers — have long understood disorganization and ugliness as an acceptable newspaper form. That form, unfortunately, fails to reflect the reality that even the most unsophisticated reader has been affected by a design environment in which practically nothing of quality remains undesigned. An exciting vehicle for journalism must be based on good design to hold on to a generation of viewers in an increasingly visual age."

As the 1980s started, some editors still asked the old questions: Why bother so much with design? Isn't content more important, and doesn't that give us enough trouble?

Of course content is more important. But content, no matter how significant or informative, is of little use if it is not **read** — and design is one way to try to improve readership.

The main purpose of newspaper design is, of course, to improve communication — to get more people to read more of the newspaper.

In the well-designed newspaper, contents are organized to help the reader and presented in simple, clear, readable form. First of all, the newspaper must **look inviting** to the reader. Then it must **help him read**.

The well-designed newspaper has a continuity of design style — in type, pictures, illustrations, maps, column headings, all graphic devices.

Clean type and clean graphics are basically simple. The well-designed newspaper bars the gimmickry of blaring headlines, contrasting headline types, kickers on headlines, odd-measure type, indented pictures and labels, doglegs of type, odd-measure leads.

Typographical chaos in the "old" Minneapolis Tribune.

The well-designed newspaper is fresh and attractive to the reader. Modular design — or block makeup — is basic. Stories are laid out in squares or rectangles. A mixture of horizontal and vertical headlines breaks up a potentially monotonous blocky effect.

Modular design is a challenge to editors who lay out pages. Its simplicity dictates awareness of the principles of design, without which pages will be dull or unattractive.

Simple design — always the most appealing — has an additional practical advantage: It is adaptable to production of computerized type and to full-page layout systems.

There's a danger here, however. As electronic miracles make use of type more flexible, the temptation to gimmickry increases. It's altogether too easy to produce type that flows around the edges of a picture cutout, for instance.

Such experiments, while visually

The task of managers should be to liberate people from the limits of structure. To do this requires a management style not often practiced in newspapers. That style allows others to participate in the decision-making process. Editors, photographers, reporters and designers all have a personal stake in the newspaper and its impact on the society it serves. Each must share in the decision-making process, from the inception of the story to its presentation on the page . . . Design is not a profession; it's an attitude, the attitude of the planner.

Robert Lockwood
Art director, The Morning Call, Allentown, Pa., in **DESIGN**, No. 1, March, 1980

LOUISVILLE Times

SATURDAY EVENING   JUNE 1, 1974 / 10¢

NEWS	SCENE	SPORTS
The news in brief...page A2	The world of Pucci...page 3	Tennis and tremors...page A7
More veteran benefits...page A2	How about this design?...page 5	Bench and the Reds roll...page A7
Artificial blood...page A2	Earning money at home...page 6	Baseball on a tightrope...page A8

Secretary of State Henry Kissinger brought back good news from his 34-day Middle East peace mission. Yesterday he spoke with President Nixon in the White House Rose Garden about the talks.

Prisoners are exchanged by Israel and Syria in the 'first stage of the end of the war'

Associated Press

Joyous crowds in Damascus and Tel Aviv greeted the first returning prisoners of war today as Israel and Syria began the exchange of wounded POWs promised in their disengagement pact.

The prisoners had been captured in last October's war.

Red Cross medical planes left the two cities minutes apart this morning carrying a total of 38 repatriated prisoners, some legless or in casts.

An hour later, 12 wounded Israeli soldiers stepped off the chartered Fokker Friendship plane at Ben-Gurion airport near Tel Aviv. They were greeted with kisses, tears and flowers from miniskirted women soldiers.

At about the same time 25 Syrians and

one Moroccan arrived to a wildly emotional welcome in Damascus. Red-bereted military police forced a crowd of hundreds from the plane to enable the POWs to disembark.

Women wailed and men cheered in Damascus as the plane taxied to a halt. But a hush fell over the crowd as the first wounded man was carried out by stretcher. Legless, he sat rigidly upright, his right hand cocked in a military salute.

"Legs are nothing. We are ready to give our souls . . ." he shouted. Cheers broke out, drowning his words.

He then insisted on being lifted from his stretcher and placed on the ground so he could bend down to kiss the soil.

Prime Minister Golda Meir, Defense Minister Moshe Dayan and Chief of Staff

Lt. Gen Mordechai Gur were among the hundreds who greeted the returning Israelis.

"This is the first stage of the end of the war," said Dayan as the men, some in bandages and in casts, boarded ambulances for a brief drive to Tel Hashomer hospital.

He pledged that Israeli troops would not budge from the Syrian front "until all our prisoners are back."

The scenes of joy contrasted sharply with the earlier POW departures from the airports.

In Damascus newsmen were barred from the airport as the Israelis were led

See FIRST SYRIAN
Back page, col. 4, this section

Trains that once flew now crawl along the tracks

By BOB KASPER
Louisville Times Staff Writer

When railroad minstrels sing about today's Chicago-to-Louisville passenger train, they won't use lively words like "Cannonball," "Special" or "Zephyr." They'll choose slow, heavy, bluesy words.

For the most notable characteristic about this Amtrak train — known as The Floridian because one of its terminal points is Miami — is that when it rolls between Chicago and here, it is one of the slowest trains in the United States.

"When it gets past Louisville, it flies. But in Indiana, it just shuffles," a Floridian passenger said recently.

Staff Photo by KEITH WILLIAMS

It's a long, slow ride from Chicago to Louisville. Mrs. Etta Faber, of Chicago, and fellow Floridian passengers relied on reading and sleeping to help pass the time on a train that usually averages only 25-30 m.p.h.

Last Saturday, for instance, the train lumbered into Chicago at 10 a.m., exactly 12 hours after it left Louisville. That is an average speed of 25 miles per hour for the 300-mile trip.

Tuesday morning it edged into Louisville's Union Station in slightly better time. On this journey the train averaged 29 m.p.h. and rolled to a stop at 7 a.m., 10 1/2 hours after leaving Chicago.

At 55 m.p.h., a car can travel from Louisville to Chicago in slightly less than 6 hours.

Buses make the trip in 7 hours and jets take less than an hour, airport to airport.

"This train is a disgrace," complained a gray-haired woman as the train chugged

through the Indiana dawn. "It is so slow . . . and the rough ride . . . I couldn't sleep last night."

"I agree," replied the porter receiving the brunt of the woman's anger.

"It is those Penn Central tracks," the porter continued. "They fixed some of the worst ones last week, but the Penn Central is bankrupt."

In a nutshell, that is the main problem with the train. From Chicago to Louisville, The Floridian rides on Penn Central track. Since 1970, when the railroad petitioned for bankruptcy, its track

See TRAINS
Page A6, col. 1

Drinking on credit doesn't go down well with the state

By LES WHITELEY
Louisville Times Staff Writer

Walk into your neighborhood tavern, where you are a regular patron, ask the bartender to let you have a drink on credit and he's likely to reply, "Sorry, but I'm not allowed to sell liquor on credit. You've got to pay cash."

But walk into a hotel, motel, restaurant or large nightclub, where you've never been before, hand the waitress a credit card to cover your drinks and she probably won't bat an eyelash.

The latter, according to the state Alcoholic Beverage Control (ABC) Board, is as unlawful as the former.

State law (KRS 244.300) is very explicit on the subject, said Porter Collier,

field director for the ABC in Frankfort. The law prohibits any retailer from selling liquor on credit, he said.

The only exception to the no-credit rule, Collier said, is the extension of "reasonable" credit by private clubs to their members and hotels to their registered guests.

Yet a large number of the liquor-by-the-drink establishments in Jefferson County — particularly restaurants, motels, hotels and large nightclubs — routinely accept credit cards as payment for drinks, either with meals or separately. In fact, some issue their own credit cards, which may be used to purchase meals and/or drinks.

Times reporters visited 12 establishments on a recent weekend and found only three that didn't accept credit cards. They were Mills Lounge, 2400 W. Broadway; the Pirates' Cove Lounge in Ben Air Manor shopping center, and Sahara Club, 3606 Bardstown Road.

Drinks were charged on major credit cards at Hasenour's, 1028 Barret Ave.; Churchill Inn, 4444 Dixie Highway; the Toy Tiger Lounge, Goldsmith Lane and Bardstown Road; the Patio Lounge, The Mall; the D-Mare Lounge, the Galt House, 104 N. Fourth St.; the Ramada Inn,

See DRINKING
Back page, col. 1, this section

Bluegrass festival brings downhome music to downtown

By ROB KASPER
Louisville Times Staff Writer

"Downhome" moved downtown yesterday as the Bluegrass Music Festival fiddled through its first day.

"When people hear 'downhome' it puts them in a relaxed mood . . . genuine, sincere, kinda folksie," said Buck White, who together with his two daughters, Sharon and Cheryl, and son-in-law Jack Hicks, played some soft and some sassy tunes on the River City Mall.

Last night a crowd tapped its feet on the Riverfront Plaza concrete to tunes provided by Bill Monroe and other bluegrass groups.

The festival, sponsored by Louisville Central Area, Inc., and Philip Morris, Inc., will be held today and tomorrow rain or shine, officials said.

The festival, in its second year, continues through tomorrow today. The 11 a.m. performance today was to be held on the River City Mall. The 7 p.m. show today and the 2 p.m. and 7 p.m. shows tomorrow will be held on the Riverfront Plaza.

Yesterday's lunch-time performance drew about 1,000 listeners. But the foot-stompin' feeling that White and others say is characteristic of bluegrass music was slow-starting.

For a while the people in the audience acted as though they were in an elevator —looking straight ahead, not talking to anyone around them, ignoring pleas of the Highwood Stringband to dance.

Then Charles B. Fort, a 51-year-old fork-lift operator at Louisville's Anaconda Aluminum Co., jumped up in dance.

"I was just down there by the stage . . . my feet were gigglin'. Finally they couldn't stand it anymore," he said.

After Fort broke the ice, a wave of warm feeling swept through the crowd, dissolving the armor that city folks wrap around their feelings, and limbering up stiff backbones.

Soon, about 15 people—an older woman in a pantsuit, college students, high school students, elementary school stu-

See FESTIVAL
Back page, col. 1, this section

Staff Photo by Paul Schuhmann

Kathleen Orndorff and her son Brennan, 4, snuggled down comfortably on the River City Mall pavement yesterday afternoon to hear the friendly sounds of bluegrass music. The Bluegrass Music Festival continues today and tomorrow on the River City Mall and the Riverfront Plaza.

Sunday may really be sun-day

If you were raised on country sunshine, tomorrow should remind you of Sundays at home.

The rain is supposed to end tonight and the sun is scheduled to be shining for tomorrow afternoon's bluegrass concert on the Riverfront Plaza.

Tonight's low temperature will be in the upper 50s and tomorrow's high will be in the middle 70s. Last night's low was 64.

Tonight will also feature a large bright moon, known among bluegrass folk as the blue moon of Kentucky.

Full weather data on Page A6.

Where to look

Comics	A11	Obituaries	A4
Names in the news	A22	Sports	A6

VOL. CLXXXI—No. 34   46 PAGES
Copyright © 1974, The Louisville Times
HOME

This page designed by Paul Back was voted best at Louisville seminar.

exciting, nearly always spell unreadability. The designer who understands the real purpose of design knows when to be adventurous. The uninitiated who experiment are taking a chance.

The well-designed newspaper is almost always the product of two minds — the designer's and the editor's. The two look at the newspaper with entirely different eyes. Both sets are needed.

The editor may be bound by tradition, but his mind must be open to change. The designer may want to do something totally new, but he must respect aspects of newspaper tradition. The resulting relationship may be one of creative tension. If editor and designer persevere, however, they may produce an attractive and exciting newspaper.

A graphics seminar sponsored by the Louisville Times in 1974 was typical of efforts now common among newspaper people who want to make newspapers look better.

The theme was sounded by Robert P. Clark, then executive editor of The Louisville Times and Courier-Journal: "We want to see if there are other ways to design newspapers so they'll be more exciting and more interesting."

And by Barry Bingham, Jr., editor and publisher of the Louisville newspapers: "Although our circulations are increasing, our percentage of penetration is going down, especially among the young. If this continues, we will become a geriatrics medium of communication. Design and content are terribly important. We should not be a fad sheet, full of gimmicks, but we should help the reader find the information that interests him."

The influence of the advertising world was dramatized at the conference. Far ahead of editors in realizing the importance of design, advertisers had been setting an example editors

Redesign of pages by Chicago advertising artists.

did not follow. But in 1971 Dan Kelly, a Chicago advertising executive, told his artists to redesign some newspaper front pages to "make them pleasing to the eye."

The results were some far-out pages that, Kelly told the seminar, brought overwhelming reaction from all over the world. The pages, he said, were "blue-sky" thinking, and ideally writers should have worked with the designers. But the interest generated by the experiment showed that more newspapers should consider redesign, he said.

Peter Palazzo told the seminar:

Newspaper makeup men and others responsible for the design of newspapers often are insensitive to what may be called GOOD DESIGN. . . The general public now appreciates attractiveness in all walks of life including their newspaper. Makeup men therefore ought to become more sensitive to what it is that distinguishes good from poor design. This SHOULD be learned by studying architecture, painting, interior decorating, etc., to enable themselves to appreciate design principles such as balance, contrast, proportion and unity.

Now, with the six-column paper, the old-fashioned makeup rules are outdated. The entire page is important, not just the top of a page. The objectives are not only to get the paper out, but to help readers read faster and more of what has been written. Furthermore, the paper should look attractive because beauty is a major cultural value in this country.

Jack Z. Sissors
The Medill School of Journalism
Northwestern University, July, 1980

Redesign of pages by Chicago advertising artists.

''We should think more in terms of a commitment to a new kind of journalism . . . and graphics, to me, is just a catalyst to this end. Graphics and editorialism have to work hand-in-hand to come up with the right answers. Only then can we put graphics in its proper relationship to journalism.''

During the 1970s, American newspapers rushed to redesign. Some editors saw the design movement becoming an end in itself, carrying a threat to consideration of content.

But so widespread was faith in redesign that failing newspapers took to it in hopes of gaining new life. Such last-minute solutions are doomed, of course, for design is no panacea. Design in the 1960s could not save the Herald Tribune; design in the 1970s could not save the Chicago Daily News, even though the Palazzo design was different and exciting.

Booming interest in design brought about founding of the Society of Newspaper Designers in 1978. The group's original 12 members grew to 160 by 1980, and its original informal newsletter became a slick publication, **DESIGN**, in March, 1980.

In early 1979 the **newspaper design notebook** was started by Roger F. Fidler, who wanted to draw together the latest information about graphics changes in newspapers.

The design movement was a tardy but significant revolution. Once editors and publishers realized the importance and practicality of design, the appearance and usefulness of American newspapers were immensely enhanced.

But the critics of American newspapers continued to point out that many newspapers were unaffected by or resisting the design movement and much still remained to be done.

A redesign for the Chicago Daily News, 1977.

Harold Evans, editor of the Sunday (London) Times and a student of newspaper design, was critical of American newspapers in an interview reported by Bill Ostendorf in the Winter, 1980, issue of Byline.

"There are no design graphics in American newspapers," Evans said. He described the newspapers as unassembled jigsaw puzzles and editors as people who couldn't quite put the pieces together.

"Design is not decoration or distraction," he said, "as many American editors tend to characterize it. It is part of the business of communication . . .

"The skills of the graphic designer, the artist and the photographer must be enlisted much earlier and in a different way. The general pattern is for words to be written by one set of journalists and passed on to another set of journalists who read them and only then start thinking about presentation. The earlier a newspaper thinks of communication as consisting of many elements, the better the newspaper's design, in the broadest sense, will be."

And further criticism:

"It's a pity that the greatest press in the world has presided over the complete bastardization of type and design . . .

"If you're going to be any good in this business, you ought to be interested in all these things. You ought to know how your paper is put together — all its parts. Any editor who doesn't know and understand how his paper works loses control over the final product. And any editor who doesn't know his typeface ought to be sacked."

Whatever the faults of American newspaper design or wherever its direction, the design concept will not and cannot be static. The 1970s brought astonishing changes and made up for years of lost time. But

Chicago Daily News / 1977

change will not stop and design must help meet the demands of the 1980s and the years beyond.

The pressures of newsprint shortages and the rising cost of paper and ink will bring about continuing changes in the way newspapers look. If the challenge is to put more news into less space, design can help do that.

Designers will have to preserve the readability and attractiveness of the newspaper while using different methods — perhaps smaller headline type, smaller but still dramatic pictures, smaller body type for features that will be read anyway.

The subject was dramatized in the fall of 1979 at a workshop sponsored by the Kansas City Star and Times. Michael J. Davies, editor of the Kansas City newspapers, put it this way in the February 1980 **Bulletin** of the American Society of Newspaper Editors:

"By and large, our newspapers do look better now. Most editors now care about good newspaper design. The shibboleth that any editor who is strong on design must be weak on content is dying. And, just possibly, the New Graphics did help circulation.

"But all that was in the 1970s. This is the 1980s and the old gods are about to be swept aside for the new. These deities will be much more demanding and far less forgiving.

"The reason for the revolution is twofold: the huge increases in the price of newsprint and periodic shortages. As cost pressures mount, more publishers will be asking editors to either use less space or to use what they have more efficiently . . .

"Will editors latch onto a new witch doctor and follow meekly in a pack, throwing out the tenets of the New Graphics and return to the dark, gray, forbidding makeup we once knew?"

This redesign of the Chicago Tribune was done by Tony Majeri, the newspaper's assistant art director, for the Kansas City seminar. It was the favorite of seminar participants.

"The hope is, of course, that we won't . . . If anything, we must create better, more eye-appealing designs even while living with a space crunch."

The newspaper whose present design is flexible enough to sustain change and whose designers and editors work together for change will be the newspaper that lasts and grows.

Whatever happens, the basic principles of newspaper design — simplicity, order, freshness — and the need for the newspaper, whatever its form, to reflect the style of its times and to satisfy its readers' needs should and must remain the guidelines.

A checklist for functionally integrated design/

Functionally integrated layouts are not created with magic words or rigid rules. They require organized and creative thinking developed through experience. And even with experience, not everyone has the visual sensitivity and judgment to become a good layout editor.

The following checklist is by no means all-inclusive. It is merely a tool for assessing layouts and should not be regarded as a newspaper design dogma.

If you can answer yes to all questions designated with an open ballot box and no to all those designated with a solid box, the page layout is probably well-designed.

Organization/

☐ Are readers guided smoothly and naturally through the page?

☐ Do all elements have a reason for being?

☐ Are all intended relationships between elements readily apparent?

☐ Are packages clearly defined?

■ Does the design call attention to itself instead of the content?

■ Does the page appear cluttered?

■ Do any type or art elements appear to be floating on the page?

■ Do any elements appear lost?

■ Are any editorial elements easily confused with advertising?

Readability/

■ Do any elements interrupt reading or cause confusion?

■ Are any legs of type perceptually truncated by art or sell lines (i.e. quotes, liftouts, etc.)?

■ Is the line width of any text too narrow or too wide for easy reading?

■ If text is set to follow the shape of adjacent art, is the story difficult to read?

■ Do any headlines or sell lines compete with headlines or sell lines in adjacent columns?

☐ Are the starting points for all stories easily determined?

Accuracy and clarity/

☐ Does the layout accurately communicate the relative importance of the stories contained on the page?

☐ Do the art elements accurately convey the tone and message of the stories?

☐ Are logos consistent and differentiated from headlines?

☐ Are the devices used in a layout appropriate for the content of the page?

Proportioning and sizing/

☐ Are all elements sized relative to their importance?

☐ Are the shapes and sizes of elements appropriate for the content of the elements?

☐ Do the shapes of elements add contrast and interest?

☐ Does the page have a dominant element or package of elements?

■ Does the shape of an element appear contrived or forced?

■ Do any logos or headlines seem out of proportion with the size of the story or column?

■ Are several elements similar in proportion and size?

Efficiency and consistency/

☐ Do all areas of white space appear as if they were planned? (When it appears as if something fell off the page, the white space is not functional.)

☐ Is spacing between elements controlled and consistent?

☐ Are areas of white space balanced on the page?

☐ Is all type, especially agate material, set at the most efficient measure for the information contained?

☐ Is the size of column gutters constant?

■ Does the number of elements and/or devices used in a package seem excessive?

Reprinted from **newspaper design notebook** Vol. 2/No. 1

Chapter

3/

Design/

How one
newspaper
transformed
itself

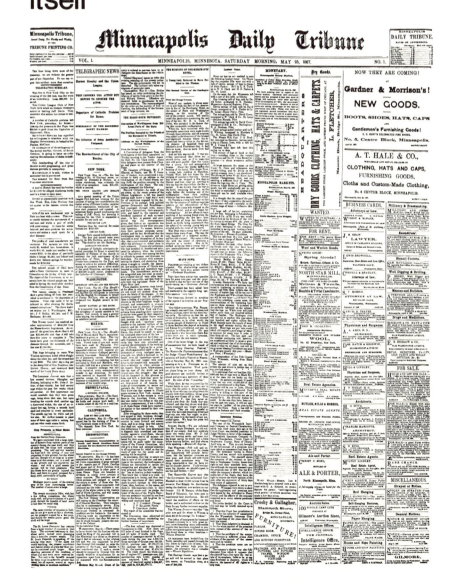

First Minneapolis Tribune/May 25, 1867

Design/
How one newspaper transformed itself

Well, we did it.

After more than three years of work, hundreds of design experiments, thousands of hours of talk and what must seem to our artists like millions of bugs, the Tribune blossomed out yesterday in its new design.

It all began late in 1967, when we asked Frank Ariss to come in to have a look at the newspaper. Actually, all we were after was a redesigned logo. It wasn't long before we were off on a complete redesign.

We're all dressed up and going places now. All we have to do is make our news content as snappy, readable, clear and up-to-date as the form in which it appears.

Minneapolis Tribune
Staff Memo April 6, 1971

Before April 1971 the Minneapolis Tribune looked like the typical American newspaper. Its editors were proud of it as a newspaper, but they didn't pay much attention to how it looked.

The Tribune then used two headline typefaces, Vogue and Futura. For Sunday advance section covers, headlines were set in Bodoni. The Tribune often embellished its headlines with underscored kickers and it went in heavily for "trick" headlines.

Its many standing features and columns were covered by label titles in differing styles, each created as need arose, according to the tastes of the artist.

Pictures were mortised and overprinted with type. If details were indistinct, the airbrush made outlines altogether too clear.

To break up body type, the first few words in every third or fourth paragraph were set in bold capital letters, preceded by a space equal to a line of type.

Tribune editors frequently used odd-measure type to set off stories from the standard, one-column size. This practice drove hot-metal printers wild, because the type had to be reset whenever an editor moved a story.

Two-column or even three-column type often was used for leads of stories on page one. Little attention was paid to squaring off type as long as headlines were sprinkled on the page at intervals considered pleasing to the eye.

Some attempt — but not enough — was made to package similar types of news.

Crowning the front page was the Old English logotype in "modernized" form — the result of artists' efforts over the years to make it look better. Crowding the logo in the page flag were bits of information set in various sizes of type.

Somehow the Tribune's editors got the idea that the logo didn't look right. It didn't seem up to date, they even said. And perhaps subconsciously they didn't like the clutter of type around it.

In any case, they decided to do something about it. Bower Hawthorne, then editor of the Tribune, took kindly to the idea of redesigning this most sacred part of a newspaper.

The search for a designer was not an easy task in those days. At the Minneapolis School of Art (now the Minneapolis College of Art and Design) in January, 1967, however, the editors found a visiting professor from London — Frank Ariss, then 29 years old.

Ariss was invited to come in to talk about redesigning the logo. The conversation was the start of a five-year relationship that would produce a complete redesign of the Tribune.

For one thing led to another and as the editors talked and listened to the persuasive Ariss they began to see how bad the Tribune looked, how it had too many typefaces, how it abused its type, how it lacked any sort of continuity of design style.

Hawthorne offered full enthusiasm and support, persuading the owners and publisher that Ariss, with the editors, should move ahead on redesign. His wise advice and patient direction continued during the project.

Ariss settled in at the Tribune, first as part-time and then as full-time consultant. Before he left the newspaper in March, 1972, he had not only completely redesigned the Tribune and produced a symbol for it, but created consistent designs for Tribune stationery, carriers' bags, the company trucks, the company airplane and even the president's office.

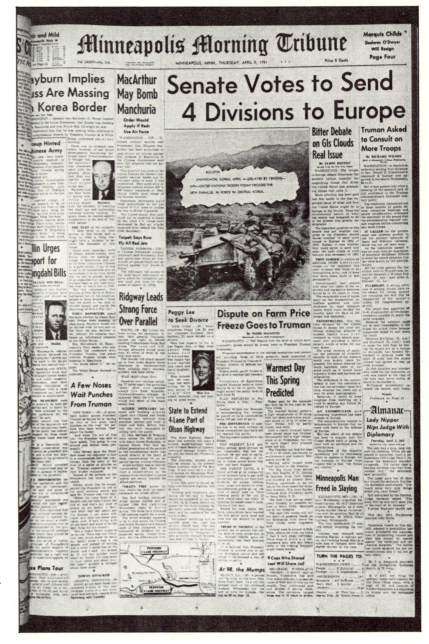

Ariss's ideas were shockingly unconventional to American editors. He ridiculed traditional ideas and reproached editors for their shortsighted reasoning: "That's the way we've always done it."

His methods were impressively thorough. He ranged through the building, talking with people in every department and learning the ways of printers, engravers, stereotypers and advertising and circulation people and the secrets of the promotion department. It didn't take him long to learn; he was unencumbered by American newspaper hangups and traditions.

All the while, Ariss was looking into the future. He saw that cold type first and then computerized production of type would soon supplant hot-metal methods. He built a "graphics engineering" concept into his redesign plans to ease production changes to come.

The image of the Tribune was important to Ariss, for he believed that the design should reflect and enhance that image. What was it the editors wanted the Tribune to be? Clean, attractive, honest, accurate, straightforward, friendly, they said. So be it in the design, Ariss replied, and complied with the requirements. Consideration of image is an essential part of planning for redesign.

Out of Ariss's self-schooling and foresight grew the plan for the "new" Tribune. His office blossomed with mockups of pages, diagrams for page flags, new labels for features and columns. His slide show on redesign was seen by key people in every department, and they became believers.

Ariss spent most of his time with editors, of course. The exhilarating process convinced them that designers alone could not do the job. (That editors could not was already too obvious.) The redesign process is a mutual one, painful at times as ideas clash, but productive in the long run.

Ariss wanted to push the Tribune's editors deep into the 20th century. They wanted to get there, but some of Ariss's early designs were too far out, too much of a departure from the familiar, for acceptance. Conversely, the editors' often stick-in-the-mud posture was irritating to Ariss.

So he pushed them forward and they pulled him back. The editors wanted a very different, very modern looking Tribune, but one that readers would accept. They wanted tradition preserved, but only in its best and most lively aspects. They looked for evolution rather than revolution.

The years from 1969 to 1971 were a period of intense and bubbling creativity, an adventure in journalistic pioneering for all who were involved in planning the redesign.

When the design was finished and approved, editors and designers felt that it was right for the times, that they had accomplished something important and exciting and that readers would respond to it well.

What sort of man was — and is — Ariss? Certainly he had one of the sharpest, most creative minds in the Tribune newsroom. He was the right man for the time, for he realized not only what the editors wanted, but what they had to have. A thorough modernist, he persevered and he succeeded.

Ariss's own words convey his persuasive directness. Some of them preface the chapter on newspaper design in this volume. Here's more of what he had to say, in an interview with Editor & Publisher in 1974:

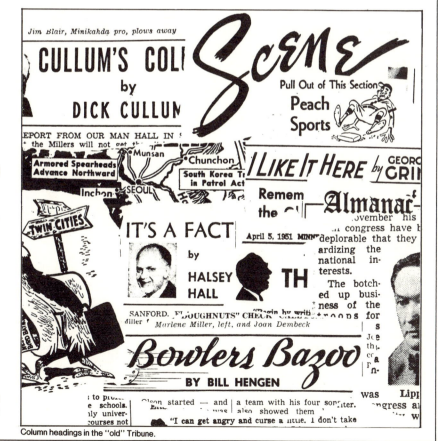

Column headings in the "old" Tribune.

"It isn't television alone that hurts newspapers. It can't compete with newspapers in depth of news. Papers are hurting themselves in their deplorable makeup. Their headlines compete against each other."

Asked how he went about redesigning a newspaper, he said:

"I can say several things in general. I would fire the art department. What good does it do? It doesn't understand design. Sure, an artist can airbrush a photo and make it look better. But that's dishonest. We should show the warts and all.

"And so many papers are still using Bodoni type. Why that was in use when King George ruled the American colonies. It was great for its time (1760) but it doesn't fit today in our new computer-style operation.

"Nor should italic type be used. It's hard to handle and tough to read. The best type for today is Helvetica. It's larger than the old typeface but takes no more space.

"Newspapers are wonderful things. They really intrigue me. They handle some 200 different subjects. Some of the more interesting people are the writers and editors themselves. But what does the promotion department do? Nothing. There is so much to promote in a big newspaper but I haven't seen one paper that does it properly . . .

"Even the ads in many papers make the news design look shabby. But sometimes newspapers stack up ads for a dreadful appearance.

"I've examined most of America's big newspapers, and their styles are wretched. They're put together in a manner 50 years behind the times. Some of the logotypes are 600 years old.

"Papers should have fewer headline styles, and they should be the same through all sections. The sections should be departmentalized. I favor

1867/

1921/

1932/

1969/

April 5/1971/

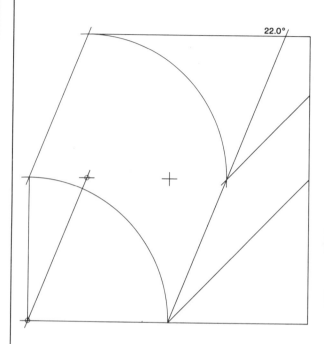

22.0°

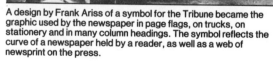

A design by Frank Ariss of a symbol for the Tribune became the graphic used by the newspaper in page flags, on trucks, on stationery and in many column headings. The symbol reflects the curve of a newspaper held by a reader, as well as a web of newsprint on the press.

photojournalism on the right side of the leading pages with short captions. So many papers are using 15th century type. They could get along with just headlines of 30- and 18-point type . . .

"Why do I set myself up as an authority on newspaper design? It's no innate talent. I have worked on design for 20 years, and each assignment required a struggle. But nothing else is as tough as the newspapers . . . There are so many different views in each paper, and it's the hardest task to design something that will bring all departments harmoniously together . . . On a scale of 100, I would rank American newspapers between one and five."

Has the passage of time changed any of Ariss's ideas? In the summer of 1980, he had this to say:

"Of course one thinks differently. Not so much about design devices but substance.

"I do not think there ever was a time when it is so important to know what is going on. This vast and credible medium of newspapers is a daily source of detailed information to learn who is shaping what, and the consequences.

"Good newspaper design can ease the words and pictures of events off the pages for the reader to better understand what is happening and so form opinions.

"With few exceptions — very few — newspapers remain blissfully unaware of this usefulness of design and its place in journalism.

"What a pity! Think of the opportunities daily lost by poor design to generate public opinion which might otherwise influence the future for the better."

But back to 1968. Once the process of redesign had started, Ariss's plan to "restock" the art department — soon to be known as the design

department — was put into effect. In the process of hiring designers, Ariss said, "I was always concerned that I was designing for my own obsolescence."

The Tribune hired Michael Carroll, a graduate of the Minneapolis School of Art, to assist Ariss. Carroll, now design director of the Tribune, was the first of a string of designers and illustrators who joined the newspaper during the next decade to bring new vitality to the newspaper's appearance.

As the redesign progressed, plans were made to introduce it. Rather than make the changes overnight, the Tribune's editors decided to phase them in over six weeks.

Accompanying the changes was a series of promotion ads explaining to readers what was happening and why, and what would come next. This proved to be a good idea.

Few readers reacted to the early changes. Most of them were on inside pages and weren't striking in themselves. But on April 5, 1971, the front page was transformed by a new headline type, a new flag with Helvetica type, a new Tribune symbol, and a new layout format, proceeding from the upper left of the page.

The "old" Tribune had disappeared. The "new" Tribune front page displayed its play story at top left, used Helvetica headline type, eliminated paragraph indentation,

Frank Ariss, left, Bower Hawthorne, center, and Wallace Allen.

dropped column rules and used a space formula to separate elements on the page. The change could hardly have been more dramatic.

Throughout the newspaper, column headings had been redesigned in a single, consistent style. All headlines were written in the same typeface, and all makeup conventions were the same. Design principles were basically simple and therefore helpful to readers. The Tribune had taken on a look of wholeness that eliminated its former clutter of styles.

Even with these major changes, reader reaction was slight — and mainly adverse. Change upsets readers, no matter how carefully it is planned and executed. But in general there was little comment from readers, perhaps an indication, the editors hoped, that the redesign had not upset them.

The Tribune surveyed readers for several weeks after April 5, asking for reactions to the design. Each survey showed a dropoff in reader concern and greater acceptance of the design as attractive.

In February 1972 the Tribune won a first-place award in typography and design among larger newspapers in the Inland Daily Press Association. The judges praised the design for its simplicity and consistency.

Hayward Blake, a judge, said the Tribune had accomplished ''the one significant change that's been made in newspaper design this past season. Rather than with art or esthetics, or through trickiness of design, addition of color, or simply a change of nameplate, the Minneapolis people designed their paper with rationale and logic. The design of the paper makes sense and can be explained easily, whereas the design of most newspapers is based primarily on tradition.''

The judges were critical, however, of inside pages of the Tribune and other newspapers in which they said

---

The Minneapolis Tribune

Thursday — February 27 1969

Minneapolis Minnesota — Volume CII Number 279 — 10c Single copy price

Enemy attack stalls 15 miles from Saigon

Reds leave quietly after one day battle — Harsh new Red push foreseen page 9

United Press International — South Vietnamese soldier helped his family leave Bien Hoa Village and Bien Hoa Air Base are only 15 miles from Saigon

3 astronauts slightly sick

Launch delay possible

Humphrey sees peril in ABM plan

Says sentinel would upset nuclear balance

Nixon renews US pledges to Germans

During visit to Bonn

Nixon names Rogers Morton GOP chairman

Rep Rogers Morton New GOP chairman

Light snow expected in Twin Cities

GM recalls 4.9 million vehicles for carburetor, exhaust checks

Editorial/Opinion	6	7
Business	14	16
Women's	19	21
Comics	28	
TV/Radio	33	
Sports	35	40
Theaters	38	

Some ideas make you think again. The Minneapolis Tribune

A 1969 design prototype by Frank Ariss.

diagonal pyramiding of advertisements hindered attractive design.

Again in 1974, the Tribune won a first place in the Inland competition. The judges then commented that the Tribune had a distinct personality because of its design. They disliked its use of two-column type for some stories, a custom discontinued when the Tribune changed later from an eight- to a six-column format.

How did the Tribune's design weather the 1970s and their great technological and economic changes?

Remember that Frank Ariss had those developments in mind in 1967. The design proved to be adaptable and resilient.

In May 1975 the Tribune changed to a six-column format. Tribune editors had wanted to do this years before, but, as is so often the case, esthetics alone is seldom a convincing reason for change. In 1975 the newsprint roll was narrowed, the page became smaller and one-column type became unacceptably narrow.

The six-column format created no problem. If anything, the design was even easier to handle, and the appearance of the Tribune was improved. Two-column type, now too wide for reading comfort, was banned, just as all type measures except one- and two-column had been in the original design. The one-column measure has remained the Tribune's basic type width.

The transition from hot metal to cold type was made in 1976 without problems. In 1977 a front-end electronic newsroom system was installed. Both writing and editing were done on terminals; typewriters, pastepots and pencils disappeared. Again, there were no problems.

The versatility of the Ariss design was demonstrated once again in the ease with which editors and printers

---

The Minneapolis Tribune SUNDAY

Vol. CIV—No. 315   MINNEAPOLIS, MINN., SUNDAY, APRIL 4 1971   Price 35 Cents

Corrections Nominee Is Prison Innovator

By Sam Newlund
Staff Writer

David Fogel

Nixon to Make Final Calley Case Ruling

By Robert B. Semple Jr.
New York Times Service

Staff Photo by Mike Zerby

Transfer students waiting for the bus to Clinton at 8 a.m. Friday at 48th St. and Fremont Av. S.

Inner-City School Draws Transfers With Multi-Culture Program

By Brian Anderson
Staff Writer

Staff Photo by Mike Zerby

Principal Robert Christman fixed an Easter breakfast for teachers and staff before school Friday.

Protesters Rally for Many Causes

By Bernie Shellum
Staff Writer

Calley Forecast Trauma That Trial Brought

By Harry Rosenthal
Associated Press

Lt. William Calley

Inside news

Foreign

National

Local

Sports

Index

Books	8, 9E
Crossword	2H
Editorial	2-4C
Movies	2, 3E
Outdoors	6H
Prizeword	7H

Robert T. Smith

Features

Almanac

Today's Weather: Little Change

Sunday, April 4, 1971
94th day;
271 to go this year.
Sunrise 5:49 a.m.
Sunset 6:44 p.m.

How to Avoid a Flap

Tribune Telephones	Want Ads	372-4242
	Circulation	372-4343
	News, General	372-4141

April 4, 1971: The Tribune the day before total redesign.

handled layout and makeup. Ariss's "graphics engineering" was seeing its best day.

After the redesign, block makeup was introduced, to eliminate typographical aberrations like doglegs and pave the way for future modular design. Editors who always yearned for rubber type now had it — but are not allowed to use it except under very special circumstances.

Simple, clean, attractive makeup is still the rule and the goal. Horizontal rules and four-sided boxes to set off a story are allowed — but not encouraged. They are used rarely and only for good reason.

So it was that the Minneapolis Tribune was redesigned and the design survived its first 10 years. The design concept is still fresh and the design principles remain unchanged.

Changes may come from future economic pressures — but they will mean adaptation, not destruction, of the design. Or change will come, as it did in 1971, in response to trends in society and readers' needs.

Minneapolis Tribune

Monday April 5 1971 | 3 Sections | 15c Single copy | Volume CIV Number 316 | M. | Copyright 1971 Minneapolis Star and Tribune Company

Saigon general says Reds downed 104 copters in Laos

United Press International

Saigon, South Vietnam
Communist gunners damaged 608 U.S. helicopters during the six-week Laos offensive, shooting down 104 of them, Lt. Gen. Hoang Xuan Lam told South Vietnam's Senate Defense Committee in a report made available Sunday.

Lam, commander of the South Vietnamese Laos operation, also said that about 150 American servicemen were killed supporting the Laotian drive.

Of the 104 helicopters Lam reported shot down, "about half were abandoned in southern Laos," he said.

Lam's statement was the first disclosure of the number of American helicopters struck by Communist ground fire in the operation. The U.S. command has never made available statistics on damaged helicopters.

The general made his report to members of the Senate Defense Committee at his Dong Ha base, northeast of Saigon.

Committee members present at the briefing included Chairman Ton That Dinh, a former general, and Sens. Hong Son Dong and Le Chau Loc.

Lam also told the senators that as a result of the Laos operation:

■ "South Vietnam's military leaders will have to confer and there should be a staff study of a reform of the army, especially from a technical aspect, to absorb losses and to make most economical use of our forces.

■ "We have to reconsider the reinforcement of our own artillery. The United States must furnish us with 175mm. guns, which have a range of 21.5 miles." (The largest artillery piece presently in South Vietnamese hands is the 155mm. howitzer.)

■ "We must research and revise our infantry weapons requirements, such as antiarmor M72s or disposable light antitank weapons.

"With a force of 30,000 men, we sacrificed 1,400 personnel (killed). This is not a heavy figure if we accept the doctrine of necessity of sacrifice. Given the odds and what we accomplished, the casualty figure should have been higher.

"Not one of our battalions was rendered inoperative or considered wiped out in southern Laos. Only four or five of more than 30 battalions suffered approximately 50 percent

Indochina
Continued on page 12A

Officials expect series of Red hit-run attacks

By Charles W. Bailey
Staff Correspondent

Washington, D.C.
Communist forces have revived a familiar scenario on a familiar stage for the latest act in the long and melancholy drama of the Vietnam War.

High administration officials regard last week's sharp enemy attacks in the northern part of South Vietnam as a likely prelude to a continuing series of hit-and-run assaults in reaction to the just-ended allied invasion of Laos.

If the forecasts are correct, a lot of familiar names will be back in the headlines in coming weeks —names like Quang Tri, Hue, Dak To, Da Nang and "the street without joy."

In separate attacks last week, North Vietnamese and Viet Cong forces struck at U.S. and South Vietnamese bases in three widely separated areas of northern South Vietnam.

■ A Communist demolition team broke into U.S. artillery base Mary Ann, 40 miles south of Da Nang, March 28. Thirty-three Americans were reported killed and 76 wounded — the highest casualties suffered by a U.S. unit in a single action in two years.

The strike occurred in the low-lying area along the shore of the South China Sea—the southern end of that coastal stretch which the French army dubbed "the street without joy" during its Indochina campaigns.

■ The next day, a strong North Vietnamese unit which reportedly had carried out a three-day forced march from Laos attacked Duc Duc, a distinct capital 25 miles southwest of Da Nang. They burned much of the town, inflicted "heavy" casualties on the local defense militia, and killed or wounded more than 200 civilians.

Duc Duc (used to be called An Hoa, and is) the scene of many previous battles —including repeated and costly "search-and-destroy" operations by a succession of U.S. Marine Corps battalions which were stationed in the area for over four years.

■ On Wednesday, Communist troops coming out of Laos attacked and overran a South Vietnamese artillery fire base seven miles southwest of Dak To in the central highlands. They inflicted apparently heavy casualties and drove out the defenders before they were finally themselves driven off with the help of U.S. air strikes.

War
Continued on page 4A

Justice unit keeps watch on political dissidents

By Richard Halloran
New York Times Service

Washington, D.C.
A Department of Justice intelligence unit that has replaced an Army intelligence detachment as the government's main watchman of political dissidence has compiled computerized dossiers on nearly 14,000 American citizens.

Officials in the department say that the interdivisional unit, known as IDIU, concentrates on black militants, opponents of the war in Vietnam, and new left advocates of the overthrow of the nation's political and economic system.

But the IDIU also maintains dossiers on elected political officials and moderates who are thought to condone or stimulate civil disobedience. One official says that "anybody like that, no matter what his politics are or what his position might be, would go into the file."

In addition, the unit collects information on those considered right-wing extremists, such as members of the John Birch Society, the Ku Klux Klan and the American Nazi Party.

The official declined to reveal the specific names on file other than those publicly identified as agitators, such as Rennie Davis and David Dellinger, both leftists.

The operations of IDIU, which was set up by former Atty. Gen. Ramsey Clark during the Lyndon Johnson administration in 1967, are another facet of the government's increasing pervasive collection of information about Americans. This controversial issue was recently explored by a Senate subcommittee under the direction of Sam J. Ervin, Jr., D-N.C.

The primary purpose of

Spy
Continued on page 5A

Israel promises talks if Arabs halt threats

By Peter Grose
New York Times Service

Jerusalem
Premier Golda Meir, outlining a tough Israeli bargaining position, Sunday promised to negotiate seriously as soon as the Arab governments show a readiness to talk rather than deliver ultimatums and threats.

Mrs. Meir's speech in Jerusalem was the keynote address of the first national convention of the United Israel Labor Party, the dominant bloc in the country's politics.

The premier refrained from publicly spelling out Israel's terms for allowing the United Arab Republic (U.A.R.) to open the Suez Canal, and for a partial interim settlement with the U.A.R., as proposed by Egyptian President Anwar Sadat.

The Israeli Cabinet discussed these terms at its weekly meeting earlier yesterday, and informants said it was decided that this subject should be pursued privately through diplomatic channels with the United States.

Guidelines for an Israeli counterproposal were understood to have been laid down at the Cabinet level. Informants said that military planners are working on two points:

■ How far can Israeli troops be withdrawn from the eastern bank of the canal and still maintain an effective defensive line in the Sinai Peninsula? Israelis accept the Egyptian contention that the canal could not be opened with Israeli forces in strength on one of the banks.

■ What means of surveillance can be devised to ensure

Mideast continued on page 12A

Pakistan rebels backed in India

Tribune Wire Services

Prime Minister Indira Gandhi's ruling Congress Party urged the people of India Sunday to lend their support to the East Pakistan independence movement.

But a resolution adopted unanimously by the party's 700 national committee members in New Delhi avoided any commitment of direct aid to the East Pakistanis.

"What we are doing is to raise our voice in the capitals of the world and in the United Nations over the brutal massacre across our borders," Mrs Gandhi said in rejecting demands from some delegates that India give arms to the East Pakistanis.

The prime minister also rejected criticism from Pakistani President Agha Mohammed Yahya Khan's government that India had no business in commenting on the developments in East Pakistan.

"India has no desire to interfere in the internal affairs of another country," Mrs. Gandhi said. "But it cannot remain silent over the oppression and wanton killing across the border"

Yahya's forces from West Pakistan are facing widespread civil disobedience from the rebelling East Pakistanis who are seeking more autonomy in the province which embraces 55,126 square miles. The two provinces, which are governed from Karachi, West Pakistan, are separated by 1,000 miles by Indian territory.

United News of India said in a dispatch from the border town of Krishnagar that Pakistani jet fighters violated Indian air space while bombing East Paki-

Pakistan
Continued on page 4A

Mrs. Indira Gandhi

Staff Photo by Earl Seubert

Wayne Frey: College means feeling depressed "a lot of the time."

Four freshmen

What is it like to be a freshman on a 40,000-student campus? The Tribune asked that question of four University of Minnesota freshmen. Their responses tell about the university and students today and, more importantly, how four freshmen from differing backgrounds reacted to university life.

First of a Series

By Brian Anderson
Staff Writer

The Institute of Technology (IT) at the University of Minnesota isn't considered an "easy" college.

Wayne Frey knew that when he enrolled in the school's mechanical engineering program last fall. But he had received A's and B's at Rosemount High School and figured that by studying three to four hours a night he would make it okay.

In the second week of the quarter he took his first test. Out of a possible 100 points, he got 18. His was the lowest score in the section.

Wayne is an intense 18-year-old man. When he commits himself to something, it is a total commitment. It is almost an obsession.

Immediately after his test, Wayne became obsessed with calculus. He almost doubled his daily study time. His study light burned until between 1 a.m. and 2 a.m. every night. The last two weeks of the quarter he spent about 100 hours just studying calculus.

The result was a satisfying "B" in his calculus course, an over-all grade average of 3.47 (A=4) and a nervous, edgy, frazzly feeling which makes him wonder if it was all worth it.

Wayne doesn't take college lightly. To him, it's a job, an extremely taxing job, which pains him and torments him incessantly. Except for those fleeting moments of satisfaction he experiences when he does well in a test, there is little enjoyment in college.

College means studying and taking tests and studying some more. It also means, according to Wayne, feeling depressed "a lot of the time."

Freshmen continued on page 4A

Inside news

Sports

Cal Luther, after agreeing Friday to leave Murray State for the head basketball coaching job at the University of Minnesota, rejected the position. Bill Musselman of Ashland College in Ohio now is expected to be named the Minnesota coach. Page 1C.

National

The Pentagon announced it is cutting back the program of remedial education for men with low scores on the armed forces qualification tests by accepting a smaller number of men with poor education. Page 2A.

Sen. J. William Fulbright said that the United States so overreacts to the threat of communism that such small nations as Israel and South Vietnam use communism as a means of "manipulating" American foreign policy in their interests. Page 3A.

Foreign

The head of the Communist Party organization in Estonia suggested to the 24th Communist Party Congress in Moscow, U.S.S.R., that regular, high-level press conferences might be an effective means of disseminating news and propaganda. According to the delegate, top Estonian officials hold about two press conferences each month. Top Russian officials are rarely available to the press. Page 16A.

The left-wing coalition government of President Salvador Allende Gossens appeared to have won a major victory in Chile's nationwide municipal elections. A tabulation showed that Allende's coalition had close to 51 percent of the ballots out of almost two million cast. Page 2A.

In his Palm Sunday homily in Vatican City, Pope Paul described some youths as being like sheep who flock after anyone who sets the pace. The pontiff said that a real Christian is not indifferent or unconscious. Page 3A.

Local

Gov. Wendell Anderson's popularity continued to decline, but at a slower rate than during his first month in office. The Minneapolis Tribune's Minnesota Poll reported that 46 percent of those questioned said they approve of Anderson and 29 percent disapprove. Fifty-seven percent had a favorable impression of Anderson when he took office in early January. Page 15A.

Two city officials have new offices on the third floor of City Hall that cost a total of $113,679. Treasurer Rey Malmquist and Comptroller Earl Arneson both said they didn't want to be moved from their old offices but Malmquist officially voted for the move and Arneson insisted on moving a wall in his private office that cost an additional $842. Page 11A.

Index

Business 13A
Comics 10B
Editorial 14A
Sports 1-6C
Theaters 10A
TV/Radio 13B

In the open

Page 1B

Features

There was a note of sadness among all the cheering as 2,500 fans at Duluth welcomed home the Minnesota high school basketball champion, Central's Trojans. Phyllis Hastings, wife of Trojan coach Jim Hastings, said she doesn't like to see the basketball season end, it's such a big part of the Hastingses' life. Page 1C.

Whatever you had planned for Tuesday night, forget it. Columnist Will Jones says no one should miss Peter Ustinov's performance as an ad-libbing Lord North in the new CBS series on the American Revolution. The program is a wildly witty hour, Jones says. Page 12B.

Almanac

Monday
April 5 1971
95 h day
270 to go this year
Sunrise 5:47 am
Sunset 6:46 pm

Today's weather
Little change

Details page 11B

Sunday's temperatures

am	1	2	3	4	5	6	7	8	9	10	11	Noon
temp	27	27	26	25	23	23	25	28	30	33	34	38
pm	1	2	3	4	5	6	7	8	9	10	11	Midn
temp	38	38	41	43	41	40	34	31	30	29	29	30

Fair weather is expected today and tomorrow in the Twin Cities and vicinity. The National Weather Service also forecasts a slow warming trend to be accompanied by light and variable winds. The high today should be 48 with almost no chance of precipitation predicted.

Predicted highs today: Minnesota, 38 to 48; North Dakota, 42 to 54; South Dakota, 44 to 58; Wisconsin, 37 northwest half to 47 southeast half.

Individually, they're not bad, but . . .

Three persons were walking down a Minneapolis street late one night when a drunken panhandler approached them. He asked if they had any spare change, and after they said they did not, they walked on. The drunk stood there for a moment, then turned and yelled after them: "Every one of you is in extremely bad company."

This is the first issue, April 5, 1971, of the completely redesigned Tribune. It was in eight-column format. One-column type was basic, but two-column was used for contrast. Block makeup was not yet emphasized.

Minneapolis Tribune

Monday May 5, 1975

Volume CVIII
Number 346
M

1A Final

3 Sections

15c Single Copy

Copyright 1975 Minneapolis Star and Tribune Company

Sugar growers reluctant to talk about profits

Farming 75

Second in a series

By Warren Wolfe
Staff Writer

Moorhead, Minn.

Here in the heart of the Red River Valley, where the earth is as rich and flat as a custard pie, the folks who make their living from sugar beets don't like to talk about the money they made last year.

That's because they made a lot. And most others in agriculture didn't.

"We kind of hate to say too much," grower Pat Benedict said as he sat in the newly remodeled kitchen of the house his grandfather built 75 years ago. "We came out all right and some others didn't do so hot. When we talk about money it sounds like we're bragging."

Just how well did growers around Fargo, N.D., and Moorhead do?

■ Earnings soared more than 425 percent in the half-year starting last Sept. 1 for American Crystal Sugar Co., a co-op owned by its 1,318

grower members, to $29.5 million from $5.6 million a year earlier. Sales for the period were up nearly 80 percent to $134.9 million from $75.3 million.

■ The average grower, who raises 154 acres of beets, already has been paid more for his 1974 crop, with a final payment yet to come, than he was paid for all of his 1973 crop. In dollars, that's $64,310 for 1974, compared with $63,985 for 1973. And that 1974 figure could rise to about $80,000 if, as planned, the final payment Sept. 30 is 20 percent

Pat Benedict    Stu Bass

of the total. All that is in spite of a beet yield that plunged 30 percent

in 1974 from 16.1 tons an acre to 11.3 tons because of a cold spring, dry summer and fall frost.

The reason, as every grocery buyer knows, is that the price of sugar more than tripled late last year, from 17 cents to 71 cents a pound, because of an apparent worldwide shortage of cane sugar.

Since the growers who own American Crystal are their own middle-

Farming continued on page 5A

Minh reported freed

Tribune News Services

Duong Van (Big) Minh, who surrendered Saigon to the Communists in the last act of his two-day presidency of South Vietnam, and 18 other former top government officials are being released from custody, Radio Saigon said Sunday.

Radio Saigon, now also known as Liberation Radio, said the decision to let Minh and the others return to their families was made following a meeting of the officials with the Military Management Committee that is administering the capital.

The 11-man committee is headed by Col. Gen. Tran Van Tra, a North Vietnamese Army soldier who is the top Communist commander in South Vietnam. The broadcast did not say where or how the officials were detained.

Although the broadcast, monitored in Bangkok, Thailand, took a conciliatory tone in the announcement, it also ordered former members of the South Vietnamese general military staff to turn themselves in or face death.

Saigon Radio said the 18 other former government officials being released included Vice President Nguyen Van Huyen and Premier Vu Van Mau.

Minh was sworn in as president April 28 and less than 48 hours later made the formal, unconditional surrender of Saigon to the Communists, giving them victory after a 35-year war against Japan, France, the United States and South Vietnam.

Nguyen Van Thieu, who resigned as president April 21, is in exile on Taiwan. Thieu was succeeded by Tran Van Huong, who stepped aside for Minh.

Saigon Radio said Saturday that a large number of officers and men of "the general headquarters of the Saigon puppet army" already have registered with the new rulers and ordered the rest to do so by this afternoon.

The radio said those who did not do so and turn in their weapons will be "severely punished," a Vietnamese

Vietnam continued on page 6A

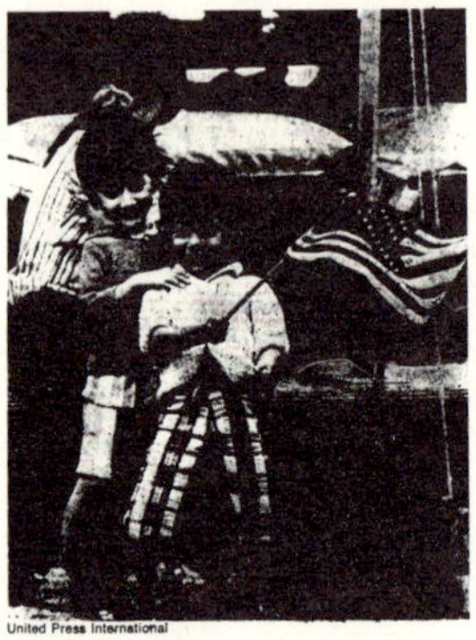

United Press International

Showing the flag

A Vietnamese child waved an American flag outside his family's temporary quarters at Eglin Air Force Base in Florida. He was among 343 refugees who arrived at the camp Sunday. (News report on page 2A.)

Fall of South Vietnam not U.S. fault, Ky says

Associated Press

Agana, Guam

The United States is not to blame for the fall of South Vietnam, says that country's former premier and vice president, Nguyen Cao Ky.

"Concerning America, and the American people, in the last 10 years, you did a lot for us — too much in my opinion," Ky said shortly after arriving in Guam this morning (late Sunday, Minneapolis time).

"But unfortunately we were not brave enough to overthrow Mr. Thieu," he said, referring to Nguyen Van Thieu, former president of South Vietnam.

"Of course, as Vietnamese, we would have liked more help, but we understand the feelings of the American Congress. There will be big problems, not only for refugees but for the United States of America," he said.

"You have your own problems. I don't want the 100,000 refugees to become a big task for your government and your country."

Ky said he expects reprisals against

Ky said he had actively plotted a forceable overthrow of Thieu to install either himself or the head of the country's Senate as the new president.

"At the time he (Thieu) lost support, he was a lonely man," Ky said. "You don't need too much force. What we needed were new military leaders. We were not interested in politics, but in military leadership."

Ky declined to name any other participants in the planning for the coup.

"Thieu and his people were corrupted and so incapable. It is not the fault of the United States Congress and the brave Vietnamese soldiers," he said of the downfall.

Ky continued on page 6A

Private colleges to cost more

By Gregor W. Pinney
Staff Writer

Students at Minnesota's private colleges will pay an average of 8 percent more next year for tuition, fees, room and board, according to a Minneapolis Tribune survey. It will be the largest increase in recent years.

In the previous four years, costs went up by about 6 percent a year.

The increase in Minnesota's private-college costs this year are the same as those in private four-year colleges across the nation, according to a survey by the College Entrance Examination Board two months ago.

While the average is 8 percent, the changes at individual colleges in Minnesota will vary greatly. Some colleges are holding the line, while others have scheduled increases of double-digit magnitude.

Six colleges are keeping their tuition and fees the same, and one—Pillsbury Baptist Bible College in Owatonna—also will freeze its room and board charges. At the other end of the scale, the cost of attending Macalester College in St. Paul will go up 14 percent, and for North Central Bible College in Minneapolis, it will rise 18 percent.

The increases do not affect all students equally, however. Gustavus Adolphus College in St. Peter has a Guaranteed -Cost Plan in which freshmen can have their costs frozen for four years. And Macalester will charge its new students $3,000 in tuition while returning students will pay $2,800.

Colleges continued on page 4A

Doctor convicted in abortion plans another one today

Associated Press

Albany, N.Y.

Dr. Kenneth Edelin, a surgeon convicted of manslaughter in the death of a fetus following a legal abortion, said Sunday night he would perform an abortion this morning. He noted that he is still employed at the same hospital (Boston City Hospital).

Edelin made the statement at a news conference on the controversy that has surrounded him since his conviction Feb. 15 in a jury trial. Asked whether he has performed any abortions since his conviction, Edelin replied, "I haven't been asked—up until Friday."

Asked how performing another abortion would make him feel, he said it was "a service that has to be rendered."

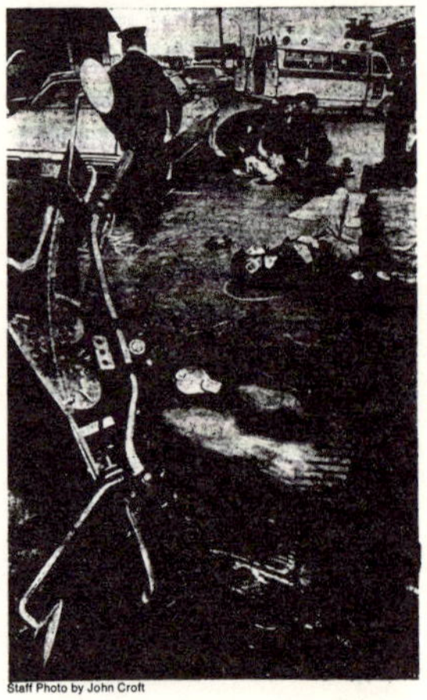

Nguyen Cao Ky

Staff Photo by John Croft

Couple injured in motorcycle accident

Policemen and ambulance attendants ministered to David and Cheryl Roberts Sunday after their motorcycle collided with a car at Broadway and Ulysses Sts. NE. Mr. and Mrs. Roberts, both 29, 4100 Nokomis Av. S., were taken to the University of Minnesota Hospitals, where Roberts had surgery for a leg fracture and his wife was under observation in satisfactory condition. There were no other injuries in the accident, which occurred at about 2:45 p.m.

Tax assessor disputes CIA on ownership of Hughes ship

New York Times Service

Los Angeles, Calif.

The tax assessor in Los Angeles County has challenged the private assertions of CIA officials and Summa Corp. executives that the Hughes Glomar Explorer is in reality owned by the federal government.

The Glomar Explorer, a ship designed to recover a sunken Soviet submarine from the mid-Pacific, is valued at up to $300 million.

The Hughes and CIA officials have said that Hughes's ownership of the ship and his intention to use it to mine the ocean floor was no more than a "cover story" concocted by the CIA to shroud, with the trappings of a commercial venture, the effort to recover the submarine.

If the Summa Corp. does own the

Explorer, questions are raised concerning possible windfall profits reaped by Hughes, compliance with federal regulations by him and others, and his liability for state and local taxes in California.

Last week, the tax assessor in Los Angeles County, where the ship has been berthed, said he now regarded it as the personal property of Hughes, and therefore taxable under the property-tax laws at a rate of about $1 million a year.

An FBI agent arranged a meeting in January between the tax assessor, Philip Watson, and "four people

Glomar continued on page 6A

To our readers:

Today's Tribune is printed in a new format, with six columns of news on each page instead of eight columns. We hope this will make the newspaper more attractive and easier to read, while at the same time enabling us to effect substantial savings in the cost of newsprint, the most expensive of our raw materials.

Each page is about one-half inch narrower than before. At the same time, converting to the new six-column format will allow us to print as much news and editorial material as we did previously, primarily because of more efficient use of space made possible by eliminating two "gutters" between columns of type on each page. There will be no net reduction in the space devoted to news because of the change.

We'd like to have your comments on our "new look." You can write to the Tribune's Readers' Representative, Dick Cunningham, or call him at 372-4450.

Nguyen Cao Ky

Almanac

Monday, May 5, 1975
125th day; 240 to go this year
Sunrise: 5:57. Sunset: 8:23.

Today's weather:
Cloudy, mild

Increasing cloudiness and a chance of showers and thunderstorms are predicted for the Twin Cities area tonight and Tuesday, with continued mild weather. The high today is expected to be in the upper 60s, with the low tonight near 50 and the high Tuesday in the mid 60s. The chance of precipitation tonight is 30 percent. **Details on Page 9B.**

'U' do something to me . . .

A couple of Minneapolis men in their late 20s were walking through the University of Minnesota the other day arguing about the students—one complaining that they are more conservative than they used to be. The other had to give up the argument. Just as he was about to respond, a student walked by wearing a Davy Crockett coonskin cap.

Business 11A	Sports 1-7C
Comics 8B	Theaters 10B
Editorial 8, 9A	TV, Radio 11B

Tribune telephones
372-4141 News General
372-4242 Classified
372-4143 Circulation

Marine tells of the last hours in Saigon

Editor's note: The writer of the following dispatch was the last marine — and perhaps the last American — out of South Vietnam in last week's evacuation. As the regional commander of embassy security guards in Southeast Asia, he directed the evacuation effort at the U.S. embassy in Saigon.

By Maj. Jim Kean
United Press International

Aboard the USS Blue Ridge

I had the dubious distinction of being the last United States Marine to leave Vietnam.

But the thing I am most proud of is that we evacuated 2,500 people

from the embassy compound without firing a shot. The only shots were fired by me and that was as we were leaving the roof of the embassy Wednesday morning. I emptied my automatic into the mechanism of a large dish radio antenna on the roof so that it could not be used.

So, I have a clear conscience, knowing that we left without firing a shot in anger despite the fact that thousands of shots were fired at us and at the helicopters evacuating people from the embassy.

We knew the end was near on Monday evening when planes bombed Tan Son Nhut Airport and firing broke out around the em-

bassy. We went on full alert. I had 42 marines on duty at the embassy compound. The others were at the DAO (defense attaché office) compound at the airport, which was to be the main staging area for the final evacuation, according to our original plan.

After we secured the compound Monday night we had a lull until about 3:45 a.m. Tuesday. Tan Son Nhut and the DAO came under attack. I got a report that two marines were killed at DAO.

The situation was getting worse after daybreak and by around 10 a.m. we knew that the critical time had arrived. The ambassador had committed us to the evacuation of around 2,500 persons from the compound. Our original plan was

the next morning (Tuesday). There were several hundred people then and by the late afternoon the number had grown to at least 10,000.

After we secured the compound Monday night we had a full until about 3:45 a.m. Tuesday. Tan Son Nhut and the DAO came under attack. I got a report that two marines were killed at DAO.

The situation was getting worse after daybreak and by around 10 a.m. we knew that the critical time had arrived. The ambassador had committed us to the evacuation of around 2,500 persons from the compound. Our original plan was

A crowd gathered outside the embassy. When police imposed a 24-hour curfew the crowd of Vietnamese dispersed for the night but reappeared shortly after daybreak

Marine continued on page 4A

On May 5, 1975, the Tribune went to a six-column format.

Design/

On the night
of April 4, 1971,
the face of the
Tribune changed...

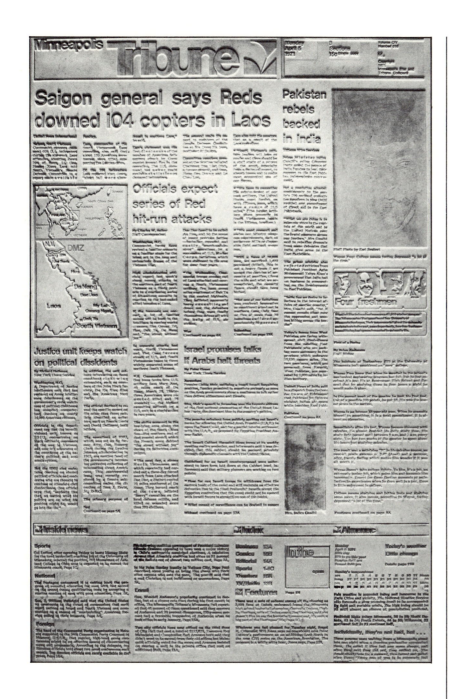

Mat produced for page one of redesigned newspaper.

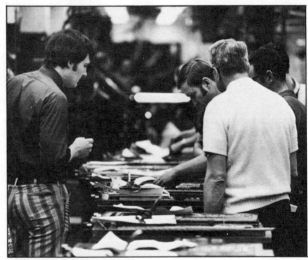

The big night . . .

It was out with the old type and in with the new at the Minneapolis Tribune the night of April 4, 1971, when the last phase of redesign went into effect. Frank Ariss, left, and Steve Ronald, above, then a news editor, watched printers making up pages . . .

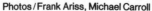

Photos / Frank Ariss, Michael Carroll

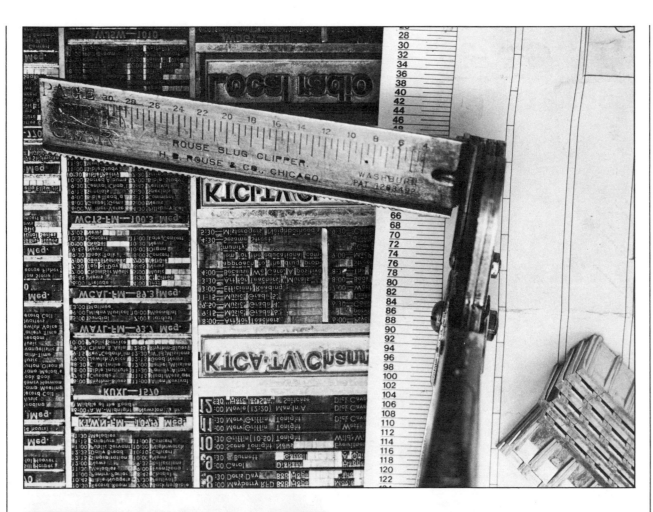

. . . hot metal type was ready and there were slugs galore. Printers used new metal grid rulers . . .

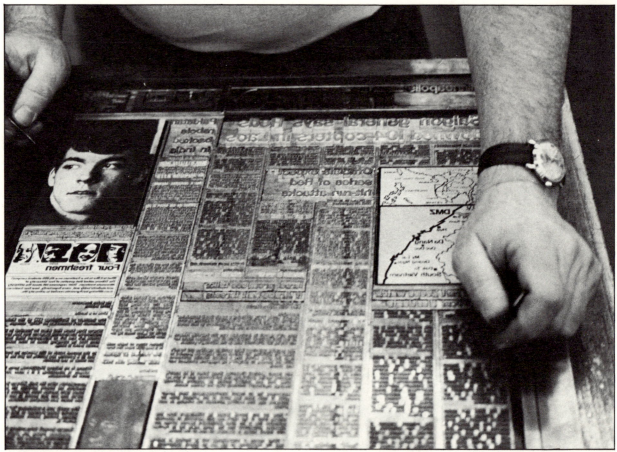

. . . page one received the printer's final touches . . .

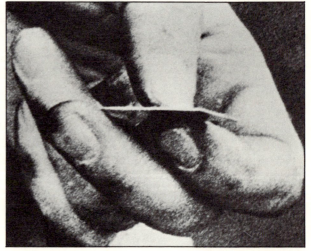

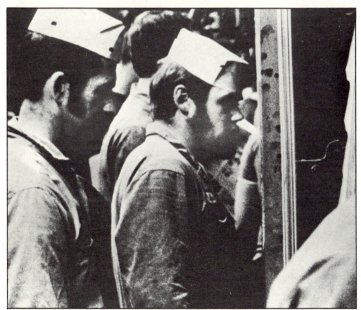

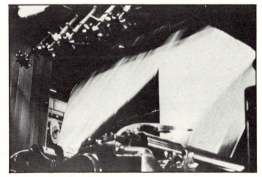

. . . the plate was cast and put on the press, the pressmen watched and a stream of newspapers dated April 5, 1971, flowed from the line.

Chapter

4/

Principles
of Tribune
design/

Rules
of Tribune
layout/

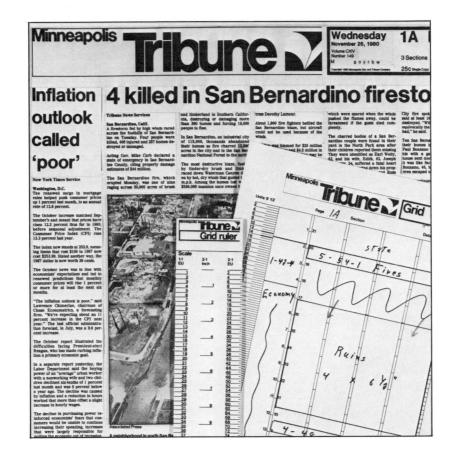

Introduction /

The layout rules spring from principles of design

The people who lay out the pages of a newspaper must understand the design approach — an undefinable process that is, more than anything, a state of mind. Design makes the difference between a page whose components are merely nicely laid out and one that reflects original thought and unity of purpose.

Design must serve content by helping readers understand what the major news stories of the day are, what stories are entertaining, what the relationship of all news elements is. The page layout person must see each page as a unit, rather than a collection of parts.

Design must bring order to the confusion of news on a particular day.

Tribune design does not allow the typographical gimmicks sometimes thought of as reader bait. Readers don't take such bait. Clear presentation of news is what they want.

Tribune design is not complicated. It requires few rules. It is not easy to use, however, because its very simplicity is demanding. The principles must be understood and the rules followed. A page put together with little thought will be as deficient in design as a page filled with typographical gimmicks. Either one guarantees a degree of unreadability.

The rules of layout spring from the design principles — the most important guidelines we have. Both principles and rules allow flexibility of layout while maintaining purity of design.

If the layout person understands and is responsive to design, the day will come when he or she looks at a newspaper page and says, "It's a unit, it communicates, **it looks right**." When that happens, a design process has taken place.

The design does not overwhelm content but helps make content more understandable. The design is unassuming, yet pleasing to the eye. The design contains elements that bear logical relationships to each other. The design tells the reader what is important. It communicates the message clearly and simply.

The principles of design/

The rules of layout

The grid/

Tribune pages are built on a grid system that requires precision of layout and pasteup and paves the way for electronic page composition.

A precise vertical and horizontal measurement is provided for every element on a page.

Horizontally the page is divided into six columns, each 12.5 picas wide. (There are 12 points between each column.)

Vertically the page is divided into 167 units, each 9.5 points deep — the depth of a line of body type.

It may help to imagine such a page with invisible lines drawn on it from top to bottom and side to side, creating 1,002 small units. Each element of a page — body type, headline type, pictures, illustrations, the page flag — must fit into a combination of those units.

Put another way, the dimensions of each element (with its necessary spacing) on a page must be divisible vertically by the basic 9.5-point depth and horizontally by the 12.5-pica column width (translated into inches in the case of pictures and illustrations).

If elements are sized correctly and placed precisely on the page, the layout will be "on the grid" and the page will be perfectly made up. **This is a basic requirement of Tribune design.**

To check the grid, place a ruler straight across a page. If every element on the page rests on a horizontal grid line, the baselines of type in each column will line up across the page.

Why bother with a grid? It's necessary for good, precise design. If the grid is followed, the page has a clean look that no other design rule can produce. The sensitive designer easily spots the page on which elements are not on the grid; for that designer the error leaps off the page as the typographical error does to the responsive editor.

Beyond this, look to the future. In an electronic page layout system, a grid will be essential and page elements will have to be precisely sized. The computer will assure precision in everything but graphics — until they, too, are computer produced.

What to do/

Stay on the grid! Size pictures precisely to keep them on the grid. Make sure pages are pasted up with spacing that keeps elements on the grid. It's not hard. It's important.

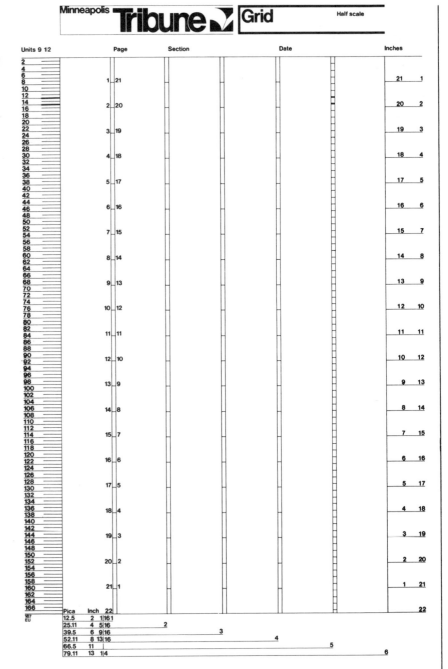

2/

The flush-left principle/

Point zero on a Tribune page is the upper lefthand corner, from which the page is built.

This establishes the flush-left principle, which dictates that each element have its own point zero, the upper lefthand corner of the space it occupies.

So headlines are flush left. Body type is flush left, without paragraph indentations.

The headlines for the play story on page one and for the major story or feature on all pages are in the upper lefthand corner instead of on the traditional right.

The flush-left principle is based on the reader's habit of reading from left to right. It follows natural design.

What to do/

Think flush left. Build a page from the upper left, whether it's a full or partial newspage. This is a major step toward consistency of design. You don't have to worry about flush-left marking of headlines or paragraphs. The computer understands the flush-left principle and sets the type accordingly.

Minneapolis Tribune

Wednesday
November 26, 1980
Volume CXIV
Number 149
M   y
Copyright 1980 Minneapolis Star and Tribune Company

1A   Final

3 Sections

25¢ Single Copy

Inflation outlook called 'poor'

York Times Service

Washington, D.C.
The renewed surge in mortgage rates helped push consumer prices up 1 percent last month, to an annual rate of 12.6 percent.

The October increase matched September's and meant that prices have risen 12.2 percent thus far in 1980, before seasonal adjustment. The Consumer Price Index (CPI) rose 13.3 percent last year.

The index now stands at 253.9, meaning items that cost $100 in 1967 now cost $253.90. Stated another way, the 1967 dollar is now worth 39 cents.

The October news was in line with economists' expectations and led to renewed predictions that monthly consumer prices will rise 1 percent or more for at least the next six months.

"The inflation outlook is poor," said Lawrence Chimerine, chairman of Chase Econometrics, a forecasting firm. "We're expecting about an 11 percent increase in the CPI next year." The last official administration forecast, in July, was a 9.8 percent increase.

The October report illustrated the difficulties facing President-elect Reagan, who has made curbing inflation a primary economic goal.

In a separate report yesterday, the Labor Department said the buying power of an "average" urban worker with a nonworking wife and two children declined six-tenths of 1 percent last month and was 4 percent below a year ago. The decline was caused by inflation and a reduction in hours worked that more than offset a slight increase in hourly wages.

The decline in purchasing power reinforced economists' fears that consumers would be unable to continue increasing their spending, increases that were largely responsible for pulling the economy out of recession.

The big news in the latest consumer price report was the jump in housing costs. Up seven-tenths of 1 percent in September, they rose 1.3 percent in October. The largest part of the change was in financing costs. After declining sharply in August and slightly in September, financing, taxes and insurance charges rose 3.1 percent in October.

That bureaucrats reflects a reversal in mortgage rates that occurred in late summer, when rates halted several months of decline and began rising again.

Economy continued on page 4A

4 killed in San Bernardino firestorm

Tribune News Services

San Bernardino, Calif.
A firestorm fed by high winds raced across the foothills of San Bernardino on Tuesday. Four people were killed, 400 injured and 257 homes destroyed or damaged.

Acting Gov. Mike Curb declared a state of emergency in San Bernardino County, citing property damage estimates of $44 million.

The San Bernardino fire, which erupted Monday, was one of nine raging across 50,000 acres of brush and timberland in Southern California, destroying or damaging more than 300 homes and forcing 10,000 people to flee.

In San Bernardino, an industrial city of 115,000, thousands abandoned their homes as fire charred 12,000 acres in the city and in the San Bernardino National Forest to the north.

The most destructive blaze, fueled by tinder-dry brush and timber, raced down Waterman Canyon driven by hot, dry winds that gusted to 45 m.p.h. Among the homes lost was a $500,000 mansion once owned by actress Dorothy Lamour.

About 1,000 fire fighters battled the San Bernardino blaze, but aircraft could not be used because of the winds.

The fire was blamed for $25 million in property losses and $4.5 million in watershed damage. Flooding may be the area's next big headache.

At nightfall, officials said that the erratic winds had subsided and that the fires "were holding." But they worried that resort communities in the San Bernardino Mountains, which were spared when the winds pushed the flames away, could be threatened if the gusts died completely.

The charred bodies of a San Bernardino couple were found in their yard in the North Park area after their children reported them missing. They were identified as Earl Welty, 63, and his wife, Edith, 62. Joseph Benjamin, 54, suffered a fatal heart attack while watering down his property to ward off the fire, and Rose Myers, 64, died while being evacuated from her home.

City fire spokesman Jimmy Jews said at least 180 of the homes were destroyed. "Without a doubt, it is unequivocally the worst fire we've ever had," he said.

Ten San Bernardino policemen lost their homes in North Park. Capt. Paul Bonnano said he tried to move his with a garden hose, but "the house next door started burning and it was like facing a flamethrower." Bonnano, 46, his wife and two children escaped unhurt and returned to

Fires continued on page 12A

Sprinkler checks falter in city

By R.T. Rybak
Staff Writer

Minneapolis fire inspectors do not know whether the sprinkler systems will work in any building constructed since 1975 because the department says it has no one who understands them.

City fire officials say that the loss of the department's only plans analyst five years ago has made it impossible to know how many sprinklers will go off and whether they will put out a fire.

There is now $350 million worth of construction going on in downtown Minneapolis. Are these new buildings safe? City Fire Marshal Marshall Bush, who signed their occupancy statements, said, "From my meager expertise, I couldn't say for sure."

Minneapolis Fire Chief Clarence Nimmerfroh said Tuesday that the fire marshal does not have the expertise to understand the complex sprinkling systems now being built. "The fire marshal looks at blueprints that I don't think he knows what he is looking at," he said.

Yesterday, Nimmerfroh informed city coordinator David Niklaus that he had ordered the fire marshal to stop signing occupancy certificates for new buildings. When asked later whether Nimmerfroh's decision will mean no new construction can occur in Minneapolis, Niklaus said, "I got Clarence's letter three hours ago and I really can't answer that."

The state building code says sprinklers, which are designed to contain a fire and cut smoke, must now be put in any building over 75 feet high.

From 1961 to 1975 new sprinkler systems were examined by the Minneapolis Fire Prevention Bureau's plans analyst Benjamin Plmon.

Inspections continued on page 4A

Associated Press
A neighborhood in north San Bernardino, Calif., lay in ruins Tuesday. It was devastated by Monday's Waterman Canyon fire.

Quake toll passes 3,000 in Italy

Tribune News Services

Naples, Italy
The death toll in southern Italy's earthquake rose past 3,000 Tuesday, and the tremors continued as Pope John Paul visited the disaster area to pray with grieving survivors.

The national police office coordinating casualty reports from the more than 100 towns and villages hit by Sunday's quake said that 2,400 bodies had been recovered and that about 700 more were still buried under rubble in a single village, Laviano, in the province of Salerno.

Whole towns were declared uninhabitable because of quake damage, and authorities said hundreds of thousands of people were homeless.

By dusk, rescue teams had still not reached villages where hundreds more people were said to be buried under tons of debris.

As the death count rose, severe aftershocks shook the already devastated area, causing the collapse of some damaged buildings.

The pope flew through the devastated region by helicopter, stopping to visit a hospital in the town of Potenza 88 miles east of Naples, then flying on to Balvano, the mountain village where worshipers were crushed in the collapse of a church wall. The pope wanted to visit the site of the church, but police and soldiers kept him away for fear that aftershocks would topple the portions of the ruins still standing.

Strong aftershocks shook the ground during his visit, causing the collapse of a fire station at Salerno, 37 miles south of Naples, and a government

Quake continued on page 4A

Sol Jacobs

City suspends head of housing unit for 13 work days

By Tom Davies
Staff Writer

The director of the Minneapolis inspections department was suspended for 13 work days Tuesday as a result of allegations that some of the housing inspectors he supervises did little or no work for the city.

Sol Jacobs, who has worked for the city for 31 years and has headed the inspections department for five, was suspended yesterday by City Coordinator David Niklaus for "the lack of management control and low productivity and falsification of official departmental documents by certain employees in the inspections department."

Niklaus said the suspension came in the midst of an in-house investigation and after review of videotapes of the WCCO-TV series on housing inspection, broadcast last week. That series alleged widespread nonwork by the city's housing inspectors.

Niklaus said the in-house investigation is continuing, but would not say if further suspensions are planned. He did say, however, that those conducting the investigation think "further suspensions are likely."

Jacobs could not be reached for comment last night, but City Council President Alice Rainville — who was present when Jacobs learned of the suspension — said he was very shown on television. The last time city officials tried to fire a housing inspector — for allegedly making racist remarks about Indians — their efforts faltered before the Minneapolis Civil Service Commission, and that case is now before the Minnesota Supreme Court.

Niklaus said city officials have been extremely cautious about discussing other suspensions for fear of jeopardizing the city's case against the specific housing inspectors

Suspend continued on page 5A

Leonard takes title back from Duran

Associated Press

New Orleans, La.
Sugar Ray Leonard regained the World Boxing Council welterweight championship Tuesday night when Roberto Duran quit late in the eighth round.

Duran cited cramps in his stomach and right arm as reason for the abrupt ending, and said he was retiring from boxing. He had won the title from Leonard by unanimous decision in June.

(Details on page 1C.)

Almanac

Wednesday, Nov. 26, 1980
331st day; 35 to go this year
Sunrise: 7:25. Sunset: 4:36.

Today's weather
Clouds, mild

Cloudy skies and a high in the mid 30s are predicted for today for the Twin Cities area.

Other predicted high temperatures: Minnesota, low 30s to low 40s; North Dakota, 30s; South Dakota, 40s; Wisconsin, low 40s.

Arts	5B	Obituaries	7C
Business	8-10A	Sports	1-4C
Comics	4B	Theaters	4,5C
Corrections	2A	TV, Radio	7B
Editorial	6-7A	Weather	5B

Tribune   372-4141 News General
Telephone   372-4242 Classified
                             372-4343 Circulation

Associated Press
Emuel and Shirley Benton, who refuse to accept welfare, stood outside their shack in New York.

One man's trash is another's home

By Timothy Harper
Associated Press

New York, N.Y.
They call their tar-paper shack home, their five children healthy and themselves happy. Emuel and Shirley Benton are carving out their own tiny corner in the concrete canyons.

Rejecting welfare, the Bentons have built and furnished a hut with other people's garbage in the lot across the street from the housing project from which they were evicted last year.

"We don't need welfare," Emuel Benton, 54, said. "What could they give me that's better than what I got?"

The family, whose sole income is Benton's $200 monthly disability check, was evicted after his second heart attack forced him to quit as a truck driver. For 28 weeks, the family slept in their battered station wagon.

Then, Emuel Benton, whose only construction experience was building a doghouse when he was 7, announced:

"They can't give us a welfare apartment that's better than our little house." Shirley Benton, 42, said.

Squatters continued on page 4A

3/

Typefaces/

A multitude of typefaces, headline styles and type widths contributes to clutter and reduces readability. Tribune design is based on one body type — Bedford roman — and one headline type — Helvetica. Helvetica is used in bold or light faces.

In general, bold Helvetica is used for hard news and light for features. Variations of body type are allowed only according to rule.

What to do/

Body type/

1/Use Bedford roman body type most of the time. The exceptions:

a/Use bold type for editor's notes, shirt-tails on stories and keys in stories.

b/Use Helvetica body type only in specific cases. These include cutlines, introductions and explanatory notes for stories that are specially displayed, the People and People in Sports columns, Then and Now in the Neighbors section, the Perspective page and feature section covers.

Such use illustrates the general principle behind use of Helvetica body type — for display of a special feature or page.

2/Use one-column type as the basic body type measure. It is set automatically by computer unless another measure is specified.

This is another basic principle of Tribune design. It means:

a/Multi-column leads should not be used.

b/Type is never set odd measure, with two exceptions:

Editorials are set 10 point on an 11-point slug, 1½ columns wide.

A variation of one-column type may be used within a four-sided box. This format should be used rarely, however. Much preferred is use of one-point rules above and below a story. These set the story off as something different, and, of course, do not require use of odd-measure type.

If the four-sided box is used, this is the way it's done:

Use one-point rules around the box. (On rare occasions, heavier rules may be needed and used, but only after consultation with the graphics editor or design director.)

Line up side rules with the body type or headline type above or below the box, so gutters outside the box are even.

The width of the type will vary according to the width of the box. Use the accompanying table to determine the width of type needed.

This is the Tribune's body type: A line set in Bedford light.
This is the Tribune's body type: A line set in Bedford bold.

Helvetica bold

Helvetica light

How Tribune type is handled in boxes/

So hard times have hit your pocket, too. The trip to Florida is out this year. You'd like to go downhill skiing, but that costs money.

Wrong. Hard times have hit the park board along with every other city agency, and the skating rink is closed. Oh, the ice is there, but the warming house is locked. The lights that used to let you skate at night

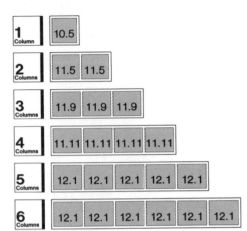

1 Column	10.5					
2 Columns	11.5	11.5				
3 Columns	11.9	11.9	11.9			
4 Columns	11.11	11.11	11.11	11.11		
5 Columns	12.1	12.1	12.1	12.1	12.1	
6 Columns	12.1	12.1	12.1	12.1	12.1	12.1

Pica widths

So hard times have hit your pocket, too. The trip to Florida is out this year. You'd like to go downhill skiing, but that costs money.

Wrong. Hard times have hit the park board along with every other city agency, and the skating rink is closed. Oh, the ice is there, but the warming house is locked. The lights that used to let you skate at night are off, too.

So hard times have hit your pocket, too. The trip to Florida is out this year. You'd like to go downhill skiing, but that costs money.

Wrong. Hard times have hit the park board along with every other city agency, and the skating rink is closed. Oh, the ice is there, but the warming house is locked. The lights that used to let you skate at night are off, too.

So hard times have hit your pocket, too. The trip to Florida is out this year. You'd like to go downhill skiing, but that costs money.

Wrong. Hard times have hit the park board along with every other city agency, and the skating rink is closed. Oh, the ice is there, but the warming house is locked. The lights that used to let you skate at night are off, too.

So hard times have hit your pocket, too. The trip to Florida is out this year. You'd like to go downhill skiing, but that costs money.

Wrong. Hard times have hit the park board along with every other city agency, and the skating rink is closed. Oh, the ice is there, but the warming house is locked. The lights that used to let you skate at night are off, too.

So hard times have hit your pocket, too. The trip to Florida is out this year. You'd like to go downhill skiing, but that costs money.

Wrong. Hard times have hit the park board along with every other city agency, and the skating rink is closed. Oh, the ice is there, but the warming house is locked. The lights that used to let you skate at night are off, too.

So hard times have hit your pocket, too. The trip to Florida is out this year. You'd like to go downhill skiing, but that costs money.

Wrong. Hard times have hit the park board along with every other city agency, and the skating rink is closed. Oh, the ice is there, but the warming house is locked. The lights that used to let you skate at night are off, too.

So hard times have hit your pocket, too. The trip to Florida is out this year. You'd like to go downhill skiing, but that costs money.

*Wrong. Hard times have hit the park board along with every other city agency, and the skating rink is closed. Oh, the ice is there, but the warming house is locked. The lights that used to let you skate at night are off, too.

So hard times have hit your pocket, too. The trip to Florida is out this year. You'd like to go downhill skiing, but that costs money.

Wrong. Hard times have hit the park board along with every other city agency, and the skating rink is closed. Oh, the ice is there, but the warming house is locked. The lights that used to let you skate at night are off, too.

So hard times have hit your pocket, too. The trip to Florida is out this year. You'd like to go downhill skiing, but that costs money.

Wrong. Hard times have hit the park board along with every other city agency, and the skating rink is closed. Oh, the ice is there, but the warming house is locked. The lights that used to let you skate at night are off, too.

So hard times have hit your pocket, too. The trip to Florida is out this year. You'd like to go downhill skiing, but that costs money.

Wrong. Hard times have hit the park board along with every other city agency, and the skating rink is closed. Oh, the ice is there, but the warming house is locked. The lights that used to let you skate at night are off, too.

So hard times have hit your pocket, too. The trip to Florida is out this year. You'd like to go downhill skiing, but that costs money.

Wrong. Hard times have hit the park board along with every other city agency, and the skating rink is closed. Oh, the ice is there, but the warming house is locked. The lights that used to let you skate at night are off, too.

So hard times have hit your pocket, too. The trip to Florida is out this year. You'd like to go downhill skiing, but that costs money.

Wrong. Hard times have hit the park board along with every other city agency, and the skating rink is closed. Oh, the ice is there, but the warming house is locked. The lights that used to let you skate at night are off, too.

So hard times have hit your pocket, too. The trip to Florida is out this year. You'd like to go downhill skiing, but that costs money.

Wrong. Hard times have hit the park board along with every other city agency, and the skating rink is closed. Oh, the ice is there, but the warming house is locked. The lights that used to let you skate at night are off, too.

So hard times have hit your pocket, too. The trip to Florida is out this year. You'd like to go downhill skiing, but that costs money.

Wrong. Hard times have hit the park board along with every other city agency, and the skating rink is closed. Oh, the ice is there, but the warming house is locked. The lights that used to let you skate at night are off, too.

So hard times have hit your pocket, too. The trip to Florida is out this year. You'd like to go downhill skiing, but that costs money.

Wrong. Hard times have hit the park board along with every other city agency, and the skating rink is closed. Oh, the ice is there, but the warming house is locked. The lights that used to let you skate at night are off, too.

So hard times have hit your pocket, too. The trip to Florida is out this year. You'd like to go downhill skiing, but that costs money.

Wrong. Hard times have hit the park board along with every other city agency, and the skating rink is closed. Oh, the ice is there, but the warming house is locked. The lights that used to let you skate at night are off, too.

So hard times have hit your pocket, too. The trip to Florida is out this year. You'd like to go downhill skiing, but that costs money.

Wrong. Hard times have hit the park board along with every other city agency, and the skating rink is closed. Oh, the ice is there, but the warming house is locked. The lights that used to let you skate at night are off, too.

So hard times have hit your pocket, too. The trip to Florida is out this year. You'd like to go downhill skiing, but that costs money.

Wrong. Hard times have hit the park board along with every other city agency, and the skating rink is closed. Oh, the ice is there, but the warming house is locked. The lights that used to let you skate at night are off, too.

So hard times have hit your pocket, too. The trip to Florida is out this year. You'd like to go downhill skiing, but that costs money.

Wrong. Hard times have hit the park board along with every other city agency, and the skating rink is closed. Oh, the ice is there, but the warming house is locked. The lights that used to let you skate at night are off, too.

So hard times have hit your pocket, too. The trip to Florida is out this year. You'd like to go downhill skiing, but that costs money.

Wrong. Hard times have hit the park board along with every other city agency, and the skating rink is closed. Oh, the ice is there, but the warming house is locked. The lights that used to let you skate at night are off, too.

So hard times have hit your pocket, too. The trip to Florida is out this year. You'd like to go downhill skiing, but that costs money.

Wrong. Hard times have hit the park board along with every other city agency, and the skating rink is closed. Oh, the ice is there, but the warming house is locked. The lights that used to let you skate at night are off, too.

So hard times have hit your pocket, too. The trip to Florida is out this year. You'd like to go downhill skiing, but that costs money.

Wrong. Hard times have hit the park board along with every other city agency, and the skating rink is closed. Oh, the ice is there, but the warming house is locked. The lights that used to let you skate at night are off, too.

50%

Use a pica of space between type and box rules on left and right and between each internal column of type.

3/Do not use leading to justify columns. If no more than eight lines of space remain at the end of a story, leave white space.

4/Use ragged right type occasionally to display special features or to break up the grayness of full-measure type. It creates white space, a key Tribune design principle, but it is a departure from basic Tribune design and should not be overused.

Ragged right should not be used within boxes or with rules above and below it. (Two variations of normal design with a single feature tend to mean over-design. There is evidence, too, that readers prefer use of a single variation.)

5/Never indent type for pictures, illustrations, labels or headlines.

6/If you turn body type past headlines or jump heads, square off the type with the first line of body type in the story or jump. An exception:

Jumps at the top of a page may be squared off with the jump head.

Headline type/

Helvetica bold and light, both in roman type, are the Tribune's basic headline types. (Examples in every size are shown on pages 57 and 58.)

1/ We don't create or use italic head type, nor do we flex type (to reduce or enlarge it). Either procedure would be a basic design change.

2/ We don't use kickers on headlines.

3/ We use decks on headlines only when they are needed for essential

headline facts. Decks should be set flush left and should use the same typeface as the main headline (bold with bold, light with light).

Decks must bear a design size relationship to the headlines they support. This is the guide:

Deck guide

Headline	Deck	Number of lines
30pt	**18pt**	2 lines
36pt	**18pt**	2 lines
42pt	**24pt**	1 line
48pt	**30pt**	1 or 2 lines
54pt	**30pt**	1 or 2 lines
60pt	**36pt**	1 or 2 lines
72pt	**36pt**	1 or 2 lines
80pt	**42pt**	1 or 2 lines

4/ We use a side headline occasionally when a story that does not merit a spread head is put into a shallow hole four or more columns wide at the top of a page. Such a story should carry top and bottom one-point rules (to avoid raw turns of type at the top of a page):

Night's fear leaves scars upon her mind

By Jay Weiner
Staff Writer

She is 26 and white and she works downtown. She occasionally smokes a cigarette and she is a strong person but she has been hurt.

Before her experiences of Wednesday night she was not exactly naive about her personal safety — what woman in the city is? — but she was,

she knows now, off-guard enough so that Friday she had a story to tell. Not a story of rape or physical contact or blood or gunshots. But a story of violence, even if today the signs of it are in her head, not on her body.

The New Year's Eve party was in St. Louis Park at a co-worker's house and she suddenly discovered she was going to be late because of this unknown man. He was walking in the

alley behind her uptown-area apartment bulding as she got into her parked car.

The man, black, in his mid-to-late 20s, thin, about 6-foot, wearing a rust-colored knit hat and rust-colored leather jacket, asked her for a ride about 9:30 p.m. He wanted a lift to Hennepin Av., just four blocks away, which seemed odd, but he was insistent.

50%

5 / We use one word for jump headlines, set in 24-point type. (A variation may be a ''spread'' jump head, which starts out with the story slug in 24 point, followed by a colon and a head angle taken from the jump.) Examples of such jump heads are shown at right.

6 / Headline sizes should conform to those in the headline style guide at the end of this chapter. No other sizes should be created.

NOTE / Tribune design flourishes with flexible headline use:

a / Consider the sense of the headline before worrying about head count. The meaning of the headline should flow naturally and clearly.

b / Copy editors are encouraged to consult with page layout people if headline orders seem restrictive. The goal, within limits of design principles, is to tell the story in the headline.

c / Short lines are encouraged. White space at the end of lines enhances design and keeps lines of type from running into adjoining heads.

d / There is no set number of lines for a one-column headline. The number may vary between two and five (at the direction of the news desk), depending on the size of the type and the length needed to convey the message.

Hospitals Continued from page 1B

said.

An unusual coalition of board members — some involved in promoting health care for low-income families, others practicing physicians — pushed for the study of obstetrics-pediatrics exceptions. Officials of many of the hospitals also have been complaining.

Here are the hospitals that have been operating specialty services that *don't* meet the health board's

Campaign

Continued from page 3B

quist does not. He believes the budget can be balanced over a number of years, and he points to the rising cost of imported oil, not the federal budget, as the economy's No. 1 goblin.

Hagedorn believes that the first step in solving our energy problems should to be encourage more domestic oil exploration; Berquist emphasizes the potential for alcohol distillation from farm products.

guidelines.

The board had voted 13 to 10 on Sept. 24 to adopt the original guidelines without studying possible exceptions. A detailed minority report was written after that meeting. The Human Resources Committee of the Metropolitan Council, which is the health board's parent organization, asked the board to reconsider the subject, which it did last night.

While the board lacks direct power

Point size range for Helvetica bold/

Drawing may be taught by tutors; but design only by heaven
12

Drawing may be taught by tutors; but design only by heaven
14

Drawing may be taught by tutors; but design only by heave
18

Drawing may be taught by tutors; but design c
24

Drawing may be taught by tutors; but
30

Drawing may be taught by tu
36

Drawing may be taught by
42

Drawing may be taught
48

Drawing may be taug
54

Drawing may be ta
60

Drawing may be
72

Drawing may l
80

100%

Point size range for Helvetica light /

Drawing may be taught by tutors; but design only by heaven
12

Drawing may be taught by tutors; but design only by heaven
14

Drawing may be taught by tutors; but design only by heaven
18

Drawing may be taught by tutors; but design only
24

Drawing may be taught by tutors; but de
30

Drawing may be taught by tutors;
36

Drawing may be taught by tu
42

Drawing may be taught by
48

Drawing may be taugh
54

Drawing may be tau
60

Drawing may be
72

Drawing may b
80

100%

4 /

Spacing /

In general:

The Tribune uses space instead of vertical and horizontal printed rules to separate elements on a page. The principle once again is creation of white space and a clean look by elimination of printed rules.

Rules of spacing must be followed in layout and page pasteup to keep elements on the grid. The space unit referred to here is the 9.5 point grid unit.

1 / Spacing elements on a page:

a / Put two units of space between six-column page logo and the first lines of type on the page.

b / Put two units of space between page logos of smaller size and type on the page.

c / Put one unit of space between RELATED elements on the page.

d / Put two units of space between UNRELATED elements on the page.

e / Put two units of space between news content and tops of advertisements.

2 / Spacing of body type:

The computer takes care of body-type spacing, placing one slug (9.5 points) between paragraphs. Otherwise:

a / One unit of space is used below bylines or credit lines when they are single lines. If they consist of two lines, no space is used between those lines, but one unit is used below the two-line unit.

b / No space is used between dateline and lead of story.

c / When 7-point or 8-point type is used, space is left at the bottom of the type to get back on the grid.

d / One unit of space is used between the last line of the story and the jump line.

e / One unit is used above and below keys or other devices inserted into a story, and one unit is used above shirt-tails at the end of stories.

f / One unit is used between a column heading or stock head and type below it.

3 / Spacing of headline type:

The computer places proper space between the lines of a multi-line

Headline grid spacing guide

Head size	Number of grid units (9½ pt units)	In points
12pt	2 grid units	19pts
14pt	2 grid units	19pts
18pt	2 grid units	19pts
24pt	3 grid units	28½pts
30pt	3 grid units	28½pts
36pt	4 grid units	38pts
42pt	5 grid units	47½pts
48pt	5 grid units	47½pts
54pt	6 grid units	57pts
60pt	7 grid units	66½pts
72pt	8 grid units	76pts
80pt	9 grid units	85½pts

headline to keep it on the grid.

(For example, 6.5 points of space will be put between two lines of 30-point type. The resulting space used, 66.5 points, is divisible by the basic 9.5 points.)

In a single or multi-line headline, the space below the last line of the headline is determined in this way:

Starting with the ascender of the last line, drop the required number of units to the ascender of the first line of text. This number will, of course, vary according to the size of the headline type.

If that sounds confusing, make it simple by referring to the accompanying table indicating the number of grid units (each is 9.5 points) allowed for each headline size.

5 /

Block makeup /

Block (or modular) makeup is basic to Tribune design. It contributes to attractiveness of layout and, while it may be difficult to use, assists clear presentation of news. Well used, it can enhance communication, assist news judgment and create beauty on the page.

What to do /

1 / Lay out all elements on an open news page in rectangular form. Square off type under headlines.

2 / On pages where ads are laid out in pyramid form, use block layout as much as possible.

3 / Use horizontal layout but vary its possible monotony by using vertical blocks of type under one-column headlines.

4 / Avoid piling blocks of type of the same size upon each other.

5 / Don't split the page with a single column of type running from top to bottom.

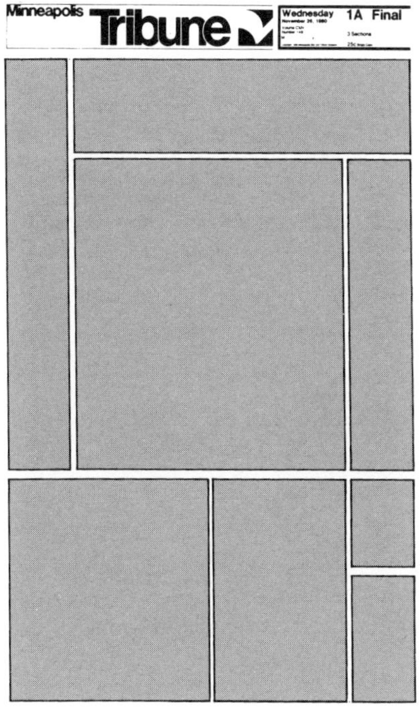

Minneapolis Tribune

Wednesday
November 26, 1980
Volume CXIV
Number 149

1A Final

3 Sections

25¢ Single Copy

Inflation outlook called 'poor'

New York Times Service

Washington, D.C.
The renewed surge in mortgage rates helped push consumer prices up 1 percent last month, to an annual rate of 12.6 percent.

The October increase matched September's and meant that prices have risen 12.2 percent thus far in 1980, before seasonal adjustment. The Consumer Price Index (CPI) rose 13.3 percent last year.

The index now stands at 253.9, meaning items that cost $100 in 1967 now cost $253.90. Stated another way, the 1967 dollar is now worth 39 cents.

The October news was in line with economists' expectations and led to renewed predictions that monthly consumer prices will rise 1 percent or more for at least the next six months.

"The inflation outlook is poor," said Lawrence Chimerine, chairman of Chase Econometrics, a forecasting firm. "We're expecting about an 11 percent increase in the CPI next year." The last official administration forecast, in July, was a 9.6 percent increase.

The October report illustrated the difficulties facing President-elect Reagan, who has made curbing inflation a primary economic goal.

In a separate report yesterday, the Labor Department said the buying power of an "average" urban worker with a nonworking wife and two children declined six-tenths of 1 percent last month and was 6 percent below a year ago. The decline was caused by inflation and a reduction in hours worked that more than offset a slight increase in hourly wages.

The decline in purchasing power reinforced economists' fears that consumers would be unable to continue increasing their spending, increases that were largely responsible for pulling the economy out of recession.

The big news in the latest consumer price report was the jump in housing costs. Up seventeenths of 1 percent in September, they rose 1.3 percent in October. The largest part of the change was in financing costs. After declining sharply in August and slightly in September, financing, taxes and insurance charges rose 3.1 percent in October.

That turnaround reflects a reversal in mortgage rates that occurred in late summer, when rates halted several months of decline and began rising again.

Economy continued on page 4A

4 killed in San Bernardino firestorm

Tribune News Services

San Bernardino, Calif.
A firestorm fed by high winds raced across the foothills of San Bernardino on Tuesday. Four people were killed, 400 injured and 257 homes destroyed or damaged.

Acting Gov. Mike Curb declared a state of emergency in San Bernardino County, citing property damage estimates of $44 million.

The San Bernardino fire, which erupted Monday, was one of nine raging across 50,000 acres of brush and timberland in Southern California, destroying or damaging more than 300 homes and forcing 10,000 people to flee.

In San Bernardino, an industrial city of 115,000, thousands abandoned their homes as fire charred 12,000 acres in the city and in the San Bernardino National Forest to the north.

The most destructive blaze, fueled by tinder-dry brush and timber, raced down Waterman Canyon driven by hot, dry winds that gusted to 45 m.p.h. Among the homes lost was a $500,000 mansion once owned by actress Dorothy Lamour.

About 1,900 fire fighters battled the San Bernardino blaze, but aircraft could not be used because of the winds.

The fire was blamed for $25 million in property losses and $4.5 million in watershed damage. Flooding may be the area's next big headache.

At nightfall, officials said that the erratic winds had subsided and that the fires "were holding." But they worried that resort communities in the San Bernardino Mountains, which were spared when the winds pushed the flames away, could be threatened if the gusts died completely.

The charred bodies of a San Bernardino couple were found in their yard in the North Park area after their children reported them missing. They were identified as Earl Weity, 63, and his wife, Edith, 61. Joseph Benjamin, 54, suffered a fatal heart attack while watering down his property in west off the fire, and Rose Myers, 64, died while being evacuated from her home.

City fire spokesman Jimmy Jews said at least 150 of the homes were destroyed. "Without a doubt, it is unequivocally the worst fire we've ever had," he said.

Two San Bernardino policemen lost their homes in North Park. Capt. Paul Bonanno said he tried to save his with a garden hose, but "the house next door started burning and it was like facing a flamethrower." Bonanno, 46, his wife and two children escaped unhurt and returned to work.

Fires continued on page 12A

A neighborhood in north San Bernardino, Calif., lay in ruins Tuesday. It was devastated by Monday's Waterman Canyon fire.

Associated Press

Quake toll passes 3,000 in Italy

Tribune News Services

Naples, Italy
The death toll in southern Italy's earthquake rose past 3,000 Tuesday, and the tremors continued as Pope John Paul visited the disaster area to pray with grieving survivors.

The national police office coordinating casualty reports from the more than 100 towns and villages hit by Sunday's quake said that 2,400 bodies had been recovered and that about 700 more were still buried under rubble in a single village, Laviano, in the province of Salerno.

By dusk, rescue teams had still not reached villages where hundreds more people were said to be buried under tons of debris.

As the death count rose, severe aftershocks shook the already devastated area, causing the collapse of some damaged buildings.

Whole towns were declared uninhabitable because of quake damage, and authorities said hundreds of thousands of people were homeless.

The pope flew through the devastated region by helicopter, stopping to visit a hospital in the town of Potenza 86 miles east of Naples, then flying on to Balvano, the mountain village where worshipers were crushed in the collapse of a church wall. The pope wanted to visit the site of the church, but police and soldiers kept him away for fear that aftershocks would topple the portions of the ruins still standing.

Strong aftershocks shook the ground during his visit, causing the collapse of a fire station at Salerno, 27 miles south of Naples, and a government

Quake continued on page 4A

Sprinkler checks falter in city

By R.T. Rybak
Staff Writer

Minneapolis fire inspectors do not know whether the sprinkler systems will work in any building constructed since 1975 because the department says it has no one who understands them.

City fire officials say that the loss of the department's only plans analyst five years ago has made it impossible to know how many sprinklers will go off and whether they will put out a fire.

There is now $350 million worth of construction going on in downtown Minneapolis. Are these new buildings safe? City Fire Marshal Marshall Bush, who signed their occupancy statements, said, "From my meager expertise, I couldn't say for sure."

Minneapolis Fire Chief Clarence Nimmerfroh said Tuesday that the fire marshal does not have the expertise to understand the complex sprinkling systems now being built. "The fire marshal looks at blueprint of new buildings before they are built but I don't think he knows what he is looking at," he said.

Yesterday, Nimmerfroh informed city coordinator David Nikitas that he had ordered the fire marshal to stop signing occupancy certificates for new buildings. When asked later whether Nimmerfroh's decision will mean no new construction can occur in Minneapolis, Nikitas said, "I got Clarence's letter three hours ago and I really can't answer that."

The state building code says sprinklers, which are designed to contain a fire and cut smoke, must now be put in any building over 75 feet high.

From 1961 to 1975 new sprinkler systems were examined by the Minneapolis Fire Prevention Bureau's plans analyst Benjamin Pinson.

Inspections continued on page 4A

Leonard takes title back from Duran

Associated Press

New Orleans, La.
Sugar Ray Leonard regained the World Boxing Council welterweight championship Tuesday night when Roberto Duran quit late in the eighth round.

Duran cited cramps in his stomach and right arm as reason for the abrupt ending, and said he was returning home boxing. He had won the title from Leonard by unanimous decision in June.

(Details on page 1C.)

Almanac

Wednesday, Nov. 26, 1980
331st day; 35 to go this year
Sunrise: 7:25. Sunset: 4:36.

Today's weather
Clouds, mild

Cloudy skies and a high in the mid 30s are predicted for today for the Twin Cities area.

Other predicted high temperatures: Minnesota, low 30s to low 40s; North Dakota, 30s; South Dakota, 40s; Wisconsin, low 40s.

Arts	5B	Obituaries	7C
Business	8-10A	Sports	1-4C
Comics	4B	Theaters	4,5C
Corrections	2A	TV, Radio	7B
Editorial	6-7A	Weather	5B

Tribune
telephone

City suspends head of housing unit for 13 work days

By Tom Davies
Staff Writer

The director of the Minneapolis inspections department was suspended for 13 work days Tuesday as a result of allegations that some of the housing inspectors he supervises did little or no work for the city.

Sol Jacobs, who has worked for the city for 31 years and has headed the inspections department for five, was suspended yesterday by City Coordinator David Nikitas for "the lack of management control and low productivity and falsification of official departmental documents by certain employees in the inspections department."

Nikitas said the suspension came in the midst of an in-house investigation and after review of videotapes of the WCCO-TV series on housing inspectors, broadcast last week. That series alleged widespread nonwork by the city's housing inspectors.

Sol Jacobs

Nikitas said the in-house investigation is continuing, but would not say if further suspensions are planned. He did say, however, that those conducting the investigation think "further suspensions are likely."

Jacobs could not be reached for comment last night, but City Council President Alice Rainville — who was present when Jacobs learned of the suspension — said he was very

shown on television. The last time city officials tried to fire a housing inspector — for allegedly making racist remarks about Indians — their efforts faltered before the Minneapolis Civil Service Commission, and that case is now before the Minnesota Supreme Court.

Suspend continued on page 3A

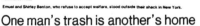

Emuel and Shirley Benton, who refuse to accept welfare, stood outside their shack in New York.

Associated Press

One man's trash is another's home

By Timothy Harper
Associated Press

New York, N.Y.
They call their tar-paper shack home, their five children healthy and themselves happy. Emuel and Shirley Benton are carving out their own tiny corner in the concrete canyons.

Rejecting welfare, the Bentons have built and furnished a hut with other people's garbage in the lot across the street from the housing project from which they were evicted last year.

"We don't need welfare," Emuel Benton, 54, said. "What could they give me that's better than what I got?"

"They can't give us a welfare apartment; that's better than our little house." Shirley Benton, 42, said.

The family, whose sole income is Benton's $200 monthly disability check, was evicted after his second heart attack forced him to quit as a truck driver. For 28 weeks, the family slept in their battered station wagon.

Then, Emuel Benton, whose only construction experience was building a doghouse when he was 7, assembled a hut with

Squatters continued on page 4A

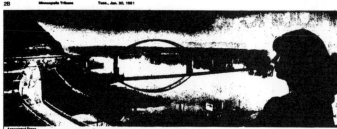

2B   Minneapolis Tribune   Tues., Jan. 20, 1981

Associated Press

A 2-mile commute has turned into a 70-mile 'hardship'

A portion of the Hwy. 18 bridge linking Prairie du Chien, Wis., and McGregor and Marquette, Iowa, has been closed, turning a 2-mile commute into a 70-mile journey for residents on both sides of the Mississippi River. The quarter-mile span of the 6-year-old bridge was closed Friday after a 4-inch crack was discovered in a steel plate. Engineers feared the crack and other structural defects could cause the bridge to collapse. Monday's rush hour brought home the effect of the shutdown on commuters in McGregor and

Prairie Du Chien, who had to drive 35 miles to Lansing, Iowa, to cross the river. Marquette Mayor Donna Kinley said the bridge closing is a hardship for that town's residents, who must drive 134 miles roundtrip if they work in Prairie du Chien. Prairie Du Chien Mayor Jim Bittner, who estimated that 50 percent of the retail sales in his town are made to Iowans, said the economic effects on his city could be disastrous. Work on the bridge was expected to begin this week, but repairs could take up to a year, officials said.

Film maker cancels
Minneapolis appearance

Wim Wenders, West German film maker, has canceled planned appearances at Walker Art Center next Monday and Tuesday, the center announced Monday.

However, Wenders has sent the Walker a print of a new film that he did with the late American director Nicholas Ray. The new film, "Lightning Over Water," has had only one previous U.S. screening, in California last month.

It will be shown at the Walker at 8 p.m. next Monday and 7:30 p.m. Tuesday. The Monday showing is basically for holders of tickets to the Walker's "Meaning of Modernism" lecture series, but some tickets may be available because of late cancellations, a Walker spokeswoman said. The Tuesday showing will be open to the public.

The schedule of films to be shown in a Wenders retrospective beginning Saturday has been changed, the Walker also announced yesterday. The new schedule: "The Wrong Move," at 2 p.m. Saturday; "Alice in the Cities," 7:30 p.m. Saturday; "Lightning Over Water," 8 p.m. Monday and 7:30 p.m. Tuesday; "Kings of the Road," 7:30 p.m. Jan. 29; "The American Friend," 7:30 p.m. Jan. 31; "The Goalie's Anxiety at the Penalty Kick," 7:30 p.m. Feb. 2.

274 die in India's cold wave

Authorities said Monday that 274 people have died in a three-week cold wave sweeping northern India.

Erma Bombeck

Last August, the Associated Press rented a tree across the street from Gov. Ronald Reagan's Los Angeles residence.

For 50 cents a day, it got exclusive rights to the tree, where its reporters could view and report on the comings and goings of the presidential candidate.

NBC rented an apartment down the street, ABC rented a garage and it was rumored CBS had exclusive rights to a fence nearby.

Why do we do it?

Why do we strip our presidents of every personal thought, every intimate relationship, every corner of privacy to satisfy our curiosity? Why do we track down their families, attack them and lay them bare for cameras and writers to feed upon?

Why is it indeed that fewer than three dozen reporters were uncovering Watergate while hundreds were interviewing President Nixon's barber?

Ironically, the White House is the only bastion in this country where freedom of speech is punishable by public scrutiny.

It occurs to me if a TV network is willing to try an experiment in the sports booth where the commentators are silenced and everyone must watch the game to see what is going on, why can't we try it for our first family?

I think we could tough it out not knowing

- How big the White House ham is for Easter.
- Who is dating a married secret service man.
- Where the president jogs and what his time is.
- Who had a history of mental illness.
- How big was the scar from his operation.
- Whether or not they share the same bed.
- How much she paid for her inaugural gown.
- Whether or not they went to church last Sunday.
- What the first family's butcher, chauffeur, brother or mother thinks of our foreign policy.

There are not a couple of life-sized toys we have put in a dollhouse in Washington to look at and manipulate. These are flesh-and-blood humans beings who have a monumental task ahead of them and who need a certain sense of self and an occasional escape from the demands to function.

I don't know President and Nancy Reagan at all.

I have a feeling that soon I will know more about them than I have a right to know.

The name for people with parents from Spain isn't always so plain

Ann Landers

Dear Ann: Ever since I can remember, whenever anyone asks me my nationality, I get the same ignorant responses. My parents came from Spain. People from all walks of life say: "You don't look Spanish." "Do your parents come from Cuba, Mexico or Puerto Rico?"

How can they be so dumb? Have they never seen a map? Don't they realize Cubans are from Cuba, Mexicans are from Mexico; Spaniards are from Spain?

The definition of "Spanish," according to my dictionary, is, "The inhabitants of Spain." Please, Ann, print this letter. I am sick to death of foolish questions and idiotic responses. I Am What I Am

Ann says: Nationality means the nation of your birth. You are an American.

I learned long ago that when people ask me, "What is your nationality?" the question they REALLY are asking is, "What is your religion?"

Some clods will ask you anything. This does not mean they are entitled to an answer. Give them a drop-dead look and change the subject.

Dear Ann: My husband has not worn his wedding ring for over a year because he developed a skin problem. The skin around his ring itched and cracked, leaving a painful raw spot. He tried leaving his ring off for a couple of weeks to let it heal, but each time he put it back, the rash returned.

Later, I told her privately that I didn't think her joke was appropriate in front of the kids. She replied, "Teen-agers know everything today. Why be hypocritical? They want to be treated like adults." What about this, Ann? Unsure

Ann says: A mother who tells a raunchy joke in the presence of her teen-agers is not treating them as adults. She is setting a poor example and confusing them. Children do not want their parents to be "pals." They want authority figures who represent something to live up to and be proud of.

Dear Ann: Our new neighbors have teen-agers the same ages as ours — 14 and 16. Recently, we invited them over for Sunday brunch. "Mrs. N." told a joke I considered off-color. My husband blushed. The kids looked pained. I was embarrassed.

Woman to marry man who adopted her son

United Press International

Melbourne, Australia

When Shirley Rider gave up her illegitimate son for adoption 10 years ago at a home for unwed mothers, she never thought she would see him again.

But now Rider, who has been married and divorced since then, is to get remarried — to the man who adopted the boy.

Rider said the first met her fiance 11 months ago and, as they discussed their life stories, it hit her that his adopted son, Shane, was her natural son. The fact was confirmed last week by an adoptions officer.

Rider has two other children, age 6 and 3, from her marriage. Her fiance, who has not been identified, has a 7-year-old daughter from his previous marriage.

Pyramidal ad layout impedes block layout on inside page.

6/

Pictures
and cutlines/

The Tribune is a visual newspaper. Photos, illustrations, charts, maps and graphs are a dramatic and helpful way of illustrating the news, orienting the reader and presenting facts quickly.

These are the guidelines:

1/Picture widths are figured in inches to make them fit on the grid. Sizes are given in the chart on page 72.

2/Cutlines are set in 10-point Helvetica bold on a 9.5 point slug.

3/Photo credit lines are set in 10-point Helvetica light on 9.5.

3/Cutlines for pictures with stories are set in lines equal to the width of the pictures.

4/Cutlines for pictures without stories are split in accordance with a formula starting with the three-column size:

Three-column/Wrap twice (set 19.2 picas)

Four-column/Wrap twice (set 25.11 picas)

Five-column/Wrap three times (set 21.5 picas)

Six-column/Wrap three times (two column)

NOTE: Use of Atex cutline formats eliminates the need to specify cutline measures. (Formats indicate the size of the picture and whether it is freestanding or with a story). For example:

⌐2collo⌐ ⌐2colws⌐

5/Cutlines for pictures without stories carry an 18-point Helvetica bold headline on top of the lines. (The headline may be light for a feature picture.)

6/Spacing rules:

a. Use no space between bottom of picture and photo credit line.

b. Use no space between picture and name line with one-columns.

c. For pictures with stories, use one unit of space between credit line and cutlines.

d. For pictures that stand alone, use one unit of space between credit line and headline and one unit between headline and cutlines.

e. If credit lines are not used, place one unit of space between picture and cutlines.

7/Half-column cuts are used in panels, never indented in type.

8/One-point rule borders are used on all pictures except half-column cuts.

HOW THEY SHOULD LOOK/ Cutline style is shown on the accompanying picture pages. One-, two- and three-column pictures are reproduced full size; four-, five- and six-column pictures are reduced to half size.

Cutlines styles for lines-only pictures/

1 column/

Making the point

Never one to let himself be long depressed, Hubert Humphrey was back on the job Monday, not as vice-president and not, after his defeat by Richard Nixon, as president — but as teacher. He had accepted a $30,000-a-year professorship that split his teaching time between Macalester College and the University of Minnesota.

2 column/

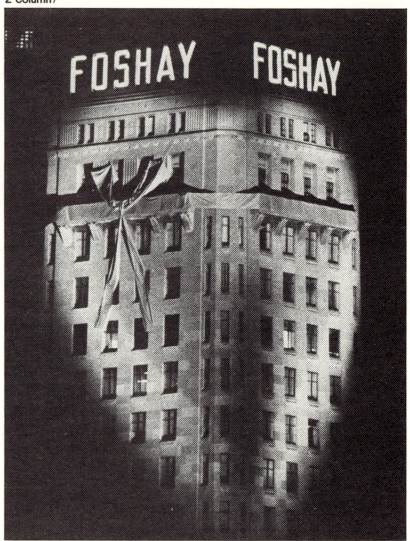

Staff Photo by Donald Black

A yellow ribbon for the Foshay

A giant sign of jubilation appeared Monday on the Foshay Tower. A yellow ribbon was draped around the building as the hour for the release of the American hostages in Iran approached. MEPC American Properties, which owns the building, had the ribbon made Monday, and workmen put it up Monday night.

100%

Cutlines styles for lines-only pictures/

3 column/

Staff Photo by Earl Seubert

A brisk wind blew, the furrows followed free

Minneapolitans took to the parks for picnics, some played in lawn sprinklers, some sat on their porches and fanned themselves Tuesday as temperatures rose into the 90s for the ninth day in a row. Still others took to the breezes and the waters of the city lakes. The sparkling waters of Calhoun and Harriet were dotted with sailboats all day. No relief from the heat was in sight.

100%

Cutlines styles for lines-only pictures/

4 column/

Staff Photo by Darlene Pfister

Even for Isaac Stern, rehearsals mean sweat and hard work

Isaac Stern, perhaps the foremost violinist of his generation, began rehearsals Friday for a series of concerts with the St. Paul Chamber Orchestra. At 60, Stern plays more than 100 concerts a year. Of the orchestra he said: ''They come to it with a smile. They haven't lost that fire of trying for something.'' Stern was working hard rehearsing the Vaughan-Williams Concerto Academico, a piece he had not played for 30 years.

5 column/

Staff Photo by Kent Kobersteen

Governors galore turned out to hear The Governor speak

Gov. Al Quie delivered his State of the State message Wednesday as five former governors listened and applauded. From left were Wendell Anderson, Harold Le-Vander, Karl Rolvaag, Elmer L. Andersen and C. Elmer Anderson. Quie gave the governors, legislators and the public only a glimmer of how he plans to solve the state's worst money shortage in years. The burning question: Does he or does he not want to raise taxes? ''There are ways to increase income and sales taxes without raising tax rates,'' said Roger Moe, Senate DFL majority leader. ''A tax in sheep's clothing is still a tax.'' Nonsense, responded IR Sen. Jim Ulland of Duluth. ''Quie really makes it clear that he will accept no income or sales tax increases, period.''

50%

Cutlines styles for lines-only pictures/

6 column/

Staff Photo by Kent Kobersteen

What is so rare as a fine iceboating day on the lake?

The wind blew gently, the sun was bright and the temperature mild Monday, to make a perfect day for iceboating on Lake Calhoun. Minnesota's mild, virtually snowless, winter continued, to the consternation of cross-country skiers and the despair of those who sell snow shovels and snow blowers. There were compensations, however, for other folks who tramped the city's streets without overshoes. Today's forecast calls for more of the same sort of weather: a chance of snow flurries, to be sure, but nothing serious; a high temperature in the mid-20s, and a bit of a chill tonight, with 2 to 7 below zero. In Phoenix yesterday the high was 76, in Los Angeles 83 and at Fairbanks 0.

50%

Cutlines styles for pictures with stories/

1 column/

Humphrey in class

2 column/

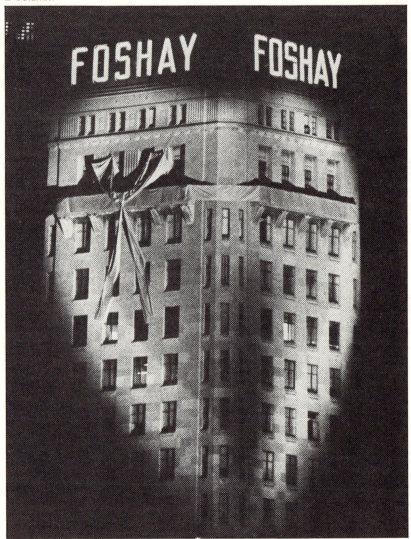

Staff Photo by Donald Black

A happy yellow ribbon for the Foshay Tower.

100%

Cutlines styles for pictures with stories/

3 column/

Staff Photo by Earl Seubert

A brisk wind helped sailors Monday on Lake Calhoun.

100%

Cutlines styles for pictures with stories/

4 column/

Staff Photo by Darlene Pfister

A towel was handy when Isaac Stern worked up a sweat during rehearsal.

5 column/

Staff Photo by Kent Kobersteen

Applauding Gov. Al Quie's State of the State message Wednesday were five former governors; from left, Wendell Anderson, Harold LeVander, Karl Rolvaag, Elmer L. Andersen and C. Elmer Anderson.

50%

Cutlines styles for pictures with stories/

6 column/

Staff Photo by Kent Kobersteen

The wind blew gently, the sun was bright and the temperature mild Monday, to make a perfect day for iceboating on Lake Calhoun.

50%

Inch equivalents to 9.5-pt grid units/

9½pt units	Inches
1	⅛
2	¼
3	⅜
4	½
5	⅝
6	¾
7	⅞
8	1
9	1³⁄₁₆
10	1⁵⁄₁₆
11	1½
12	1⅝
13	1¾
14	1⅞
15	2
16	2⅛
17	2¼
18	2⅜
19	2½
20	2⅝
21	2¾
22	2⅞
23	3
24	3⅛
25	3¼
26	3⅜
27	3½
28	3¹¹⁄₁₆
29	3⅞
30	4
31	4⅛
32	4¼
33	4⅜
34	4½
35	4⅝
36	4¾
37	4⅞
38	5
39	5⅛
40	5⁵⁄₁₆
41	5⁷⁄₁₆
42	5½
43	5⅝
44	5¾
45	5⅞
46	6
47	6⅛
48	6¼
49	6⅜
50	6½
51	6¾
52	6⅞
53	7
54	7⅛
55	7¼
56	7⅜
57	7½
58	7⅝
59	7¾
60	7⅞
61	8
62	8⅛
63	8¼
64	8⅜
65	8½
66	8¹¹⁄₁₆
67	8¹³⁄₁₆
68	9
69	9⅛
70	9¼
71	9⅜
72	9½
73	9⅝
74	9¾
75	9⅞
76	10
77	10⅛
78	10¼
79	10⅜
80	10½
81	10⅝
82	10¾
83	10⅞
84	11
85	11³⁄₁₆
86	11⁵⁄₁₆
87	11½
88	11⅝
89	11¾
90	11⅞
91	12

Picture sizes

Columns	Width in inches	
	Standard	Used only in combinations
1 col	2¹⁄₁₆	
1½ col		3³⁄₁₆
2 col	4⁵⁄₁₆	
2½ col		5⁷⁄₁₆
3 col	6⁹⁄₁₆	
3½ col		7¹¹⁄₁₆
4 col	8¹³⁄₁₆	
4½ col		9⅞
5 col	11¹⁄₁₆	
5½ col		12¹⁄₁₆
6 col	13¼	

Chapter

5/

Design/

Special
feature
sections

Design/
Special feature sections

The basic principles of Tribune design and rules of layout apply in the special feature sections of the Tribune.

There are, however, purposeful differences in design approach and use of graphics. These differences, evolving since the original design of 1971, were planned by Michael Carroll, Tribune design director.

"The objective is to make these special sections **look** special — different from the news sections," Carroll said. "So special, in fact, that when readers plow through the newspaper, a section stands by itself and says, 'I am different.' "

Just as design style in a news section tells the reader: "This is news," the variant feature design style tells the reader: "This is features."

While a different design approach makes a section **look** different, that difference does not break the continuity of design style or contradict design principles. There must be design links between different sorts of sections. The "Tribune look" must be recognizable.

The design link is forged of common principles and rules: Headline type is Helvetica, spacing rules are the same, modular layout is used as much as possible.

The differences in the design of covers or of special subject pages are major, however.

In general, the feature sections have a more relaxed appearance; Tribune design becomes flexible and fluid. Design is used to reflect the different functions of the sections. A few special daily pages are "bridges" between news and features and share design characteristics of each.

At first glance, the reader may think the Tribune has abandoned the grid system on the special section covers. In a sense, it has, although more times than not a grid is recognizable.

Body type sets up part of a basic grid. Headlines are set on the basic Tribune grid system.

"The feature section covers have what I call a 'floating' grid," Carroll says. "It's called this because it allows more freedom for the

Michael Carroll, Tribune design director.

designer, but still contains the limitations of a few standing design features.''

While editors design news covers, the special section pages are design projects. Their wide open spaces — the flag is always used at the top of the page — allow designers to work with type, illustrations, photos or graphics of any sort to best display the subject.

''For any given cover design,'' says Carroll, ''the designer has virtually the entire page to work with — space offering scope for creativity. Tribune designers have differing styles of illustration, and this allows and adds to variety of style and design from week to week.''

Difference in size is the chief design characteristic of two other Sunday Tribune sections. Picture magazine, the Tribune's roto publication, and the smaller-sized TV Week follow in general the Tribune's design principles.

In addition to the weekday and Sunday feature sections, different design features are used in two special Tribune pages, Perspective and News Plus, the ''bridge'' pages, of both news and feature nature.

Design, then, can be a means of helping the reader identify the character and content of a section — whether news, newsy features or features.

The special sections and pages/

Sunday/
The Sunday feature sections are Family/Living, Entertainment/Arts, Outdoors, Home/Garden and Travel/Adventure. They are "total" feature sections and have common design characteristics.

Sunday covers/
Cover page flags are deeper than others in the Tribune. Section names are in large, stylized Helvetica letters, outlined and shaded. Components of the flags are designed on the basic Tribune grid. A graphic key enhances the flag, sometimes referring to a feature inside the section, sometimes repeating a detail of cover art.

Anchoring the flag is a Scotch rule, a design characteristic of the Sunday sections. One-point rules run down the sides of each page.

Cover type is set 11 point Helvetica light on a 10.5-point slug in varying widths. (Helvetica body text is slightly smaller than the designated size.)

Cover art may range from photographs to illustrations, usually used large or in layouts and sometimes with color. Scotch rules may be used to separate elements horizontally on the page. A Scotch rule is used at the bottom of the page. (The Tribune's Scotch rule is made up of a one-point rule and a six-point rule, with the lighter rule on top.)

family/living

parents and children / medical care / life styles / food

Minneapolis Tribune

Sunday
November 23 / 1980

Dressing down muggers / 8FX

1F x

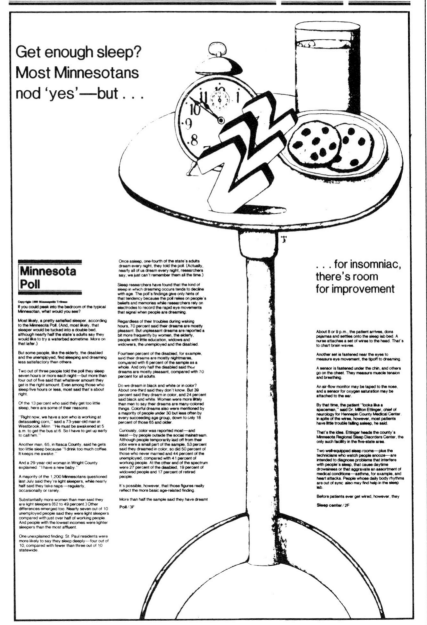

Get enough sleep?
Most Minnesotans
nod 'yes'—but . . .

. . . for insomniac,
there's room
for improvement

Minnesota Poll

Copyright 1980 Minneapolis Tribune

If you could peek into the bedroom of the typical Minnesotan, what would you see?

Most likely, a pretty satisfied sleeper, according to the Minnesota Poll. (And, most likely, that sleeper would be tucked into a double bed, although nearly half the state's adults say they would like to try a waterbed sometime. More on that later.)

But some people, like the elderly, the disabled and the unemployed, find sleeping and dreaming less satisfactory than others.

Two out of three people told the poll they sleep seven hours or more each night—but more than four out of five said that whatever amount they get is the right amount. Even among those who sleep five hours or less, most said that's about right.

Of the 13 percent who said they get too little sleep, here are some of their reasons.

"Right now, we have a son who is working at detasseling corn," said a 73-year-old man in Westbrook, Minn. "He must be awakened at 5 a.m. to get the bus at 6. So I have to get up early to call him."

Another man, 65, in Itasca County, said he gets too little sleep because "I drink too much coffee. It keeps me awake."

And a 29-year-old woman in Wright County explained: "I have a new baby."

A majority of the 1,200 Minnesotans questioned last July said they're light sleepers, while nearly half said they take naps—regularly, occasionally or rarely.

Substantially more women than men said they are light sleepers (62 to 49 percent.) Other differences emerged too. Nearly seven out of 10 unemployed people said they were light sleepers compared with just over half of working people. And people with the lowest incomes were lighter sleepers than the most affluent.

One unexplained finding: St. Paul residents were more likely to say they sleep deeply—four out of 10, compared with fewer than three out of 10 statewide.

Once asleep, one-fourth of the state's adults dream every night, they told the poll. (Actually, nearly all of us dream every night, researchers say; we just can't remember them all the time.)

Sleep researchers have found that the kind of sleep in which dreaming occurs tends to decline with age. The poll's findings give only hints of that tendency because the poll relies on people's beliefs and memories while researchers rely on electrodes to record the rapid eye movements that signal when people are dreaming.

Regardless of their troubles during waking hours, 70 percent said their dreams are mostly pleasant. But unpleasant dreams are reported a bit more frequently by women, the elderly, people with little education, widows and widowers, the unemployed and the disabled.

Fourteen percent of the disabled, for example, said their dreams are mostly nightmares, compared with 6 percent of the sample as a whole. And only half the disabled said their dreams are mostly pleasant, compared with 70 percent for all adults.

Do we dream in black and white or in color? About one-third said they don't know. But 39 percent said they dream in color, and 24 percent said black and white. Women were more likely than men to say their dreams are many-colored things. Colorful dreams also were mentioned by a majority of people under 30 but less often by every succeeding age group, down to only 18 percent of those 65 and older.

Curiously, color was reported most—and least—by people outside the social mainstream. Although people temporarily laid off from their jobs were a small part of the sample, 53 percent said they dreamed in color; so did 50 percent of those who never married and 44 percent of the unemployed, compared with 41 percent of working people. At the other end of the spectrum were 27 percent of the disabled, 19 percent of widowed people and 17 percent of retired people.

It's possible, however, that those figures really reflect the more basic age-related pattern.

More than half the sample said they have dreamt

Poll / 3F

About 8 or 9 p.m., the patient arrives, dons pajamas and settles onto the sleep lab bed. A nurse attaches a set of wires to the head. That's to chart brain waves.

Another set is fastened near the eyes to measure eye movement, the tipoff to dreaming.

A sensor is fastened under the chin, and others go on the chest. They measure muscle tension and breathing.

An air-flow monitor may be taped to the nose, and a sensor for oxygen saturation may be attached to the ear.

By that time, the patient "looks like a spaceman," said Dr. Milton Ettinger, chief of neurology for Hennepin County Medical Center. In spite of the wires, however, most patients have little trouble falling asleep, he said.

That's the idea. Ettinger heads the county's Minnesota Regional Sleep Disorders Center, the only such facility in the five-state area.

Two well-equipped sleep rooms—plus the technicians who watch people snooze—are intended to diagnose problems that interfere with people's sleep, that cause daytime drowsiness or that aggravate an assortment of medical conditions—asthma, for example, and heart attacks. People whose daily body rhythms are out of sync also may find help in the sleep lab.

Before patients ever get wired, however, they

Sleep center / 2F

family/living

parents and children / medical care / life styles / food

▼ Minneapolis Tribune

Sunday
September 23 / 1979

Erma Bombeck / 7FX

1Fx

Break a mirror and it's seven years of bad luck . . . To have a girl, sleep with a frying pan under the bed . . . The sex of the first baby kissed by a new bride determines the sex of the first child . . . If you are jealous of your lover, eat a carrot three nights in succession . . . If two letters from suitors are delivered to you at once, you will never marry either.

If you believe old wives' tales, you'll be superstitious

By Joe Kimball
Staff Writer

Lucille Wallace won't put hats on a bed. She'll put them in a closet, on the corner of a chair, anywhere but on a bed. **A hat on a bed brings bad luck,** she says, although she isn't sure why.

Wallace also won't give a friend something sharp—a pair of scissors, a knife, even a pen—unless a penny is offered in return. If Wallace doesn't receive a token payment, she fears the friendship will be cut.

Wallace, a 61-year-old Minneapolis woman, also says that:

Deaths always happen three in a row. That's usually just famous people, not necessarily people in your own family, she added.

If you enter a house through one door, you must leave through the same door, or you'll bring more company to the house.

If you sing before you eat, you'll cry before you sleep. "Some guy probably invented that one to keep his wife quiet," Wallace said.

"I agree that these are a lot of old wives' tales, but some are pretty interesting," she said. "My children are forever teasing me about these things, yet they'll adhere to them, too."

Old wives' tales, also called superstitions, or folk beliefs, typically deal with important areas

of life that cannot be faced with certainty, according to Gary Fine, an assistant professor of sociology at the University of Minnesota.

"They crop up as a means of explaining problems in the universe; they're a way of making the world intelligible," Fine said.

"If you ask most people if they really believe in old wives' tales, or superstitions, they'll probably say, 'No,'" Fine said. "They don't believe it in a scientific sense; it's more a residual belief, similar to a habit. They throw coins in a fountain because that is the thing to do."

Many believe that superstitions and folk beliefs are confined to primitive or uneducated people. No so, Fine said. "Even educated people have their own set of beliefs. **Fish is brain food and if a pregnant woman goes to an art museum, her child will be cultured** are examples," he said.

Some of the beliefs might possibly be based on occurrences. "Maybe years ago a pregnant woman ate fish, and her baby was born dumb, and that gave rise to that belief," Fine said. "But most of them are so old that we can't determine their origin with certainty."

Two common beliefs go back thousands of years:

Coins thrown in a fountain bring good luck. Good luck for the owner of the fountain, maybe. This ancient custom can be traced way back to the days when people believed spirits lived at the bottom of wells. Unless one paid tribute, the

ancients believed, the spirits would send misfortune.

Break a mirror and it's seven years of bad luck. In ancient times it was believed that mirrors could reveal the future. If a mirror broke, it was a sign that the gods did not want the beholder to foresee the bad times in store.

■

The term "old wives' tale" is in itself an old wives' tale. "The term implies that only old women are gullible, superstitious and gossipy," Fine said. "But, in fact, both men and women, old and young, gossip and hold certain beliefs."

■

However, many of the popular tales do concern old wives. And young wives and babies and pregnancy. Nearly every pregnant woman hears a sampling—usually soon after morning sickness, but before the craving for tomato ice cream.

Although not based in medical fact, these old wives' tales find their way through the generations, often from mother to daughter. In most cases, they are harmless:

If a pregnant woman takes anything belonging to another, her child will be a thief.

A pregnant woman should never walk over a grave, or the child will be born club-footed.

If a pregnant woman steps over a broom, she will bear a hairy child.

When pregnant, satisfy any craving or the child will have a birthmark in the shape of the food you were craving.

■

In parts of rural Alabama, though, old wives' tales are more commonly believed than here. And women there tend to trust this folklore more than medical advice, according to Anna Kline, of the Women Studies Program at the University of Alabama.

The University of Alabama is trying to determine why so many rural women there don't seek prenatal care, often not seeing a doctor until labor begins. The old wives' tales often take the place of medical care, Kline said. Kline surveyed 200 women in rural Alabama and found that 90 percent believe at least one of the following:

If a pregnant mother sees a deformity, her baby will be born deformed.

If a pregnant mother sees an open grave, her baby will always be hungry.

Newborn babies have poisons in their systems and should be fed a tea made of manure and alcohol to cause hives and bring out the poisons.

Babies shouldn't be bathed in water for six to 12 weeks or those hives will dry up. Instead, mothers should use urine from the diaper to bathe the baby.

Old wives' tales / 2FX

entertainment/arts

books / movies / plays / concerts / visual arts / calendars

▼ Minneapolis Tribune

Sunday
October 29 / 1978

1G

No samurai or kung fu roles for Kim: 'I loved Shakespeare'

By Mike Steele
Staff Writer

Randall Duk Kim is as American as apple pie. Also as American as pizza, lefse, tacos, chop suey and gefilte fish. He was born in Hawaii 35 years ago and, if he wished, he could trace his red, white and blue corpuscles to China on his mother's side and Korea on his father's. A good American boy, in other words.

Except that Kim early on decided to become an actor and, given American acting with its lavish concern over appearances, Kim coul easily have ended up as one of those hyphenated actors—the Oriental-American—playing houseboys, samurai, maybe an occasional kung fu role, certainly a World War II heavy and perhaps a James Bond adversary.

Randy Kim, however, also decided early on that he had no times for people who couldn't see beyond appearances. Before he was out of high school, he'd made up his mind to become a classical actor. He also discovered that Shakespeare could create characters of such richness and depth that nationality and bloodlines were as irrelevant as doubloons on Wall St. "I loved this man, this Shakespeare," he said, "and I knew I wanted to do his plays. They could make my heart weep or laugh. I wanted to do them well."

Kim first ran into Shakespeare when he read "Macbeth" while a senior in high school. At the same time, a community theater nearby was about to mount it. "Shaking and scared to death," he auditioned and was given the part of Malcolm. "I chuckled a few times when I was hailed king of Scotland, but I did love it," he said.

A year later he enrolled at the University of Hawaii as a religion major. "I knew I wanted to

Kim / 5D

Staff Photo by John Croft

"Acting," says Randall Duk Kim, "is just the craziest thing, isn't it?" He will play the title role in "Hamlet" at the Guthrie.

Shaun Cassidy, teen heartthrob, aims for separate acting, singing careers, but is having trouble keeping his rise to fame building at a slow pace. Page 5D.

Disney cartoons keep drawing, but young artists can't draw them

By Aljean Harmetz
New York Times Service

Los Angeles, Calif.
"The Black Cauldron," Walt Disney's $15-million animated film scheduled for 1980, is four years behind schedule. It will not be completed until Christmas, 1984, because the new crop of young animators the studio has spent six years acquiring are not yet competent to handle its complexities.

"The Black Cauldron," which is based on Lloyd Alexander's interpretations of medieval Welsh mythology, will be replaced in 1980 by a simpler and easier movie about animal friendship, "The Fox and the Hound."

At the same time that Disney's young animators are floundering in waters still too deep for them, classic Disney animation is enjoying a surprising artistic and box-office renaissance.

The re-release of Disney's 1967 "The Jungle Book" is bringing the studio $14 million, $2 million more than the picture made when it was first released 11 years ago. And the studio's last animated film, "The Rescuers," is outdrawing "Star Wars" in Paris, is an adult cult film in Western Europe, has earned $45 million for the studio, and has recently become the largest-grossing picture of all time in West Germany.

In November Mickey Mouse will be 50 years old, having first appeared in "Steamboat Willie" on Nov. 18, 1928. The empire he founded is robust. Disneyland and Disney World have been successful beyond even the dreams of Walt Disney who—against all advice—borrowed against his studio to build them. Last year the company earned $82 million on sales of $629.8 million. During the first nine months of this year the studio has had record revenues of $499,388,000 and record net income of $60,915,000.

Disney / 6D

entertainment/arts

Theater

Sunday
February 17/1980
Section G·Part I

books/movies/plays/concerts/visual arts/calendars

Minneapolis Tribune

Calendar/ 13GX

1Gx

PICASSO COMES TO THE PRAIRIE

OPENING NIGHTS AT THE WALKER

PICASSO IS FOR KIDS, TOO

THE INFLUENCE SPREADS

UNREALIZED COMMERCIAL POTENTIAL

Karla Bonoff's story not terribly dramatic, but might have been

By Michael Anthony
Staff Writer

"Headstrong teen-ager quits UCLA after six weeks to join rock band." From there, our story could go either way: "Band splits after debut in Elks lodge; discouraged teen-ager joins Salvation Army." Or how about "Band records hit single; teen-ager becomes star, donates Hope diamond to UCLA Music Department"?

Karla Bonoff's story is somewhat less dramatic. It is a fact, though, that she quit UCLA 10 years ago to form a band that included Andrew Gold, Wendy Waldman and the man who until very recently was her producer and constant companion, rock bassist Kenny Edwards. The band, called Bryndle, didn't play its first gig in an Elks lodge, however, though the group did sign with A&M and before disbanding recorded an album (with two Bonoff songs on it) that was never released.

Bonoff's fortunes remained at low ebb until 1977 when she signed with Columbia as a singer-songwriter. Her debut album, "Karla Bonoff," released that year, has sold 400,000 copies, an unusually large amount for a first album. And the fact that Linda Ronstadt at about the same time released an album, "Hasten Down the Wind," with three Bonoff songs on it—"Lose Again," "Someone to Lay Down Beside Me," and "If He's Ever Near"—

didn't hurt Bonoff's reputation, either. Bonoff recorded the same songs, in fact, on her album.

Two years later, there is a second Bonoff album in the stores, "Restless Nights," featuring more of her insightful, haunting love ballads, with an occasional up-tempo rocker like Jackie De Shannon's '60s classic, "When You Walk into the Room," for leavening. And at the moment, she's on the road, somewhere between a distant point and Minneapolis. Bonoff and her band will play a gig at the West Bank Auditorium tonight—two shows at 7:30 and 10:30—the last date on her winter tour. When she gets home, she said by phone from Washington, D.C., she will start work on her third LP for Columbia, which she hopes will be released early next year—a little less time, that is, than it took to put together the second album.

"I feel less afraid of it," she said of the next album, "because I've learned how to discipline myself." She had practically her whole life, that is, to come up with material for the first LP, and, like a number of performing artists, was stymied by the deadline of the follow-up album. Never having had to force herself to write songs, she worked herself into a creative funk, and the album was released nearly a year later than expected.

Bonoff/ 10G

outdoors

skiing / hunting / fitness / environment / calendar

Minneapolis Tribune

Sunday
November 23 / 1980

Ron Schara / 17C

15C

Upper Midwest ski areas schuss to new growth, not in numbers but in better facilities

By Ben Kern
Staff Writer

Upper Midwest downhill ski areas' sprawling proliferation of the last few decades has come to a halt, at least temporarily, but big things are still happening among existing areas.

Last season's vacillating weather brought only so-so business to most.

Nevertheless, more capital, some of it new, still is being invested.

Improvements, spectacular in some cases, are under way.

Among Minnesota's more interesting happenings is the $1.5 million purchase of the Lutsen Ski Area at Lutsen, Minn., overlooking the Lake Superior north shore. The George Nelson family will continue to operate Lutsen Lodge and its condominiums.

The ski-area buyer: Charley Skinner, who has owned and successfully run Sugar Hills south of Grand Rapids, Minn., and Sugar Lodge, for many years.

This summer he's been tuning up Lutsen Mountain Ski Area (its new name) with special work on snowmaking and chairlifts.

He plans an extensive Mount Lutsen Village and intends next summer to develop Moose Mountain, south of the Poplar River and lakeward from the area's Mystery run. Moose should accommodate an 800-foot vertical-rise lift line serving a lot of appealing downhill terrain.

At Sugar Hills the Ryan Development Co. has started a vastly enlarged $15 million Sugar Town with shops and condominiums overlooking the ski area and the current Sugar Town, which will be incorporated in the new one.

The first phase of the new development should be finished by the end of January.

South of Grand Rapids at **Quadna Mountain** in Hill City, Minn., a group of six (four from around the Twin Cities, two from Alexandria, Minn.) have formed Quadna Shance, Inc., and have bought the whole Quadna recreational facility.

To the ski hill they have added a four-place (quad) chair lift, the area's first chair, graded a new run totally visible from the chalet and improved and quadrupled the snowmaking.

Jay C. Diebold, press representative, said they're adding lights for night skiing and a "ski-through snack bar" and are reworking cross-country trails. They plan Friday-afternoon bus service from the Twin Cities via Jefferson Bus Lines. For more details

call Quadna at 1-(800)-662-5796 (Minnesota) or (from out of state) 1-(218)-697-2324.

Meanwhile another Upper Midwest biggie, **Telemark**, Cable, Wis., plans a Dec. 13 grand opening of its Telemark Colosseum, a new $3 million sports and convention center on a prominence northwest of where the old chalet stood.

Besides serving as a chalet, the 64,000-square-foot facility will house a main arena primarily for tennis and convertible into a hall seating 2,000

for a banquet or 3,000 for exhibitions and concerts.

Over the years owner Tony Wise has advanced the interests of Indian lore, downhill and cross-country skiing, jazz and tennis.

At the Gitchi Gami Games Dec. 15-18 he plans "the world's first indoor start and finish for a cross-country ski race."

The Colosseum will connect with Telemark Lodge by tunnel and eventually will include a ski shop,

cafeteria, rathskeller, Fjord Room restaurant and a rental shop.

South of Mankato, Minn., a new four-place chair lift will serve three new trails at **Mount Kato**. That makes seven chair lifts for Mount Kato, whose big-brother area, Afton Alps (same owners), has 18.

Paul Augustine, Afton Alps president, termed last season's Mount Kato business "pretty slow," but he's not discouraged.

He feels that mounting gasline costs

have particularly affected night skiing around the Twin Cities. "Skiers get more skiing hours for their gasoline money on weekends," he said. So do families arriving in one car, he added.

This season Afton Alps will have even more lighting, snow-making and grooming equipment than before.

Over the past summer at **Trollhaugen**, Dresser, Wis., bulldozers have been piling up a steep hill for hotshot skiers at the area's east end. A rope tow will serve it this season.

There has also been some Trollhaugen recontouring on chair-lift-served upper Storbakken head wall for a cleaner downhill shot. Snow-making capacity has been increased and 200 sets of rental equipment have been added. More comfort and more bar and restaurant service are in the big chalet.

Up at **Wild Mountain**, north of Taylors Falls, Minn., owner Dennis Raedeke reports "fantastic" business for the past season. He sells SMI snow-making machines and makes a lot of snow.

Wild Mountain has regraded many runs, has three quad chairs that whisk skiers uphill to an all-directions summit and has a year-round staff of seven. Raedeke credits the crew.

At **Birch Park / Snowcrest**, two ski areas that were merged last winter in Wisconsin across the St. Croix River from Stillwater, this season's major shot-in-the-arm went to Snowcrest, just south of Somerset, Wis.

A new snow-making system gives Snowcrest four times its previous snow-making capacity, while the chalet benefits from interior remodeling.

For Birch Park there's been general upkeep of manager Roger Lacy's excellent snow-and-grooming system.

Birch Park / Snowcrest patrons, with interchangeable lift tickets, loaded shuttle buses running on the half-hour during last winter's weekends.

Season passes for **Buck Hill**, in Burnsville, and **Powder Ridge**, at Kimball, Minn., (south of St. Cloud, Minn.) are also interchangeable.

Chuck Thompson, who has managed snow-making areas in Virginia and Tennessee, where snow-making has to be good, is in charge at Buck Hill this year. Buck's snow-making is being stepped up, and a new $60,000 Sno-Cat will help refine it.

Buck Hill's Erich Sailer and wife Ursula will continue coaching and conditioning junior racers.

Ski areas / 16C

L.K. Hanson

Running

Bruce Brothers

Running in the dark: Be careful, but enjoy, enjoy!

Back before Willie Nelson saw the light and took up running the roads, the redhead grabbed a stubby pencil and scrawled, "The night life ain't no good life, but it's my life."

"Night Life" has become an anthem for many, few of them runners, who ordinarily profess a preference for "Born to Run" or "The Long Run" or "Runnin' on Empty."

Runners historically have seemed to follow one of two schedules for training runs, either jumping into action at the promise of dawn or mucking through the day until they're turned themselves loose in the late afternoon. (The variation on either theme is the

lunch crowd, a deranged set that collectively announces it would rather run than eat, although I can count on one hand the days I haven't managed to find time for both.)

Perhaps the most convenient method of guaranteeing that no meals or runs will be missed—if you have an aversion to alarm clocks—is an often pleasant venture called the night-time run. Why so many distance runners are afraid of the dark is beyond me. Summer or winter, I have never found the simple onset of nightfall enough of an excuse to skip running.

There is no question, now that the shortest day of the year is nearly upon

us and daylight saving time is just a memory for another several months, that even those who detest such a practice will probably find themselves running in the dark anyway.

Precautions must be taken.

White or brightly colored clothing helps, as do the reflective warm-up suits, reflective strips or bands that can be added and patches that can be sewn or stuck on. Automobiles, never friendly to the runner, become even more ominous at night and should be given a wide berth.

Run where you know the route and, if possible, where it is well-lit. Keep your

eyes open and your courtesy alive, warning pedestrians with an "excuse me" so you won't frighten them out of their socks. I know one runner who carries a small flashlight. He says, "You get used to it."

A companion will offer a feeling of security, but if you are forced to run alone it is a good practice to avoid potential trouble areas and long, deserted stretches. Also, let someone know when you'll return so he or she can seek aid if you fail to show.

Some forethought and common sense are invaluable to night runners, allowing them to immerse themselves in the freewheeling aloneness and

Brothers / 18C

outdoors

fishing / calendar / fitness / camping

▼ **Minneapolis Tribune**

Sunday
June 17 / 1979
Section C · Part II

Calendar / 19C

17C

Staff Photos by Ron Schara

Dick Schara held the biggest fish he'd ever caught—a 21-pound northern pike.

After Nootin, Max Lake yields its big northerns

By Ron Schara
Staff Writer

Norway House, Canada
When the four winds blow in a single day, the waters of the Canadian North will soon lose their winter icecap, according to a Swampy Cree Indian legend.

Nootin, the wind, repeatedly switches directions to break up the lingering lake ice, smashing it into itself until it is gone.

The four winds come in mid-May—normally.

But now it was four days into June—and Nootin hadn't been blowing or switching much.

From our raven's view of Max Lake, via a Cessna floatplane, an expanse of white ice still dominated more than 50 percent of this little-known bush lake. However, the north end—pocked with islands and bays—was ice-free. Or appeared to be. Bill, the pilot, circled once, twice to make sure.

Harvey York, our Swampy Cree Indian guide and companion, waited below at a quaint outpost camp. It was located on a picturesque island, picked for its protection from Nootin

and its natural plane dock made of one mammoth boulder of granite.

The air was ice-chilled when we stepped from the Cessna's bouncy pontoons to the firm granite.

But that—chilly fishing weather—was what we expected.

And even planned—to follow the spring breakup northward, to be on Max Lake when Nootin was finished and Max had fishable waters.

So far, so good.

Or so maybe—the warmth of the wood stove in our plywood-canvas-walled tent already was inviting, and we'd barely arrived. Were we pushing the already-tardy arrival of springtime?

Would Max Lake with its partial icecap dispel the fishing tip we had chosen to follow?

At least if the tip was wrong, we had Lyle Fett in hand. And he was the purveyor of the angling promise.

Max Lake / 18C

The boats wended their way through the ice of Max Lake, above. Left, Harvey York netted one of the smaller northerns, a 12-pounder, for John Larson, center. Norb Epping was at right.

Upper Michigan is new battlefront on Indian fishing rights

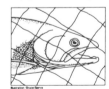

Illustration / Bruce Bjerva

By Iver Peterson
New York Times Service

Bay Mills, Mich.
The question of Indian fishing rights, already a burning issue in the Northwest, has found its way to Upper Michigan, where the conflict between sports fishermen and the Indians has everyone talking violence and a few committing it.

The fight stems from a federal-court ruling last month that denied Michigan the right to regulate fishing by members of the Chippewa and Ottawa tribes. The ruling, which is being appealed by the state, left the Indians free to fish "wherever the fish are found" in the northern parts of Lakes

Michigan and Huron and in the eastern part of Lake Superior.

The Indians say they have at last won a right assured by treaties they signed with the federal government in 1836 and 1855. But spokesmen for Michigan's multimillion-dollar sports-fishing business and the state's Department of Natural Resources contend that the Indians' fishing methods will deplete the Great Lakes of fish and destroy efforts to make the waters that hug this state self-replenishing.

So the Great Lakes join Klamath River in northern California and the Columbia River and Puget Sound in Washington as

battlefronts between the burgeoning Indian-rights movement and white sportsmen, commercial fishermen and conservationists.

In Michigan's water-bound Upper Peninsula, the decision by U.S. District Judge Noel Fox has divided the 600-member Bay Mills Indian reservation almost as deeply as it has pitted conservationists against the Federal Bureau of Indian Affairs.

Bad feelings have arisen between some of the tribe's elders and younger men who spurn the elders' efforts to forestall a white backlash by instituting tribal regulation on fishing to replace the

Fishing rights / 18C

home/garden

home life / collecting / planting / building / decorating

Minneapolis Tribune

Sunday
June 17/1979

John Gilbert / 4H

1H

Staff Photo by Richard Olsenius

Rail fences add a picturesque touch along a country road winding through rolling hills.

Fencing for privacy and beauty

By Neal Gendler
Staff Writer

Good fences are good neighbors.

Just standing around, fences protect, create and define.

Depending on how they're made, fences can protect yards from unwanted guests—animal and sometimes human; can create privacy in the midst of pandemonium, and can define areas of aesthetic enhancement.

These virtues have not escaped notice, even among people who

get along with the folks next door. People in the industry say the wood-fence business is a healthy one with growing demand from folks who want to build their own.

Home owners can make wood fences as simple or fancy as they want. They're available in prefabricated sections or as lumber plus instructions. Some suppliers also have design-idea books. Fences can be as simple as the old split rail or as fancy as basket weaves or diagonal designs. Materials include the familiar redwood and cedar and some newer types of

preservative-treated pine.

"One of the advantages of the build-it-yourself fence that is different from a prefabricated fence section is that you can adjust to the contour of your land much more readily," said Eric Canton, vice president of Canton Redwood Yard, a Brooklyn Park wholesaler.

"You can also take the same basic boards—1-by-6 or 1-by-8—and achieve so many basic designs." Canton said his firm has a book with about 20 design ideas, and "It's fun to watch

people buy the basic materials and do something entirely different from what's in our book." For example, he said, running boards diagonally or combining them with plastic panels to let through more light.

Canton said his observation, a purely personal one from driving around, is that the vertical weave is very popular right now, and he had an explanation.

"It restricts vision and at the same time permits airflow," he said. "There is a tendency to take the fence and use it for screening

purposes around a patio. The whole yard might not be fenced, but a patio may be, or a balcony." The fence "provides an area of perhaps greater intimacy— certainly to the extent that some hot tubs are going in now, and it provides an area of privacy.

"You don't have to fence your whole yard to provide a private area for a hot tub."

Privacy is one purpose for a fence; beauty is another, and the two can be combined.

"The individual who is thinking

Fences / 6H

Vertical fences remain highly popular.

A horizontal-weave privacy fence.

Two sides of fence differ in design.

I.M. Pei's architectural star is rising higher than ever

By Paul Goldberger
New York Times Service

New York, N.Y.
I.M. Pei paces his living-room floor and talks about the state of architecture. "Maybe my early training set me back. Maybe it made me too much of a pragmatist."

That is an unexpected comment from Pei, who runs an architectural office with 160

employees and numbers among its clients major corporations, real-estate developers and cultural institutions around the world. Pei questioning the value of pragmatism might seem like Morgan Guaranty Trust Co. doubting fiscal conservatism.

Yet I.M. Pei & Partners is more than a commercial architectural firm. Its work has always tried to merge serious aesthetic ideas with a professional business

sense.

At the moment, Pei's star — clear in the firmament for two decades — is rising higher than ever. He recently was named architect of the New York Convention and Exhibition Center, the $375-million project in Manhattan that was the most sought-after architectural commission New York has handed out in years.

His drawing boards are full of work from Singapore to Park Av., and next fall he will see the John F. Kennedy Library in Dorchester, Mass., a project that has eluded completion for 15 years, open its doors. He is finishing a hotel outside Peking, his first building in his native China and the first building by any American architect there since Peking-Washington relations were normalized. And earlier this month Pei received the gold

medal of the American Institute of Architects — the highest award the society gives to an architect.

It is a long way since the early 1970s, when I.M. Pei & Partners meant to many the John Hancock Tower, the 60-story Boston skyscraper whose double-paned glass windows mysteriously fell out. Pei's reputation was as shattered as the windows, and clients stayed

Pei / 6H

home/garden

home life / collecting / planting / building / decorating

Sunday
December 17 / 1978

Minneapolis Tribune

1H

Need domestic help? It's available — but be prepared to hunt (and pay) for it

By Neal Gendler
Staff Writer

You can take the drudgery from this year's holiday party-giving by hiring an inexpensive domestic worker to sterilize your house from steps to shingles, serve the food, pass the drinks, wash the dishes and clean up after everybody.

You also can walk on the moon.

Household help just ain't what it used to be.

Once upon a time there were a few rich folks and a lot of poor folks; the poor folks worked for the rich. Things have leveled off a tad now, and it's not easy to hire housekeepers, maids and other categories of people whose function, stripped of disguising titles, is to clean up other people's messes.

Like a moonwalk, it's not impossible—just difficult and expensive.

People can be found to clean a house. A number of cleaning services listed in the Yellow Pages will provide regular service—probably at prices above those of the people whose recipe cards hang on supermarket bulletin boards, but the services can provide bonded workers with transportation.

There's considerably more difficulty in finding someone to serve drinks and hors d'ouevres and do the dishes after the last dog is hung. The only listing in the Minneapolis Yellow Pages for maid service was a mistake, said the woman who answered; her firm supplies only housecleaners.

One firm advertising domestic help in the housecleaning section of the Yellow Pages never returned calls. Another, Golden Valley Domestics, offers cleaning and party service, and its owner, Donna Gillogly, said she knows of no competitors in party serving. She's been in business more than a year.

Demand for household help apparently is fierce: About 10 of 15 phone-number tabs remained on one recent week night on a grocery-store card offering maids and housecleaning, but by the time someone tried to get one of the numbers late the next afternoon, the tabs were gone, and a clerk had tossed out the card. Gillogly said she has 300 clients and a waiting list.

There are several routes to follow in trying to find someone to clean the kitchen or pass the pate: Yellow Pages listings, want ads in daily newspapers, ads in neighborhood or special-interest newspapers, state employment-services offices, notes on odd-job bulletin boards in groceries, drug stores and such places and word of mouth.

Hiring bonded firms should assure reasonable quality and dependability; hiring someone who frequently lists with a state office should help minimize risk; hiring your mother-in-law's cleaning woman may or may not work well for you or either of them, and in choosing from a bulletin board you're on your own; Gillogly advises insisting on references and going to the references' homes to see what's being cleaned and how well.

Hiring a firm is a way to obtain regular cleaning visits, unblemished by people's physical ailments, family emergencies or hangovers.

Dick Harris, who runs Twin City Domestics out of his house on 15th St., said the biggest advantage he can offer is assurance that someone will show up on schedule for general housework. He tries to assign one of his five part-time workers to the same houses among the 35 clients, but if that worker isn't available, he can deliver a substitute.

Domestics / 5H

Turn on the sunlight for house plants

Inside plants

Jack Kramer

If you want your plants to thrive in these gray days, use artificial light to make them glow and grow.

There are dozens of types of plant-growth lamps even for the modest budget. A small lamp with screw-in bulb similar to a reading lamp is inexpensive and available at plant stores. Even one lamp like this can help plants grow through the dull months.

If you use standard electric bulbs for additional light, remember to keep plants at least 30 inches from the lamp to prevent too much heat from reaching the plants.

In addition to screw-in plant lights and standard lights (both help plants), fluorescent lamps are still probably the best source of light for your plants. These lamps, sold under various trade names, furnish red and blue rays essential for plant growth.

Lamps come in different wattages. For a standard setup, two lamps of 40 watts work fine for most plants.

In fluorescent-lamp growing, keep lights on 14 to 16 hours a day; an automatic timer saves a lot of worry about when to turn lamps on and off. Place plants so they are 10 to 12 inches from the bottom of the tubes. Almost all plants benefit from artificial lights to help them grow.

If you do not want to build your own light unit using fluorescent lamps, you can buy commercial carts and trays that come with plant bins and all necessary hardware. Some are table models for a few plants; others are movable carts that accommodate many plants. In either situation, remember to water and feed plants as you would during spring and summer. Under lights, plants grow all the time.

Try to maintain a temperature of 78 degrees F. in the growing area, with a nighttime drop in temperature of, say, 10 degrees. The lower night temperature is essential for good growth.

So if your plants look wan during the winter, by all means use some artificial light, whether a single-plant grow lamp for standard sockets or a more elaborate fluorescent lamp, table or floor model.

Cacti and succulents generally rest during the winter, so keep them just barely moist, but try to place them where they will get some winter sun.

Many orchids put on a colorful display in winter and should be grown where artificial light does not hinder bud formation. Many orchids are short-day plants blooming in midwinter. Join an orchid society for more information on orchids.

As days get short it is wise to water plants early in the morning so they are dry by nightfall, and let water stand overnight in a pail for watering. Icy-cold water shocks plants and can cause harm.

Plants / 3H

travel/adventure

where to go / how to go / travel news

Minneapolis Tribune

Sunday
October 29 / 1978

1E.

THE MINNESOTA TRAVELER

Nice guys book last

By Catherine Watson
Staff Writer

Minnesotans, be proud of yourselves. You're terribly nice to travel with, your travel agents say.

There is only this one little problem. You've never really accepted the inevitable approach of winter. You just don't believe it'll happen — until it's too late.

"They never think it's going to snow till Christmas," lamented Buzz Moore, president of House of Travel agencies and newly elected Area 8 director, covering 11 north-central states, for the American Society of Travel Agents (ASTA).

"They know snow's going to be on the ground in February. I have never yet seen green grass in February," he said.

Ignoring this simple fact leads to what agents call Minnesota travelers' biggest single fault.

They book late.

On winter vacations, often so late that the best of the getaway trips they want are gone, and their travel agents have to scrounge to help them out. The agents don't like that.

Neither, quite often, do the procrastinating travelers themselves.

"The first day it snows, our phones will ring off the hook," said Joan Anderson, manager of Dayton's Travel Service at Southdale. Apparently, she said, "We like to forget that winter is coming — till it comes."

Another bookings boom occurs just after Christmas when the people who've decided they won't go anywhere this year finally give in. Said Anderson: "It's called, 'I can't stand it anymore.'"

Prime winter escape time means the Christmas holidays and the deep-winter weeks of February and the first part of March.

"Chairs space for those six weeks should've been booked 90 days in advance," especially if the traveler wanted a particular ship, stateroom or itinerary, Moore said. "If they'll take anything on any ship, they can wait three more months — but cruise bookings should be done six or seven months in advance in any case, he said.

"We can't get anything in Acapulco for February-March right now," Moore said at the end of September.

And if you wanted to spend this Christmas in Hawaii, Acapulco, the Caribbean or Aspen, you should have booked your trip by last New Year's, he added. For next Christmas, you should be thinking about it now and get it done by Jan. 1. The date of Christmas, like the existence of winter itself, ought to come as no surprise.

Any three- to four-day weekend will create a higher-than-normal demand for travel. That means school events like Teachers Convention weekend in October and the new winter energy break as well as traditional holidays. And higher demand requires more lead time on reservations. Some agents are already watching spring breaks for 1980.

Travel agents, of course, are talking about hotel space that they can confirm in advance for their customers. In foreign places, this usually means fairly high-priced hotels, ones that will reply to requests for reservations. All cities have cheaper hotels that will not bother to confirm a reservation in advance. Hardy souls and people on tight budgets often like to chance it on such accommodations, waiting until they get to a town before looking for hotel rooms. Sometimes that works. Sometimes — especially at season's peak — it doesn't, and that can be a wearying hassle, especially if the traveler's vacation time and patience are limited.

Some experienced travelers — repeaters, who know they want the same spot, same time, next year — will even make their next winter's hotel reservations when they check out this winter. Travel agents are proud of those people. They've learned from experience.

Travel agents prefer to book reservations early to make sure that clients get exactly what they want — even if the reservations have to be modified later.

Traveler / 2E

WELL, DEAR, IT LOOKS AS THOUGH IT'S FINALLY BEGUN TO SNOW IN EARNEST!

BETTER PHONE OUR TRAVEL AGENT, MOTHER—WE'LL PACK TONIGHT AND FLY TO HAWAII IN THE MORNING.

NO!

U.S., Europe

"Excellent" — Sicily

"Beautiful" — Latin countries

"What a Smasher" — Italy

"Excellent" — Spain & Portugal

"Beautiful" — Italy

"Hello, Beautiful" — Spain & Portugal

"Excellent" — Anglo-Saxon

THE EUROPEAN TOUCH/ Or I am curious — help!

By Ruth Hammond
Staff Writer

Know the difference between an Italian exhibitionist and a French exhibitionist? The Italian says: "Pssst, pssst, signorina," and the Frenchman says: "Pssst, pssst, Mademoiselle."

After spending seven months studying in Aix-en-Provence, France, and another six weeks traveling through southern Europe, I do know that the most important words for a woman to know in any language are not "please" and "thank you" but, no, no, no, no, no, no, NO!

Next to "Little Known Bathrooms of Europe," the most needed book that has never been written about continental travel is "Europe on Less than Five Molestations a Day," or, for those who want to see more and enjoy a bit of night life, "Europe on Less than 15 Molestations a Day."

This book would contain essential information on what to do:

■ When an Austrian derelict looking for a place to spend the night knocks on your shower door at 1 a.m.

■ When a middle-aged Frenchman, alleging he is a professor of photography, wants you to take off your clothes so he can see it any part of your anatomy will be useful in his work. "What's the matter? You aren't ashamed of your body, are you?"

■ When a Turk is running out of a French train station with your backpack, which he breathlessly proclaims he won't return until you get to the hotel room.

■ When, after five minutes of trivial conversation, an Italian in an art museum confides: "Do you know why I came up to talk to you? Because I've heard American girls are atomic bombs in bed."

Molest / 3 E

travel/adventure

where to go / how to go / travel news

Minneapolis Tribune

Sunday
December 21/1980

1E

Minnesotans kept fast pace during tour of Venice and 'snail' staircase project

By Margaret Morris
Staff Writer

Venice, Italy

We weren't the peppiest sightseers ever to arrive in Venice. We had been en route for 22 hours.

But we did manage a cheer once we spotted the smiling Renato Padoan, superintendent of monuments for Venice. He came to meet us with an armful of long-stemmed coral roses and four bottles of his homemade champagne.

And so our small group from Minnesota arrived in the magnificent city that rumor says is slipping into the Adriatic Sea. Don't believe it.

Venice looks better today than at any time within living memory. During the past 10 years or so, money and experts have poured in from all over the world (and not the least from Italy itself) to refurbish the major monuments. Much still needs to be accomplished, of course. But a significant portion of the outer fabric has been carefully and sensitively restored, thanks to an international campaign for saving Venice.

Scores of individuals and foundations have been involved, including the Venice Committee of the Washington-based International Fund for Monuments, which has contributed more than $3 million toward the restoration.

Eighteen of the fund committee's 140-member Minnesota chapter, organized a year ago, made up our group on this tour of Venice in early October.

The Minnesota chapter has chosen the spiral exterior staircase of the Contarini del Bovolo Palace as its project. The palace name commemorates the staircase, called the Bovolo, which means "snail" or "spiral" in Venetian dialect.

We headed for the palace on foot on our first sightseeing trip. We followed winding streets past La Fenice ("Phoenix"), the opera house with a watergate entrance, to reach the brick palace tucked behind a small courtyard enclosed by a wrought-iron fence.

The once opulent palace was built in the 13th century. The Bovolo staircase was added in the 15th century. The building is terra-cotta-colored brick trimmed in white Istrian stone. Potted red geraniums nodded from open windows in the surrounding residences, and canaries chirped in hanging cages that caught the morning sunlight.

As we climbed to the top of the four-story winding staircase, we reached an arched tower from which we could look over the wonders of the city spread out below. Red-tile roofs stretched as far as the eye could see.

To be sure, television antennae punctuated the skyline, laundry flapped on clotheslines strung between the windows and box-laden barges chugged lugubriously along the canals.

Still the view was breathtaking. It is sights such as this that attract the tourist hordes to Venice. And the Rialto

Venice/3E

Staff Photo by Catherine Watson

A Venetian winterscape:
Gondolas, churches and fog

Living in London/A whole new world for Burnsville family

By Sandi Stromberg

London, England

When we left the Twin Cities in 1979 to live in London, we had yet to realize the changes that would take place in our lives: How the move from house to apartment, suburbs to city, working mother to full-time housewife, neighborhood school to private school would affect us.

A year ago we had been the Strombergs of Burnsville, Minn., but now as we stepped off the airplane at Wold-Chamberlain Field in the Twin Cities, we were the Strombergs of London, England, back for a visit.

It wasn't until I re-entered the houses of my friends that I realized how much had happened. I found myself asking:

■ "Is it only a year ago that Erik, then 4, drove his Big Wheel into a playground full of English children who gazed in disbelief at this futuristic three-wheeler?"

■ "Is it only a year ago that I spent a frantic Thursday combing the streets of London for milk and bread, only to discover that stores are closed then?"

■ "Is it only a year ago that I suffered a near heart attack when, on returning home after our first evening out, I found that babysitters charge $3. an hour?"

In the Twin Cities once again I was struck by the ease of an American woman's life. All the things I had always taken for granted—yards for children to play in, shopping centers and supermarkets with free parking, and high school girls to babysit for $1 an hour—suddenly became total luxuries.

As in many moves, it is the women's life which changes most drastically. The husband goes off to work and although the job is new to him, he knows the company and its objectives. The mother, on the other hand, must install the family, find new stores, schools, doctors, laundromats, babysitters, playmates for the children and friends for herself. Plus adjust to a new culture and a higher cost of living.

Changes/2E

Inside pages/

Scotch rules are used at the tops of pages and to separate some elements on a page. The rules are the distinguishing design feature of the Sunday sections. They give the pages a modular look and emphasize horizontal layout as a step toward complete modular layout of advertising and news.

Column headings have been specially designed for the Sunday sections. They are consistent with Tribune style but look different from those used daily.

They are used only in one-column size, either with headlines or alone, depending on the demands of the layout. In the latter case, Scotch rules top the turns of type in a shallow layout.

4FX   Minneapolis Tribune   Sun., Nov. 9, 1980

Ambitious women succeed— in depressing everybody else

Erma Bombeck

The newspaper is so full of depressing news these days that some mornings I don't want to get out of bed.

I don't know about the world situation, but if I see one more story of a woman who works full-time, bakes her own bread, makes her own costs, works for World Peace, is running for the Senate, is carrying a child for a woman unable to have one, teaches metric at night, washes and irons her aluminum foil and whose hobby is "people," I'm going to be sick.

I feel as if I'm back in the '50s again, every magazine I picked up transported me to another guilt trip.

I have one clipping showing a woman with a freshly baked pie who, according to the story, gets up at 4:30 each morning to start the laundry and begins preparations for the evening meal. Before she leaves for work she makes sure everyone "is in a happy frame of mind." That miracle accomplished, she works all day, arrives home at 4, slips a roast into the oven and starts baking again, cleans her five-bedroom, three-bath home and—here's a Hallelujah Heloise for you—"never walks through the house unless she carries a small bucket of soapy water for wiping up baseboards, window sills and registers."

She sews all the clothes worn by the family, cans and freezes vegetables' and (I swear this is true) "is restoring a log cabin behind their home."

Good grief, she makes the Stepford Wives look like feminists.

The women of this world don't need depressing stories about women who color-code their leftovers. Give us happy stories about the women who can't shave their legs and get a hot meal in the same week. Tell us about the women who have five weeks of laundry and three rooms of furniture on the bottom steps of their two-story houses waiting for someone who is going up. Don't make us guilty when our kids send Mother's Day cards to Col. Sanders.

Tell us about the mothers who fall asleep during gum surgery, the mothers who iron only what sees daylight, the mother whose hobby is collecting boxes that say, "Just add water."

I try to get whipped up about these women who only go around once in this life and do it with all the gusto they can get, but I just feel anger and frustration.

If I were carrying a small bucket of soapy water down the hall, and someone said, "Hey, Mom, you missed a spot," I wouldn't want to be responsible for my actions.

I'm flushing as fast as I can.

More checkies with Erma Bombeck and her household, Tuesdays and Thursdays in the Tribune.

If your male belongs in dead-letter office, cancel him post haste

Ann Landers

Dear Ann: You undoubtedly are aware of the revival of the chain-letter concept in the form of a pyramid. I thought you might be interested in the one I received for my birthday. I sent it on—in two languages. Here it is to share with your readers. Still Laughing in Lima, Peru

Ann says: Chain letters are illegal in the United States, but yours is different and involves no money. Thanks for passing it on. The letter:

"This chain letter was started by a woman like yourself in the hope of bringing relief to tired, discontented wives. Unlike most chain letters, this one does not cost anything. Just send a copy to five of your female friends who are equally tired. Then bundle up your husband and send him to the woman whose name appears at the top of the list. Add your name to the bottom of the list. When your name comes to the top, you will receive 16,748 men. Some of them will be dandies. Have faith and don't break the chain. One woman who broke the chain got her own husband back. At the time of this writing, a friend of mine has received 183 men. They buried her yesterday, but it took three undertakers 36 hours to get the smile off her face."

Dear Ann: I am a recently separated female in my early 30s and live in an apartment alone. My mother is a kind soul who offers to clean up my place periodically. I am an occasional pot smoker.

On Mother's Day, while housecleaning day she went poking through my bureau drawers and found some pot and a few pipes. When she confronted me, I said, "Yes, I do smoke pot occasionally."

That put her in an uproar, and she made a scene I'll never forget. Now both Mom and Dad view me as some sort of derelict.

Is there a way to get them to see that smoking pot once in awhile is not such a terrible thing? Also, does my mother have the right to go through my bureau drawers? I feel violated, and she feels justified. Stoned Now and Then in Nashville

Ann says: If you are looking for someone to defend your use of pot, you rattled the wrong cage.

I agree that the occasional use of marijuana does not make a person a derelict, but to people of your parents' generation it means smoking dope, which is illegal, and there is no way you can put a respectable face on it.

I agree that your mother should not have been going through your bureau drawers. From now on, clean the place yourself.

Dear Ann: Bless you for putting me in touch with Recovery, Inc. I looked in the phone book as you suggested and discovered they were meeting less than a mile from my home.

Recovery, Inc., did for me what psychiatry, medicine and religion could not. I no longer am afraid to go shopping, to the movies or drive a car. I've also learned that I am not crazy, and occasional spells of weakness and nausea and heart-pounding do not mean I am going to die.

The cost? Whatever you want to give for the refreshments. After spending thousands of dollars on doctors, I consider this the bargain of a lifetime. A New Me

Ann says: Wonderful. Those who are interested and can't find Recovery, Inc., in the phone book should write to the national headquarters, 116 S. Michigan Av., Chicago, Ill. 60603.

More personal advice from Ann Landers every morning except Saturday in the Tribune.

Food allergy is nothing to sneeze at; consider it another form of addiction

The person who craves specific foods and gets relief from symptoms by eating those foods is a food addict, according to Dr. Phyllis Saifer of Berkeley, Calif.

In a recent address to the annual conference of the International College of Applied Nutrition, Saifer explained, "We cannot explain food addiction except by using the model of heroin addiction. The patient craves that to which he is allergic, and by taking some bits into his system manages to relieve his symptoms."

Saifer cautioned, "Do not suffer from the prejudice that food allergies cause bellyaches, headaches, behavior changes and muscle pain and that airborne allergens are the ones to cause runny noses and asthma. There is no connection between the allergen and the induction of a particular symptom. The symptoms are entirely dependent on the individual and his target organ, which, by the way, tends to be inherited." Thus, Saifer believes that runny noses and asthmatic symptoms can be food-based.

"The major allergenic food in the United States is milk and milk products, including cheese, ice cream, yogurt and butter, probably because ingestion begins at birth," said Saifer. New techniques of immunization to allergenic food have been developed by allergists who specialize in desensitization procedures. After a period of treatment, the patient can eat regulated amounts of the troublesome food without recurrent symptoms.

It's important to try to identify whether a food allergy is causing undesirable symptoms. Saifer speculated that you can suspect food allergies when the symptoms occur year-round and do not change when the patient takes a trip and maintains the same diet. If the patient notices relief while on a religious fast or surgical fast, a food allergy should be suspected.

Improvement of symptoms with fasting is almost a guarantee of food allergy except in the patient who may be reacting to pesticides and other chemical residues in foods. If a patient reports worsening of symptoms after meals, it is almost certain that he or she is dealing with food allergies or pesticide sensitivity.

When such as allergy is suspected, it's wise to ask for intradermal or sublingual testing to reveal the possible food culprit. If it is a single type of food such as milk, wheat, corn or eggs, it is possible to eliminate the food from the diet. Multiple allergies become more difficult to leave out of the diet, and desensitization techniques should be considered.

Here are some dairy-free recipes for those who need to eliminate milk products from their diets.

BREAKFAST RICE AND PINEAPPLE
2 c. hot cooked rice
2 tbsp. dried raisins
¼ c. well-drained pineapple tidbits
1 tsp. brown sugar
¼ tsp. cinnamon
Dash of nutmeg

Combine rice, raisins, pineapple tidbits, brown sugar, cinnamon and nutmeg. Toss well with a fork. Spoon into cereal dishes. Makes two or three servings.

POTATO-CARROT PANCAKES
1 c. shredded pared raw white potato
1 c. shredded raw carrots
½ c. finely chopped fresh onion
½ c. soya milk
¼ c. wheat flour
2 eggs, slightly beaten
¼ tsp. salt
¼ tsp. dried dill weed

Combine potato, carrots and onion in a bowl. Add soya milk, flour, beaten eggs, salt and dill weed; mix well. Drop by tablespoonfuls on a hot greased griddle. Spread batter to form a 3-inch circle. Cook until golden brown, about three minutes on each side, turning once. Makes 18 pancakes.

BANANA NUT BREAD
¼ c. vegetable shortening
½ c. dark brown sugar
1 tsp. vanilla extract
2 eggs

1¾ c. wheat flour
1 tsp. baking powder
½ tsp. salt
1 c. mashed ripe bananas
1 tbsp. lemon juice
1 c. broken walnuts

In a large mixing bowl, cream shortening and sugar together. Beat in vanilla. Beat in eggs, one at a time. Combine flour, baking powder and salt; blend into batter alternately with mashed bananas. Add lemon juice. Stir in nuts. Turn into two greased and floured one-pound coffee cans or into two 8-by-4-inch loaf pans. Bake in a preheated oven at 350 degrees for 30 minutes. Makes two loaves.

If you have a special diet problem, you can write to Jane Roth, c/o Minneapolis Tribune, 425 Portland Av., Minneapolis, Minn. 55488. Enclose a stamped, self-addressed envelope for a personal reply.

Copyright 1980 Jane Roth

Special diets
June Roth

Jeane Dixon
yo: horoscope

Sunday, November 9, 1980

Your Birthday Today

Cookbook

THE GOOD HOUSEKEEPING ILLUSTRATED COOKBOOK edited by Zee Coulson (Hearst Books, $19.95, 512 pages, color photographs and sketches).

Reviewed by Mary Hart
Staff Writer

An unusual format was selected for this book. Almost 100 pages of color photographs picture the recipes in the book and are referred to as the color index. This enables cooks to see what the finished food should resemble.

Hundreds more sketches on the recipe pages aid the beginning cook in preparing simple salads and meat dishes, while other sketches assist the more-experienced culinary artist in assembling fancy desserts and making cheese. The step-by-step sketches sometimes are in the method for fixing the food. In other instances, the sketches are auxiliary, such as cutting a fancy garnish for the food.

At the side of each recipe is the page number in the color index, the number of minutes, hours or days ahead of serving time you start the preparation and the number of servings.

The following recipe from the book didn't require any step-by-step sketches:

COLONEL'S LADY'S SALAD BOWL
(Begin 20 minutes ahead)
¼ (16-oz.) pkg. frozen peas
Boiling water
1 small head romaine lettuce
1 small head iceberg lettuce
1 small cucumber, thinly sliced
3 green onions, chopped
1 stalk (rib) celery, sliced
Dressing:

¼ c. salad oil
3 tbsp. white wine vinegar
1 tbsp. sugar
1 tbsp. chopped parsley
¼ tsp. garlic salt
¼ tsp. salt
¼ tsp. oregano leaves
¼ tsp. seasoned pepper

In medium bowl, place frozen peas; cover with boiling water and let stand five minutes.

Meanwhile, in large bowl, tear lettuce into bite-size pieces; drain peas and add to bowl with remaining salad ingredients.

Prepare the dressing: In cup, combine dressing ingredients; stir with fork to mix well. Toss salad gently with dressing to coat lettuce. Makes 12 servings.

Despite money worries, Americans retiring sooner

Golden years
Beylah Collins

Two opposing viewpoints show up in recent reports on the attitudes of older workers toward retirement.

A recent study by the President's Commission on Pension Policy reveals that 63 percent of Americans polled are worried that their retirement incomes will be inadequate to meet their needs.

At the same time, the national trend continues to be toward early retirement. Three-fourths of the workers retiring voluntarily under Social Security do so before they reach the age of 65. And this despite the fact that the age for mandatory retirement has been raised from 65 to 70 for most workers.

Both of those findings are cited by the American Council of Life Insurance in a recent report.

One part of those findings is pessimistic: People are afraid they aren't rich enough to retire. The second part is optimistic: People are retiring earlier than they have to. They are not forced out of their jobs by age —they are choosing retirement.

The conclusion from those conflicting facts has to be positive—older people look forward to retirement and are eager to get there. Many older people, far from being forced out of their jobs, are ready and willing to try out the freedom and leisure their already-retired friends have told them about. They may even have decided that working for a living until the end of their days would not necessarily be all that much fun.

With that background, the retired people of the nation are losing their negative status as poor old things put out to pasture and are becoming our new leisure class.

There is going to be more and more of that leisure class in future years. With life expectancy increasing, the American Council of Life Insurance

With that information at hand, today's retirees had better make plans to expect and to enjoy long and happy lives. And they should figure out how they are going to spend their years of leisure.

Retirement and leisure are the new raw materials they have to work with—raw materials that can be used and molded to make something of value.

Retired people who are successful members of this new leisure class generally have these things in common:

■ They have stayed mentally alert. They read, converse with friends and neighbors, make decisions, take courses, remain interested in world affairs, entertain new ideas, continue to learn and take part in community affairs.

■ They may not jog, lap dance or stand on their heads, but they exercise and move around enough so that no one could accuse them of being glued to their rocking chairs.

■ They maintain good relations with spouses, children and grandchildren, other relatives and friends. They realize that maintenance of enjoyable human relations calls for some effort and good will and that friendship is a flower they must continue to cultivate.

■ They like the stage of life they have attained. They worked all their lives to reach retirement, and now that they have reached it they plan to make the most of it.

Weddings

Ricci-Sorenson

Linda Mary Sorenson and Ronald Scott Ricci were married Oct. 18 in Bethlehem Lutheran Church.

Parents are Mr. and Mrs. George Robert Sorenson Jr., 4024 Wood End Dr., Edina, and Mr. and Mrs. Bonnie Ricci, 4341 NE McLeod St., Columbia Heights.

The couple is at home at 4101 Parklawn Av., Edina.

Buckley-Evangelist

Lynnette Mary Evangelist and James William Buckley were married Oct. 11 in St. Clement's Church.

Parents are Mr. and Mrs. John Evangelist, 1027 19th Av. NE, and Mr. and Mrs. John F. Buckley, 10228 Columbus Circle, Bloomington.

The couple is at home at 5501 Shorevew Av.

Peterson-Taylor

Martha Leigh Taylor and Milton Jerome Peterson were married Oct. 18 in Faith Baptist Church.

Parents are Stan and Eloise Taylor, 5333 Upton Av. N., and Arthur Peterson, Comstock, Wis., and LaVonne Peterson, Turtle Lake, Wis.

The couple is at home at 5100 Sheridan Av. N.

Peterson-Flannagan

Mary Helen Flannagan and Roy Walter Peterson were married Nov. 1 in St. George's Episcopal Church, St. Louis Park.

Parents are Mr. and Mrs. Arthur Walter Flannagan, 314 Meader Rd., Golden Valley, and Austin G. Peterson, 4315 Minnehaha Av.

The couple will be at home in Burnsville.

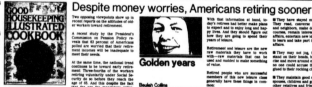

6F Minneapolis Tribune Sun., Jan. 25, 1981

Opera talent still notable in Rise Stevens's career

Margaret Morris

Rise Stevens has enjoyed two of the great careers in modern musical history—a star of the Metropolitan Opera Company and president of a major music college. If you mention the former, she'll break into smiles; if the latter, a slight pout, because she's asked about it so often.

Now she is serving as adviser and consultant to Anthony Bliss, general manager of the Met, and James Levine, music director, for the development of young artists. She also is director of auditions for the Metropolitan Opera National Council, which isn't exactly a soft job.

"I shall try to look for extraordinary talents. I'm sure they exist, but we haven't found them yet," said Stevens, who was here to be guest speaker at the midwinter dinner for the Metropolitan Opera in the Upper Midwest.

In 1975, the mezzo-soprano became president of the Mannes College of Music on E. 74th St. in Manhattan, a New York cultural landmark for more than half a century. She resigned three years later over a dispute with the board of directors.

"The board was impossible to deal with," she said. "After I left, the board of regents came in and fired the whole board. With that I said amen. They gave me an honorary Ph.D. in music. Every time I walk past the school, the kids call out, 'Hi, Dr. Stevens.' It's fun. I got the school out of the red. I raised $300,000 to $400,000 for it."

For years, Stevens led the life of a prima donna, acclaimed at the Metropolitan and other major opera houses in such roles as Carmen, Octavian, Orfeo, Dalila, Orlofsky.

As a young student, she studied at the Juilliard School under Anna Schoen-Rene. While there, she was offered a contract at the Metropolitan Opera, but turned it down on the advice of her teacher.

"I loved her dearly," she said of Schoen-Rene. "She found me when I was 17. I had just graduated from high school. She promptly steered me to Europe to study at the Salzburg Mozarteum with Marie Sutheil-Schoder."

Rise Stevens

She was engaged by George Szell for the Prague Opera in Czechoslovakia and made her debut there at the age of 22 in the title role of "Minon." Her debut as Octavian in "Rosenkavalier" soon followed at the Vienna State Opera and the Teatro Colon in Buenos Aires, Argentina.

She met her husband, Walter Surovy, a highly successful actor, in Prague. "We met at the theater where he was rehearsing, and I came to audition."

They have been married 41 years this month. For many years, he was her personal manager. He persuaded her to go to Hollywood, where she starred in "The Chocolate Soldier," "Carnegie Hall" and the Academy Award-winning "Going My Way" with Bing Crosby.

"I didn't like Hollywood. I would not have done many things if it had not been for Walter. He thought in those days broadening a career was important. He has been brilliant in steering my career."

She has toured in concert and made recordings, appeared in films and television. She was one of the most popular box-office stars on the American scene.

One of the highlights in her career was her debut at La Scala in Milan, Italy, where she created the role of Herodias in Mortari's "La Filia del Diavolo."

Her artistic home, however, remained the Metropolitan Opera for 25 years.

Why did she retire from singing? "I wanted to go out when I was on top. I had seen too many singers hang on too long. I had set an age. For three solid years I received a contract from Bing (Rudolf Bing, former general manager of the Met) with my whole list of roles on it, and each time I sent it back."

But she was chosen to be mistress of ceremonies at the gala Bing farewell. How had it happened? "By accident," she said with a laugh. "All of a sudden he called to ask me if I would be mistress of ceremonies. I had been with five different general managers. I go back to London and pre-World War II with Bing."

She was tapped to be general co-manager of the Metropolitan Opera National Company, and she developed a touring organization to provide young American singers with the experience she had to go abroad to find. She took the company from coast to coast and to Mexico and Canada. Then the Met moved to its new house in Lincoln Center, and the costs of the national company became too much.

As adviser to Bliss and Levine, she again will have the opportunity to open new doors to American singers. She ticked off some of her projects and plans.

"There are about seven in the program now, two of them national audition winners. I would like to keep it all American, but if we should find an exciting tenor from God knows where, it would be marvelous. The last decision will be up to James Levine. He is a genius."

Meanwhile, she will travel for the National Opera Council. She is going to Toronto in February and to San Antonio, Texas, for the auditions.

Beurre blanc is right light sauce for the new cuisine

Craig Claiborne

on food

New York Times Service

The sauce most frequently encountered in the *nouvelle cuisine* of France is known as beurre blanc. Although this sauce has been around for generations, it has come into prominence with the new cuisine, which eschews all sauces that burden other foods.

Without question a more delicate sauce than hollandaise, beurre blanc is a very light butter sauce (the term means white butter) made quickly and easily with reduced white wine and shallots with bits of butter beaten in. It is irresistible with simply cooked fish or seafood such as steamed shrimp or grilled salmon.

Its counterpart—somewhat less frequently found on the new menus—is beurre rouge, which is identical with beurre blanc except that the rouge is made with red wine instead of white, and it is served with dark meats such as grilled or broiled steaks.

BEURRE BLANC
(white butter sauce)
6 tbsp. finely chopped shallots
1½ c. dry white wine
12 tbsp. butter
Salt and freshly ground pepper

Combine shallots and wine in a saucepan and bring to a vigorous boil.

Let wine cook down to about one-third cup. Continue cooking over high heat, stirring rapidly with a wire whisk, and add butter about two tablespoons at a time.

Add salt and pepper to taste.

Yield: about 1¾ cups.

DARNE DE SAUMON GRILLEE
(broiled salmon steak)
1 1½-lb. salmon steak, about 1½ in. thick
1 tsp. peanut, vegetable or corn oil
Salt and freshly ground pepper
Beurre blanc (see recipe)

Preheat broiler.

Brush salmon on both sides with oil and sprinkle with salt and pepper to taste.

Arrange salmon in a shallow baking dish and place it about 6 inches from source of heat. Broil about 10 minutes. It is not necessary to turn steak as it cooks. Fish is done when center bone comes away easily from flesh. Serve with beurre blanc.

Yield: Two servings.

SHRIMP IN BEER
1 lb. shrimp in shell
Salt and freshly ground pepper to taste
1 bay leaf
6 whole cloves
1 clove garlic, peeled
6 allspice
1 c. beer

Combine all ingredients in a saucepan. Bring to boil and cook, stirring occasionally, about two minutes. Remove from heat. Serve with beurre blanc.

Yield: four servings.

BEURRE ROUGE
(red butter sauce)
6 tbsp. finely chopped shallots
1½ c. red Burgundy wine
12 tbsp. butter
Salt and freshly ground pepper

Combine shallots and wine in a saucepan and bring to a vigorous boil.

Let wine cook down to about one-third cup. Continue cooking over high heat, stirring rapidly with a wire whisk. Add butter about two tablespoons at a time. Add salt and pepper to taste.

Yield: about 1¾ cups.

STEAK GRILLE
(grilled beef)
1 2-lb. boneless sirloin steak, about 1½ in. thick
2 tbsp. peanut, vegetable or corn oil
Salt and freshly ground pepper
3 tbsp. finely chopped parsley
1¾ c. beurre rouge (see recipe)

Preheat broiler to high.

Rub steak on both sides with oil.

Sprinkle steak with salt and pepper to taste. Use a generous amount of pepper.

Place meat on a broiler rack and let it cook about 4 or 5 inches from source of heat. Broil about three to five minutes and turn meat. Broil on other side from three to five minutes. Cooking time will depend on desired degree of doneness.

Transfer steak to a hot platter and cover loosely with aluminum foil. Let steak stand in a warm place about five minutes to redistribute internal juices of meat.

Slice steak and serve hot with beurre rouge.

Yield: four servings.

This column was prepared by Craig Claiborne in collaboration with French chef Pierre Franey.

Classes in Scandinavian folk dances scheduled

Scandinavian folk-dance classes will be taught at Sons of Norway, 4511 W. Lake St., beginning Feb. 4. The classes will meet on Wednesdays for eight weeks.

A beginning class will meet from 7 to 8:30 p.m. and an intermediate class from 8:30 to 10 p.m. Classes are open to couples and singles. The cost is $16.50. Call 827-3611 for more information.

Lecture on mental illness set at Abbott-Northwestern

"Mental Illness: An Eclectic Approach to Therapy" is the topic of a lecture by Dr. Randall A. Lakosky at 7:30 p.m. Wednesday in the Watson Room at Abbott-Northwestern Hospital Education Building, 821 E. 26th St.

The free lecture is sponsored by the Schizophrenia Association of Minnesota. For more information call 922-6916.

The Tribune's Sunday business section is **Marketplace.** It carries a flag similar to those on Sunday Tribune feature sections, but its content is more news than features. Marketplace might be considered a sort of "bridge" between all-news and all-feature sections. Normal design principles and makeup rules apply on the cover and inside the section.

marketplace

business / farms / jobs / money

Minneapolis Tribune

Outlook / Just what's ahead for the economy of our region?

Sunday January 18/1981

1D

Economy / GNP growth may slip during 'double-dip'

By Dick Youngblood
Staff Writer

What a way with words these economists have.

Two years ago they were talking about the prospects for a "shallow banana" in 1979. This year it's the "double-dip" that dominates the forecasts for 1981.

It is not a banana split these folks are talking about.

It's the economy — and the prognostications lurking behind these metaphors are a mite less palatable than one of Bridgeman's ice cream specials.

The "banana," of course, was the euphemism for economic decline that Alfred Kahn, President Carter's inflation czar, invented after the Georgia Mafia told him to shut up, already, with all the negative talk about recession and depression if we don't get inflation under control.

The "shallow banana" — the widely predicted mild recession — never materialized in 1979. Instead, the economy continued growing into 1980 before tipping into a steep decline that reduced gross national product (GNP) at an annual rate of nearly 10 percent in the second quarter.

Now, after a spate of growth in the last six months of 1980, the majority of forecasters tells us we can expect another falloff in GNP in the first half of 1981. (Get it? A second dip ... "double-dip" ... well, what can you expect from people who insist on referring to a decline in GNP as "negative growth?")

And even though the outlook is for an uptick in economic activity later in the year — the product of a pent-up demand for autos and housing and the prospect of a $30 billion to $35 billion tax cut — the scenario of the majority of forecasters still is not what you'd call appetizing.

The consensus expects the worst of all worlds for at least six months:

■ GNP will begin moving upward in the last half of 1981 — but at rates of just 2 to 3 percent, well below the 6- and 7-percent levels seen in the initial stages of previous postwar economic recoveries. This, combined with a flat-to-declining GNP in the first two quarters, will leave the year with little or no real economic growth over-all — on top of a slight over-all decline in GNP last year.

■ It will also leave unemployment comparatively high, with the average for the year expected to be about 8 percent, give or take a percentage point or two, compared with 7.3 percent in 1980.

■ Yet inflation, as measured by the consumer price index (CPI), will remain firmly in double digits, thanks to the recent increase in oil prices by the Organization of Petroleum Exporting Countries (OPEC), the outlook for sharply higher food prices and the prospect that wages will jump significantly. While the inflation rate is expected to inch down from the 13.4 percent recorded in 1980, it won't be by much: Most forecasters look for a growth rate of 11 percent to 12 percent for the year.

Economy/ continued on page 10D

Agriculture / '81 should offer relief for farmers' grief

By Dennis J. McGrath
Staff Writer

This year should offer relief to farmers who watched the summer heat wave scorch their crops and felt their wallets grow lighter from the rising cost of running a farm.

At the very least, 1981 should refill their depleted bank accounts.

At the other end of the food chain, however, there will be no reprieve for consumers from steadily rising food prices. Every time they visit the supermarket, shoppers will pay dearly for the destruction wrought by the U.S. drought and other weather problems around the world.

But more important, the size of the 1981 crop will be crucial to the world's ability to feed itself and a key in determining the cost of food in the next several years.

The world's grain supply, reduced by two consecutive years of unfavorable growing weather, is at a dangerously low level. Although widespread starvation does not appear imminent, a record harvest in 1981 will be needed to avert food shortages in 1982. Anything less than record production could portend disaster.

"With stocks generally depleted, the danger looms that disappointing harvests worldwide (in 1981) would lead to widely fluctuating prices and perhaps serious food shortages in some areas of the world," said J. Dawson Ahalt, chairman of a panel of the U.S. Agriculture Department (USDA) that watches world food supplies.

"The fact that we face such a prospect just two years after accumulating our largest global stocks of grain in over a decade underscores the continued fragility of the world food situation — that the balance between too much and too little food can tilt easily and rapidly from one direction to the other," he said.

The lack of a comfortable cushion to break the fall in stocks is the result of two successive years of declines in world grain production — down 4 percent in 1979 and down another 1 percent in 1980 — because of poor weather in the Soviet Union both years and in the United States last

Agriculture/ continued on page 2D

L K Hanson

Recession / Minnesota suffered, but still may be buffered

By Lynda McDonnell
Staff Writer

Economists rarely share the same vision of the economic future. They sometimes have trouble agreeing on the past as well.

Two top diagnosticians of Minnesota's economic health, for example, offer quite different assessments of how badly Minnesota has been drubbed by the recession of 1980.

Sung Won Son, economist and senior vice president at Northwestern National Bank, and David Dahl, regional economist for the Federal Reserve Bank of Minneapolis, study different vital signs of the state's economic condition.

To Son, the past 12 months have been fairly bleak for the Land of 10,000 Lakes, largely because reduced farm income aggravated the effects of slowdowns in manufacturing, mining and housing.

Farm income estimates for 1980 are not yet available, but in general, farm income suffered considerably from high interest rates and soft prices in the first quarter. By year-end, however, prices had recovered substantially.

State unemployment, most recently gauged at 5.4 percent compared with 7.1 percent nationwide, started rising much sooner than it did nationally — mid-1979 compared with the first quarter of 1980.

Son also points out that personal income, when adjusted for inflation, fell here as it did nationally. He concludes from this that the state has suffered more than in most previous recessions.

"Recessions today are brought about by inflation, and inflation affects you whether you live in Minnesota or on the other side of the moon," he said.

Analysts at the state Department of Economic Security, which collects unemployment figures, say they must massage, adjust and bend their figures so much to conform to federal standards that they have little faith in their own figures.

Instead, analyst Dick Johnson studies employment figures, but his assessment is much the same as Son's. When calculation of figures in completed in about two weeks, he expects them to show the state's employment running about 2 percent below a year ago.

So while the state's much-touted diversified economy has kept the state healthier than the nation as a whole, it has not protected Minnesotans as well as in the past.

Dahl also studies the number of Minnesotans employed. But instead of looking at year-end numbers, he looks at the region's employment experience throughout the year. (The region includes South and North Dakota and Montana, but two-thirds of the population is in Minnesota.) His assessment of the past year is more

Recession/ continued on page 8D

Sung Won Son

Forecast / State job picture to improve slowly

By Lynda McDonnell
Staff Writer

The Minnesota job picture will improve this year, but not much and not quickly. And it may get worse before it gets better, say the state's economic prognosticators.

David Dahl, regional economist for the Federal Reserve Bank of Minneapolis, originally predicted that employment would grow by 3 percent this year in the Ninth District, including Minnesota, North and South Dakota and Montana.

But because interest rates remain high, Dahl expects employment in the district to grow by only 2 percent. This is still a healthy increase compared with the .5 percent growth he predicts for employment nationally. The gross national product will remain virtually flat, he predicts.

Sung Won Son of Northwestern National Bank of Minneapolis believes that unemployment will peak before April, reaching 8.5 percent in the nation, 7 percent in the state and 5.5 percent in the Twin Cities.

The rate will slowly fall during the rest of the year, he said. And recovery in Minnesota will be helped by strong farm income, Son said. He expects strong export demand to push up commodity prices faster than the tight-fisted Federal Reserve Board forces up interest rates.

Dave Roe, president of the Minnesota AFL-CIO, expects quite a delay before unemployment starts to fall. "I don't think we can look for any relief until late next summer or maybe next fall," he said.

In national surveys, employers say they expect the number of jobs to grow slightly this quarter. Moreover, they do say the incidence of layoffs reached its peak by the end of October.

Minneapolis employers are less optimistic. In a small survey by a temporary help firm, Manpower, Inc., Minneapolis employers predicted a depressed employment outlook for the first quarter. Only 13 percent of those sampled said they plan to hire more people while another 17 percent plan to reduce their staffs.

Job growth was predicted by employers active in finance, insurance and real estate while employers in construction, manufacturing and

Forecast/ continued on page 2D

David Dahl

Energy / An ample supply, but cost will be high

By Robert J. Hagen
Staff Writer

Barring unforseen catastrophe, Minnesota should have an adequate supply of energy this year, but it certainly is going to be more expensive.

"Our energy problem is price, not supply," said Michael Murphy, former manager of energy research at the Upper Midwest Council and now a private energy consultant.

How much it's going to cost is anybody's guess.

For example, a scenario that Murphy developed three months ago included gasoline selling for about $1.75 a gallon by the fourth quarter of this year. Since the recent round of price increases by the Organization of Petroleum Exporting Countries (OPEC), however, he has decided that $2 per gallon by the end of the year is not out of the question.

Brian Ettesvold, executive director of the Minnesota Service Station Operators Association, said gasoline prices have gone up an average of about 5 cents a gallon since the first of January. About 600 brand-name gasoline dealers in Minnesota are members of the association.

"I expect to see monthly increases of at least two or three cents a gallon for the first six months of the year," he said.

The price for home-delivered fuel oil has risen about 11 percent from last April, with most of the increase coming in the last three months. The price in the Twin Cities area has increased from a range of 97 cents to a $1 a gallon nine months ago to about $1.10 a gallon today. In areas farther from pipelines, the price is two or three cents a gallon higher.

OPEC raised the maximum price for crude oil to $41 a barrel last month, which was followed by increases of from $2 to $4 a barrel. Saudi Arabian crude, an OPEC benchmark price, went up $2 to $32 a barrel.

"I've seen some forecasts that include a price of $45 a barrel," Murphy said. "That's a very depressing scenario. And the real question is whether the U.S. economy, which may be in a recession anyway, can take that kind of shock."

Canada, which has been gradually curtailing its oil exports to the United States, raised its export tax by $6 per barrel early this month, bringing the price of its crude to $42 a barrel. It also boosted the price of natural gas it exports to the United States by about 11 percent.

Shortly after the Canadians increased their oil price, Koch Refining, Minnesota's largest refiner, raised its wholesale gasoline price by 5 cents a gallon and Ashland Oil, the state's second largest refiner, increased its price 3 cents a gallon.

Koch's refinery at Pine Bend in Rosemount gets between 70 and 80 percent of its crude oil from Canada, depending upon the season.

"You never know what the Canadians are going to do, but it appears right now that we won't have any problems with supply," said Glen Shore, Koch director of public relations. "The price will be something else again.

Energy/ continued on page 2D

**The Sunday magazine/
Picture** magazine, as its name
implies, is the Tribune's showcase for
photographs. Emphasis is on
pictures, although type is used
extensively. Picture is a rotogravure
section. Its design principles are
those of the Tribune's other special
sections: Helvetica type is set 9 point
on 9.5, a four-column grid is used, the
nameplate is in Tribune style and
standing layout rules are used.
Layout of the magazine is done by a
designer, with the magazine editor
and chief photographer involved.

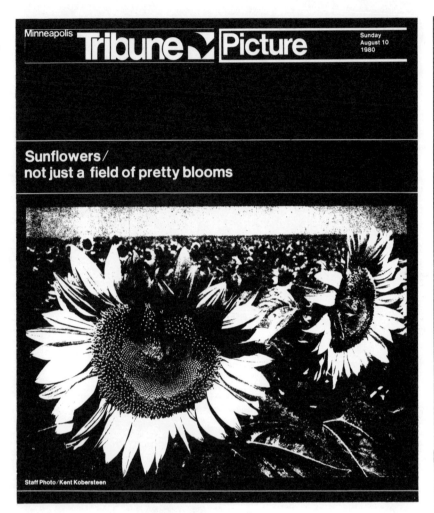

Minneapolis **Tribune** / **Picture**

Sunday
July 20
1980

Confirmation/it's still a rite of passage

Illustration/L.K. Hanson

Cover subject is expanded on next two pages.

Confirmation/the revised version

John Nelson, center, surrounded by some of the 41 other confirmands at Prince of Peace Lutheran Church in Burnsville. From left and going clockwise: Sherry Brunes, Denise Madsen, Jane Johnson, Jon Eidsness, Doug Bestul, Kris Bai- ley, Patti Crowl and Julie Mueller.

Staff Photos by Bruce Bisping

**By Brian Jones
Staff Writer**

They talked baseball, not Exodus, at one table. Other teen-agers strolled freely in and out of the church workroom. There was an occasional rattle-rattle, ker-chunck as coins begat soda pop in a machine around the corner.

Another Wednesday afternoon in confirmation class.

Confirmation class?

That scene might appall old-line Lutherans for whom confirmation meant at least two years of Saturday mornings in straight-back chairs, endlessly repeating " . . . Leviticus, Numbers, Deuteronomy . . . " and sleeping with catechisms creeping through the brain.

All that is passe in hundreds of Lutheran churches that have adopted a modern, multimedia, flexible-schedule confirmation program. Rote memorization has given way to learning packets and discussion groups. The confirmation class at Prince of Peace Lutheran Church in Burnsville is one example.

Next to the open Bible in front of most of the teens was a cassette tape player. In front of them was a video slide viewer. Confirmation students at several of the tables followed lines of the Bible with scanning fingertips, while earphones were perched on their heads.

If older Lutherans squeezed their ears between those earphones, they might be even more astonished at the lesson than at the classroom scene. The "Star Wars" theme introduced one tape before a lecturer stated, "As you begin to listen to this

tape, be sure that you have the following items in your possession: (1) A Bible opened to Genesis 1 . . . "

"There is learning going on here. Why does learning have to be oppressive? Why do you have to make the kids hate it?" asked the Rev. Andrew Jensen, associate pastor of Prince of Peace (the kids call him Pastor Andy).

"The student sets the pace here. There are some kids in here six hours a week, but others haven't found the church yet. The schedule is flexible. If a boy has football in the fall, he can skip confirmation class for practice and rejoin the program later on," Jensen said. Some students finish the confirmation program in a year; others take two years.

Perhaps the most marked change in approach is that students aren't put on the spot by being asked questions in front of their classmates. Instead, the teens are quizzed, usually once a week, in smaller conferences with their teachers.

"This program is nicer than some of my friends' (confirmation classes), who go to other churches. It seems like they have to just sit and memorize," said John Nelson, 15, who was confirmed at Prince of Peace Church on Pentecost, May 25.

Anne Pankow, 15, was also confirmed at Prince of Peace Church on Pentecost. She said, "When you start out, you know the basic parts of the Bible—but when you finish, you know more deeply what it is about."

Apparently, lots of other students and lots of Lutheran congregations agree. Since Jensen developed the multimedia approach to confirmation class in 1971, about 1,900 congregations nationwide have adopted the learning program. Jen-

sen said it takes a 3,000-square-foot warehouse in Burnsville to store all the materials marketed in the program.

While the heat is off the kids, Jensen insists they learn as much as they did under the older, stricter method.

For example, the learning packet on Genesis—one of 16 such packets leading from the Creation through the modern Lutheran Church—requires students to be able to list the six main characters in Genesis, discuss the theme of purpose presented in Genesis and consider the relationship of God to history and to their own lives.

Students read scriptures with accompanying tapes and filmstrips, read supplemental books, then write reports on selected topics. At group quizzes, teachers test the students' grasp of the Biblical concepts and assign further work in weak areas. ▶

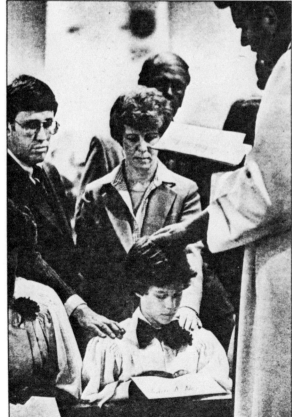

At left, John Nelson knelt, his parents placed their hands on his shoulders and Pastor Andrew Jensen read the Bible verse that he had selected: Jeremiah 29:11—"For I know the thoughts that I think toward you, said the Lord, thoughts of peace, and not of evil, to give you an expected end." At top, John and his parents left the service and headed home for a special dinner with John as guest of honor. Above, the robe with carnation attached and the bow tie came off and landed on John's bed as soon as he got home.

94

TV Week, the Tribune's Sunday television and radio magazine, is a quarter-fold size publication produced on an offset press. Helvetica type and a three-column grid are used and the nameplate is Tribune style.

Minneapolis **Tribune** **TV week**

March 4-10 1979

Moving week in the Twin Cities Changes in network affiliations of KSTP, WTCN and KMSP mean TV dials will be spinning overtime
Page 7

Minneapolis **Tribune** | **TV week**

February 1-7 1981

Joanne Woodward as schoolteacher Federal-state clash over racial integration
is re-created in CBS-TV's 'Crisis at Central High'
Page 19

Wednesday/
The **Perspective** page design bridges news and features. The page is a vehicle for articles, often quite long, that provide more explanation and content — and even opinion — than they do new facts.

Since the page is **not** news and **not** features as they are commonly known, its design must tell the reader that it is something different. The page flag is very different from the standard daily style, and odd-measure Helvetica light body type, set 10 point on a 9.5-point slug, is used.

Perspective

Minneapolis Tribune
Wednesday
July 23/1980
11A

Build a better mousetrap, it is said, and the world will beat a path to your door. But if you raise a more productive dairy cow, a whole lot of dairy farmers eventually go out of business. Then why do dairy farmers keep hoping to find such an animal?

The search for the perfect cow

By Mark Kramer

As everyone has heard by now, America is losing its farmers. Since World War II, acreage per farm has doubled and farm population has halved. Today, six percent of all farmers grow half our food. We can take a detached, aesthetic sort of pride in the inventiveness and organization that enable the surviving farmers to get so much done; but the cost in neighbors is high.

Because so few jobs remain as unambiguously useful as farming, the loss of half these jobs must be considered a serious latent consequence of the arrival of the new agriculture. Nowhere in the country has increased productivity ruined a greater percentage of farmers than it has in New England. In richer areas, farms have combined; the fields, if not all the people, still grow food. My Yankee neighbors, with farms locked between hills, swamps, and city streets, sell farmland to developers. Massachusetts has only a few thousand full-time farmers left; Connecticut, fewer; Rhode Island, only a few hundred.

This incredible change, as devastating to an established way of life as any revolution, has resulted neither from conspiracy nor from public vote. The cause is systematic: Farmers, competing with each other for the privilege of supplying our food, are eager for the ever-more-productive technology offered by manufacturers competing for the privilege of supplying farmers their tools, backed by investors competing for decent returns, backed by banks, backed by governments, backed by armies, backed by us.

Along the way, the losers have been as eager for progress as the winners; that is the built-in paradox of progress. Take, for example, that elegant development of modern technology, the Holstein-Friesian milk cow. In the postwar era, milk demand has remained constant, but the milk is now supplied by one third as many cows, each producing triple the amount of milk produced in 1945. In the same period, new hardware has allowed (or required) the remaining dairy farmers to more than treble the size of their herds. The result? Few farmers producing lots of milk.

The paradox is this: Although dairy farmers wink out like city lights at midnight, there has never existed one — future winner or future loser — who didn't wish his cows gave more milk. That yearning for an edge on the farmer next door, that inescapable and unneighborly desire, has been the making of farmers, and their undoing. And it all started a long time ago.

Cows have been domesticated for millennia — there are bovine remains in Neolithic Swiss lake dwellings. The modern milk cow, as distant from the wild beast as the poodle is from the coyote, is a reflection of nature at her most genial and compliant. To understand the genetic perfection of cows, one must understand the tastes of their predators.

In all of natural history, no predators have transformed animals more ambitiously to suit their own omnivorous needs than humans. We have modified the very competence of the cow, creating an animal completely dependent on us for survival in its present form. What we have bred into the innocent *Bos typicus* is a flesh both tender and built of grass, a powerful body, a submissive temperament and — most important here — a capacity to produce far more milk than its own young require.

These days, the first 9,000 or 10,000 pounds of milk a cow gives in excess of the needs of its own young pay the cost of keeping the farmer in business. With good cows, the profit over costs increases with each subsequent ton up to about 20,000 pounds, a production average met by the herds of only the best dairy farmers. According to the publication Hoard's Dairyman, some cows still at work in Ethiopia yield only 1,000 pounds of milk a year. A cow yielding only 4,000 or 5,000 pounds would have been tolerated in the average American dairy herd until about 1950. It took at lot of those cows to slake America's thirst, and there were a lot of dairy farmers. Now things are different.

In Rochester, Ind., in a box stall, in a Quonset barn, with adjacent paddock replete with well-nibbled apple trees, there dwell three mascot sheep, several friendly geese, and the modern queen, the reigning bovine, the Cleopatra of all dairy cows, whose name is Beecher Arlinda Ellen. Queen Ellen is the Roger Bannister of dairydom. She has broken the equivalent of the four-minute mile for milk production during a measured 305-day period. She went over the 50,000-pound barrier with 314 pounds to spare. That's more than 20,000 quarts of milk from one cow.

Beecher Arlinda Ellen, at the top of her production, eats 60 pounds a day of 16-percent-protein grain, and also 70 pounds of alfalfa hay. She drinks nearly 60 gallons of water a day.

The accelerating pace of dairy breed improvement makes more farmers poor than it makes rich. It serves to concentrate milk money in fewer and fewer farmers' pockets. It puts poorer farmers out of business. It forces all farmers, regardless of inclination, to participate in a mad race to keep up with the Beechers.

Ellen is nursed and tended with care. Her proprietor, Harold Beecher, says, "No water ever fell on her back." Her record milk production run earned him about $5,000. Her progeny, male and female alike, are enormously valuable breeding stock, worth tens of times the value of her milk. The shadow of Beecher Arlinda Ellen darkens the ruminations of somber and ambitious farmers the nation over. But for all her worthiness, can she sit on velvet cushions on a high throne, and languidly nibble hay cubes? Can she snooze, munch kudzu, romp with young calves and young bulls, leading games of follow the leader?

Hardly.

Cows, even lesser cows, exhibit their competence to exist these days by going about their business continually. Dairy cows' business is eating. The wild cows of yore also had to *find* food and keep themselves out of danger. But with humans in charge, the food was delivered and the danger institutionalized.

Eating is the only job left, and cows must go about it with a will. All animals, of course, eat and turn food into flesh. Lactating mammals turn food into milk as well, and dairy cows, having been bred to the chore, turn lots of food into lots of milk. Beecher Arlinda Ellen is the queen of hunger. She's too hungry to loaf. She's condemned by her genes to a lifetime of insatiable hunger. She was born to crave food, to feed, to metabolize food and make milk of it at a rate that fascinates dairy scientists, and to eat more while they stand about fascinated. She eats instead of sleeping.

Beecher Arlinda Ellen eats while cartels complete for the honor of buying her calves still damp. Her daughters will be raised to test and compete with Mother. Her sons will remove to fine pastures and will soon enough be at stud. The stakes in these subsidiary Beecher Arlinda Ellen enterprises, like the bureaucracy needed to sustain the complex dairy-breeding industry, are enormous. The breeding industry's procedures are costly and complex, the results quixotic. Beecher Arlinda Ellen keeps on eating.

Beecher Arlinda Ellen represents the pinnacle of accomplishment in the vast and dispersed effort that dairy farmers undertake to put each other out of business. What successful dairy breeders have to sell is an economic edge over one's neighbors, and a way of "milking" more money from *Bos typicus*. The accelerating pace of dairy breed improvement makes more farmers poor than it makes rich. It serves to concentrate milk money in fewer and fewer farmers' pockets. It puts poorer farmers out of business. It forces all farmers, regardless of inclination, to participate in a mad race to keep up with the Beechers.

The dairy breeding industry is built on the work of a minority of farmers who strive to make finer genes as well as fuller tanks of milk. Eighty-five percent of dairy animals in America are Holstein-Friesians. There are about 9.5 million of what are called "grade" Holsteins, which are pureblooded cows but without pedigree papers. A twentieth of Holstein cows — about 500,000 animals — are "registered," nearly all with the Holstein-Friesian Association of America (HFAA). The infrastructure supporting the HFAA demonstrates the complexity, and the structural, unplanned, automatic, business-as-usual nature of the forces that make farming today a race for technological improvement.

To start with the 500,000 registered cows: At a cost to a farmer of perhaps $15 a year per cow, a production testing supervisor from the Dairy Herd Improvement Association (DHIA — a testing service run by the Department of Agriculture) shows up in farmers' barns, usually once a month, to record with unimpeachable honesty the milk yield of each cow and the butterfat and protein content of the milk. From these tests are extrapolated yearly yield averages. (Many "grade" cows are on DHIA test programs too, because the results guide efficient feeding and culling choices.)

Farmers owning registered animals file sketches, bloodlines, and registry numbers for each cow with the HFAA. Owners of purebred stocks are basically interested in coming up with choice bull studs whose daughters will milk more than the daughters of the other bulls. They are also occasionally interested in breeding not only for production but for "type" — for daughters whose udders are higher, whose hooves are sturdier, whose faces are nobler of aspect, who conceive and calve more easily, who resist disease more heartily and stand more proudly than do the daughters of other bulls.

But mostly, they are interested in breeding bulls whose daughters make more milk.

It is not easy to establish reliably whose daughters do these things. One must raise up a purebred bull until breeding age (about two years), breed it artificially to sixty or eighty cows in scattered herds, await the birth of thirty or forty female calves (that takes about ten more months), raise the calves to join their respective milking herds (another two years), and then milk them for a season (ten more months). It's six years before the results are in. This is costly — it is estimated that it costs at least $40,000 a bull. But thousands of novice bulls are aspirants each year for the role of father superior.

The motive of farmers for engaging in bull testing is the chance for profit, and the joy of speculating on a prideful bit of uncertainty amidst the plodding routines of daily farm life. The motive for the Holstein-Friesian Association of America is fiscal soundness, and, as their publications benignly put it, "the good of the breed." And it's true. Their hand is forced too. If they let up, Brown Swiss, Jersey or Guernsey will forge ahead.

'Think of what my milk check would be,' farmers think, 'if my cows gave twice as much milk each day.' If all cows gave twice as much milk, the check would be about the same, and business would be tougher.

HFAA certifies and keeps records of the winners, those rare beasts whose "predicted difference" — a statistical index of progeny improving upon a farmer's herd average — for both milk and type is high. HFAA is at the center of the information flow; it performs the massive quantity of secretarial service needed to isolate these fancy bulls reliably.

What seems miraculous is that a cooperative effort requiring broad funding exists even though few participants benefit and many are harmed by the results. Most farmers keeping registered Holstein animals do not make very much from the fact of their cows' registration. HFAA's drab empire, built on farmers' dreams, works to the detriment of many dairy farmers. There is obviously no malevolent intent in this. It's just that HFAA provides a high-technology sort of information that enables the most ambitious farmers to crowd out their neighbors. The fields we see growing up to brush along the sides of New England's highways, blocking once-opened vistas and closing in land where food once grew, are casualties of the increased efficiency afforded by such tools as the HFAA provides.

In the meantime, dairy farmers persist in dreaming about the new improved cow. "Think of what my milk check would be," farmers think, "if my cows gave twice as much milk each day." If all cows gave twice as much milk, the check would be about the same, and business would be tougher. The profit of a high-producing cow isn't merely in its productiveness, but in the rareness, the timeliness of its high production. When other cows catch up, that's how productive cows will have to be simply to avoid the butcher's block. And cows are improving rapidly. The public wants only so much milk. But the national herd average is improving at an amazing 300 or 400 pounds a year, these days, after decades of slow improvement and centuries of no improvement.

And there are consequences. Because cows are better, more money can be spent on keeping them and milking them. It pays well to buy the best stall for a cow to sleep in, the best system to milk a cow, the best feed to keep cows' production rolling, and the best semen for breeding herd replacements. All this means more business, more financed agriculture, more low-labor, capital-intensive farming systems, and even fewer farmers.

Two new lines of endeavor, currently the subject of intense research by scientists in both private and public sectors, will almost certainly further alter the world of dairy farming suddenly and strongly when they come of age. It is probable that they will develop soon, and it is certain that, when they do, the dislocations seen so far in the changing nature of dairy farming will be repeated on a grander scale.

The first of these developments is semen sexing. Scientists are working to develop a process that will enable stud companies to sell semen guaranteed to produce offspring of predetermined sex. Of course all farmers not engaged in breeding stud bulls will always choose to have their cows spring heifer calves. Sexed semen will double the efficiency of calf raising, since now half of a farmer's calves are not of the desired sex. With more heifer calves to choose from, one may expect herd averages to climb, decreasing still further the total population of cows — and of dairy farmers — needed by the nation.

It will be delightful to the farmer in the short run to have such control. In the long run, such increases in efficiency, given a fixed demand in the marketplace, inevitably result in a continual shakeout of "less efficient" producers.

The more Faustian and far-reaching scientific innovation, now far along in development, is that of ova transplants. When perfected, ova tranplants may result in as sudden and significant a rise in dairy production per cow as that caused by the introduction in the early 1950s of frozen bull semen from top bulls. Ova transplants are now done by a surgical process in which a veterinarian flushes a cow's uterus to recover eggs recently inseminated. The uterus flushed is that of a "top cow," perhaps of Beecher Arlinda Ellen, or one of her sisters. The process releases up to twenty fertile eggs.

Awaiting blessed events in a nearby barn are twenty guest mothers, their estrous cycles synchronized by drugs with that of the donor cow. The recipients are implanted with the fertilized eggs — this used to be surgical procedure, too, but recently has been accomplished without surgery — and produce healthy calves. The calves, a score at a time, are all prize stock. In the future, a farmer may be able to take fertile eggs from his best cow and have a barnful of her daughters at a single throw. Needless to say, that would result in quantum leaps in milk production in every herd that used it.

And, further in the future, what will happen to farmers when Beecher Arlinda Ellen can be cloned?

Illustration/ John Miller

It's a cow . . . It's a perfect cow . . . It's Bo Dairy (artist's conception).

Perspective

Minneapolis Tribune
Wednesday
December 5 / 1979
7A

The American friends of West Germany's neo-Nazis

Graphics / Al Bloharnan

By Alfons Heck
Pacific News Service

The neo-Nazi movement in West Germany is not only gaining ground but is turning to political violence. Few Americans realize that the United States serves as a major support base for this movement, or that Lincoln, Neb., is its financial and propaganda capital. In this dispatch from the Pacific News Service, writer Alfons Heck reports on recent developments.

In the middle of the recent trial of six neo-Nazi terrorists in Bueckburg, West Germany, reporters in the courtroom were shocked when a number of trial observers rose in reverent respect for the only witness to testify for the defense — a young American.

Why was a U.S. citizen appearing in a West German courtroom defending the activities of self-proclaimed Nazis?

The answer involves a complex international network of Nazi members and sympathizers who look to the unlikely city of Lincoln, Neb., as their movement's financial and propaganda capital. And 26-year-old Gerhard Lauck, born in Milwaukee of German parents, is the man who put Lincoln at the center of the Nazi map.

As such, Lauck is better known — and more despised — in West Germany, where the neo-Nazi movement is rigidly suppressed, than he is in the United States, where he is allowed to operate in the open.

The four-month trial at which Lauck appeared as star witness was widely covered in the West German press, for it stemmed from a significant departure in neo-Nazi tactics. It resulted in conviction of six West German neo-Nazis for crimes including armed robbery, bodily assault and theft of arms. The latter charge grew out of an incident early this year in which Dutch NATO soldiers on maneuver were waylaid and robbed of their automatic weapons.

Like other right wing extremists in Europe, West German Nazis no longer limit their activity to illegal rallies or inflammatory speeches. They have turned increasingly to acts of terrorism reminiscent of the better-known ultra-left wing organizations.

As his testimony at the trial revealed, Gerhard Lauck has played a central role in this tactical change.

From his Nebraska headquarters, Lauck heads the NSDAP AO (the initials stand, in German, for National Socialist German Workers Party in Reconstruction) and allegedly directs numerous clandestine cells inside West Germany. In 1976, Lauck was expelled from West Germany as persona non grata after spending four and a half months in a prison for political agitating and smuggling propaganda.

For the last six years, Lauck has edited the American Nazi Party's publication "New Order," and has published a bi-monthly German-language version of it, called NS Kampfruf (National Socialist Battle Cry) in addition to articles calculated to stir racial hatred and anti-Semitism, it unabashedly calls for the overthrow by force of what it calls West Germany's "Jew-oriented" government

Lauck testified at the Bueckburg trial at the request of one of the six defendants. 25 year old Michal Kuehnan, the acknowledged intellectual leader of the six and a member of Lauck's organization since 1977. West German authorities at first balked at Kuehnan's request but eventually granted Lauck a safeconduct and immunity from prosecution — although they kept him in virtual custody for the two days he appeared at the trial.

"We shall eventually succeed in restoring the Nazi Party," he told one reporter at the trial, "because not only moral right but public opinion is on our side. Why should the Communist Party be allowed to operate legally by the Jew-influenced Bonn government while we are persecuted?" Many West Germans, although they despise the neo-Nazis as an anachronistic embarrassment, share the sentiment that the party should not be suppressed.

Hans-Joseph Horsch, the director of Hamburg's Office for the Protection of the Constitution, a sort of German FBI, is among high officials in the police organization who believe that it is both unrealistic and dangerous to suppress the neo-Nazis. He predicted a year ago that doing so would lead inevitably to acts of terrorism, and he suggested that the various groups be allowed to operate openly, as they do in the United States

Kurt Rebmann, West Germany's chief federal prosecutor, does not agree, though he admits to a "growing concern" on the subject

In light of the neo-Nazis' suppression in West Germany, Lauck's work in the United States is critical. He produces vast quantities of neo-Nazi propaganda to send to West Germany, a task nearly free of risk. According to Nazi hunter Simon Wiesenthal, Lauck's mailing list contains between 10,000 and 20,000 names in West Germany alone.

The May-June issue of "Kampfruf" was the prosecution's exhibit A in the Bueckburg trial. On the back cover it depicted, under the headline "Freedom of Revolution," a young Nazi blowing up a TV tower, presumably during the German showing of the NBC production "Holocaust." It was presented as evidence that the publication advocates violence.

That edition also contained articles stating that "only lice were gassed in Auschwitz" and that it was "a myth" that the Germans killed six million Jews

Lauck's testimony may have harmed Kuehnan, although he tried to dismiss the back cover illustration as "rhetoric." The prosecutor considered charging Lauck with perjury because the content of his publication contradicted his testimony. But he was saved by his American citizenship, and the grant of temporary immunity.

Back in Lincoln, Lauck explained that he does condone violence, "but only in self-defense to what has been and still is being done to our German comrades." He added that he could not have admitted that to his West German interrogators.

But it is not only with his publications that Lauck's work in behalf of the neo-Nazi movement is significant. As unofficial treasurer, he funnels funds to neo-Nazis all over Europe, but especially in West Germany.

In addition to proceeds from the sale of Nazi publications and paraphernalia, and membership dues, Lauck boasted that he gets funds "from virtually every place in the world, although we haven't had any contributions from Tel Aviv lately.

Though the active membership of neo-Nazi groups in the United States is not huge — a reliable estimate puts it at no more than 2,000 members — there are many thousands of anonymous sympathizers. On the matter of arms shipments he is evasive: "I just can't comment, for obvious reasons, you understand."

**Thursday and Friday/
Thursday Food** and **Friday
Special** sections are purely feature
sections. Their design is similar to but
different from Sunday sections.

Flag design emphasizes the day of
the week, screened letters repeating
the name of the day across the top of
the page, with the titles **Food** and
Special in bold Helvetica. Flags are
shallower than those used Sunday
and have fewer segments.

The pages are highly designed, with
large photos and/or illustrations.
Helvetica light body type, ragged
right, is used according to the same
specifications as on Sunday covers.

thursdayfood

Minneapolis Tribune   April 24/1980   1C

**readers
recipe
contest
3rd annual
cookbook**

Contents/

Appetizers/**2C**	Nonmeat main dish/**20C**
Salads/	Quick breads/**22C**
Vegetables/**6C**	Yeast breads/**23C**
Meat/**9C**	Nonbaked desserts/**24C**
Poultry/**14C**	Baked desserts/**26C**
Fish/**18C**	Photo/Earl Seubert
Design/Michael Carroll

hursdaythursdayfoodthu

Minneapolis Tribune   December 28/1978/1C

Department store eateries offer honest, if dull, dining downtown

By Bonnie Miller Rubin
Staff Writer

After a week of wining, dining and general excess, there is something very comforting about a department store restaurant.

Even if you have not set foot in one in years, rest assured that nothing has changed. Mothers still take their little boys to the ladies' room. Egg salad on whole wheat (with or without trimmed crusts) is still the overwhelming favorite and the "house" dressing is still a gloppy bottled French.

Here you will be safe from ferns, sprouts and menus on gasoline cans. No one will ever say, "Hi! My name is Muffy and I'll be your waitress."

On the contrary, department store waitresses tend to be named Edna or Helen and they are pros — the kind of waitress that can carry five plates up her arm at one time. There is no Muzak, just the constant clatter of silverware.

The post-Christmas mayhem, when everyone is returning and refunding, provides a perfect time for rediscovering this remnant of our youth. After being sent from department to department, you may discover that the ceramic ash tray, which came in a box bearing the name of a local retailer, really came from a roadside stand in Tijuana. Three hours later you still have the ash tray, along with a headache, two very sore feet and a tremendous appetite. There's only one solution: It's time to get something to eat . . .

Donaldson's — The North Shore Grill at Donaldson's is always bustling — and with good reason. While the atmosphere is nondescript, the food is remarkably well prepared. We made two trips at the height of the lunch hour during the peak of the season, and the quality of the food never wavered.

Donaldson's specialty is fish. The kitchen staff has mastered the basic techniques of broiling, frying and sauteeing — no small feat judging by the abundance of dry, overcooked fish that is served today. We sampled the walleye ($4.50), the salmon steak ($3.80) and the trout ($3.10). All were comparable to what we've had at fine restaurants for twice the price.

Chicken salad ($3.10) is usually a pedestrian dish, especially when served at a department store. But at Donaldson's, it was chock full of big pieces of real off-the-bone chicken, and served in a glass flower pot. Unfortunately, the Skyliner ($2.70) a cheeseburger topped with bacon, was far from top-flight. The off-gray burger was not helped by the cold French fries.

Save room for dessert, because Donaldson's makes its own pies. The apple is second only to Peter's Grill — packed with apples, not filler, into a deftly prepared crust. The service tends to lag at times, but the food for the price is hard to beat.

Young Quinlan — The Young Quinlan Fountain Room is a throwback to another era and therein lies its charm.

This is where ladies — not girls and not women — come to lunch. You'll probably see more fox boas (the kind with the beady eyes and the little claws) here in one afternoon than you've seen in the past decade. A Young Quinlan lunch is an outing, a reason to come downtown — especially if it's Tuesday, and you can see a fashion show along with your doilied chicken pot pie.

There are a few small distinctions that set Young Quinlan apart from other department store restaurants. This is the only spot where you take the order. (A check and a pencil are left on every table.) This is the only place where you can make reservations or rent a small private room, free of charge. And Young Quinlan undoubtedly takes the most pride in its bread, miniature bran muffins and sticky caramel rolls, which are a definite improvement over the all-too-common foam-rubber white.

A favorite of mine is the rare roast beef salad ($3.50). Order this when you're dieting, but don't want to feel deprived. Rosy strips of tender beef over lettuce, with green pepper rings, hard-cooked eggs, wedges of surprisingly good tomatoes, radishes and onions, are served with a puckery lemon marinade dressing on the side.

Another boon to dieters is the seafood bowl ($3.75), which had very high-quality white tuna and shrimp. Our only criticism is that it crams all this stuff in a small dinner salad bowl, making it impossible to toss without getting it on the table.

Department continued on page 3C

Blending of food and theater a long-standing habit with Donahue

By Trudi Hahn
Staff Writer

John Donahue, director of the Children's Theater Company, inhabits an office that may be the world's most exclusive dinner theater.

At one end of the long room is a butcher block dinette table with caned-seat chairs. At the other end is a modest kitchen, an example of efficiency apartment design. Stretching between them, a wall of cream-colored curtains covers an expanse of glass looking down on the stage and audience of the Children's Theater Company. Donahue's guests can eat a meal and watch the play for dessert.

Donahue's unusually strong involvement with food and theater began about 15 years ago in an abandoned police station in south Minneapolis, where the company of players, then known as the Moppet Theater, stayed alive by eating communally at the station's kitchen.

"It's the only way we could live; nobody made any salaries."

Donahue broke off as Michael, a dog of Irish wolfhound and miscellaneous extraction, nuzzled his visitor's knee for attention. "He's been with us since he was big enough to fit in this basket," Donahue said, reaching toward a slice of French bread to accompany his minestrone and wine.

The chic, warm decoration of the apartment-like office shows how far the theater company has come since the police station days. The visitor's chair is imitation Tudor with carved wooden arms and a high tapestry back. A system of wooden shelves spans the wall facing the curtains. Low white sofas are grouped on oriental rugs. Michael stays off the sofas but has been known to rear up to investigate the kitchen countertop.

Donahue uses the office's kitchen to prepare luncheons for heads of corporations and suppers for people like Helen Hayes and Ray Bolger. At meal's end, the curtains are drawn back for a look at the performance.

"It's a great way to introduce the theater to people."

And a great way to introduce people into the company's circle of food and friendship. "Breaking bread together is one of the best ways to make friends with people . . . That's why it's important to have food on the premises."

Donahue said the Children's Theater building has three kitchens. A tour of the other two, with Michael padding along, revealed that "kitchen" is really an overstatement. More accurately, the others resemble glorified utility cupboards.

The single piece of kitchen equipment in both is a compact, multi-use unit that contains sink, refrigerator and stove. In the kitchen near the ground-floor lobby, food and drink is prepared or kept warm for sales in the second-floor lobby before the performance. (The first choice for that kitchen's location was needed for handicapped restroom facilities on the second floor.)

The other glorified utility closet adjoins the actors' green room, where the company retires to relax before or after a performance. "I always wanted a big kitchen off the green room, but I couldn't ask for that" in the new building, completed in 1974; "it wouldn't have been understood."

Donahue envisioned a big kitchen with a fireplace that would be the center of a community of people, like the kitchen of a house, where you could chat, smell the simmering pot and contribute to the meal.

"Preparation and sharing are an important part of nourishment for the

Donahue continued on page 2C

John Donahue in the kitchen off his office.

100

ay friday friday Special frid

Minneapolis Tribune

June 15 / 1979 / 1C

No longer CBS's 'wise man,' Eric Sevareid finds place to be alone with his thoughts

By Nan Robertson
New York Times Service

It is to a primitive log cabin in a clearing in the woods near the Blue Ridge Moutains that Eric Sevareid has repaired for peace of mind over the last 28 years. Now that he is retired, he comes more often, to fish in the still waters of his pond for bass and blue gill, to hunt quail and ruffed grouse and to refresh his soul.

"You could not spend three days here and not relax," Sevareid mused aloud the other day. A child of the North Dakota prairie, of landlocked wheat fields billowing toward a limitless horizon, he came in his maturity to cherish the solitude of forests, of stands of trees shadowing a greensward.

It is a place where a reflective man, cast in a public career, can take refuge with his thoughts. For many years Sevareid was the resident wise man of CBS, and not just a rough-hewn, handsome face on television proffering instant analyses.

Some, he knows, find him pompus. "I am cursed with a somewhat forbidding Scandinavian manner," he acknowleged, "with a restraint that spells stuffiness to a lot of people."

Adlai Stevenson saw through "that unfortunate facade," according to Sevareid. "He knew that inside I am mush, full of a lot of almost bathetic

sentimentality about this country, the Midwest, Abraham Lincoln and the English language. Adlai saw through to your heart."

For more than four decades after his graduation from the University of Minnesota, Sevareid was a reporter, editor, war correspondent, radio newscaster, columnist and television commentator. He was one of "Ed Murrow's boys," one of the brilliant newspapermen hired by CBS in 1939 as World War II loomed.

Right after the war, he wrote his book, "Not So Wild a Dream," reissued recently with a new introduction by the author and the subtitle "A Personal Story of Youth and War and the American Faith." Historian Arthur Schlesinger Jr. said the republication "restores to a new generation one of the significant American documents of our time." It has become a popular book on campuses 33 years after its debut.

Sevareid, 66, has been retired for a year and is loving it. He is more relaxed. He is sleeping nights. He has time for long lunches with old friends and for his five grandchildren and his 14-year-old daughter, Cristina, who went to live with him in his big stone house in Bethesda, Md., after Sevareid and his second wife were divorced. (The twin sons of his first marriage, Michael and Peter, are 39 and prospering in their chosen careers in television production and the teaching

Sevareid continued on page 4C

Sevareid continued on page 4C

Yesterday's advice on dating seems like ancient history to today's teen-agers

IT'S BEEN THREE DAYS AND BRAD HASN'T **CALLED!** MAYBE...MAYBE I'M NOT A REAL **WOMAN** TO HIM...

By Leslie Bennetts
New York Times Service

New York, N.Y.
The faded little book caught her eye one day in the biology classroom, where it was wedged among others on a shelf. Curious, she started leafing through it. Soon she and her fellow 14-year-olds were hooting with laughter. First published in 1959, it was called "On Becoming a Woman," and to them it read like a relic of another civilization.

"They had certain costumes you had to wear," marveled the blue-jean clad ninth-grader, who lives in Manhattan. "It goes on and on about a navy blue sheath as a fundamental part of how you're supposed to dress! And the whole structure of the date, all the rituals of it — it's so different for us now!

"And there was all this stuff about never calling a boy on the telephone. I feel totally free to call a boy; it doesn't make me feel awkward to be more aggressive. The whole thing about how girls were supposed to wait by the phone is just not the way it is."

In addition to the specific mores of another era, however, she was struck by the larger implications of what she read.

"At first I thought it was all very funny," she mused. "But when I stopped to think about it, and the whole idea of pleasing the boy that runs all the way through it, I started getting kind of angry. There were all these lists of things on how you should please a boy, and nothing about how a boy did anything for you — as if it was your duty just to please, and boys didn't have those duties, only girls."

The little book, written by Mary McGee Williams and Irene Kane and published by the Dell Publishing Co., concluded with a chapter called "It's Not Too Soon to Dream of Marriage" ("After going steady," the authors wrote, "comes marriage, if life is to proceed in an orderly fashion, and it generally does.")

The book went through 17 printings and sold hundreds of thousands of copies over the years. An entire generation of young women were influenced by it and others like it. Books that presented the basic facts of life and discussions of dating and sex, but mixed the information with heavy doses of cultural conditioning about how to be a successful female in American society.

In dealing with boys, this feat was

Dating continued on page 4C

Dating continued on page 4C

The view from the top . . . of a high-rise project

By Jeff Strickler
Staff writer

It is the first thing everyone looks at. Come upon a high-rise construction site and the eyes automatically turn to the top. And the higher the building gets, it seems, the stronger the fascination becomes. We crane our necks and squint into the sun as our eyes strain to reach the summit, drawn to it like iron to a magnet.

But no matter how high the building is, there is always at least one person up even higher: Brad Wood or his colleagues, the men who work the cranes that dot the Minneapolis skyline.

It takes a special kind of person to climb up a ladder several hundred feet above the ground and crawl into an office that hangs over so much empty air. In the words of one of Wood's land-based associates, "You gotta be crazy."

"Aw, it's not so bad," Wood said, allowing as how he has learned to live with some of the vagaries of life in a crane, little things like swaying in stiff winds. "That first time I saw the end of the boom drop about five feet I wondered . . . But I've never heard of

one of these tipping over."

Wood spends up to half his life (during the summer, 12-hour shifts are not uncommon) in a small glass cage suspended 240 feet above the Gateway area of downtown. He operates one of the two giant Kraus-Anderson of Minneapolis, Inc., cranes at the 100 Washington Square site on Marquette and Washington Avs. It is a perch that offers an unparalleled view of downtown life.

"I can't quite see over all the buildings yet," he said. "But I should be able to soon." Before the job is done, Wood's crane will be half again as high as it is now, leaving him 360 feet up in the sky.

In the meantime, he settles for peeking over the Post Office to watch the barges on the river. And, of course, the obligatory girl-watching. "I've got just a great view of the (Towers condominiums') swimming pool," he said.

Wood's job, obviously, is not a good one for either the claustrophobic or those less than comfortable at great heights. The traditional rule of "don't look down" doesn't apply. Wood's job is to look down.

"Adjusting to the height bothers you," he admitted. "All that space below you . . . But you get used to it."

Still, there are drawbacks to being up so high, he said. The biggest is the simple fact that it is a long walk to the office. Once Wood is in his chair, he stays there for the duration of his shift. There is no kibitzing with co-workers over coffee or trading one-that-got-away fish stories at lunch. Even if everyone else takes a break, Wood can't, because there is no place for him to go.

And, Wood said, one of the first things a crane operator learns is that when you go to work in the morning you do your best to make sure you don't forget something important (like your lunch) back on the ground.

But there are advantages, too, said the 29-year-old native of Murdock, Minn.

"I enjoy the quiet," he said. "I can't hear

Crane continued on page 4C

A 22-story office

Brad Wood and his "office" have become part of the downtown skyline.

Crane continued on page 4C

Inside pages/
Design style is identical with daily style and the same layout rules are followed. Column headings are identical with daily headings except that the three-sided boxes are shaded instead of bold.

A standing feature of Friday Special is **The long weekend**, a calendar of events.

The long weekend

Minneapolis Tribune
Friday
November 7 / 1980
5C

Special events/

Living/Learning/

Music/

Theater/

Saturday

Today

Sunday

Neil Spencer and Lany Wendel find time for romance in the comedy "The Real Inspector Hound," 8 p.m. tonight and Saturday in the Arena Theater at the University of Minnesota's Rarig Center.

Film/

Today

Saturday

Sunday

Dance/

The University of Minnesota Marching Band will take a load off its feet when it takes the stage in Northrop Auditorium at 3 p.m. Sunday to present its 19th Annual Indoor Concert.

Saturday/
The Saturday Tribune is called **Saturday**. Combining both news and feature sections, it is as different from daily and Sunday newspapers as Saturday is from other days of the week.

Because its name is different and because Saturday is a transitional day between the weekday newspaper, with its news emphasis, and Sunday, with its heavy feature content, **Saturday**'s design is different — and transitional.

The page one flag shouts **Saturday** at the reader in type larger than the Tribune's name. Otherwise the page is a typical Tribune news page.

Other section flags emphasize content, in a style that anticipates Sunday's design. Graphic devices are used in flags for the Sports and Shelter sections and on the News Plus page, a full page of background on a current news situation.

The **Neighbors** section is distinctly different from any other **Saturday**, weekday or Sunday section, and its design dramatizes this difference. An oval nameplate, still in recognizable Tribune design style, is used.

The cover format is usually the same, for the sake of reader recognition and familiarity. Layout style is deliberately low key. The format is basically five column. Bedford body type is used.

Inside the section are two special pages with their own flags — a picture page and the Reader's page, whose content is written by readers.

Minneapolis Tribune **Saturday**

August 23/1980
5 Sections
25¢ Single copy
Volume II
Number 53
1A. Final

Ranier man fights government for his land

By Eric Pianin
Staff Correspondent

Washington, D.C.
To the Department of the Interior, Clarence Oveson, 71, a pleasant, industrious family man from Ranier, Minn., is little more than a squatter or trespasser.

For 13 years the department has been trying to pry loose Oveson's 40-acre home on Rainy Lake, in northern Minnesota, to add to Voyageurs National Park. But the government refuses to pay Oveson for the land, valued at $50,000, because of a defect in the title dating back to 1913, when the land was first homesteaded.

"There is no apparent basis for a claim of equitable title on the part of the Ovesons," a top department official said recently. "As far as we can ascertain, they and their predecessors have always been trespassers on land of the United States."

Oveson was shocked by the government's pronouncement. After all, he said, he and his wife had bought the property "in good faith" 37 years ago. They raised three children there, operated a mink farm and commercial fishery, and regularly paid county property taxes.

"How would you feel if you lived on a property for nearly 40 years and then they come and tell you you're trespassing?" Oveson said Friday. "That's kind of hard to take."

With the help of Rep. James Oberstar, Eighth District DFLer, Oveson is attempting to fight back. Oberstar has introduced legislation to require the government to pay Oveson $50,000 for his land or to grant him clear title. Oveson and Oberstar testified on behalf of the bill yesterday before a subcommitee of the House Judiciary Committee.

Although the subcommittee deferred action until it heard from government witnesses, many of the members said they sympathized with Oveson.

"It sounds like you've had a gigantic run-around for years" said Rep. William Hughes, D-N.J."

The problem began in 1913, when the land was homesteaded by Irvin W. Hunstable. Hunstable transferred his interest in the land to Harry Smith in 1914, before Hunstable had technically secured ownership from the federal government.

In 1916, Hunstable withdrew his application to buy the property, and the U.S. government refunded his homestead fee. At that point, the land technically belonged to the federal government.

Nonetheless, it was sold and resold by a series of "owners" and was car-

Oveson continued on page 4A

U of M Hospitals plan major revamping

By Lewis Cope
Staff Writer

University of Minnesota Hospitals officials announced a $232-million plan Friday to replace and remodel their facilities. It's the most expensive hospital construction proposal in Minnesota history.

While the broad outlines of the plan have been known for 18 months, the hospital's application to the Metropolitan Health Board provides details and starts the critical Certificate of Need process.

The proposal will be reviewed by the Metropolitan Health Board, whose members are expected to look closely at its size and might insist on cutbacks before giving their endorsement.

The state's Certificate of Need Act is aimed at controlling hospital costs by making sure no unneeded hospital facilities are built. With the average hospital occupancy rate in the Twin Cities area running below 75 percent in recent years, there is a generally acknowledged surplus of beds that health planners see as costly inefficiency.

However, University Hospitals officials said that their institution plays two unique roles. It's the base for teaching future doctors and other health professionals. It also serves as a regional referral center for highly specialized care. The average occupancy rate at University Hospitals has been running at 76 percent in the past year.

"This (proposal) is replacement and renovation, not expansion," said Robert Dickler, senior associate director of University Hospitals and project chief. Here's what the plan — which includes flexibility in the number of beds — calls for:

■ The hospital, which now has 715 beds in operation, would be designed to operate at a maximum of 713 beds and minimium of 653 beds. That is, the hospital would reduce the number of beds in operation periodically if occupancy rates didn't meet Health Board guidelines, cutting the staff (and in that way operating costs) in the process.

Health Board members will closely examine this approach, looking at it from both over-all size and operational viewpoints. Some existing hospitals close sections when their patient census is low, but University Hospitals officials said their plan is designed to make this more efficient to do.

■ The proposal calls for building a new 10-story core hospital on land where a relatively small Powell Hall office building stands (on the far south side of the existing hospital-medical school complex).

The existing main hospital building would be remodeled. Part of the renovated space would be used for medical school offices, classrooms and other nonhospital purposes. Newer existing parts of the hospital complex, such as the cancer and heart hospital units and the clinic building, also would be retained, in some cases with renovation.

■ The timetable calls for completing the Certificate of Need process by November, seeking approval from the Legislature early next year, starting construction next summer, completing the new core building by mid-1985, and finishing the renovation work by 1987.

Hospital continued on page 4A

Inflation cooled in July despite increase in food prices

By Clyde H. Farnsworth
New York Times Service

Washington, D.C.
Consumer prices did not rise in July, the first time there has been no monthly increase in the over-all cost of living in 13 years, the Labor Department said Friday.

The big factor behind the unchanged consumer price index — after increases of nine-tenths of 1 percent or more in each of the preceding 18 months — was the decline in the cost of buying a house. The drop, the first in seven years, reflected lower mortgage rates in late spring.

Other elements of the index, particularly the food component, continued to rise, suggesting that the inflation relief may be only temporary, government and private economists said.

An increase of nine-tenths of 1 percent in consumer food prices in July and a 3.8 percent increase in the recently reported wholesale price of consumer foods, still waiting to be passed on, could mean the end of moderating food prices, said Howard Hjort, the Agriculture Department's chief economist.

A contributing factor is the recent drought that reduced livestock and grain supplies.

"The decline in mortgage rates in May and June finally showed up in the index," said Michael Evans of Evans Econometrics, a forecasting firm in Washington. "But most people only buy a house every seven or eight years. They go to the grocery store every week, and those prices are up."

The Carter administration took credit for the improvement. Alfred Kahn, the president's anti-inflation counselor, told the Joint Economic Committee of Congress that although inflation is still a "clear and present danger, we are out of the double digit range." He said it was "hard to imagine anything more gratifying than zero," and "I hope you will not begrudge me a certain measure of joy."

But Ronald Reagan's economic adviser, Martin Anderson, likened the situation to being in the "calm eye of the hurricane, thinking the worst is over." He said double digit inflation had not ended and warned that danger signals were flashing on supermarket shelves.

Because of technical factors in compiling the index, mortgage costs will

Economy continued on page 5A

Associated Press

Some youngsters in Austin, Minn., found that a dirt hill made a good takeoff ramp for an impromptu long-jump competition. The mound of earth was next to the basement excavation for a new house.

Win or lose, Fridley woman is devoted to John Anderson

By Lori Sturdevant
Staff Writer

When John Anderson took her hand and focused on her with his sharp blue eyes Friday morning, Janet Jacobson couldn't help telling him how she feels about him.

"I'm committed to the end," she said. "I don't care if we win or not."

"Oh, we'll win, we'll win," the independent presidential candidate responded.

(Teachers' union backs Carter; Reagan woos Christian group. Page 6C)

Illinois Congressman John Anderson is running for president to win.

Fridley homemaker Janet Jacobson is working for his campaign because she admires and respects him.

But to win? "I guess I'm ambivalent about that," she said at a breakfast meeting for Anderson volunteers. "Some days I think he has a chance, other days I don't. But I believe in him. Even if I was absolutely sure he couldn't win, I'd still work hard for his campaign."

Janet Jacobson

It's volunteers like Jacobson — and she is typical, state Anderson coordinator George Soule said — that give the Anderson "Unity Campaign" the aura of a crusade. That feeling has prompted comparisons — unwelcome to those involved — with the McCarthy Kids of 1968 and the Goldwater conservatives of 1964.

"You know, the types who'd rather be right than win," an Independent-Republican insider commented as he scanned the crowd at an Anderson rally Thursday night in Minneapolis.

Minnesota's Anderson volunteers have "made more progress in an organizational sense" than their counterparts in any other state, Anderson said Thursday. They've given him "an excellent chance to win in Minnesota," he said.

But they haven't given him a campaign that's long on political experience.

Jacobson, 36, has very little political experience or inclination. She usual-

Anderson continued on page 6A

Financial aid scheme nets criminal charges

By Margaret Zack
Staff Writer

The former financial aids officer for Minneapolis Community College and four former students have been charged in five separate complaints with an alleged scheme that diverted at least $100,000 of the college's money for personal use.

Al G. Frost Jr. was named in all five complaints. In May he was charged with theft by swindle and misconduct of a public employee. The new charges are five counts of theft by swindle and one of aggravated forgery. He has been suspended without pay by the college.

Nathaniel Allen, who the complaint said was an assistant to Frost, was charged with two counts of theft by swindle. Nathaniel Shannon, who also allegedly worked in the financial aids office, is also charged with theft by swindle.

Frost continued on page 6A

Polish officials, strikers unit report progress in first meeting

Tribune News Services

Gdansk, Poland
Government officials and delegates from the joint strike committee at Gdansk's Lenin shipyard met for one hour Friday night and reported progress in the 9-day-old general strike.

It was the first direct contact between the two opposing sides.

(Additional articles on 1C.)

Florian Wisniewski, one of the three delegates sent by the strike committee, said the head of the government's negotiating team, First Deputy Premier Mieczyslaw Jagielski, had agreed to visit the strikers today at the shipyard.

Elated by the outcome of their talks, the delegates honked the horn on their auto repeatedly as they drove back to the shipyard and shouted, "Victory. Victory. Jagielski's meeting us tomorrow."

In other developments yesterday:

■ Chancellor Helmut Schmidt of West Germany called off a summit meeting with East Germany's Communist leader, Erich Honecker, because of the Polish crisis. A government spokesman said the summit, scheduled next Thursday and Friday, had been canceled because "developments in Europe" made prospects for its success "unfavorable."

He made no mention of Poland, but in a separate statement Schmidt's Social Democratic Party linked the decision to "concerns which are relat-

Poland continued on page 7A

Helmut Schmidt

Almanac

Saturday, August 23, 1980
236th day; 130 to go this year
Sunrise: 6:24. Sunset: 8:07.

Today's weather
Thunderstorms

Cloudy skies and thunderstorms are forecast for the Twin Cities area today. A high temperature in the mid to high 80s is expected.

Details on Page 7D

Arts	7D	Editorial	8A
Business	4-6C	Sports	1-5D
Comics	6D	Theaters	6-8C
Corrections	2A	TV, Radio	9C

Tribune telephones

Auditor investigating utilities commissioner

By Robert J. Hagen
Staff Writer

Katherine Sasseville, a member of the Minnesota Public Utilities Commission (PUC), is being investigated by the Office of the Legislative Auditor over alleged irregularities or improprieties in travel expenses, the Minneapolis Tribune has learned.

"I can only say that we are (investigating), and I cannot say any more until our investigation is complete," Eldon Stoehr, the legislative auditor, said Friday.

Sasseville said early yesterday that she had not been notified of the investigation.

"No one has talked to me about this or asked me to provide any information, and I find it very irritating that I had to learn about it from a reporter," she said.

She later called Stoehr, who confirmed that an investigation had begun. She also requested and obtained a meeting with his representatives.

"I gave them my files covering five years and I am certain that when they examine my billing records that they'll see that there's no truth to the allegations that have been made against me," she said. "They declined to identify the person who accused me."

Sasseville said she was told Stoehr's office is investigating whether she took trips to conferences at the state's expense and then accepted honorariums from associations or in-

Investigation continued on page 6A

104

neighbors
Minneapolis Tribune

R.C. Wray has lived at 4343 Scott Terrace in Morningside for 54 years.

Saturday
April 14 / 1979
1B

Larry Batson

When my sister was about 4, she had a pet chicken named Betty. We lived, my parents, sister and I, in a converted chicken house behind a little gas station and repair shop my father ran. I don't remember where Betty lived.

But my sister and the chicken spent a lot of time together on the grounds of our estate, which included a garden patch, a pile of worn-out parts from the shop, some magnificent weeds along the gravel highway and behind the privy and a rock fence that sheltered colonies of scorpions.

Betty would take the lead, scratching and pecking. My sister came just behind. In one of the sunbonnets Mom made for her, bending down to examine whatever Betty had uncovered and proposed to eat. When Betty felt a certain urge, she would cluck nervously and my sister would pick her up and run to the house.

She would place Betty on the quilt covering the cot where she slept, shush everybody in the house and plop herself down on the floor beside the cot. Then, her nose almost touching Betty's beak, the two would cluck and croon together until Betty had laid an egg. A noisy celebration would follow.

There was a little talk around the village about whether such close contact with life's mysteries was seemly. But my sister grew up as prim and proper as any of the girls who didn't know for certain how eggs got here.

However, she maintained a strong interest in animals. When Pop set up as a dairy farmer, she was 11 or 12, and was most interested in seeing a calf born. As months passed and the opportunity never came, she was about to bust.

The practice in the hills was to arrange things so that cows calved in January or February. That way the cow would give gushets of milk for a couple of months, transforming the fat it had accumulated into food for its calf — which we intercepted. Then green grass would appear about the time the cow's ribs began to stick out and the milk would flood anew.

Clever, unsentimental exploiters, we dairymen.

We didn't run to warm stalls or calving sheds, but we had 60 acres of woods and the climate was mild. Our cows usually made hiding places in the woods, had their calves at night and waited for us to find them in the morning. It was an ancient ritual. The cow never made a sound as we passed nearby. You had to find her fair and square. Pop or I would put the calf on our shoulders and carry it to the barn, often half a mile or farther, with the mother bawling and butting along behind.

So my sister saw newborn calves aplenty, but never was witness to the process as she had been with Betty.

Till one miserably wet, raw Saturday when we left her alone on the place. Pop and I were hauling hay for a neighbor, trading work. Mom went along to visit and help cook for the bunch. We'd all be home to milk, we told my sister, who had a cold or some such reason for staying behind.

Old Spook chose that day to have her calf. The cattle were in a cane field, eating from shocks of the sweet, fermenting delicacy. They had slavered for the cane all summer and fall, but it was tightly fenced, for in its green state it was poisonous. A hard frost made it safe to eat, triggering some chemical reaction.

A critter would pull a thick stalk loose from a pile, start chewing on the butt end and close its eyes blissfully as the sugary juice ran out the corners of its mouth. Hardly anything would coax it away. But my sister saw Spook leave the cane field and cross to the woods, moving in a straight line at the swift shuffle cows use when they have urgent business. My sister put on a jacket and followed.

Spook had picked a spot beside a fallen tree. It was sheltered and carpeted thickly with oak and hickory leaves. Now these were dense woods, thick and brushy, unlogged and unburned for many years. Hunters sometimes got lost in there. The cow had a half-mile head start, yet my sister found Spook and plopped herself down on the tree trunk.

Spook was a large, nervous and dangerous horned animal and this was not a time when she wanted company. Yet somehow my sister established rapport.

She sat there, that skinny little girl, cold rain soaking her, for hours. Past noon dinnertime, into the afternoon, past milking time.

It was dark when she came home. Mom had checked with the neighbors and was in the house, waiting for word. Pop and I were milking, for nothing interferes with that on a dairy farm. My sister walked into the milking parlor.

She was muddy, scratched, soaked, shivering and gaunt with exhaustion.

"Well now," Pop said softly, "your mother was worried. You'd best go tell her you're back."

My sister nodded wearily and then smiled.

"Spook had a heifer," she said.

Morningside, a town that was, lives in the hearts of those who live there

Staff Photos / Darlene Pfister

E. Dudley Parsons, 72, Morningside's unofficial historian: "Everybody knew that the only way Morningside could survive was to get involved. You couldn't sit back and let the other fellow do it because, quite often, the other fellow was doing something else. It's true there was an economic barrier between Morningside and the rest of Edina; our kids were not accepted in the play groups of the country club kids. We looked to each other for a sense of community, a sense of community that is perpetuated today. Morningside didn't lose its character when it was annexed into Edina."

Walking up Scott Terrace.

Kids played on the sidewalk on Drexel Av.

By Tom Sorensen
Staff Writer

Poor Morningside.

The village seceded from Edina almost 60 years ago because of sidewalks that Edina wouldn't provide. Edina, mostly farms and pastures at the time, had better things to do with its money than build sidewalks so the swells who lived near W. 44th St. and France Av. S. could keep mud off their shoes.

So Morningside set up its own government and built its own sidewalks. The next 45 years were good ones, old-timers say. But the good times ended when the 240-acre village got caught up in the winds of high finance and big government. In 1966, the village's 2,011 residents voted whether to retain their independence or rejoin Edina. When the dust settled, Morningside had voted two to one to hook up with Edina, by then the Edina we'd come to know and love.

Last summer the Edina street department told Morningside residents it was going to rip up their old sidewalks, build new ones and pass the costs along to the homeowners. That angered Charles Griffin, 4200 Branson Rd., who said his sidewalk didn't need to be replaced. Patched like the sidewalks in the wealthy Edina Country Club area had been, yes, but not replaced.

"We feel like we're Edina's poor kin," said Griffin, who has lived in Morningside seven years. "I think a lot of people wish we could secede again."

Sidewalks and secession. The Morningside Story. Getting our wouldn't be as easy as it was in 1920 when Morningside residents petitioned the courts for the right to establish an independent community. Now, according to the League of Municipalities, Morningside would have to be annexed to another city — either St. Louis Park or Minne-

Morningside continued on page 2B

If you're looking for family fun...

See See this this play play

Recalling one of history's more memorable rainstorms, the Mixed Blood Theatre Company will present "Noah" at the Walker Art Center at 1 p.m. today and Sunday. The actors portray, among others, Noah, God and the animals. No admission charge. The play is in the art center's information room. The art center, attached to the Guthrie Theater, is on Vineland Place across from Loring Park.

Easter in Sweden

Happy Easter! They're having an "Easter in Sweden" program at 3 p.m. Sunday at the American Swedish Institute, 2600 Park Av. Admission to the institute is $1 for adults, 50 cents for students, 25 cents for children under 6.

Give the cook a night off

If you have to cook a big dinner tomorrow, you might want to take tonight off by going to the Steak Fry at VFW Post No. 1149, 3018 17th Av. S. Top sirloin steak with all the trimmings is $5. Serving is from 6 to 9 p.m. The dinner is put on by the auxiliary. Profits will help support Camp Courage.

Easter in the park

The folks who run Como Zoo (also known as The Old Zoo, The Little Zoo, The St. Paul Zoo or The Other Zoo) want you to know that the zoo will be open from 8 a.m. to 5 p.m. on Easter Sunday. (Today, too.) And, to answer all your questions ("How many quilts in a porcupine?"), they have a Zoo Answer Booth set up today and tomorrow in the main building.

You can't get Karen's goat

This is mostly for kids, grades one through eight, interested in science. The Science Museum of Minnesota has what it calls the Saturday Science Clubhouse. The "clubhouse" meets once a week for discussions and demonstrations on scientific subjects, such as "Computers" (April 21) and "Presenting Sound" (April 28). Today's clubhouse is about "Karen's Critters" and will feature an African pygmy goat and a red fox. Two places to go: At 10 a.m. today, the clubhouse meets at the Science Museum, 30 E. 10th St., St. Paul. At 1 p.m. it'll meet at the Minneapolis Public Library, 300 Nicollet Mall. Cost is $1 for non-members, 75 cents for members. For more information on the Saturday Science Clubhouse, call 221-9488 or 372-8543.

Tantivy! Tantivy! Tantivy!

The Hennepin County Park Reserve District is sponsoring three egg hunts today and Sunday. No. 1 is at noon today at Eastman Nature Center in Elm Creek Park, west and north of Osseo. Stop by to find clues and look for a prize. No charge. No. 2 is an old-fashioned family Easter egg hunt at 2 p.m. Sunday at Lowry Nature Center in Carver Park, west of Victoria. This one costs $1 per family and you must make a reservation. Call 472-4911. No. 3 will be from noon to 4 p.m. Sunday at Richardson Nature Center, 8737 E. Bush Lake Rd., Bloomington. Stop by any time during those hours to search for prizes that will not cause cavities. No charge, but reservations are required. Call 941-7993.

More family fun/6B

neighbors
Minneapolis Tribune

3B

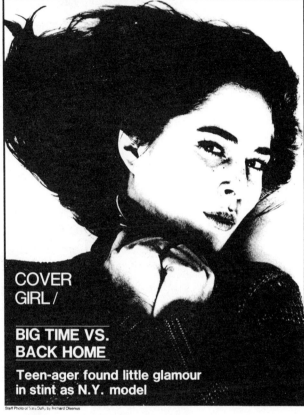

COVER GIRL /

BIG TIME VS. BACK HOME

Teen-ager found little glamour in stint as N.Y. model

Staff Photo of Sara Duffy by Richard Olsenius

COVER GIRL

"A freshness, a certain spirit, a certain, what would you say, aliveness."

By Tom Serensen
Staff Writer

Sara Duffy, whose face and neck were featured on the October cover of Seventeen Magazine, was sitting at a booth in a downtown restaurant, a cup of coffee on the table in front of her and a Navy peacoat at her side.

Although the bus on which she had arrived from Benilde-St. Margaret's High School was late, the important thing was that she had arrived at all. Duffy had made it clear during an earlier telephone conversation that she considered herself a regular teen-ager, and if she were about to be portrayed as an on-the-verge starlet or a high-school cover-achiever, then she didn't want to be portrayed at all.

O.K., you're a regular teen-ager. But that's where the problem comes in. Regular teen-agers are not often written about in newspapers. Regular teen-agers go to school during the day and sell hamburgers two evenings a week plus Saturday afternoons. Those who are written about have to do something out of the ordinary, like breaking an all-time single-game conference scoring record on a basketball court or leading the rope on a high-speed chase and ending up being tried as adults.

"Sara lives a very normal life," said Mary Duffy, who is Sara's mother. "She runs around with a bunch of high-school kids and does the same things they do. When she's a model, she's a model, and when she's at home, she's at home."

And when she's at a downtown restaurant, she's at a downtown restaurant. Her looks are not the bombshell kind, which may explain why on this cold, drab, Tuesday afternoon, the heads of passersby have not turned in her direction. Then again, it's tough to be a bombshell this early in the week. But bombshell or no, looks are her ticket. While other teen-agers might use a soft jump shot to attract college recruiters or engage in a high-speed chase to get attention from the law, it's Duffy's face that's helping her make a name.

Only 16 and a high-school junior, she spent last summer in New York City at the behest of Eileen Ford, who is quite famous in fashion circles. Still, an invite alone is no guarantee. That's a tough market out there, the major leagues. But by the end of the summer, Duffy landed the cover shot along with several other Seventeen assignments, and turned down additional offers so she could return to Minneapolis — she lives in the Bryn Mawr Neighborhood — and school.

Her success was not without precedent. She signed with the Eleanor Moore Talent and Modeling Agency when she was nine and landed her first commercial the same year, helping a hardware store peddle a boy's bike that a girl could ride, too. She was the girl. The clerk tried to convince her that she should buy a girl's bike, but Duffy was adamant. Finally, the clerk gave in and sold her the boy's bike. In commercials there are no surprises. The bike was on sale.

Teen-ager continued on page 2B

Jim Landberg

Writes for the vacationing Larry Batson

There was this guy in college, see, a rather pleasant type who, though generally popular, had a habit of freeloading. Not in a major way, mind you. But in a manner some cohorts found mildly irritating.

Seems The Flicher liked to sometimes sneak a drink of pop out of several friends' pop cans and bottles. Often. Well, often enough.

The Flicher was, from time to time, goaded about this by dorm cronies, but he truly thought his habit not an unreasonable one. Why shouldn't buddies share a bottle of soda, he reasoned. He didn't realize that, while pals all, they were tiring of his habit.

Besides, The Flicher serviced upwards of

Flicher continued on page 4B

If you're looking for family fun...

A taste of mushing

You can learn all about dog sledding at 1 p.m. Sunday at the Lowry Nature Center. An experienced musher will tell about selection of sleds, equipment and dogs, and a dog-sledding demonstration will follow. Reservations are needed at 472-4911. The center is in Carver Park, north of State Hwy. 5 on Carver County Rd. 11 (about five miles west of Chanhassen).

'Shoemaker and the Elves'

The Grimm fairy tale, "The Shoemaker and the Elves," will be enacted in a puppet show at 2 p.m. today at the Augsburg Park Community Library, 7100 Nicollet Av. S., Richfield. The story is about an overworked shoemaker and some helpful elves. The show, staged by Pat Mertes, will include an audience sing-along.

The fine art of scrimshaw

Scrimshaw — engraving on bone and ivory — will be demonstrated at 2 p.m. Sunday at the Eastman Nature Center in Elm Creek Park, located near Osseo at State Hwy. 152 and Territorial Rd. A naturalist also will tell about the history of scrimshaw.

At the movies

Some old favorites and a new version of a classic story are on film programs this weekend. "Meet Me in St. Louis," the Vincente Minnelli musical about childhood and American dreams at the jurn of the

century, will be shown at 2 and 8 p.m. today at the Walker Art Center. The 1944 film stars Judy Garland, Margaret O'Brien, Mary Astor and Leon Ames. Adult admission is $2.50 ($1.50 for senior citizens); admission for children under 12 is $1 for the matinee, $1.50 for the evening show. At the Minneapolis Institute of Arts, the 1941 film "Topper Returns" will be shown at 8 p.m. today. Joan Blondell plays a ghost who helps an amateur detective investigate her death in an eerie mansion. Admission is $2. The University Film Society is presenting a new Czech version of "Beauty and the Beast" at 7:30 p.m. Sunday at the Bell Museum Auditorium, 17th and University Avs. SE. The film will provide "great, spooky fun," the society staff says. Admission is $3 for adults, $1.50 for children. The movie is paired up in a double feature with a Slovakian romantic film, "Cruel Love."

Holiday bird count

An annual holiday bird count will be held today at the Richardson Nature Center. A naturalist will lead walks at 8 a.m., noon and 3 p.m. to identify and count various species of birds. The results will be included in the National Audubon Society's annual Christmas bird count. After each walk, a program will be given on attracting and feeding birds during the winter. Reservations are needed at 941-7993. The center is in Hyland Lake Park, 8737 E. Bush Lake Rd., Bloomington.

More family fun/6B

---

the neighbors
by Jerry Van Amerongen

"Come to think of it... he bit you last year, too!"

106

A story in pictures

Staff Photos Richard Olsenius
Minneapolis Tribune

Saturday / December 6 / 1980 / 3B

The movie's over at St. Louis Park Theater but the Art Deco lobby lives on, and it was crammed wall to wall recently with celebrities who came to be seen at the gala opening night of two party shops.

Not really celebrities so much as ordinary Twin Cities folks who looked like celebrities. Close to 250 stars, some of whom have already appeared in the obituary columns, came to the party at 4835 Minnetonka Blvd. on a recent Sunday: Orphan Annie, John Belushi, Scarlett O'Hara, Mae West, Roy Rogers and other glamorous types, most of them acting their parts as they collected hugs from the hugging clown and nibbled at refreshments displayed on mirrored tables.

The four hostesses of the gala had better know how to give a party to beat all because that's their business. They are the owners of Give My Regards To — Susan Gray of Golden Valley and Susan Glassberg of St. Louis Park — and the owners of Party Decor — Reva Lear and Shirley Rivkin of St. Louis Park. Both shops moved last month from a much smaller space next door into the 1930s-era theater. The theater closed six months ago; the auditorium and marquee had to be torn down to make space for a new high rise for senior citizens.

Gray says the owners have maintained the theater's image, with its stucco and marble exterior and the mirrored lobby and octagon-shaped lighting inside. Give My Regards To sells gifts, candy, invitations and "paperware" and does custom invitations and stationery. Party Decor rents and sells party centerpieces and sets up and takes down parties. "We're trying to bring a little of New York and Hollywood to Minneapolis," Gray said.

Could that be Marilyn Monroe and her agent? Or was it really Britt and Owen Husney dressed up that way for the opening night party.

That old theater lobby was overflowing with celebrities

Dolly Parton (Tanya Bickerstaff) with Irving Husney (as himself).

You thought it was Miss Piggy, but it's really Susan Gray of the Give My Regards To shop; Alfalfa was played by her nephew Benjy, 9.

Of course the Marx Brothers were represented; Sophie and Jerry Teener were Harpo and Groucho.

Superman (Bud Gruenberg) and Phyllis Diller (Riva Gruenberg) — and that's Harpo again.

neighbors
Minneapolis Tribune

Readers write for readers

Saturday/January 17/1981/5B.

Fond memories of running the old Caryville ferry

James Alf

I remember the evening at the old farmhouse table when my dad, Bill Alf, sat hardly eating, top lip white with tension, saying little. It was the first days of 1949 and he had been to Menomonie, Wis., and "got the job."

The job was a one-season contract to operate the Caryville ferry, across the Chippewa River ten miles west of Eau Claire. It was the first of 16 annual appearances he was to make before the ferry committee, where each time he successfully stood against all other applicants for the contract.

With the job came a four-room house (pitcher, pump and path, no electricity) a gravel road 15 feet from the front door and a gravelly garden spot. Thirty years later my mother still remembers emptying our eight-room farmhouse into the four-room house that was to hold her, Dad, four boys and Fido.

We boys ranged in age from 17 to 4 and we all had the privilege of helping Dad run the ferry. Fred was already old enough to take cars across. As he got old enough to work away I began helping, then Rodney did, and finally Art. Art was 21 in 1966, when a bridge took the place of the ferry, so it all worked out perfectly for Dad.

There were some mishaps at the ferry, but never a loss of life. Dad came home one day to find the ferry mid-river with only the railings above water. On one railing sat Freddy and two county truck drivers "like crows in a row." The county truck was wheels-up in the river. They couldn't row to shore because the lifeboat was under the truck. It turned out that someone had gotten out of the truck and left the brake off.

The ferry was officially closed from midnight to 6 a.m., but Dad was allowed to charge a small fee if he wanted to get out of bed for someone. One such time he crossed to get a persistent horn-blower on the other side, and as he walked past the car to raise the loading apron he chanced to smell the driver's boozy breath. After getting the ferry under way he said, "Mister, this is going to cost you a buck."

Back came the reply. "You can take the buck and . . . ." The rest was lost to grinding gears and rattling planks — Dad told for years of the magnificent plume of water in the air, then the slowly dimming lights. The next morning Sheriff Walters found the sobered fellow in a neighbor's haystack, and a county truck pulled the car, by now well soaked, out of the river.

My turn came on an inky, starless night when Rick Donnelly was taking a carload of us home from roller skating. I was taking him across, but halfway over we discovered the afterdeck under water. Rick got everyone into the rowboat, I got wet to the waist, and Rick's '41 Chevy spent the night with fish swimming in and out the windows.

Although the ferry's purpose was one of utility, it was still quite a tourist attraction — and never more so than on any nice Sunday afternoon. Some Sundays more than 300 cars crossed, and there was always much picture taking and a general air of excitement and enjoyment.

There was no charge for crossing, so some folks crossed twice. Others parked their cars by the river and rode back and forth without them.

Sometimes a feature story about the ferry would appear in one of the Twin Cities papers and bring an extra deluge of business. One Sunday that such an article came out, the ferry was out of commission. There were lots of disappointed folks that day who had driven a long way for a ride across the river.

When Polaroid cameras came out, I bought one with Dad's help and sold souvenir snapshots of folks on the ferry for 50 cents. If patrons waiting on the shore wondered why it took so long to take a couple of cars across, it was because I had to get in two sales pitches and two 60-second developments during the three-minute crossing.

The other unrelated enterprise we carried on was fishing. Almost any time people approached the ferry, they might find one of us fishing over the railing.

Fishing between crossings was a light-hearted catch-as-catch-can affair. My dad was a relaxed kind of fisherman who liked to "give the fish time to swallow it." Late one afternoon he was fishing just that way, letting a fish haul his line slowly around the bottom. When it got out a ways, he set the hook.

The fish shot out, stood on its tail "tall as a man against the setting sun," Dad said, flopped down and parted company. The fish was gone but Dad measured his success in terms of working the rest of the day on wobbly knees.

Bill and Alice Alf live in an apartment in Eau Claire now, safe from midnight crossings and great fish. Cars cross the river on a bridge, but the old ferry house still sits nearby, much the same as it was when the ferry ran.

Ah, those were the days.

James Alf lives near Onamia, Minn. He is a lumber sawyer.

Everyone's a photographer

Nancy Campbell, of Wayzata, sent us this interesting photograph of the child with a daisy for a face. Neighbors invites you to submit your favorite print or slide, and some information about it, for possible use on this page. Because we print in black-and-white, please submit color pictures only if color is not essential to the photo. Prints must be 4 x 5 or larger, and color prints should be accompanied by the negatives. Send your photos to Hal Quarfoth, Neighbors editor, Minneapolis Tribune, 425 Portland Av., Minneapolis, Minn., 55488. Enclose a self-addressed stamped envelope if you want your photographs returned.

A letter to Gramma, across the miles and years

Velma Alt

(Almost 68 years ago, when she was eight years old, little Velma Woods sent this letter to her grandmother, who lived some distance away and had little information from Velma's family since Velma's mother died. It was found in the grandmother's belongings after her death, and returned to Velma. Now a grandmother herself, she says she knows how much it must have meant.)

Rowley, Iowa
May 2, 1913

Dear Gramma,

I got your letter yestorday and I was glade to here from you once again. I hope you have not the room a tizom. now have you got it. I hope you havent. it is twelve a clock and Harold and papa have not come from the field yet to have dinner. Luella popped a dish pan fool of pop corn yesterday and it is not etoten yet. They was a rag man come here yesterday and wanted some rubish but Luella said they was not any. he gave Luella a nickle for some pop corn to. We have some rubish and she says now it is a quarter worth of rubish. but she said we did not have any etail. Erma cant walk yet. I guess that is all. Form Velma Woods

Velma Alt now lives in Kalona, Iowa. She spends summers in Minnesota, at Leech Lake. She says she is glad now that Grandma kept her letter, and especially glad that she wrote it.

Slide-show technique: Boring from within

Robert W. Branham

From time to time the Tribune has given helpful hints on how to take good slides. I now think it's high time that some guidelines were thrown out on how to *show* slides.

As any self-respecting photographer knows, the basic prerequisite for showing slides is a captive audience. And we photographers must be continually on the lookout for new sources of bodies to make an audience. Look for business acquaintances who don't know you too well; new neighbors are always good, as are old friends whom you haven't seen for many years.

The first step is to ask them over. You may have to put out a few drinks and some snacks. After a while, during a lag in the conversation, inquire quite innocently, "Would you like to see a few slides?"

Now, a query such as this directed to close friends or relatives would invariably be greeted by a chorus of prolonged groans. Not your new-found friend, however. Unless he is a complete clod, he will murmur something like: "Oh, great," or "Gee, I'd like to." After all, what else can he say — he's drinking your booze. Just the other night I acquired several new victims using this very ruse.

As they descend the stairs to the recreation room, I softly lock the hallway door.

First I show them my so-called "good" slides — those masterpieces so badly misjudged by the photo club over the last ten years. Then it's on to Hawaii: carousel after carousel.

By now they are bleary-eyed, they want water, they want to go to the bathroom.

But there is no stopping me now; I show no mercy. Drunk with power, I take them to Germany, Austria, then Switzerland, and the *piece de resistance*, Italy.

By this time they have been uniquely privileged to see some 600 slides. Not only that, they have listened to an intelligent, detailed commentary on each and every one. As a bonus, I pass along innumerable statistics as well as photographic advice.

But alas, finally, "Conscience makes cowards of us all." Reluctantly, I must release my hostages. Bedraggled and exhausted they shuffle up the stairs. Gently, I assist one whose eyesight has temporarily given out.

But me? I am triumphant, secure in the knowledge that I don't just take slides — I show them!

Robert W. Branham lives in south Minneapolis. Consider yourself warned.

Robert W. Branham

A midwinter morning's dream of summer harvests

Gladys I. Pearson

A seed catalog arrived in the mail today. I page through its contents, envying the perfect illustrations. Through the kitchen window I can see the garden only by the raspberry canes poking through the snow.

I dream on a cold winter day and remember the harvests of that garden.

First of all there is the harvest of produce. There are the first snappy radishes and crisp lettuce picked in early summer. Later there are tender peas and string beans just right for eating. Then there are the myriads of vegetables of late summer and autumn — corn, tomatoes, broccoli, carrots, squash and onions, to mention a few. Not only are these enjoyed during the summer, but the surplus is canned, frozen or stored to be used throughout the year.

But every seasoned gardener knows he also reaps a harvest of frustration. There is the late frost in spring or the early one in autumn that can destroy much. There are the times when it rains too much and the plants stand in puddles, and the hot, dry days when they droop from thirst.

Occasionally one finds tomato plants neatly severed by hungry cutworms. Sometimes root maggots invade the onion patch or dine on the tiny root hairs of broccoli or cabbage, causing the plants to die. Or suddenly hundreds of potato beetles begin devouring the flourishing potato vines. Strawberries can bloom profusely but produce only tiny berries with a hard core caused by an invisible mite. Raspberries can give signs of a healthy crop only to develop a blight that will produce shrunken berries.

And then there are the animals! It doesn't take long for that pretty little rabbit to consume a row of lettuce or peas. Woodchucks love garden greens. What a disappointment it is to come to gather the first ears of fresh corn only to find that the wily raccoon has been there first. One day three deer sailed gracefully over the fence right into the middle of the garden.

And the weeds! The everlasting, persistent weeds!

But there is a third harvest — the harvest of joy. What greater joy than to stand on some sun-filled, dew-fresh morning admiring a garden that has flourished in spite of obstacles? There is the joy of being linked in the miracle of creation: sifting the warm, damp humus through one's fingers and pondering its potential, planting the seed, with the reminder from scripture that that seed must die but in so doing will bear fruit.

Also, in essence, one harvests the sun in all its varying degrees of intensity, the life-giving rain, the winds whether gently cooling or blustery. And there is the harvest of bird song — pure joy issuing from the throats of purple finches perched high in the treetops.

It is late afternoon and the catalog still lies in my lap. It has accomplished its purpose. In the spring I will plant another garden!

Gladys I. Pearson lives in Bemidji.

A chilly sound-effects concert on the shore

Sharen Neumann Kaatz

Winter has come to the Trade Lakes in southern Burnett County. An early-morning "sound effects" concert by Mother Nature has left no doubt.

While dressing for my morning walk to the public access, I could hear strange noises while I was inside the house. Maybe a couple of tomcats in a territory fight?

When I stepped outside, the sound of honking geese flying high and fast greeted my ears. They must be a last flock, late in getting started south. But no — strange noises again, another larger flock of noisy geese in a hurry and flying high.

Again a strange loud sound echoing over the woods; it sounded like a rifle shot even though deer hunting is over for this year. Next came a rumble like a giant's upset stomach, the sound carrying clearly in the frosty morning darkness.

A good time to walk, 6:30 in the morning: no traffic, no dogs out, plenty of solitude.

Another overwhelming noise, this time like a massive piece of tin being shaken. An owl flew off his perch on top of an electric pole, startled by the weird sound.

Another rifle-shot sound; a cottontail rabbit dashed away, his white tail bobbing in the early light.

They were ice noises — the continuous sounds of freezing and expanding echoing from Big Trade Lake and Little Trade Lake. Each seemed to be trying to outdo the other in response to the 28-degree morning.

The cirrus clouds were high and dark blue against the ever-lightening sky. Tree branches stood out bare and black. No reds or pinks in the winter sky this morning. The colors went with the dramatic mood of the morning.

The crescendo of lake noises reached its peak and then, as the sky lightened, stopped as if on cue.

It's hard to leave the warmth of a cozy wood fire and go out for that early-morning walk, but never had I been so stimulated and rewarded for my trouble.

Why, after living here for 17 years, had I never heard such an intense winter concert before? Is this to be an unusual winter, unusually warm or unusually cold?

That first chill wore off in a hurry, listening to the concert of the lakes. How small and insignificant I felt. I finished my walk in awed silence.

Sharen Neumann Kaatz lives near Frederic, Wis.

news plus
Minneapolis Tribune
Saturday
January 17 / 1981
11A .

'The clock ticks...'

With those words, State Department spokesman John Trattner this week tried to describe the building intensity of negotiations for the release of the 52 American hostages held in Iran. In the final days of the Carter administration, there were indications that agreement was imminent. Articles on this page deal with some of the key diplomats involved in the long negotiations, including Warren Christopher of the United States and three Algerian intermediaries, and with others who have had roles in the drama that began more than 13 months ago.

Associated Press

Carter's praise reflects Christopher's importance

By B. Drummond Ayres Jr.
New York Times Service

Washington, D.C.
Deputy Secretary of State Warren Christopher has seldom enjoyed being in the limelight, so it probably suited him fine Friday afternoon to be absent from the White House when President Carter named him one of 15 recipients of the Medal of Freedom, the nation's highest civilian honor.

But even though Christopher was 4,000 miles away in Algeria, making one final effort to negotiate freedom for the American hostages in Iran, Carter nevertheless got the slim, taciturn Californian on the phone to praise him for service to country.

"Warren Christopher," the president said, reading the official proclamation honoring the 55-year-old No. 2 State Department official, "has the tact of a true diplomat, the tactical skills of a great soldier, the analytical ability of a fine lawyer and the selfless dedication of a citizen statesman. His perseverance and loyalty, judgment and skill have won for his country new respect around the world and new regard for the State Department here at home."

As the top aide to Secretaries State Cyrus Vance and Edmund Muskie, Christopher has handled some of the most sensitive diplomatic problems faced by the Carter administration.

He helped smooth the way for passing the much-disputed Panama Canal treaties, helped win approval of shipments of high-technology arms to Arab nations and went to Taiwan to reassure the Nationalist Chinese government after the United States and China moved to strengthen diplomatic ties. While in Taipei, Christopher's limousine was damaged by angry demonstrators and he suffered several cuts and bruises.

When Soviet troops invaded Afghanistan, Christopher was dispatched to Europe for talks with allied governments about imposing sanctions. For the last several months, he has concentrated almost exclusively on efforts to free the hostages. He has shuttled between Washington and Algiers, the meeting point for intermediaries, often going for long stretches without rest but always emerging from the work sessions with the proper, unrumpled demeanor expected of a diplomat.

Christopher's greatest strength is said to be his ability to negotiate. Unfailingly courteous and soft-spoken, tightly organized and prepared, he is reported by associates to have a knack for winning concessions without making his adversary feel boxed in. "Never get mad except on purpose," is his advice to aides.

While negotiations are under way and, more to the point, once the negotiations are over, Christopher avoids the media as much as possible. In a town where egos are almost always a factor, he sometimes seems to have none. One of Christopher's longtime friends says privately that his lack of flamboyant ego and his great caution are the main reasons he has never held a Cabinet-level post in three decades of being in and out of Washington.

Other Washington figures and observers say Christopher has never been given a Cabinet job because he is not true Cabinet material. "More a mechanic than a philosopher," Rep. Benjamin Rosenthal, D-N.Y., once said when asked whether Christopher should be named secretary of state.

When Vance resigned as secretary of state last spring to protest the abortive raid to free the hostages, there was speculation for a few days that Christopher might be moved up.

Christopher was born Oct. 27, 1925, in Scranton, N.D. His father, a banker, was hit hard by the Depression and illness and eventually the family ended up in the Los Angeles area. After serving in the navy, Christopher earned a law degree in 1949 at Stanford University, and did so well academically that Supreme Court Justice William Douglas asked him to serve as Douglas' clerk for a year.

Christopher later worked as a lawyer in California and dabbled in Democratic politics.

Eventually, his political associations led him to Washington, where he served first as international trade negotiator, then on a study group looking into the causes of urban riots, then as deputy attorney general in the Johnson administration.

In 1973, Christopher was approached about becoming the special Watergate prosecutor. He turned down the job, however, arguing that he had not been promised enough freedom and flexibility.

When Christopher completes his tour at the State Department at noon next Tuesday, he is expected to return to his Los Angeles law firm.

Canadian recalls a great escape

By Peter Costa
United Press International

Six U.S. diplomats were smuggled out of Iran three months after the American Embassy takeover in a daring escape plotted by Canada. Armed with Canadian passports and wearing Canadian lapel pins, they posed as tourists at Teheran Airport.

"They passed straight through customs with their new identities," Canadian Consul-General Kenneth Taylor said recently in describing the maneuvers used to spirit the Americans to freedom.

The Americans bought caviar and other Iranian souvenirs at the airport to convince customs officials they were just average tourists, said Taylor, now head of the Canadian Embassy in New York.

One of the Americans, who had worried that his pronounced Southern accent would giving him away, was asked questions by the Iranian officials that required only yes or no answers. He was not detected.

The Americans were given false passports and identity papers after a secret Canadian Cabinet meeting Jan. 4, 1980, Taylor said. The Americans left Iran Jan. 28, 1980.

Taylor, 46, said the Americans fled to Canada's embassy in Teheran shortly after the U.S. embassy takeover on Nov. 4, 1979. Two were housed in Taylor's villa, while the others hid in a home of "another colleague nearby," Taylor said.

"They didn't leave my house except to visit the other house and they did that about every three weeks. Even though our residence was large and the Americans were able to move in the house freely, we were always aware that the unpredictable could happen.

"One of our concerns was that one or two newspapers in the United States and Canada had this story and we worried whether the story would break and we would be discovered."

During the month of January, the Canadians reduced the number of their own embassy staff to facilitate a quick evacuation if necessary. The day before the Americans escaped, Taylor said, the staff consisted of only six military personnel, three diplomats, Taylor and his wife.

Taylor's wife left Iran the day before the Americans departed and flew to Paris. Taylor left a day after the Americans and flew to Copenhagen.

Taylor said the Canadian Embassy was closed soon after his departure and would reopen only after the hostages were freed.

According to the U.S. State Department, this is what has become of the four other escapees:

Robert Anders is serving with the U.S. Embassy in Oslo, Norway.
Mark Lijek and his wife, Cora, are with the U.S. Consulate General in Hong Kong.
Henry Lee Schatz, former agricultural attache, has returned to the Department of Agriculture in Washington.

Upon reaching freedom, the diplomats agreed to withhold detailed comment until the hostages were released.

Algerian mediators receive high marks

Tribune News Services

Washington, D.C.
State Department officials have been lavish in their praise of the three Algerian intermediaries at the center of the negotiations in the hostage crisis.

The Algerians were chosen by their government after the Iranian parliament announced Nov. 2 that Algeria would be used as the official channel of communications with Washington.

Algeria began representing Iranian interests in Washington earlier in the crisis when U.S.-Iranian relations were broken. Swiss diplomats have represented the United States in Teheran.

The Algerian team, described by State Department officials as "three equals, with no clear leader," consisted of:

Abdelkarim Ghareib, Algerian ambassador to Iran; Rehda Malek, Algerian ambassador to the United States, and Seghir Mostefi, chairman of the Algerian National Bank.

As they shuttled between Teheran and Washington, the Algerians amassed documents in three languages. They also earned a reputation of being close-mouthed, refusing to speak to newsmen as they hustled in and out of the two capitals.

None of the three speaks fluent English or Farsi, so the Algerians conducted their negotiations in French, which was then translated. Farsi was used in case of conflict or ambiguity.

The major negotiating problem — compounded by the language differences — was the complexity of the bargaining, involving international transfers of large amounts of money and terms of Iranian and American law.

Included in their traveling file were about 60 sample presidential edicts that the United States was prepared to issue to put the hostage deal into effect. At one point, the Iranians complained that the United States was using the mass of paper to confuse and delay the negotiations.

In Washington, the Algerians were given a short course in U.S. constitutional law, outlining what the president could do and what he could not. Consequently, they were able to reply to Iranian questions that were not specifically answered in U.S. documents.

Officials in Algiers characterized their role initially as that of a "postman." It was only recently that they admitted that the Algerian envoys had taken an initiative, by asking the Americans — and presumably the Iranians — to make their messages crystal clear to the Algerians before transmitting them to the other party.

The Algerians also provided a detailed description of 1980 Christmas visits with all 52 hostages and met in Washington with members of about 20 of the hostage families to describe their encounters with the captives.

It was the first time since April that all hostages had been seen, and it came at a time when rumors began to arise that some of the Americans were in poor health, or possibly even dead.

Deputy Secretary of State Warren Christopher, who headed the U.S. team of negotiators on trips to Algiers, said of the Algerians, "They have done a job of great skill and professionalism."

Warren Christopher

Abdelkarim Ghareib

Rehda Malek

Seghir Mostefi

14 hostages had shorter ordeal

Fourteen Americans captured at the U.S. Embassy in Teheran on Nov. 4, 1979, have been allowed to leave Iran. They were blacks, women and one ill white man.

Before they left Teheran, Iranian leader Ayatollah Ruhollah Khomeini announced that blacks and women "who were not spies" would be permitted to leave, because Iran considers blacks oppressed and Islam respects women.

The first three — Kathy Gross, 23, of Cambridge Springs, Pa.; Sgt. William Quarles, 24, of Washington, D.C. and Cpl. Ladell Maples, 24, of Earle, Ark. — were flown out of Iran 15 days after the embassy seizure. The next day, 10 more hostages were freed, bringing to five white women and eight black men the number released by Thanksgiving.

Two women and a black man remain in Iran: Kathryn Koob, 43, of Jesup, Iowa; Elizabeth Ann Swift, 39, of Washington, D.C. and Charles Jones Jr., 40, of Detroit. The last hostage to win release was Richard Queen, 29, of Lincolnville, Maine, who was suffering multiple sclerosis. He was freed after 250 days of captivity.

Queen adjusts well from captivity to freedom

E. Michael Myers
United Press International

Washington, D.C.
Richard Queen removed his glasses, blinked into the glare of the bright lights and wiped tears from his eyes. He was home.

Queen was among the Americans seized at the U.S. Embassy in Teheran by Islamic militants in November, 1979. But his ordeal ended nine months later.

Queen, who was the vice consul of the embassy, suffers from multiple sclerosis. His growing paralysis dumfounded his captors but promptly convinced an Iranian physician that he was ill.

His captivity, including months in a dark cellar, ended July 11, 1980, after 250 days.

Queen may be the best evidence of the resilience of the Americans to overcome the psychological pressures of being held hostage.

Queen appears to have endured the captivity in good mental and physical health except for signs of the disease that afflicts the central nervous system.

He coped well with his enforced isolation. His captors called him "the perfect hostage."

"I like to read," Queen told reporters on his return. "We had lots of books, a wealth of books, literally thousands.

"(Reading) was my way of dealing with the world," he said.

Queen was held for two or three months in a dank, darkened basement but later was moved to an individual room with a view of the mountains.

His captors generally treated him well, he said.

"And I tell you the truth, I feel somewhat guilty, a little bit, that I'm here now and they're not," Queen said. "Mentally they're coping pretty well. They're pretty strong people."

sports

Saturday

January 17/1981

Minneapolis Tribune   comics   1C.

Kicks derail Detroit

By Special Correspondent

Pontiac, Mich.

Ricardo Alonso checked out of a Minneapolis hospital and into the Minnesota Kicks' line-up Friday, just in time to score the deciding goal as the Kicks dumped the Detroit Express 2-1 at the nearly empty Silverdome.

The Express, which went into the match with a five-game losing streak and without leading scorer Pato Margetic, who had been suspended, attracted 3,492 fans to the 60,000-seat stadium.

Those who showed must have felt as if they were watching a chess game. The Kicks failed to get a shot on goal in the first period and finished with just 16. Detroit managed 12 in the supposedly action-packed, high-scoring version of soccer under confinement.

"It was a funny game," said Kicks Coach Geoff Barnett. "Not a lot of chances, but we stuck to our task and won it."

The visitors notched both goals within the first 2:03 of the second half to raise their record to 8-3. Alan Willey knocked in a Chico Hamilton shot off the boards just 11 seconds into the half to break the scoreless tie.

"I didn't have a decent chance the entire first half," said Willey, who tallied his 16th goal to set a Kicks indoor record. "It was a bloody tight game."

Less than three minutes later, Alonso registered his 15th goal, beating Express goalkeeper Gene DuChateau to a pass from Tim Clark in the goalmouth and sliding in a quick shot to make it 2-0.

"Super pass," said Alonso, who had been hospitalized with a groin infection until yesterday morning.

Alonso, in fact, said he was looking forward most to a hearty dinner after the game because he had been fed intravenously in the hospital and had not eaten solid food for a day.

Kicks continued on page 6C

'Fix' charges prompt probe

Newton, Mass.

Boston College officials said Friday they will offer full cooperation to the U.S. Justice Department in connection with allegations that some former basketball players engaged in point-shaving in the 1978-79 season.

Athletic Director William Flynn confirmed that federal authorities are looking into "fix" charges stemming from statements by an informant.

Point-shaving entails holding the margin of victory under the established betting line.

Flynn said that the investigation is disturbing, but he stressed that none of the allegations pertain to current coaches, administrative personnel or players.

"We are convinced that all of our present basketball players are excellent people, as well as being good players," he said.

Flynn said the players allegedly involved no longer attend the school. He refused to say how many players were involved and said he did not know which games authorities were looking at.

One of the Boston College players named by a source close to the inquiry as allegedly having taken money to shave points was Ernie Cobb of Stamford, Conn., a 1979 graduate who unsuccessfully tried out for the New Jersey Nets last summer.

Cobb, a 5-foot-11-inch guard, could not be reached for comment, but his mother said, "That is something he's denying. He says it's not true."

An unidentified source said the outcomes of at least three Boston College games during the 1978-79 season were affected by point-shaving.

"It got to be a joke by the end of the season," the source said. "Many bookies wouldn't even put BC on the card."

The Boston Globe reported the three games in which players allegedly were paid to shave points were against Fordham, which Boston College won 71-64; against St. John's, which it lost 65-76, and against Connecticut, which it lost 91-74.

Boston College Coach Tom Davis called the allegations "shocking and disappointing." He added, "When the Justice Department first talked with us about the allegations, I thought back as to whether there were any games in which I felt that any player gave less than his best effort. Even with the benefit of hindsight, I can think of none." The Eagles posted a 21-9 record in 1978-79 under Davis.

The Washington Post reported that the allegations surfaced last July during an unrelated investigation into the December 1978 theft of $5.8 million from a terminal at Kennedy International Airport in New York.

A key informant in that investigation, convicted felon Henry Hill, told federal authorities he paid at least two players — reportedly $1,000 to $2,000 per game to each — to fix games, the Post reported.

Two major point-shaving scandals have rocked college basketball in the last 30 years. In 1951, 31 players from seven schools were implicated. Ten years later, the charges involved 28 players from 17 colleges.

Staff Photo by Pete Hohn

Minnesota defenseman Mike Meadows slid to the ice in front of goalie Jim Jetland to stop a blast by Wisconsin's Dan Gorowsky Friday night in a Western Collegiate Hockey Association game at Williams Arena.

Gophers rip Wisconsin 6-3

By John Gilbert
Staff Writer

The University of Minnesota hockey team returned to peak form Friday night, ripping Wisconsin 6-3 before 7,764 fans, the biggest hockey crowd of the season at Williams Arena.

Goalie Jim Jetland came up with a strong 32-save performance to hold the victory, while cocaptain Steve Ulseth scored three goals and Butsy Erickson added two.

The question now is whether the Gophers' effort — clearly their best since beating Denver 7-0 and 4-1 in November — was their true form or just a flashy performance they won't be able to maintain in tonight's 7:30 rematch.

"It was a big win for us," said Gophers Coach Brad Buetow. "It gives us a lot of confidence. The second period (when Wisconsin got only two shots) was as good as we've played defensively."

Jetland, feeling added pressure after his dispute with Buetow last weekend, allowed goals only on rebounds after he had made good saves.

"I hope I answered some questions," said Jetland. "I just tried to go out and play my game."

The teams probed for chances through the high-tension first 10 minutes. Then Erickson and Ulseth made it look as if the Gophers would run away and hide, scoring three times in less than three minutes on Wisconsin goaltender Jamey Gremore.

Erickson's shot from the right side hit Gremore and popped in the air, landing in the crease and sliding barely across the line at 11:19.

Pal Ethier went off for removing Jeff Teal's helmet with a high stick at 12:04, and Ulseth went to work. Aaron Broten, whose play had generated the first goal, held the puck in at the left point and fed a diagonal pass to Ulseth at the right circle, where he drilled a shot at 12:30.

It became 3-0 at 13:53, when Brad Doshan set up Ulseth with a superb play, curling back from the blue line on the left side before feeding a pass across to the right to Ulseth, who was breaking in alone.

The runaway slowed down when the Badgers pumped in two goals, both on rebounds after Jetland saves. Peter Johnson scored with the rebound of Therna Weish's power-play blueline shot at 15:34. A minute and a half later, Weish broke up the right side of a 2-on-1, and when Jetland blocked his hard shot, Weish reacted in time to hold his own rebound in.

That cut the gap to 3-2 at the first intermission, and it might have been 3-3.

'U' hockey continued on page 6C

Gopher, Illinois players know each other well

By Jon Roe
Staff Writer

Champaign, Ill.

Trent Tucker well remembers those high school basketball games against his cousin, Craig Tucker, back in Flint, Mich. And Derek Harper well remembers his high school teammate, Darryl Mitchell, back in West Palm Beach, Fla.

But the times, they are a-changin'. Today, when Trent Tucker, Mitchell and their University of Minnesota basketball teammates take on Craig Tucker, Harper and their University of Illinois teammates at Assembly Hall (3:05 p.m., Ch. 9), those days will be nothing more than ancient history.

"Any special meaning going against Mitch?" asked Harper, the Illini's superlative freshman guard. "No, nothing more than that I'd like to win the game. And I guess it's going to be the same for him. Sure, I want to play my best against him, but he's probably thinking the same way. It's just another game that we'd like to win to show that we are a good team."

"That's the role I have here, too. My whole job is to help set things up for the other guys. That's what you're supposed to do when you're the point guard. Goes with the job."

Illinois Coach Lou Henson said it can be the toughest job in college basketball, especially for a freshman. But Harper, who was considered to be the best high school guard in the country last year, is already leading the Illini in assists.

"He's not as good as he's going to be in a month," said Henson. "And he's not as good as he's going to be next year. There have been a lot of ups and downs, just like any freshman is going to go through. But the only thing that's hurting him right now is his inexperience."

Craig Tucker has had more experience; he played for two years at a junior college before joining the Illini this season. He has started eight of 12 games and is averaging 12.6 points a game as Illinois has built a 10-2 record, 3-1 in the conference and 18th place in the national ratings. Henson has been rotating Harper and Tucker with junior Perry Range in the Illini backcourt.

"I gave a lot of thought to going to Minnesota," said Harper, who is averaging nearly eight points a game. "Mitch and I talked several times and he told me why he felt Minnesota had been a good place for him. But I sorta felt that just because some place had been good for him didn't mean it was going to be good for me, too.

"And at Illinois, I knew I had a chance to be a starter, if I worked hard and earned the spot, right away. The Illinois coaches told me

Mitchell and Harper were teammates for one high school season, when Mitchell was a senior and Harper a sophomore. "I think I led the state in assists that year," recalled Harper. "And a lot of those passes went to him, and he'd get the bucket.

"One thing I know for sure," said Trent Tucker, "I'm positive that Craig is going to be sky-high for this game because he just hates to lose to me. Back in high school, our teams really had some battles. It'll probably be the same thing in this game."

The Gophers made a recruiting pitch for both Craig Tucker and Harper a year ago, but neither even visited Minnesota. There has been speculation that neither was anxious to be on the same college team with a cousin or a former teammate.

'U' basketball continued on page 6C

Craig Tucker   Trent Tucker   Derek Harper   Darryl Mitchell

shelter

Minneapolis Tribune   Want ads inside

Saturday

January 31/1981

1S

Real estate industry is changing — What it means to you

By John Kostouros
Staff Writer

It looks as if home buyers and sellers are going to get some help from an unlikely source — the recession.

According to some industry watchers, the downturn in the economy, which has hit real estate firms especially hard, is forcing mergers and company closings. And it also is speeding the purchase of smaller firms by larger ones, a trend that began several years ago.

While not everyone agrees on what the consolidation will eventually mean to the consumer, if things go as the optimists say they will, it could mean better-trained sales agents, more services and just maybe a reduction in the cost of hiring a real estate company to sell your home.

An increase in competency among real estate agents would be a welcome improvement in an industry that has suffered in the past from high turnover of salespeople and a lack of formal training.

Four of every five people who come into the business last less than two years. With that high a turnover rate among agents, there is little time to effectively teach salespeople the intricacies of real estate marketing and finance, according to Dan Diebold, a real estate broker, consultant, teacher, and author.

The Minnesota industry addressed the problem of undertrained real estate salespeople three years ago by requiring applicants to have 30 hours of classroom education before they can be licensed as agents. Once licensed, agents must take more training.

But that effort has critics. The law allows agents to get credit for courses that don't really improve service to the consumer, according to some.

While the predicted consolidation should take a few more years, the process has begun. Two years ago Coldwell Banker, a national firm, bought the Spring Company. Recently Edina Realty merged with Award Realty, Eberhart bought Fox-Her-

furth Realty, and Burnet Realty bought the two top-growing Century 21 franchise holders. Several smaller agencies have simply closed, and countless others have shrunk dramatically, according to Diebold.

Author/Realtor Thomas Ervin predicted in his recent book "Real Estate Revolution — Who Will Survive?" that the business will soon be dominated by fewer than five giant national companies. Ervin's predictions are echoed by local real estate professionals.

"There's a frenzy in the marketplace about who's going to last," said William Saunders, head of Coldwell Banker's residential sales division. Many companies are expanding rapidly, mostly by buying smaller firms and opening new offices, on the theory that growth is the only alternative to being overwhelmed by the more aggressive companies, Saunders said.

The race to grow has produced fierce competition for clients and of-

Agents continued on Page 4S

Thoughts about a city of yellow ribbons . . .

By Bernard Jacob

A look at architecture

Our obelisk was decorated last week, the Foshay Tower sported a yellow ribbon. Audaciously and beautifully it carried its ribbon, as if on behalf of the entire city. And for all of us it carried the message of compassion, gratitude and loyalty.

The message was repeated many times throughout the city, on storefronts, on windows, doors and everywhere. Spontaneously and wonderfully the city was decorated and unified by one theme.

These occasions are rare. One thinks of Christmas time, when added lights and decorations signify joy and celebration. But Christmas is a recurring holiday and therefore it can be planned. The release of the American hostages had been anticipated only a very short time.

The ribbon around the Foshay Tower took an inspired idea and much planning. But it had to occur very quickly and indeed it appeared overnight. The ribbon, 4½ feet wide, with 40-foot loops and 30-foot streamers, was to scale, just the right size for the building, and it sent the message effectively and quite simply. The concept became reality very quickly. This contrasts with the time it took to build the Foshay Tower and all buildings in the city.

It sometimes takes years from the inception of a building to its comple-

tion and occupancy. Some take longer than others to erect and complete. Cities, however, take forever — a city is never complete, never finished. A completed city would be a dead city (a cemetery is never completed either).

The present construction and reconstruction downtown will be finished in a few years and when projects currently under way are occupied, new ones will have been planned. The central business district is being enlarged, the heart of the city is growing in all directions.

The shape of the city, its texture and its civility are a direct result of its architecture: the quality, grace and beauty of its buildings. Between buildings are streets and from building to building are skyways. And the manner in which these accommodate traffic — both pedestrian and vehicular — also sets a tone, a tempo, an ambience.

Planning decisions leading to the treatment of streets and the creation of skyways are not easy and, once made, it still takes years before they are implemented.

Good planning and perseverance

create Nicollet Malls, Orchestra Halls and successful urban centers. However, all the planning and all the architecture in the world cannot specify the spontaneity, the joy, the accidental encounter, the necessary noise and bustle that make a city. A plan, however, can set the framework for the city's daily life.

City planning is difficult in a democracy where we prize individual freedom above all else. We believe in freedom of expression and in spontaneity, yet we must live together. So we agree to legislate certain safeguards and standards. We do not legislate the design of buildings, even of

very important buildings, or building complexes, even though they affect the city very significantly.

Expressions of joy or compassion are temporal but buildings last a long time. They outlast their planners and architects and go on to affect future city dwellers. Thus, buildings in the city requires tact, grace, vision, courage and, above all, a healthy sense of responsibility — which, even if we wanted to, cannot be legislated or planned.

Bernard Jacob, a regular contributor, is a practicing Minneapolis architect.

At the Government Center   On the Foshay Tower

At Dayton's

Home, garden show expects bumper crowd

By John Kostouros
Staff Writer

Don Engebretson, who has been putting on "home and garden" trade shows for years, remembers a time when you had to almost bribe people to get them to attend.

"In the old days you used to bring in Dolly Parton, Liberace, somebody to attract attention, then hope that the people that came to see them also owned a home," said Engebretson, producer of the Minneapolis Home and Garden Show (Thursday through Sunday, Minneapolis Auditorium).

That was before the children of the baby boom became homebodies. Since 1976, attendance at the Minneapolis show has tripled. Last year the show drew 75,000 in six days. This year the promoters expect the same number in four days.

(Promoters were forced to cut the show back to four days because of booking conflicts for the auditorium but are promising to expand it next year to 10 days, the length of the original 1976 show.)

In doing research for the show, Engebretson found another reason for the high level of interest in home improvements. He says Upper Midwest residents spend more on their homes than folks in any other region.

Home show continued on Page 2S

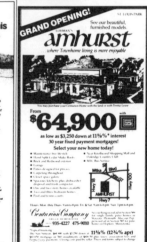

Editorial/Opinion pages/

Minneapolis Tribune

Established 1867

Charles W. Bailey Editor
Wallace Allen Associate Editor
Frank Wright Managing Editor
Leonard Inskip Editorial Editor

Donald R. Dwight Publisher

6A   Tuesday, January 27, 1981

Namibian negotiations off the track

South Africa's scuttling of the United Nations conference on Namibia this month poses an early challenge for Ronald Reagan's African diplomacy. The failure of the talks threatens to undo several years' work of five Western nations, including the United States, for an end to guerrilla warfare and an internationally recognized Namibian independence. It also threatens to intensify hostilities in Namibia and Angola between South African troops and the South West African People's Organization (SWAPO). The challenge for Reagan diplomacy is to steer a course between two polarizing pressures that will intensify because the new administration's African policies are not yet known.

Black southern Africa's frontline nations will probably ask for comprehensive sanctions against South Africa in the United Nations Security Council next month. They will tend to read the American response as a test of this country's commitment to black self-determination and against apartheid in white-ruled South Africa. Strongly backing the frontline countries will be Nigeria, perhaps willing to use the weapon of oil in persuading the West to be harsh on South Africa.

South Africa, though, will probably press Reagan to back off from the U.N. and Western plan for a Namibian settlement. It would prefer American assent to an internal settlement sponsored and arranged in Namibia by South Africa. South Africa will tend to read the U.S. response as a test of American commitment against Soviet influence in SWAPO itself and elsewhere on the continent. And South Africa will not be shy in reminding Washington that South Africa's minerals and strong economy are important to the West.

Neither of these pressures — for sanctions or for backing off — should simplistically determine the American approach to Namibian independence. To signal approval of a South Africa-sponsored internal settlement would settle nothing. On the contrary, it would guarantee widening of the warfare, further openings for Soviet interference and strained friendships with the black African nations on whom stability throughout the region depends. However, encouraging a move toward anti-South African sanctions would accomplish equally little. It would not end the warfare. But it would undercut South African support for Namibian independence, would weaken the liberal wing of South Africa's National Party and would do worse damage to black states that rely on South Africa for trade, transport and food than it would to the economy of South Africa itself.

Pe

By Ja
The N

Washi
The h
politics
months
loving
their
there i

Few variations of design mark editorial pages

The editorial / opinion pages follow normal Tribune design principles and layout rules.

All type except editorials is set one column, 9 on 9.5. Editorials are set 10 point on 11, on one and a half columns.

The Tribune grid and the flush-left principle are followed. Bylines are set in Helvetica type, 10 on 11, with hairline rules above and below.

The following pages illustrate page design and special column headings.

Editorial/
Opinion pages/

Minneapolis Tribune

Established 1867

Charles W. Bailey Editor
Wallace Allen Associate Editor
Frank Wright Managing Editor
Leonard Inskip Editorial Editor

Donald R. Dwight Publisher

10A . Thursday, January 15, 1981

Merge interior, energy departments? No

Now comes Michael Halbouty, irrepressible Texas oilman and Reagan energy adviser, to propose that the Departments of Energy and Interior be merged into a new department of energy and natural resources — on grounds that it would satisfy President-elect Reagan's pledge to abolish the Energy Department and would "save billions of dollars and cut down on the government work force."

Halbouty can be excused the naivete of believing, if he really does, that any reorganization can save billions. He's merely accepting the snake-oil pitch so often used to sell reorganization to a skeptical public. If Halbouty's plan *did* save substantial sums, it would be one of few in a long line of state and federal reorganizations to achieve that oft-promised goal.

Savings aside, to Halbouty the oilman the plan no doubt makes sense. It reeks of rationality. The Energy Department sets policy for the use of natural gas, oil and coal, but the Interior Department controls the leasing of public lands holding those resources. What could be more reasonable than compressing these natural-resource interests into one agency? Stir in the Department of Agriculture's forest service, various and sundry other small agencies, and, *voila*, you've created a one-stop natural-resources center.

Of course, energy involves, or should, more than oil, coal and natural gas. And interior has responsibility for such non-resource items as Indian affairs and trust territories. But the central problem with Halbouty's proposal is that rational government does not always translate into good government. In this case, a strong brief can be developed for seemingly irrational current arrangements.

The Interior Department is a special organism. It acts, in a sense, as an adjudicator of competing claims on public lands. At the direction of Congress, it works to strike a complex, ever-changing balance — among those who prize public land for its wildlife habitat, wilderness, recreation, cattle grazing, mineral extraction, energy development and half a dozen other uses. And whatever the use to which a portion of the public domain is put, interior has a special stewardship: to insure the land is not abused, to protect it not only for now, but for generations that will follow. Differences exist about how best to carry out that requirement of sound stewardship, but not about its existence.

To meld the Energy Department into Interior would destroy those fundamental adjudicatory and stewardship roles. The Energy Department is explicitly, and rightly, an advocate of resource exploitation. It represents only one of the competing uses that the Interior Department must balance. Mix the two departments and the likely result is domination by a philosophy of exploitation. Even the proposed name — energy and natural resources — suggests a preponderance of bulldozers and drilling rigs. No hint exists there of the other values interior has come to embody as the nation's groundskeeper. Natural resources would become only grist for the energy mill. The worry is that this, rather than rational, less-expensive government, is precisely what Michael Halbouty has in mind. Which is a goal worthy of early and vigorous thwarting.

Owen Wangensteen

"From empiric craft to scientific discipline" sums up the monumental history of surgery that Owen Wangensteen wrote, with his wife Sarah, after his retirement. The phrase also captures the change Wangensteen brought to teaching surgery at the University of Minnesota Medical Schools and Hospitals. By insisting for 40 years that his students not only be skilled with scalpels but also understand intellectually how the body functions and how disease proceeds, Wangensteen was key in making the university a major medical center. His death this week, at age 82, has inspired tributes from around the world.

Indeed, as chief of surgery from 1931 to 1967, and in retirement as an active professor emeritus, Wangensteen won worldwide respect. From research under his direction — and from students he taught — came pioneering advances in open-heart surgery and eventually heart transplants. "Wangensteen suction," developed in the 1930s, is standard procedure still for preventing intestinal blockage after abdominal operations. And what he once called "my least-recognized contribution" was to think through and start an early-detection program for catching cancer before too late to treat it.

But international prominence never long drew Wangensteen away from his native Minnesota. He was born and grew up on a farm near Lake Park. He took his schooling and degrees at the university. There he found his calling as a great teacher and outstanding scientist. Until his death he stayed active and creative in the department he had headed. The Minnesota community will miss Owen Wangensteen.

At the reunion, yesterday's moonlight

By Richard N. Livingstone

Hampton, N.H.
She came up to me after dinner and introduced herself, and I never told her how much I was hoping she would be there or that I had looked around more than once to see whether she was. We talked for a minute or two and then we edged around to the table to look at the old photographs where we all stood frozen in time with long dresses and baggy pants and crew cuts and the bright and eager eyes of the youngsters we used to be.

I asked her where she was living now and whether she had any children, and she said no, just a husband and a cat. It was getting late, and we agreed that it had been a great reunion and fun to see everyone from the old church group again and then we said good-by. And she walked out the door and up the asphalt driveway by the church to her car.

She looked older now, of course, with lines in her face — still attractive, I thought — but I could still see in her face the same girl I had seen in the moonlight so many years ago, and remembered ever afterward. She had come to only a few of the meetings, at least the ones I went to, but that night we happened to leave together, and we walked up the driveway beside the church.

We both agreed that it was a beautiful night, and then she turned her face toward me, and in that instant I saw the moonlight reflected in her long black hair and soft black eyes, and I thought how beautiful she was. I thought then that I must call and ask her out, but I never did, and that was the last time I saw her until the reunion, as her family moved soon afterward to another town.

When I saw her again, I wanted to tell her how I had felt that night. But she would have thought I was foolish or crazy or trying to seduce her, she with the husband and cat and probably a trim split-level house in a nice neighborhood and her weekly women's group. Reunions are not the place to bring up such things, but places of merriment and loud laughs and hearty handshakes and a demure kiss on the cheek. It is the time to guess who she or he is, and for bursts of recognition, and to remember when, and for dinner and coffee and drinks that toward the end of the evening turn bitter in the mouth.

We go to reunions to meet people, to see old friends from another time and another place and who are now strangers to our lives. But do not be deceived. We go to reunions to find a part of ourselves. We go to find again the boy or girl we used to be, another self we knew long ago and still remember and chase and try to catch like an elusive wisp of smoke. The people we know are there, and in our conversations we strike chords of our former selves, but that is all. We find that we cannot escape so easily, that only our hopes and dreams, our expectations and ambitions, are changed, and not us.

We are still inarticulate. We chitchat, as we chitchatted with our old friend who died last month of cancer, as we chitchat with our mother or father, our brother or sister, our wife and our sons and daughters and everyone who means more than the world to us. We still, at age 50 or more, cannot bring ourselves to say "I love you," as though we shall live forever and have time through eternity. And the moments go and are lost and never come again.

And at reunions we see these moments and know again that we cannot live them over. They are gone and will never return. We find a part of our long-ago selves and we are sad, but not so much for the moment that has gone, for all the girls we will never see again in the moonlight and for all the times of our lives that have vanished like smoke in a summer wind, but for ourselves and all the words that waited for another time.

Richard N. Livingstone is an editor.

Letters from readers

A hit-run death

I am sick and furious. I witnessed a hit and run in Minneapolis. Had it been a person, perhaps I would have gotten some action. Sorry to say, it was only a dog — a beautiful German shepherd, somebody's pet, which won't be coming home today. I called the police department, and the police informed me that they were not interested and that I should call the dog pound. I called the dog pound to see whether they would like the information regarding the driver of the vehicle who ran over the dog. They informed me that they didn't think they needed that information.

I am not an "animal-lib"-type person, nor do I have any pets of my own. I am simply stunned by the lack of caring or concern exhibited by our local authorities. I am sure the owners of this animal are also saddened by this event, the only consolation being that their pet did not suffer. — **Johnnie Martin, Northfield, Minn.**

Stealing from the blind

I am blind in one eye and nearly blind in the other. While walking on Franklin Av., to Heller's Grocery, I was bumped from behind by a man. He said he was sorry — only running for a bus. I thought nothing of it and proceeded to the store. I tied up my dog and discovered my wallet was missing. Thank you, thief, for sparing my faithful seeing-eye dog. Next time you won't be so lucky. — **Mrs. C. Hudson, Minneapolis.**

"Let me guess, OK? Russia, Brezhnev. Right? Germany, Schmidt. France, Whatsisaame . . . ?"

History's verdict on Jimmy Carter

By Russell Baker
The New York Times

New York
A group of learned men quoted in the paper the other day gave it as their opinion that Jimmy Carter will not go down in the history books as much of a president. Possibly so. A George Washington doesn't come along very often, and even if one did, under our present system for choosing presidents he would probably be wiped out in the polls for showing badly fitted false teeth in his television smile.

Jimmy Carter

Trying to guess what history will say is tricky business. A hundred years from now school children compelled to study American history from John Kennedy to Ronald Reagan are more likely than not to lump all five presidents of the era under the label of "General Confusion" and let them go at that.

This is what most Americans do nowadays with the presidents between Andrew Jackson and Abraham Lincoln and those between Andrew Johnson and William McKinley. Even people who have read some history have trouble telling you whether Franklin Pierce preceded Millard Filmore, where Zachary Taylor fitted in, how he differed from John Tyler, which Harrison was Benjamin and which William Henry, and what Chester A. Arthur did that was different from what Rutherford B. Hayes did.

John Tyler

People a hundred years hence are probably going to be equally baffled about the five presidents we have had since 1961. When presidents come and go as rapidly as they have come and gone in the past 20 years, they are apt to leave nothing but a blur in the history books.

Among these five, Carter has as good a chance as any of being remembered honorably, if at all. Imagine for a moment that you are situated in the year 2081 and cramming for a test on 20th-century presidents.

You can handle Theodore Roosevelt easily enough. The last hero of American optimism. William Howard Taft, OK, he was the fat man, fattest president in history.

Woodrow Wilson? A snap. World War I. League of Nations. Intellectual.

Warren Harding, Calvin Coolidge, Herbert Hoover. Lump them all together under "Roaring Twenties." Harding was sexy and produced Teapot Dome; Coolidge did not choose to run; Hoover got caught in the stock-market crash. Franklin Roosevelt: the big fellow; you know enough to write a 25-word essay on him. Harry Truman: gave 'em hell, big Cold War leader. Dwight Eisenhower: war hero, presided over eight years of unprecedented American prosperity and power.

With John Kennedy, however, you run into a confusion of rapidly changing presidents and incomprehensible political snarls such as, in 2081, only a Ph.D. in history can hope to grasp. You probably know that Kennedy was assassinated, and possibly, if you prefer scandal to history, that he liked to play around.

But did Kennedy come before or after Richard Nixon? Well, Nixon was the one who had to quit because of Watergate, whatever Watergate was, and then he was succeeded by the vice president who had been appointed instead of elected. Was that Carter or Johnson?

Millard Fillmore

It couldn't have been Johnson because the fellow who succeeded Nixon was a nice guy, and Johnson was not a nice guy, but the one who had to quit because he made a mess of the Vietnam War.

It will probably take you a while to remember that it was Gerald Ford who followed Nixon, and even if you do remember you are probably going to forget altogether to include Carter, as people nowadays forget to include James K. Polk when trying to remember who came between John Tyler and Zachary Taylor.

Students who are cunning about grades may be able to keep things properly sorted out by using the phrase "a very wet November breeze" as a memory device in which "A" stands for "Assassinated" (Kennedy), the "v" in "very" for Vietnam (Johnson), the "w" in "wet" for Watergate (Nixon), the "N" in "November" for nice guy (Ford) and the "b" in "breeze" for breezy (Carter). Why does "breezy" instantly bring Carter to mind? Because he was the first president who insisted on being formally addressed in the breezy style, by his nickname Jimmy rather than James.

Zachary Taylor

This, admittedly, is not a great distinction for a president, but on the other hand it is not discreditable either. It is certainly not as bad as being remembered by "Vietnam" or "Watergate" and, in the long run, far preferable to being remembered by "assassinated." It is not so pleasant, to be sure, as being remembered by "nice guy," but it is better than not being remembered at all, for if Carter can get himself remembered way up there in the future some student may be moved to ask the teacher what Carter did.

I fancy the teacher will have to reflect a minute before saying something like, "Well, he really didn't do anything terribly dreadful at all." For the era 1961-1981, that is not a bad notice from the history critics.

The menace of Watt is exaggerated

By George F. Will
The Washington Post

Washington
Sneak up behind an environmentalist and shout "JAMES WATT!" and you will induce an interesting tautness of nerves, like that which afflicted Macbeth when he saw the ghost of Banquo. Although I share many of their anxieties and most of their values, I think environmentalists are exaggerating, as is their wont, when they describe the menace posed by the next interior secretary.

Whatever you think of his fervent "developmentalist" ideology, there is no reason to impugn his honor. His duties as secretary will be different from those he had in the job he is leaving. He has been director of a hyperactive legal foundation supported by corporations and specializing in court challenges to federal environmental regulations. At interior, his duty will be to perform more complicated balancing functions, and he deserves the ordinary assumption that he will do his duty as defined, often strictly, by law.

When his critics, practicing preemptive indignation, say he is a "fox sent to guard the chicken coop," their rhetoric suggests that interior's sole function is to "guard," meaning preserve or conserve, the nation's natural assets. Actually, preservation is only part of interior's mission.

The laws that substantially dictate what a secretary shall do, do leave important matters to his discretion, which will be used. Watt's views mirror those of the man who just carried 44 states. Ronald Reagan ran strongest in the region where Watt — a Wyomingite who has been living in booming Denver — has been a leader in the fight for less restrictive environmental regulations.

When Watt says he sees the West "not simply through the eyes of a summer traveler but as a native," he is the authentic voice of the "sagebrush rebellion." Indeed, he is the Robespierre of Western resistance to Washington's intrusiveness. The principal cause of Western seething is federal ownership of so much Western land.

How much? Some percentages of federally owned land are: Nevada 87, Idaho 67, Utah 65, Alaska 60 (it was 96 before last year's legislation), Oregon 52, Wyoming 48, California 45, Arizona 44, Colorado 36, New Mexico 34, Montana 30, Washington 29. (East of the Mississippi, the highest percentage of federal ownership is 12 in New Hampshire.) This huge federal presence is one reason why in 1980 in 14 Western states an incumbent Democratic president won an even smaller percentage of the popular vote than George McGovern did in 1972.

Reagan's goal is to return to the states "primary responsibility" for environmental regulation so as to "increase responsiveness to local conditions." But one can understand the West's (more precisely, many but by no means all Westerners') desire for that without considering it sound policy. The doctrine of "states' rights" seems especially strained when used to dilute the component of national interest in obviously national needs such as water, timber, minerals and wilderness and recreation areas.

Environmentalists must consider Watt's warning that if development of the West's vast energy reserves is impeded until a crisis comes, development then may be especially ravaging. For Watt, development by "free enterprise" is a fighting faith. And if presidents are to ease their burdens by practicing "Cabinet government," Watt may be the model of what presidents need: Cabinet officers who share the president's beliefs, passionately, and who relish conflict.

Reagan can reasonably claim a mandate to review environmental policies, but environmentalists need not fold like accordions. The real mandate is murky. The electorate is at it again: willing ends but not willing the means to those ends. Much environmental regulation preceded, or proceeded without sufficient understanding of, the "oil shocks" and regulatory excesses and other factors which have now focused attention on America's declining productivity. Illegal command economics no longer generates wealth as easily as it did, and because the world is more competitive, Americans are now more sensitive about the costs of things, including environmental improvement.

But they still strongly support environmental goals. If that support conflicts with Reagan's mandate for lightening the weight of government, that only means that Americans are, as usual, conflicted, and not unreasonably.

Furthermore, nature is impervious to election returns. God sendeth rain on the just and on the unjust, but not equally on all regions. Many things — from making shale oil to washing the tennis togs of those anticipated immigrants from the declining East — require more water than much of the West has handy or can organize without rearranging those things — water rights — that have occasioned the West's fiercest conflicts. It is, therefore, good that when Watt says he anticipates "tremendous conflicts," he seems like a man to whom conflict, the more tremendous the better, is the syrup on the flapjack of life.

Editorial page flag/

Minneapolis Tribune

 Established 1867

Charles W. Bailey Editor
Wallace Allen Associate Editor
Frank Wright Managing Editor
Leonard Inskip Editorial Editor

Donald R. Dwight Publisher

12A   **Sunday, January 25, 1981**

U.S. should not act hastily on Iran

"Anger and haste hinder wise counsel," says an English proverb. The proverb itself is wise counsel now. Americans are justifiably angry at the abuse their countrymen suffered in Iran. The revelations of barbaric treatment unleashed a 15-month store of frustration and outrage. Good; the emotions should be got out.

ernment" has only a fragile hold on power. Iraq pounds away. If the United States took action that further destabilized Iran, a process dangerous to world peace might be set in motion. Iran could disintegrate into a number of hostile ethnic states — with the Soviet Union ready to exploit opportunities in such a vacuum. A Soviet move would threaten the West's vital stake in the Persian Gulf region.

Editorial page graphics/

Letters
from readers

1 column graphic

Letters
from readers

2 column graphic

100%

Editorial page graphics/

James Shannon

1 column graphic

Point of View
Charles W. Bailey

Bylines/

James Shannon

2 column graphic

100%

Put inauguration day in December

By George F. Will
The Washington Post

Washington
Tinkering with the Constitution is generally unwise, even impertinent, but the time has come to change one word, replacing "January" with "December" in Section One of the 20th Amendment: "The tenure of the President and Vice President shall end at noon on the 20th day of January . . . ."

A recurring question today is: Are

an invasion in the weeks after the election, Carter's ability to organize such solidarity would have been even less than it was in the best of his days.

Even a narrow election victory imparts something that is difficult to acquire, even more difficult to keep, and indispensable to energetic government: mo-(forgive me, George Bush)-mentum. Yet such is the inescapable toll taken by our unduly prolonged transition periods that when President Reagan stepped forward to deliver his inaugural address, he

— that seemed designed to repair the damage done to the public's understanding of his economic intentions by too much talk during the too-long transition.

During a transition, and especially early in one, there is an unusually high ratio of journalistic energy to real news, so news reports contain an unusually high ratio of speculation to substance. In addition, nothing is more fun to report than disagreements within an administration, and the process of looking for them can produce them, especially

Chapter
7 /

Design /

How graphics
are used in
the Tribune

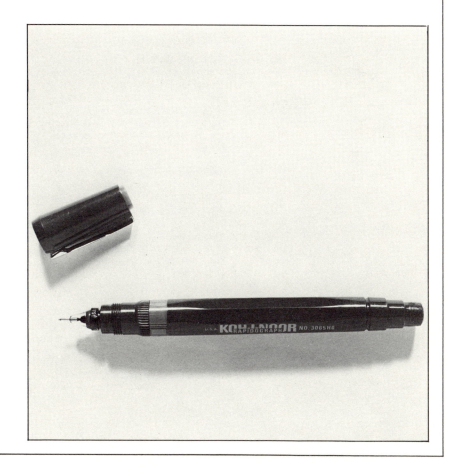

Introduction /

Simplicity is the keynote in graphic style

A major purpose of the Tribune's redesign was to achieve a consistency of graphic style throughout the newspaper.

Before the redesign, Tribune artists created standing heads for features as they were added to the newspaper, each artist in his own style.

Each standing head reflected the content it covered. No one thought of its place in the newspaper as a unit. The result, of course, was a hodgepodge of unrelated styles.

For the redesign, all the old standing heads were discarded. More than 200 graphic devices were redesigned. All were drawn to achieve a consistency of style and to fit the Tribune grid.

Simplicity is the key to Tribune news graphics as it is with its total design. The objective is artwork that will communicate its message to the reader clearly but unobtrusively. Designers keep in mind, too, the need for producing artwork that will print cleanly.

Several examples of base artwork are shown in the following pages. From them grow the graphics used in the newspaper, also shown.

Column headings follow similar styles, with slight differences between daily and feature sections, as indicated.

When the Tribune runs a series, a graphic name device is created in Tribune style, to be used from day to day.

Maps, charts and graphs are important visual aids for readers. This chapter shows how they are made.

Design /

How graphics
are used in
the Tribune

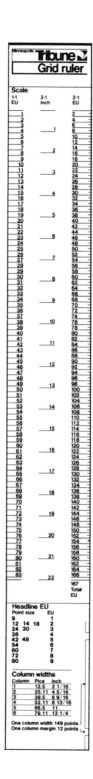

Tribune logotype/

1969/

Letterforms for new logotype (Helvetica)/

April 5/1971/

Logotype/April 5/1971/

Graphics at right show the evolution of the logotype from the original of 1969 to the logo used today. In the second panel, Frank Ariss was experimenting with a Letraset production of the Helvetica letters used in the logo. He then enlarged the letters and used them as the basis for designing the stylized final logo.

Daily flags/

Minneapolis

Tuesday **1A** **Final**
January 13, 1981
Volume CXIV
Number 190
3 Sections
M   y
Copyright 1981 Minneapolis Star and Tribune Company   25¢ Single Copy   Section A/Part I

National/World news

 Minneapolis Tribune
Tuesday, January 13, 1981   .2A

Metro news **1B**
Comics/TV-Radio

3B.
State news
Tuesday/January 13/1981

Sports/General news **1C.**
Tuesday January 13 1981

50%

Sunday base flags/

outdoors

hunting / fishing / fitness / environment / calendars

Minneapolis Tribune

Sunday

home/garden

home life / collecting / planting / building / decorating

Minneapolis Tribune

Sunday

1H

entertainment/arts

books / movies / plays / concerts / visual arts / calendars

Minneapolis Tribune

Sunday

1G

travel/adventure

where to go / how to go / travel news

Minneapolis Tribune

Sunday

1E

family/living

parents and children / medical care / life styles / food

Minneapolis Tribune

Sunday

1F

Base artwork
30% black screen in letterforms

50%

Sunday flags /

outdoors
hunting / fishing / fitness / environment / calendars
Minneapolis Tribune

Deer hunting / 10C

Sunday
February 1 / 1981

home/garden
home life / collecting / planting / building / decorating
Minneapolis Tribune

Sunday
February 1 / 1981

1H

entertainment/arts
books / movies / plays / concerts / visual arts / calendars
Minneapolis Tribune

Calendar / 6G

Sunday
February 1 / 1981

1G

travel/adventure
where to go / how to go / travel news
Minneapolis Tribune

Sunday
February 1 / 1981

1E

family/living
parents and children / medical care / life styles / food
Minneapolis Tribune

3F

Sunday
February 1 / 1981

1F

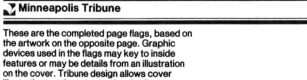

These are the completed page flags, based on
the artwork on the opposite page. Graphic
devices used in the flags may key to inside
features or may be details from an illustration
on the cover. Tribune design allows cover
illustrations at times to overlap the flag.

50%

Perspective flag/

Minneapolis Tribune
Wednesday
January 21/1981
13A

Thursday food flag/

hursdaythursdayfoodthu

▼ **Minneapolis Tribune**   **January 22/1981/1C**

30% black screen in letterforms

Friday special flag/

ayfridayfridaySpecialfrid

▼ **Minneapolis Tribune**   **January 23/1981/1C**

30% black screen in letterforms

50%

Saturday flags/

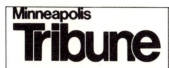

Saturday

January 31/1981 Section A/Part 1

Volume III
Number 28
M   y

5 Sections
25c Single copy

Copyright 1980 Minneapolis Star and Tribune Company

1A   Final

Minneapolis Tribune

3B

Saturday
January 31/1981
1B

30% black screen in letterforms

 **news plus**

Saturday
January 31/1981

Minneapolis Tribune   TV logs   1C

 **shelter**

Saturday
January 31/1981

Minneapolis Tribune   1S

 **sports**

Saturday
January 31/1981

Minneapolis Tribune   comics   1D

The graphic on the sports cover is changed from season to season, as shown at left.

50%

Column graphics base artwork/

18 grid units

1 column base artwork / 12.5 picas

9½ points

9 grid units

2 column base artwork / 25.11 picas

3 column base artwork / 39.5 picas

100%

Column graphics/

Robert T Smith

30 point Helvetica bold / set solid 30 / 30

1 column graphic

Robert T Smith

6 points

2 column graphic

Robert T Smith

6 points

3 column graphic

100%

Sunday graphics/

18 grid units

Scotch rule —

24 point Helvetica bold set solid 24/24

12 point Helvetica light

1 column base artwork / 12.5 picas

You and your children

Jan Rigert

1 column graphic

8 grid units   6 points —

1 column base artwork / 12.5 picas

Minnesota authors

1 column graphic

5 grid units

2 column base artwork / 25.11 picas

Scotch rules are used in Sunday graphics only, in contrast to the six-point open box used daily.

Minnesota authors

2 column graphic

100%

Series graphics/

H.R. Haldeman

The ends of power

1 column graphic

Dutch elm

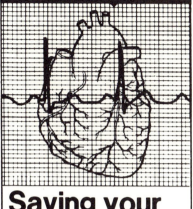

Saving your heart

Indian youth/
The disappearing student

Graphics for series of articles are specially designed to fit the subjects.

World oil/
How safe is our supply?

The changing American farm

Tribune maps/

The curved lines on a map are simplified into basically straight lines. Borders are strengthened for clear reproduction.

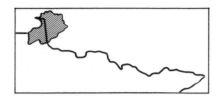 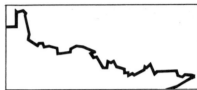

Only Helvetica light and bold type is used on maps and charts.

Helvetica bold

Helvetica light

On Tribune maps, open squares denote major cities. Closed squares are used for smaller cities and towns.

Capitals—countries/ Example/Warsaw

Capitals—major cities/ Example/Twin Cities

Towns/ Example/Rochester

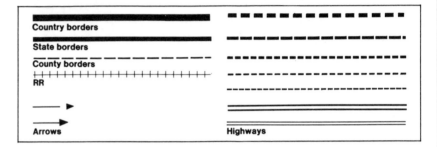

Country borders

State borders

County borders

RR

Arrows

Highways

Borders are available in tape format.

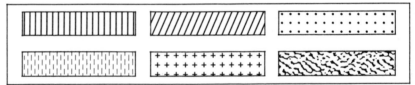

These are screening techniques used.

Wire service maps are converted into Tribune style.

131

Tribune maps/

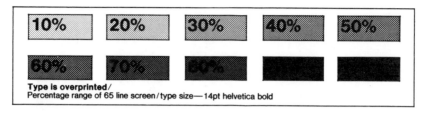

Type is overprinted/
Percentage range of 65 line screen / type size— 14pt helvetica bold

Sixty-five-line screen is used on Tribune maps and charts.

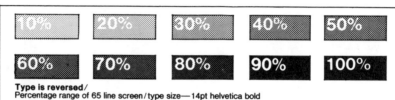

Type is reversed/
Percentage range of 65 line screen / type size— 14pt helvetica bold

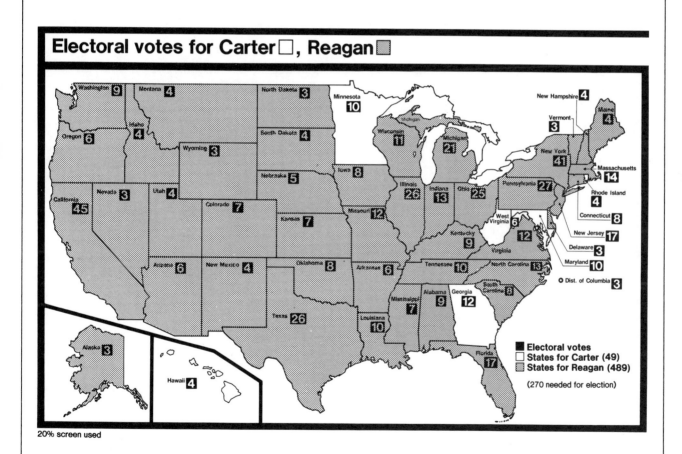

20% screen used

Tribune charts/

Projected food price increases

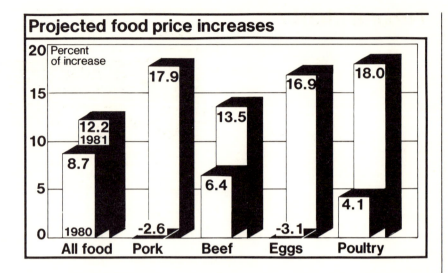

Percent of increase

	All food	Pork	Beef	Eggs	Poultry
1981	12.2	17.9	13.5	16.9	18.0
1980	8.7	-2.6	6.4	-3.1	4.1

Budget Dollar/Estimate for fiscal year 1982

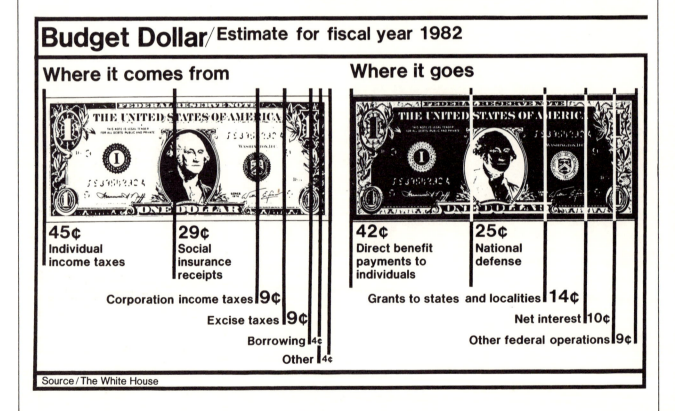

Where it comes from

45¢ Individual income taxes

29¢ Social insurance receipts

Corporation income taxes 9¢

Excise taxes 9¢

Borrowing 4¢

Other 4¢

Where it goes

42¢ Direct benefit payments to individuals

25¢ National defense

Grants to states and localities 14¢

Net interest 10¢

Other federal operations 9¢

Source/The White House

100%

Tribune charts/

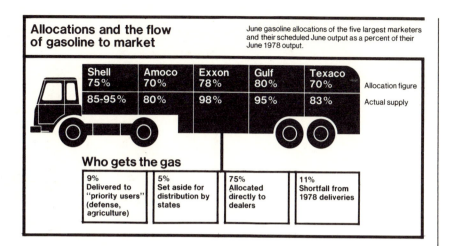

Allocations and the flow of gasoline to market

June gasoline allocations of the five largest marketers and their scheduled June output as a percent of their June 1978 output.

	Shell	Amoco	Exxon	Gulf	Texaco	
	75%	70%	78%	80%	70%	Allocation figure
	85-95%	80%	98%	95%	83%	Actual supply

Who gets the gas

9% Delivered to "priority users" (defense, agriculture)	5% Set aside for distribution by states	75% Allocated directly to dealers	11% Shortfall from 1978 deliveries

Dow Jones chart/

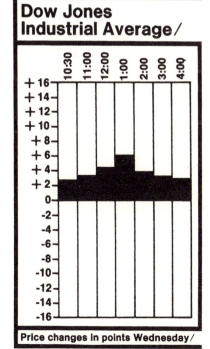

Dow Jones Industrial Average/

Price changes in points Wednesday/

Price changes in points Monday/
Price changes in points Tuesday/
Price changes in points Wednesday/
Price changes in points Thursday/
Price changes in points Friday/

100%

National weather map/
Before redesign/

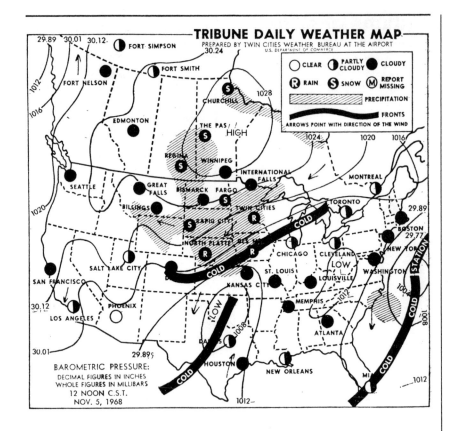

This map, furnished by the Weather Bureau, was used in the Tribune before adaptation of the regional weather map on the opposite page.

Regional weather map/
Tribune style/

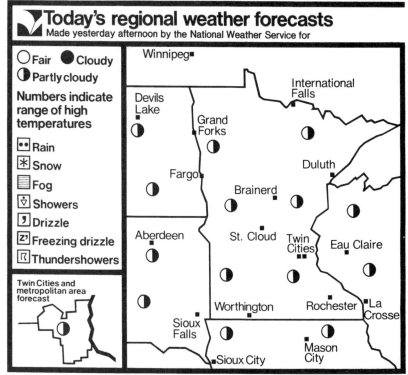

Today's regional weather forecasts
Made yesterday afternoon by the National Weather Service for

○ Fair ● Cloudy
◑ Partly cloudy

Numbers indicate range of high temperatures

•• Rain
✳ Snow
≣ Fog
▽ Showers
ʃ Drizzle
Zʼ Freezing drizzle
ℝ Thundershowers

Twin Cities and metropolitan area forecast

Winnipeg
International Falls
Devils Lake
Grand Forks
Fargo
Duluth
Brainerd
Aberdeen
St. Cloud
Twin Cities
Eau Claire
Worthington
Rochester
La Crosse
Sioux Falls
Sioux City
Mason City

The Twin Cities air pollution index is reported daily in a recorded telephone message by the Minnesota Pollution Control Agency. It's available after 2 p.m. weekdays, except holidays, at (612) 633-6698.

20/25	25/30	30/35	35/40	40/45	45/50	50/55	55/60	60/65	65/70
20/25	25/30	30/35	35/40	40/45	45/50	50/55	55/60	60/65	65/70
20/25	25/30	30/35	35/40	40/45	45/50	50/55	55/60	60/65	65/70
20/25	25/30	30/35	35/40	40/45	45/50	50/55	55/60	60/65	65/70
20/25	25/30	30/35	35/40	40/45	45/50	50/55	55/60	60/65	65/70
20/25	25/30	30/35	35/40	40/45	45/50	50/55	55/60	60/65	65/70
20/25	25/30	30/35	35/40	40/45	45/50	50/55	55/60	60/65	65/70
20/25	25/30	30/35	35/40	40/45	45/50	50/55	55/60	60/65	65/70
20/25	25/30	30/35	35/40	40/45	45/50	50/55	55/60	60/65	65/70
20/25	25/30	30/35	35/40	40/45	45/50	50/55	55/60	60/65	65/70

National weather map/

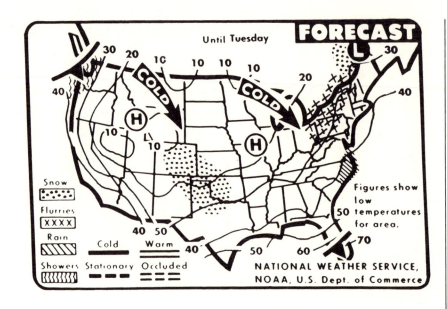

National weather map/ Tribune style/

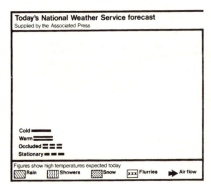

Base artwork

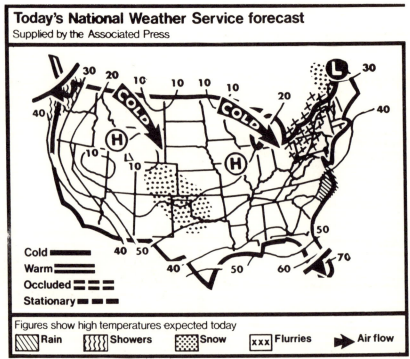

National forecast map/

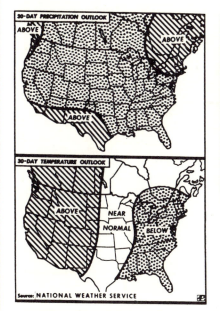

National forecast map/Tribune style/

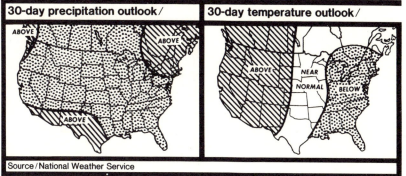

100%

Monthly weather chart/

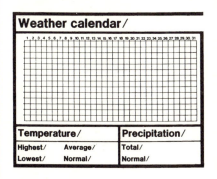

January/ July/
February/ August/
March/ September/
April/ October/
May/ November/
June/ December/

Base artwork

Weather calendar/April/

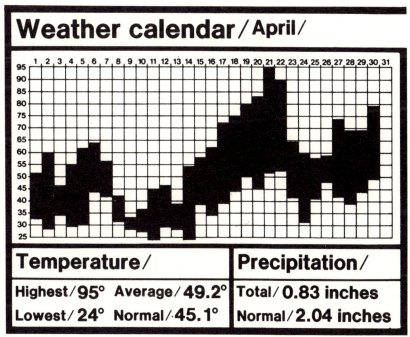

Temperature/

Highest/95° Average/49.2°

Lowest/24° Normal/45.1°

Precipitation/

Total/0.83 inches

Normal/2.04 inches

138

Yearly weather chart/

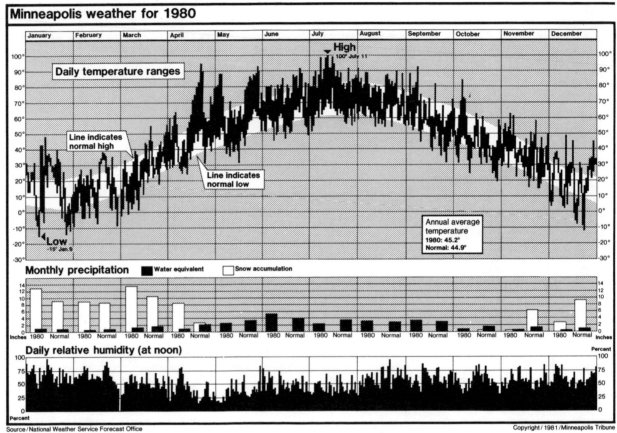

Minneapolis weather for 1980

Daily temperature ranges

Line indicates normal high

Line indicates normal low

High 100° July 11

Low -15° Jan 9

Annual average temperature
1980: 45.2°
Normal: 44.9°

Monthly precipitation Water equivalent Snow accumulation

Daily relative humidity (at noon)

Source/National Weather Service Forecast Office

Copyright / 1981 / Minneapolis Tribune

This chart showing the year's weather is
produced by the Tribune design department
annually. It's published in the newspaper and
then offered for sale on heavy stock.

50%

Chapter
8/

Design/

The results of redesign: Newspapers in the 80s

The Courier-Journal

THE·EMPORIA·GAZETTE

THE KANSAS CITY STAR.

THE MORNING CALL

The New York Times

The Providence Journal

St. Petersburg Times

San Francisco Examiner

Telegraph Herald

TIMES-UNION

The Washington Star

Introduction /

The redesign process raises some questions

What did American newspapers look like at the start of the decade of the 1980s?

How much had they been affected by the design revolution?

What paths to redesign had newspapers pursued?

How did designers and editors relate to each other in the redesign process?

Did newspapers continue to use redesigns in their original form? If not why not — and what changes were made?

How satisfactory had the work of designers been?

For hints of the answers, take a look at the news and feature pages of a few newspapers — large and small — around the country and judge for yourself.

Editors and design directors were asked to describe their newspapers' redesigns and how they came about.

The narratives here do not pretend to tell the whole story. In some cases stress is on the creative process; in others, on the details of redesign. They do offer glimpses of the redesign process — which differs from one newspaper to another — and they shed light on some of the complications of redesign.

The newspapers are not meant to be a cross-section. Others might have been chosen, and certainly many more could have been used, perhaps with greater reason.

But the experiences these newspapers have had may be typical of others. Tips and ideas flowing from them may help editors and designers in the present and in the future.

The stories describe the various ways newspapers have grappled with redesign. Some have found the results satisfying; others have gone on struggling. Some have asked a designer to do the work for them, and then have changed the design. Some have used editors as designers.

The variety of ideas is startling. So are the differences in design approach taken by the various editors. One newspaper says there can't be too many rules governing design and layout; another says any rules at all are too many.

Most newspapers stress that design must be flexible. Most find their designs constantly changing. It all leaves us with more questions:

Has knowledge of design theory been acknowledged as necessary background for those who lay out pages of newspapers?

Are the reasons for and methods of redesign well understood and well used? What is the real role of the designer?

Why have newspapers hired designers, adopted their plans and then proceeded to change them?

What is the best way to proceed on redesign: Revolution or evolution?

These questions and the following narratives and page reproductions are offered more to stimulate thinking than to suggest answers or imply conclusions.

It is worth noting again, however, that we think the Minneapolis Tribune's redesign of 1971 is as fresh and usable today as it was ten years ago. Tinkering along the way has been discouraged. At the same time, the design has been expanded and enriched, as described in the chapter on the Tribune's special sections.

The Courier-Journal/

'Designing a page for print is not art'

A pioneer in modular design, the Courier-Journal allows its news art staff considerable freedom in layout. But, as news editor Ben Post acknowledges, design must conform to the "character" of the newspaper, based on its traditions and development.

"Of course, all decisions on what goes on page one and the position a story gets on the page are based on news value," Post said. But when he is laying out a page, he tries to visualize a package that "will not only give the proper emphasis to individual stories but to the page itself."

"A design — whether a newspaper page or a painting — reflects the personality (preferences) of the designer," Post said. "And my page ones reflect my preferences. I like rules that border art, I like ruled packages, I like odd-measure type when used properly, I like balance and I like variety (within limits of the page). And I like emphasis — sometimes strong (grab the reader) and sometimes subdued (ease them into the page)."

Johnny Maupin, the Courier-Journal's news art director, expresses the newspaper's design philosophy in words about his own work:

"Every feature page that I approach I try to bring order, clarity and directness to that page. I try to make it look special, and at the same time be compatible with the over-all look of the newspaper.

"Like all designers, I want to use the combination of word and image to communicate as effectively as

---

LATE KENTUCKY EDITION — Louisville, Ky., Wednesday morning, August 6, 1980 — 25¢

The Courier-Journal

Iranians are freed after giving identities

Shelby votes to fix disputed bridge

Sen. Henry Jackson, D-Wash. (left) shared a laugh with Sen. Edward M. Kennedy, D-Mass., before the two held a meeting on Capitol Hill yesterday to talk about efforts to "open" the Democratic National Convention. Kennedy said he is considering Jackson and Senate Majority Leader Robert C. Byrd for the No. 2 spot if he wins the Democratic nomination. (Story, Page A 2.)

Carter, Kennedy agree to early vote on key rule

Support for president erodes in Graves County

'If Carter is the nominee, I'm not voting'

George Miller, left, wants to head the rubber workers' local in Mayfield. David Herndon holds the post.

Reagan calls for tax cuts to help inner-city areas

INSIDE

The Courier-Journal/

possible.

"I have a lot of preferences when it comes to designing a page, but I know that the printed page should not be a medium for self-expression. Designing a page for print is not art. Designing is a highly skilled, sensitive, creative craft. It is in no way related to painting."

Maupin describes the Accent page shown here:

"The strong image of Custer was used to draw attention to the accompanying story. The line conversions and rule lines were used to give the story a feeling of the past.

"The bottom story on the Bedford stonecutters gave me the opportunity to use a special typeface to fit the mood of the subject. The cluttered backgrounds of the photos were dropped out. I used line conversions of the monuments in order to show more detail."

Herman Wiederwohl, a member of the news art staff, describes his design for the Accent page shown:

"I take a somewhat spontaneous and natural approach to design and illustration. I get absorbed in the story and hopefully reach a point of understanding and caring about the subject. Since I'm the father of two small children, my feelings for the death of a child were predictable.

"From my first reading I knew I wanted the mood of the page to be soft and delicate and dignified. I had no clear image in mind but I wanted to put a lump in the reader's throat. The final solution for this page came about during the research for my first idea.

"I was going to create a montage, using a photo album and various

---

The Courier-Journal, Monday morning, July 28, 1980   B 5

ACCENT

NOSTALGIA

Before Custer was sent back to the Indians

By JEAN HOWERTON COADY
Courier-Journal Staff Writer

THE SCENE is a grand ball at Louisville's second Galt House at First and Main 108 years ago. The man in the full-dress black uniform with the Imperial Cross of the Russian royal family is Grand Duke Alexis, son of Czar Alexander II, who is on a good-will tour of America.

The tall gent with the bright golden hair and beard, clad in an olive-gray uniform lavishly tinseled with gold braid and set off with a large scarlet necktie, is Gen. George Armstrong Custer, Civil War veteran and Indian fighter.

What on earth brought these two together? Custer, who was living in Elizabethtown, Ky., at the time, had been engaged to take the duke on a "grand buffalo hunt" in Nebraska. It was from Elizabethtown that the ducal train pulled into Louisville on Jan. 30, 1872.

The 22-year-old duke upstaged the general on this occasion, for Louisvillians had been preparing a welcome for the royal visitor since his arrival in New York two months earlier.

A crowd of 1,000 greeted the train and "a few impertinent street Arabs shouted 'Howdy, Aleck'," according to The Courier-Journal. Flags and bunting were out and throngs lined the streets "and all the windows were filled, many with charming ladies who waved their lacy handkerchiefs as the cortege passed."

Kentucky Gen. William Preston, who had been U.S. minister to Spain, welcomed the duke, speaking of "the unaltered friendships between our two great countries. May this strong bond never be severed."

The duke was said to be "visibly affected" and grasped Preston's hand in "a good old-fashioned Kentucky handshake."

The newspaper reported that the Galt House "was in a blaze of glory" for the ball. "The radiance that streamed from the stately chandeliers lit up a scene that is witnessed but once in a lifetime . . . All of Beauty and Fashion had gathered to do honor to the royal guest . . . It was an outpouring of Kentucky's fairest daughters and most gallant sons, and with what exquisite grace the Kentucky belles floated through the measures of the lancers, the polka and the waltz!"

The duke led the Grand Quadrille with Mrs. Preston. Mrs. Custer, in blue grosgrain with white satin piping, was the partner of General Preston. A Mrs. Johnston "danced gracefully with Count Bodisco, the Russian Consul General, in a gown of pale green satin looped with black velvet ribbon and scarlet morning glories." (Presumably Mrs. Johnston and not the consul general wore the gown.)

"Forty carefully selected musicians" were concealed behind a screen of rosebuds. There were 68 dishes on the menu. So much for Grand Duke Alexis.

As for General Custer, he took up residence in Elizabethtown with part of his famous Seventh Cavalry in 1871 and stayed there two years. After the Civil War, in which he was the youngest Union Army general at 23, he served five years on frontier duty, then was sent to Kentucky "to break up illicit distilleries and to control the Ku Klux Klan and carpetbaggers."

Custer kept a racing stable and a pack of at least 40 hounds. His wife wrote in her book, "Boots and Saddles," that dogs were all over the house in bad weather. "The steam from their shaggy coats was stifling, but the General begged so hard for them that I taught myself to endure the air at last."

The Custers were active in the social life of Elizabethtown, and the general was noted for changing his costume from uniform to civilian clothes several times a day. His book, "My Life on the Plains," was written in what is now the Brown-Pusey House there.

Custer's humdrum life as a country squire was broken when he was summoned to military police duty after the great Chicago fire of 1871 and again by the buffalo hunt with Grand Duke Alexis.

In the spring of 1873, Custer and his men were sent West to deal with Indians.

In 1876, Custer and his 264 men were wiped out by Indian tribes which had been united by Sioux Chief Sitting Bull at the Battle of the Little Big Horn in Montana.

Custer's widow survived a long time. She visited friends in Kentucky in 1880. When she was interviewed in 1926 on the 50th anniversary of her husband's death, she spoke with fondness of her stay in Elizabethtown. She died in 1933 at the age of 90.

BEDFORD STONECUTTERS: MASTERS' MEMORIALS

By LARRY GREEN
© The Los Angeles Times

BEDFORD, Ind. — They are called cutters. They have worked in the limestone hills here for more than 150 years, tearing giant blocks — 5, 8, 10, 20 tons — from the ground.

Some labored in mills slicing the cubes into building slabs for the Pentagon and Rockefeller Center, the National Cathedral, the Canadian Bank of Commerce and rails across the country.

Others carved the bas-reliefs and friezes for the cornices of some of America's most impressive buildings. The gothic crown of the Chicago Tribune Building and the clockwork statues on top of Grand Central Station are monuments to the craft.

This the artisans did for money; it was their job. But there are other monuments to their work, sculptures cut from love and shaped in sorrow. They sit in the center of town here, not far from the county courthouse square, in the Green Hill Cemetery, delicate stone memorials to children, parents, colleagues.

Evaldo Dau, who died in 1894 at the age of 7, rests beneath an empty pair of high-button shoes, so carefully carved that they appear soft. Next to them leans her straw hat, a ribbon of stone tied tightly around its brim. And a delicate dove is perched, an olive branch in its beak.

Not far away is a remarkable reproduction of a stonecutter's workbench, the nails, cracks in the wood, even the grain of the wood, reproduced in minute detail. Atop the bench is a stone cornice and atop it are the tools of a stonecutter: a hammer, chisels, mallets, a broom and a carelessly tossed, wrinkled apron.

This incredible monument stands over the grave of Louis Baker. He was a 23-year-old apprentice stonecutter who died in 1917. Bessie Wilson, 81, the cemetery's caretaker, said that young Baker died on a weekend and that he was so loved by his fellow workers that they reproduced the workbench exactly as their young colleague left when he went home, for the last time, on Friday night.

Tom Bardon died in 1937 pursuing one of his loves, golf. A life-size statue of him standing next to a meticulously carved golf bag and complete set of golf clubs marks his grave.

Michael F. Wallner was 22 when he was wounded in World War I. From July 20, 1918, until his death on June 3, 1940, he was hospitalized. His grave is marked by a doughboy, carved so precisely that every crease in his uniform is there. "They say it looks just like him," caretaker Wilson said.

There are other monuments: angels that might have been decorating the finest cathedral, little sheep carved over the graves of children and one giant column topped off with a statue of a stonecutter, his apron tied carelessly around his waist.

In his hands are the tools he used to earn his living and to carve his love.

The grave of Mitchael P. Wallner, wounded in World War I, is marked by a doughboy, carved so precisely that every crease in his uniform is there

Other examples of the stonecutters' surprisingly delicate art include this grave site surmounted by tender hearts

This incredibly detailed monument stands over the grave of Louis Baker, a 23-year-old apprentice stonecutter who died in 1917. He was loved by his fellow workers that they reproduced the workbench exactly as their young colleague left it when he went home for the last time.

It's not only colleagues who are recognized by the stonecutters. This child, complete with ruffled collar and air of innocence, stands atop another grave site

The Courier-Journal/

childhood toys to convey the notion that we are left only with the memories and some tangible remnants when a child dies.

"While browsing through my family albums, I happened upon a closeup of my daughter at age 3 as well as a series of photo studies I did of tulips in various states of bloom. The two images clicked.

"The idea of a tulip petal dropping off to signify the end of life pretty much hooked me and the page fell together naturally from here on.

"My main intent is always to find an appropriate image and to wed that image with appropriate typography to create a visual mood which suits the content of the story."

The Courier-Journal redesigned its section flags and logos in late 1978, to achieve a bolder look and a consistency of design style.

ACCENT   G

When death takes your child

By JOE WARD, Courier-Journal Staff Writer

> 'A child's death is out of sequence. It is loss of control, loss of expectation. All the dreams you had for that child are gone, maybe with one phone call. You don't know what that's like until it happens to you.'

IT IS A basement room — bare concrete floor, acoustical ceiling tile, folding tables set up in the center, folding chairs around the tables and along the walls.

The men and women in the chairs make up a noticeably non-homogeneous group. They are of different ages and economic levels, and at first there is not much interaction.

But as the business begins, their bond becomes clear. "I'm Janet Wilder," one woman says. "My son, Dudley, was killed almost four years ago in a house fire. He was 12."

The people listen. "I'm Julie McGee," another says. "My daughter, Julie, was 24 when she was killed in an automobile accident two and a half years ago."

The next woman introduces herself, and then a man does. It is a grim progression. It covers death by accident, disease, murder; death that was expected and death that wasn't. The victims were children or in their 20s.

Occasionally a person shakes his head without speaking, indicating he cannot, and the turn passes. Some make an effort to speak only to have their voices tremble and go out of control. There cannot be a throat in the room without a lump in it.

But there is something that is not grim there, too, something positive that is noticeable with the first introductions, that becomes marked as introductions lead into discussion. The people respond to one another.

A young woman straining to control her voice complains that her mother will listen all day if she says she's having problems with her husband, but will change the subject immediately when it touches on her dead child.

Blank faces along the wall kindle with recognition and sympathy. They understand, and it is a relief to all of them that they do.

People who have suffered the death of a child, Julie McGee said later, don't get much real comfort from people who have not.

"A child's death is out of sequence," she said. "It is loss of control, loss of expectation. All the dreams you had for that child are gone, maybe with one phone call. You don't know what that's like until it happens to you."

The bereaved are plunged into a nightmare world of nagging questions: How could I let this happen? What if I had been more careful? Why my child? They go over all the details again and again, looking for the fatal flaw, trying to find an answer that will explain it for better or for worse and let them be.

All the feelings are there, she said: "Pain, sorrow, anguish, extreme weariness, betrayal, guilt, anger, self-pity — fear that you're losing your mind."

Friends and relatives say, "Be strong," and after awhile they suggest it's time to stop crying. And the bereaved, Mrs. McGee said, see that people don't understand. They worry that no one will, that the pain will never go away and they cannot survive.

When they meet someone who does understand, who has survived, it is a revelation and a relief.

Mrs. McGee discovered that the hard way, thrashing about disconsolate and hopeless after the death of her grown daughter, until she met a woman who had lost a son and who understood.

"I learned that you won't find peace until you find people who can help you out some of your worries to rest," she said.

The woman she found was Janet Wilder, and the two joined with a third woman — Grace Manske — to form an association of people who have suffered the death of a child. There are people who attend the meetings who can't imagine life without the organization.

Those three women were not the first to discover the need of bereaved parents for the company of those who have suffered the same loss. The group they formed — in November, 1978 — was a local chapter of what already was an international organization: The Compassionate Friends, founded in England in 1969.

The Rev. Wayne Willis and Nancy Lange had noticed the same need at Norton-Children's Hospitals, where Willis is chaplain and Mrs. Lange was a nurse. Hospital staff members would come to know parents of children in the hospital, and then lose touch with them when their need was perhaps greatest — after their children had died.

Mrs. Lange herself lost a child 11 years ago, and she was especially concerned that something be done for such parents. "I can't even describe the emptiness you feel when you walk out of the hospital with nothing," she said.

A group called Bereaved Parents has been meeting monthly at the hospital since 1977. Like that of The Compassionate Friends chapter, its structure is informal and its meetings are open to anyone who has lost a child and to siblings and other relatives of a dead child.

The meetings give grieving parents a chance to talk about some of the things that are happening to them, things that need to be talked about but that other people don't seem to understand.

The groups, Willis said, are there to "support people — to reach out and say there's help, there's hope, you can make it."

But they also are there, he said, so that people can learn from one another how to go on, not to have "unrealistic expectations."

Life, he said, is never the same for a person who has lost a child. "Even when you're old and gray, there will still be some grief." He conceded that he might sound pessimistic.

But things that are pessimistic to some people aren't necessarily so to others. Discussion at a meeting of bereaved parents has its own perspective.

At a recent Compassionate Friends meeting, for example, Barbara Calhoun talked about a wrenching visit to a dentist's office. She had experienced a bad reaction to a local anesthetic — it made her cry — and had been sent to another dentist who used gas. That was worse. "I was hysterical," she recalled. "I was terrified. The dentist asked me what I was afraid of, and I said, 'I'm afraid I'll die. I don't want to die.'"

The dentist switched off the gas, brought her around with oxygen and suggested they delay the dental work, and it is not clear what he thought. But the people at the meeting were not horrified.

They knew, as Mrs. Calhoun went on to say, that it was a positive experience.

"It was the first I knew I didn't want to die," she said. "Since then things have begun to look up. I realized I can live again."

"You learn," Julie McGee said, "that you have survived the worst thing that can happen to you."

Mrs. Calhoun worries that there are bereaved parents in the community who don't know about the groups.

Her 18-year-old daughter, Kim, was killed in a traffic accident 20 months earlier. She had allowed the girl to go to Greensburg for a weekend and she got the call from there.

She refused to believe it. She felt extreme anger toward her sister for calling her and telling her a thing like that when it wasn't true. She called the mother of another girl who had taken the trip with her daughter and said not to worry, that there had really been no accident.

"There's no explaining it," she said. "I lost my parents, a brother, a sister, a brother-in-law, my father-in-law, and I could have sworn I knew what hurt was. I woke up the next morning and was totally amazed that a car was driving down the street. I thought the whole world had stopped."

Four or five weeks later, the pain was only worse. "It's real pain," she said. "It feels like somebody is tearing your guts out. I was going berserk. Nobody understood what I was going through."

A friend saw an article about The Compassionate Friends group and brought her a clipping. "I went totally insane," she said. "I thought, 'Somebody cares and somebody will know how I feel.'"

Grace Manske, whose phone number she found in the article, happened to be out of town, and Mrs. Calhoun dialed the phone "constantly" for three days. Finally, someone answered.

"I don't want anybody to have to go through what I went through those first weeks," she said.

The Compassionate Friends group meets monthly and has a list of members who are willing to talk with bereaved parents at any time. The group can be reached through the Louisville Crisis and Information Center, 589-4313.

The Bereaved Parents group has spawned two other general groups — at Corydon, Ind., and Elizabethtown, Ky. — and one specialized group, for parents who have suffered miscarriages and stillbirths.

Willis, who can be reached at Norton-Children's Hospitals — 589-8175 or 589-8000 — has information on those groups.

Mrs. Calhoun said she and others are in the process of establishing another specialized group — for the siblings of dead children. She can be reached through The Compassionate Friends.

AS ANYONE knows who has ever tried, it is difficult to talk to a parent who has lost a child.

Julie McGee, coordinator of the Louisville chapter of The Compassionate Friends — an organization of bereaved parents — says no one who has not lost a child can really understand how it feels.

She says bereaved parents themselves recognize how misguided were their past efforts to console a friend or relative in the same situation. So the organization has compiled a list of do's and don't's.

Do

✔ Be available, to listen, to run errands and to help with housework and other children.

✔ Say you are sorry about what happened to their child and about their pain.

✔ Allow them to express grief without holding back. Listen if they want to talk about the child, as much and as often as they want to.

✔ Encourage them to be patient with themselves, not to expect too much of themselves and not to impose any "shoulds" on themselves.

✔ Talk to them about the special, endearing qualities of the child who has died.

✔ Give special attention to the child's brothers and sisters, at the funeral and later.

✔ Reassure parents about the care their child received, but be careful not to say anything that is obviously not true.

Don't

✔ Avoid them because you are uncomfortable.

✔ Say you know how they feel unless you have lost a child yourself.

✔ Tell them they've grieved long enough and "ought to be feeling better by now." Your guess at an appropriate timetable probably is short. Avoid telling them, in general, what they "should" feel and do.

✔ Change the subject when they mention their dead child.

✔ Worry about mentioning their child's name. You won't make them think of him; they probably are doing that anyway.

✔ Try to point out some bright side. They don't want to hear, "At least you have your other children," or, "At least you can have another child," or, "At least you had the child for a while."

✔ Try to commiserate with them by saying the child's case was bungled by the doctors or the hospital or someone else involved. They will be plagued by guilt and feelings of inadequacy without any help from you.

— By Staff Artist Herbert Borchardt

The Emporia Gazette/

W.L. White's redesign dates back to 1958

The Emporia Gazette was a pioneer in redesign. A frequent winner of awards for typography, the Gazette stands out because of the size and elegance of its headline type and its airy appearance.

The late W. L. White, then editor of the Gazette, told how the redesign came about, in the September 1979 issue of SEMINAR Quarterly.

White began to redesign the Gazette in 1958, when he said it was "a mixture of thick, black Gothic type, indistinguishable from the mass of big and little city papers except for some arty-minded ones who had gone to Bodoni and a few who stuck with Caslon."

White first eliminated all black type, which, he said, "burns out everything for a considerable distance around it — making the body type look thin and pale and unreadable — like a small star near a full moon."

Emphasis is necessary, White said, and he got it by "careful use of white space, and not by squirting thick gobs of black ink in the reader's eye."

Which font, White asked, was the most readable?

"My rule here," he decided, "is that the letters should not be distorted. All condensed fonts were immediately eliminated, and of course I decided that my headlines should be upper and lower case."

White had no use for publishers who were shortening ascenders and descenders so "those smart guys could crowd more lines into a column

---

THE·EMPORIA·GAZETTE

91st Year, No. 13 — Wednesday, the Sixteenth Day of July, MCMLXXX — Thirty Pages

Industrial Production Declines
Recession

U.S. Economists Say Drop Signals Additional Layoffs

Racial Violence Erupts in Miami
* * *

Policemen Reported Wounded

City Commission To Meet Tonight

Two Accused Of Abduction
Crime

Emporans Are Held In Kidnapping Here

By Lee Markowitz Ringler

Good Evening

Today's Forecast
EMPORIA and VICINITY

Emporia Weather

A BAD YEAR FOR ROASTING EARS—The corn crop in Lyon County, as in most of the Midwest, is suffering from the prolonged heat, lack of moisture and hot winds. (Photograph by Gert Miglelicz)

Draft Registration to Begin Monday
At Emporia Post Office....
By Jerry Underwood

Heat Wave Death Toll Jumps to 44
TOPEKA, Kan. (AP)

Florida's Congressman Is Indicted on Tuesday
Abscam Probe....

WASHINGTON (AP)

Reagan-Ford Ticket Being Discussed
Republican National Convention....

DETROIT (AP)

Iranian Council Closes Borders To Stop Conspirators' Escape

The Emporia Gazette/

inch." The price, he said, was unreadability resulting from loss of white space between lines and a possible confusion of similar looking letters.

"If a line of type is to be readable," he wrote, "differences between letters should be emphasized so that there can be no possibility of confusion. Generous ascenders and descenders achieve this . . . and produce a paragraph with plenty of white space between lines."

White found his typeface in Cloister, a descendant of a type designed by Nicholas Jenson, who got his inspiration from the majestic capitals on Trajan's column in Rome.

White recalls that when he ordered Cloister from Linotype in Brooklyn, "they almost panicked." Why? Cloister was used only for books and Bibles, he was told: "Nobody would think of using it in a newspaper!"

"That only convinced me that I was right," White wrote. "For the publishers of books and Bibles seek high readability and are far more skilled knowing how to get it than the average newspaper publisher, who has one eye on his cash register, thinking of shortcuts and how to save paper."

White decided not to mix type families, for the sake of readability. He used the italic version of Cloister — one without too much slant — for contrast and emphasis.

The Gazette, White said, was one of the first newspapers to drop column rules; again, the reason was readability.

Headlines do not shout in the Gazette. White foresaw no newsprint shortage, we may assume, but he had a good reason for choosing small

THE·EMPORIA·GAZETTE

91st Year, No. 17 — *Monday, the Twenty-first Day of July*, MCMLXXX — Eighteen Pages

Bolivia:

Miners Battle Rulers

★★★

Fighting Reported In La Paz

LA PAZ, Bolivia (AP) — Miners in southern Bolivia said they were still battling the new military government and reported heavy casualties as sporadic gunfire continued in La Paz through the nightly curfew. Troop convoys traveled the capital's streets all night.

The junta that overthrew the civilian government on Thursday claimed in a communique it had eliminated all resistance. It threatened to fire all workers who did not abandon the general strike against its rule that began Friday.

The mine workers' clandestine Democratic Solidarity Radio said the miners in the southern Santa Ana district on Sunday fought the troops sent there by the junta and captured three tanks. The broadcast reported "many casualties" and "a lot of working-class blood has been shed."

The miners' radio also reported heavy fighting in the mining city of Huanuni, and sources in La Paz said air force jets were strafing the miners. But other reports reaching La Paz said there were only minor skirmishes in the mining districts and that the troops returned to their barracks.

No confirmation was available of any of the reports.

The commanders of the three armed forces took over the government to prevent leftist ex-President Hernan Siles Zuazo from being elected president by the new Congress, but Siles Zuazo escaped and went into hiding. He sent a taped message to the news media Sunday calling on Bolivians to support the general strike and overthrow the junta.

He said the junta, which ousted interim President Lidia Gueiler and named the army commander Gen. Luis Garcia Meza as president, would make Bolivia "a huge cemetery in the very heart of South America. This regime of national destruction will not consolidate itself as long as there is a people ready to fight against it."

Siles Zuazo appealed to the Roman Catholic Church, the International Red Cross and human rights organizations to "demand the names of the dead, so the sad story of missing people in other countries under military regimes will not be repeated."

BOTTLENECK – Zack Henning, age 7, of Americus, concentrates and leans every inch he has over the rail at a "Bottle Pitch" game at the Americus Days festivities. The soft drink prizes were a big lure for the booth Friday through Sunday. (Photograph by Owen Stayner)

Planners to Meet On Tuesday Night

The Metropolitan Area Planning Commission will begin its annual review of Emporia's comprehensive plan at its meeting Tuesday at 7 P.M. in the Civic Building.

The planners will consider a request to vacate an alley easement in the Ranchview Addition, and they will discuss possible changes in the zoning regulations pertaining to nonconforming uses.

☆ ☆ ☆

Budget on Agenda For School Board

The Emporia Board of Education will give preliminary approval to 1980-81 district budgets at its meeting Tuesday at 4 P.M. at Village Elementary School.

The board will approve 1980-81 student and faculty handbooks for Lowther Middle School, and, in closed session, will discuss property acquisition.

☆ ☆ ☆

Baghdad:

Iraq Rejects U.S. Proposal

Diplomatic Relations Will Remain Severed

BAGHDAD, Iraq (AP) – Iraq has rebuffed American proposals for restoration of diplomatic relations despite increasing trade between the two countries and shared views on Iran and Afghanistan, Western diplomatic sources say.

The sources here in the Iraqi capital say President Saddam Hussein's government also rejected overtures, relayed through third parties, for a meeting between Secretary of State Edmund Muskie and Foreign Minister Saadoum Hamadi.

Relations "will remain severed until a substantive change occurs in the U.S. position on the Arab-Zionist conflict," said Hamadi in a recent interview with the Beirut magazine Monday Morning.

"The severance of relations with the U.S. was not prompted by secondary or bilateral considerations, but by American hostility toward the Palestinians and support of Israel. The United States seizes every opportunity to try to persuade us to restore relations, but we refuse, and we will continue to refuse until a major change occures in the American position."

"It's just that one thing that's in the way," said one diplomat.

Iraq broke diplomatic relations with the United States during the 1967 Arab-Israeli war. However, a U.S. Interests Section staffed by 14 Americans operates in the Belgian Embassy. It monitors commercial and political affairs and issues visas.

☆ ☆ ☆

Extended Forecast

Kansas extended forecast, Wednesday through Friday – Little or no precipitation. Lows in 60s northwest and 70s elsewhere. High 95 to 105.

Iran:

Plotters Executed In Tehran

Parliament Elects Militant Moslem Cleric as Speaker

By the Associated Press

Five officers died in the first executions of the military plotters against Ayatollah Ruhollah Khomeini. Meanwhile, the new Parliament elected a militant Moslem cleric as its speaker, and Khomeini called on it to purge the government of those who are not "100 percent Islamic."

The five military men, a retired brigadier general and four air force officers, were executed at 1 a.m. Sunday by firing squad at Tehran's Evin prison, Radio Tehran reported.

The five were among some 500 Iranians, many of them military men, who were rounded up a week ago on charges of plotting to overthrow the government.

Radio Tehran said a special Islamic court convicted the five men Saturday of planning to "establish an American social-democratic system and bring back the treacherous fugitive Bakhtiar, preparing 35 to 50 jet planes for the operation and for bombarding the Imam's (Khomeini's) reesidency, bombarding other sensitive places and highly populated areas, and preparing printed material to be distributed in various cities."

Shahpour Bakhtiar was the last prime minister appointed by Shah Mohammad Reza Pahlavi before Khomeini's revolution overthrew him. Now an exile in Paris, he escaped an assassination attempt last Friday.

The new Parliament, or Majlis, elected as its speaker Hojjatoleslam Ali Akbar Rafsanjani, a leader of the powerful Islamic Republican Party which controls the assembly. Many of the party's members want the 52 American hostages, who today spend their 261st day in captivity, to be tried as spies.

The election of the speaker was the final organizational step for the Majlis, and it can now turn to such business as the election of a prime minister and members of his cabinet, such pressing matters as economic reconstruction and the fate of the hostages.

In an address to the nation, Khomeini criticized the army and government for "indecisiveness" and told the it "must decide on a government which is 100 percent Islamic and not accept anv minister like some of the present ministers."

"The Majlis should not accept anybody with the slightest doubt of his commitment to Islam," the leader of the revolution said.

This was viewed as a call for a cabinet of Moslem militants rather than Westernized moderates favored by President Abolhassan Bani-Sadr.

Good Evening

One gardener reports his green beans have turned into "has-beans."

☆ ☆ ☆

Today's Forecast

KANSAS – Partly cloudy with scattered thunderstorms, mostly west and south tonight. Cooler tonight. Low around 60 northwest, around 70 southeast. Sunny Tuesday. High around 90 north, mid 90s south.

EMPORIA AND VICINITY – Clear to partly cloudy tonight and Tuesday. Cooler tonight, lows in low to mid 60s. Highs Tuesday around 90. Northeasterly winds diminishing to less than 10 mph tonight.

☆ ☆ ☆

Emporia Weather

1 P.M.	85 degrees
High Sunday	105 degrees
Low last night	72 degrees
Barometer	30.11 steady
Humidity	55 percent
Winds	NE 9

☆ ☆ ☆

State Department Workers Welcome Freed Diplomat

WASHINGTON (AP) – Fighting back tears, freed American hostage Richard Queen returned to the State Department today to a tumultuous welcome, telling his cheering colleagues that "You all know how much I love to be back."

Thousands of department workers crowded into a lobby to greet him. He was hugged by two secretaries freed from Iran in November. "This is just the first step back for the other 52," Secretary of State Edmund S. Muskie said.

At a press conference, Queen said his Iranian captors were mostly dedicated Moslem students who made no real effort to turn him against the United States.

"There was no brainwashing," Queen said. He said he was treated well by the militants who have held the U.S. Embassy in Tehran since November, although there were "a few S.O.B.'s."

The 28-year-old diplomat, set free because of a neurological illness, said he was out of touch with most of the 52 other American hostages, but he was confident that they would survive their ordeal.

"I think they are pretty strong people," the bearded former vice consul said.

Queen told a news conference after the ceremony that he taught himself French during more than eight months in captivity, played penny-poker with a roommate and read hundreds of books from the U.S. Embassy library.

He said his captors "didn't care what we did as long as we didn't escape."

Queen, who can speak Farsi, said some of the militants were "really fine people" while there were "a few S.O.B.s."

He flatly rejected any suggestion that those who seized the embassy last November and have held it since were Communists.

"They were zealous, Islamic – and, as far as I know, students," Queen said.

Budget:

Joblessness To Reach 8.5 Percent

Tax Cut Plan Rejected by Carter Administration

WASHINGTON (AP) – The Carter administration, rejecting any tax cut plan at this time, officially conceded Monday there will be no balanced budget in fiscal 1981, but instead a $30 billion deficit.

In addition, the administration says its fiscal 1980 deficit will jump from an estimated $36.5 billion to $61 billion, reflecting the country's decline into recession, higher defense spending and surprise events including the eruption of Mt. St. Helens and the flood of Cuban refugees.

The administration – in its mid-year budget review – also predicted that the recession will push unemployment to 8.5 percent by the end of this year. Joblessness will remain at about that level through 1981, it said.

Some private economists expect the jobless rate to reach close to 9 percent.

Even the 8.5 percent projection is far higher than the 7.2 percent jobless rate predicted by Carter's economic advisers in March.

The overall economy should decline by 3.1 percent this year and then rebound modestly by 2.6 percent in 1981, the new forecast says.

Inflation, meanwhile, will increase by 12 percent between 1979's fourth quarter and this year's fourth quarter – slightly less than originally predicted and by just under 10 percent in 1981 – a bit more than expected.

Currently, consumer prices are rising at a 10.9 percent yearly pace.

"These economic prospects are not acceptable to the administration," said James T. McIntyre Jr., director of the Office of Management and Budget.

To combat the deteriorating economy, McIntyre said, "It is quite likely a tax cut will be desirable in 1981."

But, he stressed: "It is not appropriate to propose one now."

"The administration believes strongly that the last months of a congressional session, in an election year, are not the time to make the judicious decisions needed for a skillfully-designed tax program to improve economic performance," said McIntyre.

That tax reduction should be aimed heavily toward increasing investment and productivity, he said.

In contrast, Republican presidential nominee Ronald Reagan is calling for quick enactment of a $36 billion tax cut, effective Jan. 1, and congressional Democrats are hoping to unveil a plan of their own by early September.

Senate and House hearings on a tax cut begin this week.

No Crowd at Post Office. . . .

Draft Registration Begins Here

By Lynn Bonney

When the Emporia Post Office opened for business at 8:30 this morning, a dozen people were waiting. They had not come to register for the draft. The lone man in the line was obviously of retirement age. The 11 others were women.

Nine minutes later, two 20-year-old Emporians became the first local men to register for the draft.

Bobby Armitage of 1213 Frontier Way was born Feb. 20, 1960, and Michael Hirt of Rt. 2 was born Jan. 2 of the same year. Each filled out a card giving his name, sex, date of birth, current and permanent addresses and Social Security number.

After postal clerks check the information against other identification, such as driver's licenses, the forms will be returned to the Selective Service. Within 90 days, registrants will receive, instead of draft cards, verification letters from the Selective Service.

As of now, there is no draft and has been none since 1973. President Carter has said he has no intention of asking Congress to reimpose the draft. But reinstating registration, which stopped five years ago, could shorten by almost a month the time it would take for a callup, if one became necessary, officials say.

"Who really wants to be drafted?" the young men joked as they prepared to fill out the cards.

"If the country really needed us, we'd go," Mr. Hirt said, "but I don't think anything that's going on now is a real crisis."

"I didn't think it would happen, but it's happening," Mr. Armitage said.

It almost didn't happen.

Late Friday, a Federal court of appeals blocked registration as unconstitutional because the process excludes women. That ruling was reversed Saturday by Supreme Court Associate Justice William Brennan. However, the full Supreme Court will have to decide the constitutionality of the Selective Service Act.

In explaining his order, Justice Brennan indicated that the Supreme Court could go either way in the case. But he said a failure to proceed with registration in the meantime could cause foreign policy and military problems, while the government could destroy the computerized information it has collected if the law is eventually found to be unconstitutional.

Four million men are expected to register at local post offices during the next two weeks. Men born in January, February or March of 1960 are to register today. Those born in April, May or June register Tuesday, those born in July, August or September register on Wednesday, and those born in October, November or December register on Thursday. Men who are unable to register on the scheduled day may register on Friday.

The same schedule will be repeated next week for those born in 1961. Men with 1962 birthdates will register in January. After that, all young men must register on their 18th birthday anniversary.

Failure to register carries a maximum penalty of five years in prison and a $10,000 fine.

Despite the possible penalties, leaders of draft protest movements planned demonstrations across the country. Several peaceful protests, including one near the White House, were held over the weekend.

Police were called to the Emporia Post Office about 10:15 this

(See Draft, page 2)

Ground Shifting. . . .

Heat, Drought Causing Breaks in Water Mains

By Lea Markowitz Ringler

There is a problem underfoot.

Emporia City Engineer Lee Stolfus said Emporia is suffering the same conditions as the rest of the Midwest. That is, the extreme heat and drought are causing the ground to shift, resulting in damage to underground pipes.

As an example, a water main under 12th Avenue split about midnight Sunday. The longitudinal crack was estimated to be about 12 feet long.

That crack is not the only water main problem the city has dealt with during the current heat wave. Mr. Stolfus said similar splits have ocurred and will probably continue to occur. The situation is "not routine, but its not abnormal," he said. "It is something we can anticipate, though."

Twelfth Avenue from Union Street to Exchange Street was barracaded to traffic after the split was discovered. Mr. Stolfus said city crews were working to replace the split section of cast iron pipe and repair the street. He said he hoped to have the avenue reopened by noon today. Another smaller crack was discovered in the main about two blocks east of the first crack. Mr. Stolfus estimated it would be repaired by this afternoon.

"The extreme heat has shifted the top few feet of ground," Mr. Stolfus said. The older cast iron pipe cannot take the added stress. Mr. Stolfus added that water mains are now made of a pipe that is also cast iron, but has a greater flexibility. Water mains are buried about five feet below the surface. He indicated that the newer pipe has withstood the stress so far this summer.

City water customers in the immediate "split" area were without water. Mr. Stolfus said that included the Cambridge House Apartments and businesses along 12th Avenue. "We will get (the main) repaired as quick as we can, though," Mr. Stolfus said.

OPPOSES REGISTRATION – Edward Rehwinkle, a member of an anti-draft registration group, explains his activities to Emporia police officers Cris Ramirez, left, and John Green. Mr. Rehwinkle's group is handing out anti-registration information at the Emporia Post Office, where registration began this morning. (Photograph by Geri Migielicz)

The Emporia Gazette/

headline type.

The newspaper, White said, was designed to be read in your lap — not on a newsstand or pinned to a wall. So why use big headlines? Viewed from a distance, White admitted, The Gazette looks gray. Not so if it's held in the lap, he said.

Many of these design ideas — adopted by so many newspapers since 1958 — gave White what he wanted: a more readable newspaper. His goals were similar to those of designers since his time:

"We get contrast and emphasis, yes, but nothing is done which will detract the reader from the meaning of what he is trying to read."

The results, said White in 1969:

" . . . The Gazette has been winning awards with monotonous regularity since 1960, when we were the smallest paper ever to win the Ayer award."

Page 4

THE GAZETTE

William Allen White, 1895 - 1944
William Lindsay White, 1944 - 197?

Rev. James Beals, *Sports Manager* — Glenn Edward Johnson, *Promotion Foreman*
Glen Albert Bradshaw, *Production Manager* — Durrell Lee Rangel, *Circulation Manager*
Everett Rex Call, *Managing Editor* — Elizabeth Thomas Robinson, *Advertising Manager*

THE GAZETTE, EMPORIA, KANSAS — Monday, July 21, 1980

The Rustmobile
By Russell Baker

Misfire

VIRTUALLY every day for the past two weeks someone has called to ask if The Gazette will publish William Lindsay White's powerful "Prayer for Rain."

The prayer first appeared on April 27, 1935, and that night a three-inch rain broke the drought that had parched Emporia...

You Should Read

Prayer for Rain

AS a dues-paying member of the Congregational Church, the writer is entitled, under its creed, to address his Maker directly in prayer, without the intervention of prelate, saint, parson or priest, in any place, on any subject, at any time, and in our own language.

So here goes: O Lord, in Thy mercy, grant us a rain, and by that we don't mean a shower...

Discovering Detroit
By Mary McGrory

20 Years Ago

40 Years Ago

W. L. White

The Kansas City Star/

Goal of redesign was to channel creativity

"Behind The Star redesign are a few basic concepts," the newspaper's design manual states. "Closely adhered to, these ideas will present the reader with a newspaper that has a distinct personality. A consistent personality will strengthen our acceptance by our readers. We will become part of the reader's daily routine. A familiar friend.

"These ideas, while restrictive in a sense, must be followed to insure consistency. This is not an effort to curb creativity, but to channel it. The burden of visual interest should rest with the photo and art departments and in the work they produce, not typographic gimmicks. Editors will have a format they are familiar with and will be freed to spend more time on story ideas than layout ideas."

The Kansas City Star appeared in its new design in April, 1980. Randy Miller, then editorial art director for the Kansas City newspapers, was responsible for the redesign.

The layout style of The Star is modular. "That is," the manual says, "each story or package (related stories) should form one rectangular shape. Story, headline, photo or art must all form one unit. . . On inside pages, you should think of the page as a series of rectangles.

"Since the paper will be modular, it will be simple to box stories. Boxes should be used only when needed. Generally that will be when heads are bumped . . ."

The Star's redesign called for use of the old body type — 8/9 Aurora — except for editorials. One of the few changes made since redesign was an

THE KANSAS CITY STAR.

Tuesday evening, July 8, 1980, Main Edition, 24 pages 25c

Old temperature records melt as mercury heats up

Four temperature records have been broken in downtown Kansas City this summer. The numbers above the shaded area represent the years in which the record temperatures were set.

For those without 'air,' relief has no spelling

By Robert J. Pessek, staff writer

In the kitchen cabinet, the peanut butter is as warm as freshly set street tar.

It's 2:30 a.m. It's hot. Again. Still.

The nights bring scant relief from the torrid weather of recent weeks. And after the long hours of another hot night, the eastern horizon turns a raw red. Electric fans push tired air over the unclothed—or nearly so—bodies of fitful sleepers.

The days—and nights—have been long on discomfort, short on relief. Monday was no exception—another record high of 106, and a low of only 88.

"Suffer, suffer, is the word—suffocation. If I could I'd give every poor person in America an air-conditioner . . . ." said Miss Gloria Jean Dunlap, of 3804B Montgall.

The magic words—air conditioning: central air, units in windows and in cars, chilled atmosphere at work. The refrigeration of the air we move in and breathe has made an important difference in how we survive broiling summers.

It seems to be everywhere. But it isn't.

Miss Dunlap and her roommate, Miss Luella Sykes, sat on a shaded front porch and rubbed ice wrapped in towels over themselves—not much of a replacement for air conditioning, they said.

Those who live or work without air conditioning describe the effects: Appetites diminish, sleep is more difficult, work is harder, tempers are shorter and general discomfort shoots up with the thermometer.

The constant sweat can leave the stale, sour smell of a wet rag kept too long in a closed drawer.

And not surprisingly, those without air conditioning—generally the elderly, people on fixed incomes and minorities—don't have it because they can't afford it.

Preston Wyatt and his sister Brenda sat on their deep stone porch overlooking the heavy traffic of U.S. 71 at 4015 Prospect. Like many without air conditioning, they spend a lot of time on the porch. And do as little as possible.

"You can't go and cook and eat in there—it's too damn hot," he said. "So it's sandwiches—peanut butter, baloney."

"The cooking's down to zero," said Mrs. Corrine Baker, from the porch of her apartment at Linwood and Brooklyn. When she must heat food, she uses a grill outside.

"A lot of salads, a lot of juices and stay out of the sun," Mrs. Baker said. "We even have to wash the children down with water because they get so irritable."

"We're on this front porch from about six in the morning to two in the next morning. We spend about four hours (a day) in the house," she said.

Across town at 507 W. 36th, retired Army veteran Clarence Hamilton sat bare-chested in his studio apartment. He dabbed himself with a towel hung around his neck.

"Don't cook at all," he said. "God, I've been living on juice, iced tea, ice water for a week. Don't cook nothing."

"It ain't worth a damn," he said about

See Relief, pg. 8A, col. 1

Without air conditioning, the porch eases the heat for Mrs. Corrine Baker, her granddaughter, Keela Baker, 1, and the baby's mother, Mrs. Joy Baker. (staff photo by Jim McTaggart)

Pro-ERA GOP plank rejected

By the Associated Press

Detroit—Republican platform writers today voted to abandon the party's 40-year support for the Equal Rights Amendment and to place instead in the 1980 Republican platform an assertion that the issue "is now in the hands of the state legislatures."

ERA backers called the near-unanimous vote by the human resources subcommittee a major defeat and vowed to appeal to the full 106-member platform committee and to take it to the convention floor if necessary.

Sen. John Tower, R-Texas, chairman of the full committee, said he did not expect his panel to reverse the subcommittee. He called the language "a compromise" and told reporters, "I hope there aren't any more controversies."

The plank came with the blessings of aides to Ronald Reagan, who opposes the ERA.

The subcommittee approved the plank after flatly rejecting, by a 11-4 vote, a proposal by John Leopold

See GOP, pg. 8A, col. 5

Carter offers a hand in cranking up automobile industry

By the Associated Press

Detroit—President Carter huddled early today with automobile industry and union leaders, unveiling a set of proposals to help the ailing industry make the expensive transition to manufacturing smaller cars.

In announcing his aid package, Carter said, "I believe this is a major step forward in providing for the American consumer a high-quality, fuel-efficient auto that will be required in the months ahead."

His proposals included:

• An expedited hearing on complaints that the U.S. automobile industry is being hurt by imports of foreign cars.

• Regulatory changes that would save the industry $500 million in complying with federal anti-pollution standards. New legislation might be required.

• A less costly way of complying with regulations that protect workers from toxic lead and arsenic.

• A program to provide at least $50 million next year to communities and firms hurt by the industry slowdown.

• Special loans totalling between $200 million and $400 million to help dealers finance their car inventories.

• Speed-up of a Treasury Department proposal that should allow the industry faster depreciation tax writeoffs for plants and equipment. Carter also said that when the time is right he will propose a general tax cut and the automobile industry obviously will have special consideration.

Carter said, "We have literally worked day and night" on the plan.

Carter's whirlwind, 55-minute visit to Detroit came as Republicans were gathering for pre-convention activities: GOP leaders said the visit was purely political.

The president arrived from Plains, Ga., on his way to a memorial service in Tokyo for Masayoshi Ohira, the Japanese prime minister who died last month.

It is the Japanese who have cut most deeply into the U.S. car market. The Japanese makers have been selling smaller, more fuel-efficient cars for years; as gasoline prices rose in the past decade, imports have steadily increased their share of the U.S. market.

Japanese imports accounted for 22 per-

See Automobile, pg. 8A, col. 3

Border Patrol believed close to identifying smugglers

By the Associated Press

Ajo, Ariz.—The Border Patrol, using "hard-core, firm identification" from survivors, says it is closing its net on the "coyotes" who smuggled a group of Salvadorans into the United States and let 13 die in the scorching desert.

Once they recuperate from their ordeal, the survivors—13 El Salvador natives and one Mexican—will be moved to Tucson and held as material witnesses, Border Patrol officials said.

"This time we have some hard-core, firm identification," said E.J. "Jerry" Scott, senior Border Patrol agent here. He said chances are good of capturing and convicting the smugglers.

He lamented the fact that the first three survivors found had lied about their companions.

"The first three men we found on the highway told us there were no others in the desert," Scott said. "That was on Friday, and if they had told us about the other people out there we probably could have saved them all."

The survivors have described their guides as "three Mexican youths," according to agent John Rockhill.

To spur the investigation, Gov. Bruce Babbitt offered a $10,000 reward, and he wrote to U.S. Attorney General Benja-

See Smugglers, pg. 8A, col. 1

Children will get to camp

By The Star's staff

About half of the 100 inner-city children who saw plans for summer camp fizzle twice may finally get to attend camp.

Perhaps as many as 45 children will attend a camp late this month in Raytown as the result of the efforts of the Greater Kansas City Camping Collaboration.

A two-week camp program in mid-June, sponsored by the Upper Room Jesus Center, 4808 Troost, folded after only two days because of insufficient supplies and facilities.

A refusal by church officials to release the names of the children later blocked efforts by the Camping Collaboration to send some of the disappointed children to area camps without charge.

Upper Room officials, including its director, The Rev. John Birmingham, said unfavorable publicity about the failure of the camping trip had discouraged them from making any more such attempts.

Ms. Beth Shirk, camping services coordinator for the Collaboration, however, received a list of names and addresses from Al Brooks, assistant city manager, late last week.

Parents of about 30 of the children

See Camp, pg. 8A, col. 5

Inside

Abby 2B
At Your Service 1B
Bombeck 2B
Bridge 5B
Business/Financial 5A
Comics 5B
Crossword 5B
Deaths 4C
Editorials 6A
Movies 3B
Sports 1-3C
TV 5B
Want Ads 4-10C

Vol. 100, No. 253

Weather

Clear to partly cloudy tonight and Wednesday with a 30 percent chance of thunderstorms is the National Weather Service forecast for the Kansas City area. The low tonight in the mid to upper 70s. The high Wednesday in the mid 90s. The temperatures:

*Unofficial
Precipitation in 24 hours ending at 6 a.m.—none.
River Stage—4.7 feet, up .1.
Lake of the Ozarks—3.3 feet below full reservoir.

Starbeam

Predictions: Baseball—National League 8, American League 6; high temperature—about the same, again, as what's on the gasoline price signs.

The Area

The St. Louis school district has done what the Kansas City has been unable: Spend millions of dollars to regain its "AAA" state rating. Page 3A.

Weather-caused high consumption results in inadequate water supplies for areas of Jackson and Cass counties. Page 3A.

George Brett of the Royals says he is afraid he won't play well when he returns to the lineup Thursday. Page 1C.

The Nation

Inflation moderates at the wholesale level as prices in June take a relatively modest rise of 0.8 percent. Page 2A.

Star Style

Your bedroom decor can reveal your personality. Page 1B.

Where to Call

Star City Desk (816) 234-4300
Star Business/Financial News 234-4370
Classified Advertising, (816) 234-4000
Circulation, (816) 234-4545
Sports Scores, (816) 234-4380
Other Departments, (816) 234-4141

The Kansas City Star/

increase in text face size to nine point; the eight-point was judged hard to read in the wider measure column size adopted (five columns on section fronts and six columns inside).

Another chapter in the ragged right debate was written in Kansas City. The original redesign called for ragged right text in feature sections. Readers, already smarting from what they perceived as smaller body type (actually, it was larger, but a new heavier headline face made it appear smaller), protested the addition of ragged right type. All type in The Star is now justified.

The Star allows use of four-column-wide type on section covers, but "there is no bastard measure. There cannot be any mixing of type widths on a page."

The Star's headlines are set down style, in Goudy X-Bold. "No exceptions," warns the manual. "That means we do not use italic type, art type, kickers, dropouts or any other kind of typographic manipulation. The one choice you have is to use a deck when you cannot say all that is necessary in the head . . ."

The Star's page design calls for one dominant piece of art — a single photo or a layout — conforming to the feature approach of an afternoon newspaper. A second piece of art used on a page must be smaller.

All photographs, even half-columns, have hairline rule borders. Wild photos are put into a hairline box with one pica of white space surrounding them. Photos with stories carry hairlines only on the edges.

Marty Petty, editorial art director, describes the challenge of keeping department editors thinking art and graphics "when they initiate

---

[The right portion of the page is a reproduction of a newspaper section front:]

STAR STYLE

Sunday, April 6, 1980, Page 1C

inside

A pixie-faced boy's disappearance has evoked a normally withdrawn neighborhood's compassion, help and prayer—Page 6C.
Short evening dresses: ruffles, flourishes, flirty flounces—Page 7C.
Also in Style: Kansas City People and Betty Beale—Page 3C. Ann Landers and Norman Vincent Peale—Page 4C.

Passive men, wild women

Real differences between sexes perpetuate woes

By Dr. Pierre Mornell
Special to The Star

Like a fine wine, capital's social whirl best when sipped

By Bette Lind
Society editor

See Washington, pg. 2C, col. 3

Sojourn in District of Columbia begets fond memories

By Bette Lind
Society editor

See Passive, pg. 2C, col. 1

Born again, they found inner peace

By Michael Bauer
Staff writer

A tiny shawl collar and striped belt add tailored, bright accents to the knit top and sharkskin skirt modeled at the Woodside Racquet Club. (fashions by Tennis Warehouse/staff photo by Jan Housewerth)

See Faith, pg. 8C, col. 1

White rallies to win back points on court

By Marjean Busby

The Kansas City Star/

assignments, **not** the day before publication. Both Randy and I have found this education to be the key to successful packaging of the daily product."

The morning Kansas City Times also has been redesigned but not, Petty said, as an overnight project like The Star.

"The philosophy in its redesign," she said, "was to communicate to the readers that The Times was a hard news morning paper wanting to appear authoritative, tasteful and conservative. . . . Overall, The Times was fighting to create an image totally separate from its sister paper The Star, both in content and appearance."

Saturday

The Bond Cabinet
Take a look inside governor's inner circle
Page D-1

Weekend
Art builds into an exhibition
Page C-1

Sports
Martina's image improves with age
Page E-1

The Kansas City Times

Metropolitan Edition ★ ★ January 17, 1981 25c

Hostage agreement reportedly near

U.S. begins to convert Iran's gold, securities

From the Washington Post, AP, New York Times and Los Angeles Times

WASHINGTON — The United States on Friday transferred about $1 billion in Iranian-owned gold to London and began converting $1.2 billion in Iranian securities to cash in preparation for an agreement — possibly coming today — for release of the 52 American hostages.

The actions were ordered by President Jimmy Carter as senior administration officials met with executives of 12 American banks to formulate a U.S. response to Iran's latest proposals for settlement of the 14-month-old hostage situation.

The American response was sent late Friday night to Deputy Secretary of State Warren Christopher in Algiers, to be relayed by Algerian intermediaries to Tehran. The response is in the form of an international agreement between the two countries, according to White House press secretary Jody Powell.

"If they accept it, we will have an agreement," he said. If they accept promptly, he said, the hostages could be released by Tuesday, Inauguration Day.

Powell and other officials cautioned that Iranian acceptance is not certain, especially in light of the many disappointed hopes of the past months. Adding to the uncertainty are statements from officials in Tehran insisting that financial issues are already resolved. In Washington this was denied.

At the State Department, Treasury Secretary G. William Miller and representatives of the 12 banks were unable after a seven-hour meeting to reconcile differences between the United States and Iran over the total of Iran's frozen assets.

Iran claims about $14 billion in assets were blocked by President Carter, but the United States puts the total at about $9.5 billion.

Miller reported "good progress" in talks with the bankers but said, "We are still at a point where we do not have an agreement," adding that consultations would continue.

Miller and White House counsel Lloyd Cutler then went to work drafting a U.S. response to Iranian financial demands.

"The reason we are trying to be so precise is that no one wants to make an agreement in which there is so much vagueness that there could later be an abortion of an agreement because of the misperceptions of the amounts," Miller said.

Despite Miller's comments, there was a keen sense of anticipation, including rare public expressions of optimism, that freedom for the captive Americans may be the last spectacular event of the presidency of Jimmy Carter before he gives up the office to Ronald Reagan on Tuesday.

Reagan, who in recent days had refused to give what he called "a blank check" for any agreement to be made by Carter, said Friday that, as he understood the details of the proposed deal, "I thought that (they) made sense . . . I continue to be optimistic."

Reagan told reporters he was "being kept up minute-by-minute" on the government's efforts to obtain release of the hostages.

The timetable for a settlement remained uncertain as the clock ticked toward the end of Carter's term, but

See HOSTAGES, Page A-4, Col. 1

Associated Press

Activity increased the world over as agreement neared on the hostages' release. At right, Deputy Secretary of State Warren Christopher arrives at the U.S. Embassy in Algiers while presidential counsel Lloyd Cutler (left) leaves the State Department in Washington. Meanwhile, U.S. and British bankers flew from London to Algiers for talks on the financial arrangements. The transactions will reportedly be handled by the Algerian Central Bank, pictured at center. If a deal is struck, it is believed the hostages will take a commercial jet from Tehran to Algiers, then transfer to the U.S. military base in Wiesbaden, West Germany.

State of the Union finale

Carter finds perils, progress

New York Times News Service

WASHINGTON — President Jimmy Carter, in a final State of the Union message to Congress, warned Friday that the United States confronts serious problems, including unemployment and inflation rates that are unacceptably high and an increasingly tight world oil market.

In a 76-page written message that summarized both the achievements of his administration and the policies it would have pursued in a second term, Carter drew attention to what he sees as a continuing Soviet threat to the integrity of Poland.

"Although the situation in Poland has shown signs of stabilizing recently," he wrote, "Soviet forces remain in a high state of readiness and they could move into Poland on short notice." He added that Moscow had been advised that such a move would have "severe and prolonged consequences for East-West detente, and for United States-Soviet relations in particular."

Administration officials have said privately that they were convinced the Soviet Union was about to intervene in Poland in early December and was deterred at the last minute by concerted warnings from the Atlantic Alliance. Nonetheless, they still believe an invasion by Soviet forces remains a high probability.

In normal years, the State of the Union message is a major occasion. The president usually presents his summary in person before a joint session of Congress. This year, however, with Carter in his last days in office and President-elect Ronald Reagan already in Washington in anticipation of his inauguration Tuesday, it was a much-diminished event.

The text of the message was released by the White House late Friday

See CARTER, Page A-14, Col. 1

Inside

Vol. 113, No. 114 76 Pages

Departments

Cold, cold facts

The freeze puts squeeze on Florida citrus crops, residents . . .

By Robert Unger
National Correspondent

ORLANDO, Fla. — The nation's crazy weather, after sowing confusion and worry over most of Middle America all winter, made a shocking assault this week on the East and South.

In New England, the weather quickly became a deadly enemy, threatening to freeze its human constituents, and, sadly, sometimes succeeding.

In Middle America it remained a fickle friend, allowing calm pleasures while withholding the vital moisture that must come if the nation is to be fed.

And here the weather was disconcerting to all, infuriating to many, and disastrous to some. At best it offered itself as an ugly bully in the country's winter playground.

While Middle Americans still smarted under word that their utility rates would increase because they had used too little power, Florida utilities had to rotate blackouts to keep up with the demand for heat.

Psychologically and otherwise, few here were prepared.

"As late as noon Monday no one was predicting the kind of freeze we had," Jerry Chicone Jr., an orange grower near Orlando, said. "We knew it was going to get cold, but no one knew it was going to be as bad as it was."

Orange growers call 27 degrees their break-even point. They can take temperatures that low for up to four or five hours. Anything colder than that or lasting longer than that means big trouble.

"We ended up with temperatures down to 21 degrees. And in some places it stayed below 27 degrees for as long as 10 hours," he said.

The Tuesday morning low in Jacksonville was 13 degrees. Then Tuesday night, temperatures in some areas dropped below the record of the previous night.

By Wednesday afternoon some or-

See FLORIDA, Page A-4, Col. 1

. . . While crisp, sunny winter is mixed blessing for Midwest

By Bill Prater
Energy/Environment Writer

Wade out into central Missouri's Bennett Spring this weekend and you'll not only get cold, you'll be competing for space with about 100 trout fishermen, happily ignoring that it's the middle of January.

At the Mission Hills Country Club, 15 to 20 enthusiasts a day are following their golf balls around the private course — which is normally open this time of year for cross country skiing.

Kansas City street maintenance crews are out repairing road shoulders and potholes instead of spreading salt and clearing away snow and ice.

And Rex Philipps' snow removal equipment gathers dust in a corner of his lawn and tree service in Raytown, while he waits resignedly for warmer weather and work reseeding customers' yards seared brown and lifeless by last summer's record heat wave.

Signs of early spring are everywhere but on the face of a thermometer — which shows not a heat wave, but temperatures slightly below normal so far this winter.

While grapefruits blister and freeze on the trees in Florida, and resort operators curse the warmth and absence of snow across the Colorado Rockies, Missouri and Kansas are in an awkward zone halfway between the two extremes.

A blanket of drought protects this area like Mother Nature's umbrella.

See AREA, Page A-4, Col. 5

John Spink/Staff

The snow shovel business hasn't been very good for John Hardman at Strasser's Hardware, 910 Southwest Blvd.

The biggest question on Carlin's energy tax: Who's going to pay?

By Laura Scott
Kansas Correspondent

TOPEKA — Envision the ideal tax: It raises millions if not billions of dollars each year. It requires no complicated forms. And, most important, no one has to pay it.

Of course, such a tax doesn't exist. And — despite all the recent marveling at the political wisdom of Gov. John Carlin's proposed $200 million tax on oil and gas production — the age-old question still applies to it: "Who will pay?"

Carlin and his aides say the 8 percent severance tax will be paid by the oil, gas and coal producers, the people who take the minerals from the ground.

But energy producers say the ultimate taxpayer will be the customer. At first, they say, he or she will pay through higher electric and gas bills and later through higher gasoline prices.

Each side is right, to an extent.

A close look shows that almost every utility customer in Kansas will pay higher electric or gas rates if the tax is enacted by the Legislature.

Some Kansans will pay even more — among those the people who live in and educate their children in counties that depend heavily on oil properties for the local tax base.

But for most Kansans, the ultimate costs will be offset by the benefits that Carlin has built into his plan — lower property tax rates statewide, reductions in farm equipment taxes and income tax reductions to help pay for the anticipated increased energy costs.

Here is who would be affected by the severance tax and how:

Utility customers

Kansans who live in homes heated by natural gas — or by electricity produced from gas — and commercial users of gas will feel the pinch most. That is because most natural gas contracts allow the producers to pass on their increased costs to the utilities, which in turn pass them on to their customers.

Although 84 percent of the increased tax will be paid by out-of-state gas producers, $18 million is expected to

See CARLIN, Page A-8, Col. 1

Musicians, association to vote on compromise

By Laura Knickerbocker
A Member of the Staff

After weeks of on-again, off-again negotiations, a decision to cancel the symphony season and some maneuvering by Mayor Richard L. Berkley, both sides in the 15-week Kansas City Philharmonic strike may accept a compromise today that could end the labor dispute.

If they do, the canceled season would be revived on Jan. 22 and run for 30 weeks.

The executive committee of the Philharmonic Association and the musicians will vote separately at 4 p.m. today to accept or reject recommendations made Friday by a fact-finding panel appointed by Berkley.

These recommendations call for adding one week to the orchestra season the first year of the three year contract, two weeks the second year and three weeks the final year. Salaries would remain at the level of management's final offer.

Despite the associations's repeated statements that financial resources are already strained to the limit and the musicians' assertions that ratification amounts to capitulation, some representatives on both sides believe

See ORCHESTRA, Page A-14, Col. 1

THE WEATHER

Mostly sunny and not so cold today and Sunday with southwesterly winds 10 to 20 miles an hour in the National Weather Service forecast for the Kansas City area. High today in the upper 30s. Low around 20. High Sunday in the middle 40s. Details on Page B-4.

THOUGHT FOR TODAY

A learned fool is more foolish than a wise fool.

— Moliere.

The Morning Call/

Its designers take part in news judgments

"Our design is flexible. We have a philosophy of a changing front page that responds to the changing news. The design of that page is dictated by the pressures of the news rather than a preordained idea of how the page should look. We think the design is appropriate to the content and the readers we serve."

The words are those of Robert Lockwood, art director of The Morning Call of Allentown, Pa. Lockwood, with design editor Jeff Lindemuth and then executive editor Edward D. Miller, was responsible for the redesign.

The change came near the end of the 70s, when Miller made Lockwood art director and sought a new method of packaging the news. Miller thought first in the conventional terms used by most newspapers considering redesign: Create a design format and lay out the news in conformity with it.

Lockwood had other ideas: Involve designers in the everyday production of the newspaper, he suggested, and let the news dictate the design. Miller agreed, after a year's experimentation. Lindemuth was named design editor, with authority to make news judgments.

In early 1979, Miller said, The Morning Call became the newspaper he had been seeking.

"When the paper arrives at my house in the morning, I am just as surprised as anyone by its content and appearance," he said in an article in newspaper design notebook (Mar/Apr 1979).

What happened grew out of Miller's

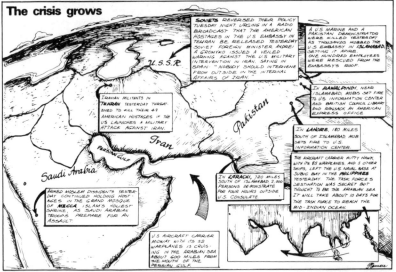

See A Second Front Page A3

THE MORNING CALL

LEHIGH VALLEY'S GREATEST NEWSPAPER

ALLENTOWN, PA. 18105
THURSDAY, NOVEMBER 22, 1979

NO. 28,695 (USPS 363-060)

20¢

Index

BRIDGE D4
CALENDAR D1
CLASSIFIED D6-18
COMICS D3
DEATHS D6
EDITORIAL A28
FAMILY B17-30
FINANCIAL C12,13
LETTERS A29
MOVIES A3
MOVIES D6
RESTAURANTS D6
SPORTS C1-11
TV D1

Weather

Partly sunny today (excellent for turkey plucking); cloudy, chance of showers tomorrow. For details, see Page D1

The crisis grows

THE IRANIAN CRISIS: DAY 19

Americans rescued as embassy burns in Pakistan

ISLAMABAD, Pakistan (AP) — Thousands of enraged Moslems, some firing rifles, stormed the U.S. Embassy here yesterday and set it afire in rioting that killed one U.S. Marine guard and one demonstrator.

Thirty-seven other persons, including two unidentified Americans, were injured as Pakistan troops dispersed the mob and rescued more than 100 American staffers, some from the roof of the burning building.

One staffer, Thomas G. Putscher, an aid editorial, was captured on the embassy grounds and held hostage for more than five hours before being released unharmed at a nearby university, American officials said.

Pakistan's Moslem president Gen. Mohammed Zia ul-Haq spoke to President Carter by telephone and expressed deep regret and apologies for the attack. White House spokesman Jody Powell said State Department officials announced later that Secretaries of State Cyrus R. Vance ordered the departure from Pakistan of non-essential

▶ Marine slain. A12

U.S. government personnel and about 300 dependents of government employees.

The Moslem crowds, reacting to erroneous reports that Americans were involved in the takeover Tuesday of the Grand Mosque in Mecca, Saudi Arabia, shouted "Kill the American dogs" and stormed the gates with guns blazing, witnesses said.

A leader of some 300 students who led the attack said the group believed rumors that American Jews were responsible for the mosque takeover, adding "We regret the lives lost and the destruction."

Another student said "We got news that Jews had taken the Khana Kaaba and 300 hostages including 300 Pakistanis. We simply wanted to express our protest peacefully and then a shot was fired from the

Please See PAKISTAN Page A12▶

Militants vow to kill hostages if U.S. attacks

TEHRAN, Iran (AP) — Iranian militants vowed yesterday to kill the 49 American hostages and blow up the occupied U.S. Embassy in Tehran if the United States launched a military attack against Iran A government spokesman said Iranians "would dig the grave of America" if it used force.

More than a million Iranians, responding to a call by revolutionary leader Ayatollah Ruhollah Khomeini, marched through the streets of Tehran shouting "Mar bar shah, mar bar Carter — Death to the Shah, death to Carter."

The day marked the 1,400th Islamic New Year and the beginning of the 29-day month of Moharram, a mourning period for Iran's majority Shiite Moslems.

In Washington, White House spokesman Jody Powell warned Iran's leaders they will be "strictly accountable" if the hostages are harmed. The Carter administration has ordered the aircraft carrier Kitty Hawk and five escort ships from the Philippines onto the Indian Ocean to join the carrier Midway, now cruising 600 miles south of Iran.

A statement to militants who seized the embassy Nov. 4, demanding that the exiled Shah be returned for trial, said, "We have been informed that the Americans intend to attack Iranian territory. We are hereby warning the American government.

"If these threats materialize all the hostages will perish. The slightest military aggression against Iran will also threaten the lives of all Americans living in Iran and immediately the American embassy will be blown up."

An Iranian government spokesman said the movement of the U.S. carriers was probably a bluff. But "we are determined to resist to the last person and to the last breath, and we shall dig the grave of America or any other country here if they commit the slightest

Please See MILITANTS Page A13▶

INSIDE

Islam's new fervor

The world's 800 million Moslems entered Islam's 15th century yesterday with a new fervor fueled by oil dollars and manifested in Iran's radical fundamentalism. A2

A crowd estimated at up to two million people converged on the occupied U.S. Embassy in Iran, where militants threatened to kill their 48 American hostages if the United States attempts to use military force against Iran. A2

Soviets change broadcast tune

A Soviet-controlled radio station that broadcasts to Iran now is urging the release of American hostages at the U.S. Embassy in Tehran, making "180-degree shift" from its previous stance. A2

U.S. has several military options

By FRED S. HOFFMAN
Of The Associated Press

WASHINGTON — A buildup of U.S. Navy carrier striking power on the Indian Ocean-Arabian Sea area will enable President Carter to order retaliatory strikes against Iran if American hostages are killed.

The Carter administration is carefully avoiding any public commitment to an option or set of options, but the threat of possible retribution is considered the most plausible course of action for the United States if the Americans held in the U.S. embassy in Tehran are slain.

Military planners discount the practicality of any rescue mission into Tehran, saying such an effort most likely would lead to the instant deaths of the Americans, who have been prisoners of Iranian students for 17 days.

Please See OPTIONS Page A13▶

Uncontested Divorce $395—434-2101
Legal Services Atty. H.G. Burchill

Allentown Toy & Trade Show
Agriculture Hall Nov 24-Dec 1

Sheepskin Coats & Seat Covers
The Shepherds Hut
Trexlertown Pa 395-5710

Both Brass Rail Restaurants
Closed Thanksgiving Day

McDonald's® Will Be Open
Thanksgiving Day Regular Hours

The Morning Call/

conviction that most designers are decorators, that designers must have control over news judgments, that designers must be on the news desk to work out the design dictated by the day's news.

Said Miller:

"If I gave anybody any rules, it was to throw away all the rules. It was not a question of, well, you've got to have two picas of white space here, or I want a lead story, or I want a six-column format. What I wanted was a newspaper that would reflect the events of the world, the events of the community, and some idea of interpretation and feeling about those events . . ."

How is this unconventional approach worked out? Miller explained:

"If you hit a day when the College of Cardinals elects a new pope, you can believe you're in a one-story day. Most days have multiple stories, multiple pieces of information that are of interest to a multiple readership. So you may have anywhere from five to 50 items on your front page. There is no formula, there is only human ingenuity and awareness of watching the news as it comes in and having the common sense to know how to design it for a consistent body of readers. . . .

"Days have different patterns, different textures, different colors, different feelings, moods and events, and they have to be blended and presented in a way that reflects those differences.

"And if the structure of the paper is so rigid and so demanding that it is not elastic enough to tolerate all those differences, it will create an artificial order that does not really exist.

Index

BRIDGE	D4	FINANCIAL	C11
CALENDAR	D1	LETTERS	A13
CLASSIFIED	D6-18	LOTTERY	A2
COMICS	C12	MOVIES	D2-4
COURTS	B6,7	PORTER	C11
DEATHS	D5	RESTAURANTS	C6-9
EDITORIAL	A12	SPORTS	C1-6
FAMILY	B8-10	TV	D1

(C) 1979 Call-Chronicle Newspapers, Inc All rights reserved

NO. 28,578 (USPS 363-060) ★ ★ ★

THE MORNING CALL

LEHIGH VALLEY'S GREATEST NEWSPAPER

ALLENTOWN, PA. 18105
FRIDAY, JUNE 8, 1979

Weather

Hazy, humid, chance of thunderstorms today and tomorrow. For details, see Page D1

20¢

DC-10 GROUNDINGS

✔ Air travel continues at less than full efficiency

DC-10 probers check for design flaw

WASHINGTON (AP) – Aviation experts in four cities ran computer tests, probed engine wreckage and checked documents yesterday in an effort to determine if there is a basic design flaw in the engine mounting of the grounded DC-10 jetliner.

"It's a long, slow, plodding process of sifting and re-sifting through the evidence," said Federal Aviation Administration spokesman Fred Farrar.

"We're trying to find out what happened, what is causing the cracks in the engine mounts, was something overlooked in the certification process, is there a basic flaw in the system?" he said. "It's arduous work."

FAA chief Langhorne M. Bond suspended the certificate of the DC-10 Wednesday, saying there might be a design defect in the engine mounting assembly.

The action grounded all 138 DC-10s operated by U.S. airlines. Although the order does not apply to 143 foreign-registered DC-10s, the FAA said yesterday that all foreign carriers that operate the aircraft had voluntarily taken their planes out of service.

The moves disrupted travel plans for tens of thousands of persons around the world.

The grounding was the fourth for the troubled plane since the May 25 crash of an American Airlines DC-10 in Chicago that killed 275 persons in the nation's worst aviation accident. An engine fell off the big plane as it was taking off and the aircraft plunged to the ground and burned.

Please See DC-10 Page A8 ►

No rush now — Associated Press

An Athens-bound couple settles down for a long wait at Newark International Airport yesterday after arriving early in the morning to find that the plane replacing the DC-10 originally booked for their charter flight was full. Seventy passengers were told that an attempt would be made to get them on another airline later in the day.

Airline operations hampered

By The New York Times

NEW YORK – Hampered by the grounding of 281 DC-10's around the world, airplane travel continued at less than full efficiency yesterday with airlines switching planes, flights and passengers in an effort to compensate for the absence of the wide-body jumbo jets.

Simultaneously, the airlines appear to be taking pains to assuage public fears about the grounded planes. Both United Airlines, which has 37 DC-10's in its fleet, and American Airlines, which has 30, are telling passengers wherever possible that they have faith in the reliability of the DC-10's.

"We're not selling," said David Lobb, a representative of American, "but if we're asked we say we have complete confidence in the aircraft, because we do."

Please See HAMPERED Page A8 ►

A breakdown of DC-10 orders

McDonnell Douglas accounts for the DC-10 on a 400 airplane program, assuming that with the delivery of 400 planes it will have recovered the development costs incurred in the start-up phase of the program. As of April 30, 1979, McDonnell Douglas had these orders for DC-10's:

277 DELIVERIES
Planes that have been paid for and delivered to airlines

63 FIRM ORDERS
DC-10's for which a deposit has been accepted and a delivery date assigned

70 OPTIONS
Planes that customers have the right to purchase, or planes on conditional order

410 TOTAL ORDERS

Food prices drop 1.3% in May

WASHINGTON (AP) – The biggest decline in wholesale food prices in more than three years in May gave hope to consumers yesterday that the torrid pace of inflation is easing, especially at the supermarket counter.

The government said overall wholesale prices increased just 0.4 percent in May, down sharply from the first four months of 1979 and the smallest monthly increase since August. Prices had increased 0.9 percent in April.

In another encouraging report, the government said the nation's businesses plan to increase investment spending by nearly 13 percent this year, or 4.5 percent after discounting for inflation.

"It enhances our confidence that we'll be able to avoid a recession," said William Cox, the Commerce Department's deputy chief economist.

President Carter, in a speech before the newly formed United Food and Commercial Workers International Union, vowed once more that he will not resort to mandatory wage and price controls in the battle against inflation.

"I will not slap mandatory government controls on wages and prices just through the 1980 elections and then later watch inflation skyrocket out of control," the President said. "I will never fight inflation by deliberately throwing millions of Americans out of work."

In its monthly wholesale price report, the Labor Department said food prices declined 1.3 percent in May, the sharpest drop in any single month since February 1976. The price of beef and veal fell 6.9 percent, reversing five consecutive months of increases.

Although prices of fuel and non-food goods were up sharply again, Carter administration economists said the decline in food prices, if it continues, should restrain the overall rate of

Please See PRICES Page A10 ►

BEEF 6.9% — PORK 10.1% — GASOLINE 4.2% — FUEL OIL 5.4%

While May's food prices dropped, fuel costs rose sharply

Weekend gas supplies tight but no major problems seen

►Schlesinger sees supplies improving. A8
►Driving to energy war in a diesel. B1

By The Associated Press

Americans hitting the road this weekend probably won't have any major problems finding gasoline. Although many gas stations will be closed tomorow night and Sunday, those stations that are open should have plenty of gas.

And there are signs that the tight gasoline situation is easing a bit.

On the whole, government and industry officials said yesterday, the weekend will probably not be too much unlike the last couple of weekends, with sporadic spot shortages but no major problems.

Please See GASOLINE Page A10 ►

Weekend availability

DELAWARE
Most stations will be closed all weekend.

MARYLAND
Despite good supplies, many stations will close Sunday.

NEW JERSEY
More than three quarters of the state's stations will close Sunday as gas supplies continue tight.

NEW YORK
Most stations will be closed tomorrow night and Sunday, especially in and around New York City, but supplies are described as adequate.

OHIO
Most stations will be open all weekend.

PENNSYLVANIA
"Sunday is the big problem," said John O'Donnell of the Pennsylvania Service Station Dealers Association, with 80 percent of the state's stations closed. Supplies are generally tight.

Pope visits hometown

Pope John Paul II waves to huge crowd of faithful in downtown Wadowice, his birthplace, yesterday. It marked his first return to the town since becoming Pope. The pontiff was in the seventh day of a visit to his native Poland.
A2

Doctors remove 200-pound benign tumor from California woman

SAN FRANCISCO (AP) – A huge ovarian tumor weighing more than 200 pounds has been removed successfully from a young woman by a team of doctors at the University of California Medical Center, the team's chief surgeon said yesterday.

The benign growth, estimated at a yard in diameter, had been growing inside her for about 15 years, said Dr. Russell K. Laros, Jr., head of the seven-member team which performed the 4½-hour operation May 24. He described the tumor as one of the largest in medical history.

Laros said the woman had been gaining weight since her teens, but assumed she was simply getting fat.

The woman, who weighed 380 pounds when she was admitted to Moffitt Hospital complaining of abdominal pain, was released Tuesday weighing about 180 pounds, Laros said. He declined to identify her except to say that she was from the San Francisco Bay area.

Laros could not explain how such a mass could go undetected for so long. "How do women carry full-term babies without realizing it?" he said. "I suppose there's an element of denial involved."

The woman is perfectly capable of bearing children with her remaining ovary "if she desires," Laros said. Laros said that tumors weighing more than 20 pounds are very rare.

Flood faces ethics violation charges

WASHINGTON (AP) – The House ethics committee yesterday accused Rep. Daniel J. Flood, D-Wilkes-Barre, of 25 counts of violating House rules.

The committee voted during a closed-door meeting to file the charges, which correspond to federal charges lodged against the 16-term congressman last year.

Flood has 21 days to answer the committee's accusations. Depending on what the committee and the full House decide, Flood, if found guilty, could face a fine, a reprimand or expulsion from Congress.

REP. DANIEL J. FLOOD

Flood, 75, currently hospitalized for possible eye surgery, was indicted by a federal grand jury in October on charges of taking more than $50,000 in bribes in return for using his influence as chairman of an important congressional subcommittee on labor, health, education and welfare.

His first trial on those charges ended in a mistrial Feb. 3 after jurors voted 11-1 for a guilty verdict on some of the counts. His retrial, scheduled for June 4, was postponed indefinitely because of his ailments.

The ethics panel also voted yesterday to hold public hearings on allegations that Rep. Charles Diggs, D-Mich., violated House rules. Diggs was convicted of mail fraud and filing false payroll vouchers.

The Morning Call/

"And I think readers will sense this over a time. But when they see the diversity reflected in their newspaper, it will make that newspaper far more credible."

The Morning Call encourages the "development of news people with a wide range of skills necessary to produce a product as complex as a newspaper," Lockwood said. "That means we need artists who can make sound news judgments and editors who include visual skills as part of their own job requisites"

What actually happens in the Allentown process is shown in these sample pages.

On a day when the Iranian crisis intensifies, The Morning Call devotes its front page to a single subject. A normal front page appears on page 3 of The Call.

Another front page offers charts, lists and shadow boxes to present information clearly and efficiently.

A sports page is devoted to a single major feature — opening of the fishing season. Black keys with reverse type give readers news bulletins and tell them what's inside the section.

A food page carries two related stories, boldly presented, with the headline far down on the page knitting them together.

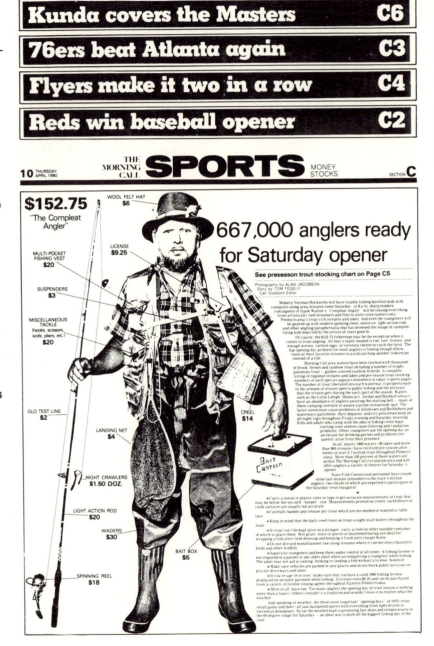

Kunda covers the Masters C6

76ers beat Atlanta again C3

Flyers make it two in a row C4

Reds win baseball opener C2

10 THURSDAY APRIL 1980 · THE MORNING CALL · **SPORTS** MONEY STOCKS · SECTION **C**

$152.75
"The Compleat Angler"

WOOL FELT HAT $6

MULTI-POCKET FISHING VEST $20

LICENSE $9.25

SUSPENDERS $3

MISCELLANEOUS TACKLE (hooks, scissors, knife, pliers, etc.) $20

GLO TEST LINE $2

LANDING NET $4

CREEL $14

NIGHT CRAWLERS $1.50 DOZ.

LIGHT ACTION ROD $20

WADERS $30

BAIT CANTEEN

BAIT BOX $5

SPINNING REEL $18

667,000 anglers ready for Saturday opener

See preseason trout-stocking chart on Page C5

Photography by ALAN JACOBSON
Story by TOM FEGELY
Call Outdoors Editor

The Morning Call/

FOOD

"Culinary Arts" is a cookbook attractive enough to be placed on the coffee table, but it's so full of good recipes that it is bound to be in the kitchen most of the time.

The newly published Allentown Art Museum cookbook is just in time for last-minute Christmas gifts ($10.95 for spiral bound and $15.95 for cloth bound. It's also available by mail. Write The Culinary Arts, The Allentown Art Museum, 5th and Court streets, P.O. Box 117, Allentown, 18105. Include 6 percent state sales tax and $1.50 for postage and handling.)

The book is perfect for the hard-to-buy-for person. And the chronicle of Lehigh Valley foods is a compact solution for presents that have to be mailed.

But the cookbook also commemorates a red-letter day in museum history — the 20th anniversary of the December day in 1959 when the museum first opened its doors along 5th and Court streets.

"Culinary Arts" is not your ordinary amateur community cookbook of hastily printed lists of neighborhood recipes.

You will find old favorites, new discoveries, personal variations and family food traditions among the book's nearly 400 recipes. It's a slick, clean presentation produced with the help of Rodale Press designers.

You'll also come across recipes hard to find anywhere else. Don't be afraid to try Vincent Price's recipe for Italian Sausage Creole (the well-known character actor was a museum visitor). Weigh in, after you've made Blair Creek's (the Inn) Chocolate Cheese Cake — a recipe that calls for three pounds of cream cheese, six eggs and six ounces of chocolate, among other calorie-laden ingredients. And Ballietsville Inn's Souffle Grand Marnier is bound to impress dinner guests. Stuffed Chicken En Croute with Champagne Sauce, courtesy of The Sign of the Sorrel Horse, is another sample of what awaits readers in the special restaurant section.

Terry Kovel, an Ohio resident who lectures at the museum occasionally and also coauthors a weekly antiques column that appears in the Sunday Call-Chronicle, managed to submit a recipe that sounds old — "Six-Week Muffins."

Author Ruth Spira ("Naturally Chinese") has several recipes in the book.

Food favorites that have been served at museum functions also are included in the book — everything from Southern Brown Sugar Bars and Chocolate Mint Bars to Lobster Cheese Chowder, Dilly Dip and Sesame Baked Chicken.

The book's content ranges from gourmet dreams — "Lobster Stuffed Tenderloin of Beef" and "Creamed Strawberries With Chocolate and Rum" — to plain and simple foods. There's an Apple Crisp recipe. Henry McIlhenny, a collector and friend of the museum, has submitted an Indian Pudding recipe which includes 1797 directions — "If having a brick oven, bake all night." Today's cooks can make the dessert by baking it for three hours in a 300-degree oven. A 19th-century recipe for curing gout is included in the beverage section.

"Chicken Breasts Supreme" is included for cooks who are frequently in a hurry. The recipe contains make-ahead and freeze directions.

The 17 full-color illustrations include paintings and illustrations of culinary utensils in the museum's collection. Examine the art in the book, and you won't be able to hold back a smile when you come to Henry O. Tanner's 1886 painting "Lion Licking Paw."

Members of the Society of the Arts (SOTA) produced the book which was edited by Connie Hansell and Jeanne Beldon. Thousands of hours went into creating the book. Some people say the publication could have been an encyclopedia rather than a cookbook if time spent was the only measure of content.

SOTA members planned the book carefully. Recipes are printed so they cover no more than two pages. That way, pages needn't be turned to continue a recipe when a cook's hands are liberally dusted with flour. No abbreviations were used in the recipes, so there is no excuse for adding a tablespoon of an ingredient when the recipe calls for a teaspoon.

Most important: The book's recipes were thoroughly tested by teams of volunteers. That's why Connie Hansell swears by "Danish Herring" appetizers and reports, "The low heat method for filet mignon really works. You end up with a delicious, medium-rare main course."

The book, a blend of recipes from local cooks and from "outsiders" who have visited the museum as guests or lecturers, also represents a blending of ideas.

Before SOTA began its monumental project, other museum cookbooks (proven fund-raisers) were studied.

Committee members examined art cookbooks from Denver, Dayton and Boston, Worcester, Baltimore and St. Louis art museums to learn how the cookbooks were designed and check the contents.

There were gorgeous "arty" productions that cost well over $25 a copy. "They looked classy but wasted a lot of space," according to Beldon.

They also saw cookbooks that screamed "amateur" — hundreds of recipes and a few specks of art all crammed into the pages.

SOTA's goal — a book that obviously was an art museum production but one that would be useful to cooks.

The cookbook planners talked about concentrating on appetizers or desserts rather than preparing a general cookbook.

In the end, however, they settled on a general cookbook — a publication that would be of the most use to the most people. They considered including special sections for persons who own food processors or microwave ovens but scratched this idea. They decided those people would buy cookbooks specially suited to their purposes.

Before committee members could decide on the cookbook's sections, they had to wait and see what kind of recipes the museum's members submitted.

SOTA sent out pleas to all 3,200 members to ask for family recipes like "your special steak marinade, Aunt Matilda's chocolate cake, two ways to cook veal or a meal in a dish like crabmeat casserole."

Responses to the request for recipes numbered nearly 1,000. Some persons sent 5 or 10 recipes. Others copied down a single special family recipe. A list of the returns sounds a bit like "The Twelve Days of Christmas." A sample — the cookbook committee received 12 recipes for chocolate cake, 9 for cheesecake, 8 seafood appetizers, 5 zucchini breads, 4 kinds of mushroom soup and 3 apple crisp recipes. Appetizers and desserts led the submissions.

SOTA members had to eliminate roughly half the recipes to keep the book at a manageable size. Some recipes were eliminated because they were duplicates, others were put aside because their senders had already had recipes selected for the book. Extremely common recipes — those found in practically every cookbook — were also eliminated.

Teams of volunteer testers sorted out additional recipes for elimination when the recipes were incomplete, unclear or simply didn't yield good results.

Sections that made the final cookbook: appetizers, soups, eggs, breads, salads, meats, game, poultry, fish, seafood, vegetables, pasta and rice, relishes, cookies, desserts, beverages and restaurants.

Here are some of the appetizers from the cookbook, in time for you to try them during holiday entertaining.

Superb shrimp toast

1½ lbs. shrimp, cleaned and shelled
1 small onion
1 piece fresh ginger (size of a quarter)
7 water chestnuts
4 Tbsps. wine (rice or sherry)
2 tsps. sugar
1 tsp. salt
Liberal dash pepper
Cornstarch (as needed to thicken)
¼ cup water
12-15 slices stale bread
2 cups sesame oil

Mince shrimp, onion, ginger and water chestnuts. Add wine, seasonings and water. Spread on stale bread triangles, which have been decrusted. Deep fry both sides (spread side down first) in sesame oil until golden brown. Drain on paper towel. Serves 12.

Broiled chicken bits

2 chicken breasts, boned and skinned
½ cup Sake (or dry sherry)
⅓ cup sesame oil
1 Tbsp. freshly grated ginger
½ cup soy sauce
1 garlic clove, pressed
⅓ cup sesame seeds, lightly toasted

Cut chicken into 1-inch cubes. Combine sake, sesame oil, ginger, soy sauce and garlic in a glass bowl. Marinate chicken cubes in mixture for 20-30 minutes. Drain, skewer on bamboo sticks. Broil over charcoal or in broiler 4-5 minutes until nicely browned. Dip in toasted sesame seeds and serve. Serves 4-6.

Corner cafe cheese ball

2 8-oz. pkges. cream cheese
½ lb. Cheddar cheese spread
½ cup mayonnaise
¼ cup finely chopped onion
¼ cup finely chopped chives
Dash Worcestershire sauce
½ tsp. lemon juice
1 Tbsp. dry sherry
Sesame seeds
Chopped walnuts

Mix all ingredients at room temperature. Divide into two balls. After chilling for an hour, roll in chopped walnuts and sesame seeds. Can also be rolled in parsley for added color. Yield 2 balls.

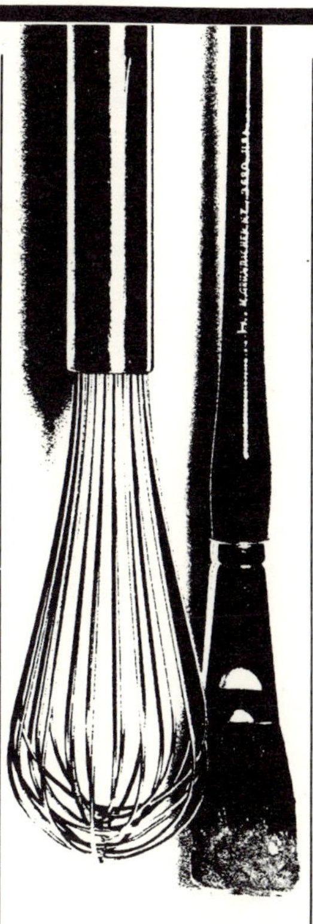

THE CULINARY ARTS

The slick new cookbook published by the Allentown Art Museum — just in time to toast a 20th anniversary — makes a good last-minute Christmas gift.

Story by Diane Stoneback, food editor.

SLIM GOURMET

'No frills fare' good eating for dieters

By BARBARA GIBBONS

If you fly a lot, you should know about the "no-frills fare" dieters can order as an alternative to the fattening, nonfilling toy food served on most flights. While airline "special diet" meals will never win any gourmet awards, the food is definitely superior, not only in nutrition but in taste and quality, too.

Wouldn't you rather have simple baked chicken or fish, or a lean tenderloin steak, plus some real vegetables and fruit?

You don't have to be a first-class, full-fare passenger or a VIP. If your ticket entitles you to a meal, it also entitles you to a special meal, if that's what you need or want. It's a service that virtually all major domestic and most foreign airlines provide.

Don't feel sensitive about asking for a low-calorie meal. (Anyway, most "special meal" fliers I've seen are slim, poised executives who look as if they know where they're going.) In case you're wondering, the airline will not embarrass you in any way by calling attention to your special meal. You won't hear, "Hello, this is your captain speaking. Will the obese person who requires a special meal kindly identify himself or herself to the flight attendants? Stand up so we can all get a look at you, Fatso!" What they will do is say: "Passenger (Your Name), please push the call button."

You can avoid even that amount of public notice by identifying yourself to the first steward you see when you enter the plane door: "Hi, I'm (your name) and I get the low-calorie meal." The flight attendant will note your seat number. This may also save you from being served last, one of the admitted disadvantages of being "special."

You can even specify poultry, seafood or meat. Or nonmeat: in addition to low-cal, you can also order vegetarian. Or kosher. Or diabetic, low-cholesterol, salt-free or bland. (I've tried them all, and if you ask me, the last four are interchangeable with low-cal.) Occasionaly, I snitch some lime slices from the bar cart to squirt on the plain baked chicken. On one occasion, when I was returning from a TV cooking show, I retrieved some soy sauce from my underseat luggage to jazz up the airline's plain cooking. "Fussy," mumbled the stranger in the next seat. However, he was eating a glubby-looking macaroni UFO while I had steak, really green, green beans, sliced carrots, fresh orange salad, Swedish crispbread and a real apple for dessert.

How do you get this service? When you arrange for your ticket, tell the travel agent or reservation clerk that you want a low-calorie (or other) meal on all your meal flights. In theory, your special meal will also show up on all continuing and connecting flights, even those on other airlines.

Human error being what it is, however, you should take extra precautions to get what you want. My experience is that special meals are "no-shows" about a third of the time . . . because somebody didn't push the right button or fill in the right blank. You won't go hungry; you simply get served what everyone else is having. This is especially vexing on long flights or if a special meal is medically mandated . . . salt-free or diabetic, for example.

You can increase your chances of getting what you want if you follow these tips:

►Book well ahead of time. Some airlines say they require 48 hours, others say six hours' notice. To be on the safe side, book your special meal request as early as possible.

►Ask the reservation agent's name when you make your special request. This puts him or her on notice that the airline will be able to fix blame if you wind up eating greasy lasagna somewhere over Toledo.

►At least six hours before flight time, call the airline to confirm your special meal request. There is still time for the meal to be arranged. Get that person's name, too.

►Arrive for your flight one hour ahead of time (a good idea in any case). When you pick up your tickets, ask the ticket agent to confirm that your special meal request is on the manifest. If not, chances are there may still be time for the ticket agent to pick up the phone and ask the catering company to add a special meal to the food cargo.

►Don't be put off at this point. If the counter person doesn't want to be bothered, he or she may tell you it's too late. Insist that the caterer be called. Demand that every effort be made to provide the service the airline agreed to when you arranged your flight. (One way to transform an attitude of surly indifference into courteous solicitude is to request a supervisor so that you may arrange a complaint in writing.)

Finally, if you do wind up over Toledo with greasy lasagna, do file a complaint. If every passenger who fails to get the special meal needed takes assertive action, meals and service may improve.

Some breakfast cereals are ten times as fattening as others. For a complete calorie, fat, protein and carbohydrate guide to nationally marketed cereals — by brand name — send a stamped, self-addressed envelope and 35 cents to Slim Gourmet cereal guide, in care of The Sunday Call-Chronicle, Sparta, N.J. 07871.

The New York Times/

A master plan merges consistency, surprise

"There are two ways to go about a visual transformation of a newspaper. The first is to develop a tight cohesive format for the entire paper, relate all elements to each other, change the whole thing in one major step, keep the execution in tight adherence to format."

The speaker is Louis Silverstein, assistant managing editor-editorial art of The New York Times. The place is a newspaper design workshop at Chicago in September, 1979. Silverstein is explaining how The Times decided to redesign.

He continues:

"The second is perhaps less logical but realistically more acceptable for many papers, especially the bigger ones. This is to change a step or a section at a time, but keep a consistent character as you go along — let each piece fit into a master plan in your mind, so to speak.

"This is the path we've followed at The Times.

"Each new section has a strong character, a definite sense of structure, and a definite styling, and in these senses, is carefully formulated. But we depend very heavily on day-to-day creativity in execution.

"So we attempt a juggling act — careful control, consistent character, yet with great emphasis on surprise, flexibility and inventiveness in content as well as design.

"I like to stress what can be described as the design of the total paper with questions of space planning and strong design in alliance

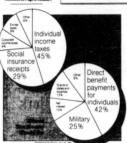

The New York Times — "All the News That's Fit to Print" — NEW YORK, FRIDAY, JANUARY 16, 1981 — 50 CENTS

The New York Times/

with, not defeated by, the presence of ads. My emphasis is on configuration relationship of ad space to editorial content, and especially the relationship of the new feature sections to each other, and to hard news.

"This is the structure or the architecture of a paper."

The Times pages printed here show some of the changes in Times design approach.

One of the two front pages is typical, Silverstein says. The other, less typical, ties a big news event to a special picture layout.

"In both cases," Silverstein says, "it is characteristic that the headlines and design attempt to communicate levels of importance of the stories."

In the daily feature sections (Home, Living, SportsMonday, Science Times and Weekend), says Silverstein, "we worked to give each section a strong magazine-like identity of its own, and yet keep them related to each other and to the paper as a whole. The format and photography attempt to do this — allowing plenty of room for day-by-day creativity, and yet keeping a recognizable ongoing consistent character."

The New York Times

LATE CITY EDITION

VOL.CXXIX....No. 44,590

NEW YORK, WEDNESDAY, MAY 21, 1980

25 CENTS

BUSH WINS MICHIGAN; REAGAN AND CARTER ARE OREGON VICTORS

CALIFORNIAN NEARS MAJORITY

Results Leave Him Just Shy of 998 Delegates Needed to Capture Republican Nomination

By ADAM CLYMER

50,000 Warned of Volcano Flood Threat

Scientists See Danger In Overflow of Lake Dammed by Debris

By WALLACE TURNER

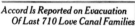

In what he called "a stroke of luck," Vern Hodgson, an amateur photographer of Lynnwood, Wash., was setting up his 35mm camera on a tripod when Mount St. Helens began to erupt Sunday morning. He took these pictures from a distance of 15 miles, using 400 ASA color print film. In all, he made 16 pictures in about four minutes, shifting from a 75-100mm zoom lens with an extender, making it the equivalent of a 300mm lens, to a 50mm lens and finally a 35mm wide-angle lens as the cloud from the eruption widened to about 20 miles.

QUEBECERS DEFEAT SOVEREIGNTY MOVE BY DECISIVE MARGIN

Cabinet Resigns In South Korea As Riots Grow

More Deaths Reported in Huge Kwangju Protest

By HENRY SCOTT STOKES

A TRUDEAU VICTORY

Many French Canadians Join English-Speakers to Back Federalism

By HENRY GINIGER

U.S. Scolds France on Soviet Talks And Britain Over Sanctions on Iran

By BERNARD GWERTZMAN

157 ELDERLY WOMEN DIE IN JAMAICA FIRE

14 Missing at Institution — Police Charge Arson Was Involved

Accord Is Reported on Evacuation Of Last 710 Love Canal Families

By ROBIN HERMAN

CONFEREES' ACCORD ON BUDGET SNAGGED

5 Liberal House Democrats Balk at $6.1 Billion Rise for Military

By MARTIN TOLCHIN

INSIDE

Decision on Cubans' Status
The White House said arriving Cubans would be treated as applicants for asylum, so Congress need not be consulted on the number admitted. Page A24.

New York to Get U.S. Funds
New York State will get the Federal money it needs to make $40 million in Medicaid payments to New York City hospitals and nursing homes. Page B3.

Miami Police Inquiry Is Set
The Attorney General announced that a team of Federal prosecutors and agents would study alleged abuses by the Miami police. Page A22.

Around Nation	A26	Music	C15,C26
Art	C13	News on People	B4
Books	C30	Obituaries	A33
Bridge	C30	Op-Ed	A30
Business Day	D1-19	Real Estate	B5
Chess	C30	Shipping	D13
Crossword	C21	Sports	A28-22
Editorials	A34	Theaters	C28-26
Going Out Guide	C22	TV / Radio	C31,C26
Living Section	C1-21	U.N. Events	A4
Movies	C28	Weather	B6

News Summary and Index, Page B1

The New York Times /

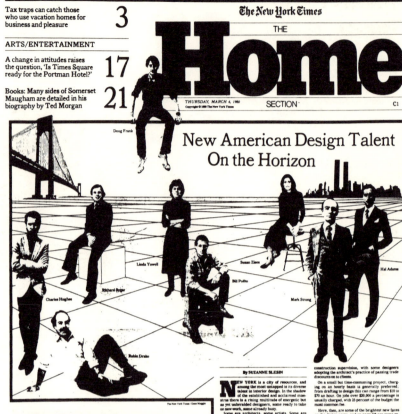

Tax traps can catch those who use vacation homes for business and pleasure — 3

ARTS/ENTERTAINMENT

A change in attitudes raises the question, 'Is Times Square ready for the Portman Hotel?' — 17

Books: Many sides of Somerset Maugham are detailed in his biography by Ted Morgan — 21

The New York Times

Home

THE

SECTION

THURSDAY, MARCH 6, 1980
Copyright © 1980 The New York Times

C1

New American Design Talent On the Horizon

By SUZANNE SLESIN

Continued on Page C8

An Old Factory Holds Tiffany Archive

By JANE GENTESSE

Silver vase made for William Cullen Bryant.

Continued on Page C8

Shopping for a Stereo System With a Budget of Under $600

By MICHAEL deCOURCY HINDS

Sam Goody's

Rabsons

Continued on Page C8

The New York Times /

TUESDAY, AUGUST 21, 1979
Copyright © 1979 The New York Times

Science Times

With Education,
Style, Arts,
Sports

The New York Times

C1

Scientists See Peril In Wasting Helium

By MALCOLM W. BROWNE

HELIUM, as commonplace as the gas-filled children's balloons sold at the zoo, is under intense new scrutiny because of a warning by scientists that wasting it will imperil the world's technological future.

The warning has compelled Government policy-makers and energy experts to reexamine the unique properties and potential uses of helium, a substance so elusive that after its existence was discovered on the sun in 1868, three decades elapsed before it was also found to exist on earth.

Scientific witnesses testified at a Congressional hearing this month that helium is the key to a "superechnology" by which global energy starvation can be held at bay. While helium itself is not a fuel, it can vastly extend the usefulness of such nonrenewable fuels as oil, coal and uranium because of its ability to remove all "friction" from the flow of electricity, a characteristic known as superconductivity.

Ultra-efficient motors, electrical storage systems far better than any chemical battery and new transportation systems are among the expected benefits of superconductivity. Some working prototypes have already been built, but government and industry have so far been unwilling to make the financial investments needed for large-scale application.

Scientists' statements received a sympathetic hearing by the House Subcommittee on Energy and Power, and experts hope a bill enforcing conservation of helium may be passed in the next session of Congress.

But many earlier attempts to enact such a law have failed.

Despite the fact that helium cannot be replaced by anything once it is lost, the scientists said, some 13 billion cubic feet of the precious gas is being dumped into the atmosphere each year, mainly by the companies that pull it out of the earth along with the natural fuel gas they sell. Existing stockpiled reserves of helium are vastly larger than required by the current small demand, and a helium-based "superechnology" has yet to become a reality. Consequently, gas companies have considered the cost of separating and

Continued on Page C2

Helium, the refrigerant needed for the new technology of superconductors, can be efficiently cooled to near absolute zero in Stirling heat engines like the one below. Mechanical power is used to compress the gas, counting it to heat (1). The heat is ducted away and the helium is then allowed to expand, thus chilling it (2). The cycle is repeated until the gas is so cold it liquefies (3).

Only three small blimps like this one are in service in the United States today, but huge, helium-filled airships have been proposed as the freight haulers of the future.

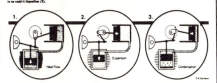

1. Heat Flow
2. Expansion
3. Condensation

U.S. Expects To Learn From Soviet Space Effort

By BAYARD WEBSTER

THE two Soviet astronauts who lived for six months 200 miles above the earth in a compartment the size of a small house trailer are expected to provide biologists and physicians with a wealth of scientific data about living and working in space. But eager American space scientists likely will have to wait until the end of October to learn of any new Soviet findings or why one of the astronauts complained after landing of having trouble speaking normally.

Lieut. Col. Vladimir Lyakhov and Valery Ryumin, an engineer, orbited the earth in a 6 space station for 175 days, breaking the previous record, also held by Soviets, by more than a month. The United States record is 84 days in Skylab. They returned to earth safely on Sunday in a Soyuz spacecraft.

Dr. William Shumate, a medical scientist who is deputy chief of medical sciences at the Johnson Space Center in Houston, said that although there are as yet no scientific reports from the astronauts' record-breaking flight, a joint American-Soviet manned space flight working group has exchanged information on earlier flights. And on Oct. 25, a 13-man Soviet team of scientists and physicians will come to the space center to present the results of their research on the Salyut manned flight.

He noted that of the two reported comments made by Mr. Ryumin after he landed — that he felt twice as heavy as he was told he would feel, and that he had trouble articulating words — the latter was puzzling, and the former expected.

"We didn't find any vocal inarticulation problems with our astronauts, and I've tried to think of a reason why it might have that effect. We're really anxious to have that one explained," Dr. Shumate said.

"But the feeling-heavy problem is normal when most astronauts return. Ours have often remarked when they got on the ground that they felt like their pants were going to fall off. In space, of course, the pants are weightless."

Dr. Shumate expects data from the Salyut mission to be "a major contribution to man's space endeavors. We know a lot about the effects of living in weightless space from the shorter orbital flights," he said in a telephone interview, "but a flight of this

Continued on Page C7

EDUCATION

New Test For 'Black English'

By DENA KLEIMAN

"I'M gonna be showing you some pictures. Some about kids and some about other things. After I show a picture, I'm gonna ask you some questions about it. Ain't no right or wrong answers — just say what you must."

These are the instructions, to be read by a teacher, at the beginning of a test to determine whether elementary school students speak "black English," a dialect found in many black communities.

The test, developed by the staff at Marymount Manhattan College in New York, has been proposed as one of the steps a school district in Ann Arbor, Mich., might take to comply with a Federal district court decision in the so-called "black English" case.

Under the ruling by Judge Charles W. Joiner, black English must be recognized as a dialect that differs systematically in phonology and grammar from standard English and has its own set of rules. It should not be perceived in any way as indicative of a youngster's inability to learn, he must be understood as a barrier to learning standard English.

In his ruling, which focused national attention on the issue of black English, Judge Joiner directed the school district to devise a teacher-training plan. The school district, which has decided not to appeal, last Friday submitted to the judge a 30-hour course designed to teach faculty members about the dialect, how to identify youngsters who

Continued on Page C4

Pompeii Dead 1,900 Years, but Vesuvius Lives

By LINDA CHARLTON

Vesuvius, as it erupted in 1944.
The New York Times

It was just after one o'clock on a sunny August afternoon in the bustling resort city of Pompeii when residents and tourists noticed the strange cloud that seemed to be rising out of the nearby mountain named Vesuvius. Oh, there had been earthquakes in the past few days, but they were common enough in the area. No one realized it was the last day of Pompeii.

Pliny the Younger, whose description is the only known eyewitness account of the eruption, wrote that by the evening of that first day, most people in the area were convinced "that the final endless night of which we have heard had come upon the world." He himself, he wrote, was curiously consoled by the thought that "all mankind were involved in the same calamity, and that I was perishing with the world itself."

It was Aug. 24, 79 — 1,900 years ago this Friday — that Pompeii died and became immortal. The 12 feet of ash that buried the city of about 20,000 persons obliterated what had been a prosperous provincial Roman coastal resort, about 16 miles from Naples. But it also preserved it in a state of suspended animation. There was no time to prepare for death, so it was life in mid-breath that reappeared when chance excavations in the middle of the 18th century turned up evidences of the buried and forgotten town. Since then, and increasingly as archeology has become more sophisticated, Pompeii has become one of the Western world's fascinations.

It was not, of course, the beginning of a last endless night. And although we now know much about volcanoes in general and the heat and pressure inside the earth that spawn them, we don't know precisely why Vesuvius erupted that day or what caused its more recent eruptions or, for that matter, when it may erupt again. But Ve-

suvius remains the volcano in the popular imagination, mostly, according to the volcanologist Martin Prinz, because "people love disasters."

As Dr. Prinz explained, volcanic action is responsible for the planet we live on, its waters and its atmosphere. The cause of volcanic activity is the continuing movement of the earth's crust, specifically of the tectonic plates of crust that slide slowly about the earth a few inches or less per year. An explosive eruption, of the type that destroyed Pompeii, is the venting of material under high pressure, with the volcano's crater serving as the vent. The interior of a volcano contains molten material or magma in which gases such as carbon dioxide, ammonia, chlorine, methane, sulfur dioxide and carbon monoxide are dissolved. When volcanoes do explode, they emit ash, steam, gases, stones, lava — all intensely hot — but not fire itself, as high as 35 or 40 miles into the air.

The scientific study of volcanoes suffers from a major handicap: The interior of the beast is inaccessible to the scientists who study them. Because of this, Dr. Prinz notes, "No one can predict what's going on inside; you can only measure it" after something happens. As to why a volcano, such as Vesuvius, erupts when it does, "We have no idea, as far as I know."

From observation, it is known that many volcanoes, including Vesuvius, erupt cyclically — but, Dr. Prinz cautions, it is a "very, very rough cycle." Vesuvius, since 1036, has been in what is called a phase of basaltic eruption, meaning the exudation of liquid, tarry material, perhaps with some "fire fountains" or small blobs of red-hot material spurting 1,000 feet or so. But the eruption of 79 A.D. was an explosive one, an ash eruption, as were those that followed until it went into the new phase in 606.

There is some speculation as to what influences the type of eruption. For ex-

Continued on Page C2

THE DOCTOR'S WORLD

On Alert for The Potentially Fatal D.T.'s

By LAWRENCE K. ALTMAN, M.D.

AS an intern in San Francisco I treated a business executive, a member of a prominent West Coast family, who went to surgery for repair of a hip that he broke in a fall. Although he denied drinking more than an occasional cocktail, my suspicion — based on limited experience as a medical student at Boston City Hospital where alcoholism was a commonly treated problem — was that he was an alcoholic with impending delirium tremens, or the D.T.'s. It was something about his manner, perhaps the way he answered questions. My suggestion to the orthopedic surgeon in charge was that the man be treated for this potentially life-threatening condition.

The surgeon disagreed. He voiced surprise that someone would consider a man of such stature a silent alcoholic, let alone one who faced the D.T.'s.

But at 3 A.M. the nurse called, asking me to examine the patient, who, now in a cast, was agitated, restless and unable to sleep. When I arrived at his room, he was hallucinating. The diagnosis was clear: florid D.T.'s. He described spiders and other

Continued on Page C2

Woodcut depicts effects of delirium tremens.
The Bettmann Archive

ARTS: Fay Kanin, new head of film academy, discusses her 'Friendly Fire,' page 9/ **BOOKS:** Dyson's 'Disturbing the Universe,' page 11

STYLE: In California, a commune for single parents that works/ A restaurant that's a second home for dancers in the Berkshires, page 13

The Providence Journal/

Its redesign offered some startling ideas

The design philosophy of Peter Palazzo took form in his redesign of The Providence Journal. Known for his redesign of the Sunday New York Herald Tribune in the early 1960s, Palazzo was hired a decade later by the Journal and Bulletin to suggest ways to revitalize the newspaper's graphics.

Palazzo explained his design views and his methodology in The Bulletin of the American Society of Newspaper Editors (July / August 1974).

"There has long been a fear that adding graphics to print news presentation could only obscure or diminish the news value or communication of the printed word," he wrote.

"Ten years ago the Sunday New York Herald Tribune proved not only was this not so but also that the opposite was true — that an exciting visual presentation not only stimulated reader interest in the news, but, if done effectively, even enhanced and dramatized the editorial value of what might ordinarily be dull, routine news items."

On Dec. 2, 1972, the morning Journal and evening Bulletin were combined into one Saturday edition. The Palazzo redesign was used. During 1973 the design was applied to the Sunday newspaper and then, over time, to the daily Journal.

Palazzo's specifications were startling to some editors. His front page was divided into three blocks: one for pictures, whether they accompanied stories or were free-standing; another for news briefs, summarizing the contents of inside

The Providence Journal

Published in Providence, R.I. Monday, February 19, 1979 Two Sections/36 Pages 20 Cents; $1.20 per week by carrier

CITY EDITION

State

JOHN M. BROWN, new warden of the state prison, says conditions have "improved enormously" since he took over in October. Page A-3.

SEN. JOHN H. CHAFEE says that he favors passage of a constitutional amendment that would limit federal spending, but believes the move should be initiated by Congress rather than by the states. Page A-3.

THE DIRECTORS of the North Kingstown Chamber of Commerce draft a statement expressing concern that the Town Council's attempts to halt construction work on the Electric Boat plant could seriously hurt local businesses. Page A-3.

APPRAISERS HIRED by the Providence Housing Authority say a 256-unit North End housing project could carry a price tag of between $2.2 to $5 million. Page B-1.

International

BRITISH UNION and local-government officials wait for the Labor government to approve a deal they worked out to settle the strike by 1.5 million public-service workers. Page A-5.

National

A NEW ORLEANS firemen's union leader urges off-duty firemen to join striking police on picket lines. Mayor Ernest Morial offers amnesty from discipline to strikers who return to their jobs by noon today. Page A-6.

THE SON of Sen. Alan Cranston, D-Calif., is charged with arson and attempted murder for allegedly trying to kill his former girlfriend. Page A-2.

IN A SUBURB of Chicago, "Defense Technology '79," an exhibit of modern-day weapons expertise and seminars, opens to a private audience as thousands of protesters pray and shout outside. Page A-2.

Financial

TAX SAVINGS have been created for almost everyone by the 1978 Revenue Act, and columnist Sylvia Porter explains the new breaks. Page B-4.

INVESTORS ARE BECOMING more interested in Treasury bills, notes, bonds and money-market certificates, but the mathematics of calculating the yields on such investments is hard to understand. Page B-4.

Sports

COLIN AHERN'S goal with 50 seconds remaining lifts Providence College to a 4-3 hockey victory over Cornell. Page A-7.

RUDY WILLIAMS' phenomenal 92-foot basket stands an excellent chance of going into the record books as the longest field goal ever recorded. Page A-7.

CUMBERLAND AND MIDDLETOWN win divisional titles in R.I. Interscholastic sectional wrestling championships. Page A-12.

Weather

A CHANCE of light snow today. Clearing tonight. Sunny tomorrow. High today in the 20s. Low tonight in the upper teens. High tomorrow in the 30s. Complete report on Page A-2.

Index

A gentle kiss, words of praise

President Carter comforts Mary Ann Dubs after calling the slaying of her husband, Ambassador Adolph Dubs, a "despicable act of violence." Story on this page.

—UPI Photo

Rescued from the sea

Aviation Machinist Mate 2nd Class Mark Torr, right, sits in a helicopter at Hyannis, Mass., after being pulled from the sea after the chopper he was riding in, below, crashed. The Coast Guard helicopter was rescuing an injured man on a Japanese trawler about 180 miles southeast of Cape Cod. Torr was the only known survivor of the crash. Story on this page.

—UPI Photos

Chinese warned by U.S.S.R. to halt warfare

Vietnamese assert they are checking the advance of Chinese army troops and tanks

The New York Times

HONG KONG — Vietnam asserted yesterday that it was "checking" China's attack across their border and had destroyed 46 Chinese tanks and killed hundreds of Chinese soldiers.

But information about the fighting remained extremely sketchy, and analysts here said it was impossible to tell how far the Chinese had advanced into Vietnam, or what Peking's real objectives were.

• • •

CHINA ITSELF released no news at all yesterday about the attacks its troops launched early Saturday along much of the rugged 480-mile frontier. The troops were supported by tanks, artillery and warplanes.

United States intends to stay out of Indochina conflict. Page B-5.

It did appear, however, that Peking remained anxious to limit the fighting, and perhaps intended only a lightning raid to "teach the Vietnamese a lesson," as one source suggested yesterday.

Repeating a Chinese-government statement made Saturday, the Chinese Communist paper *Jenmin Jih Pao* said in an editorial yesterday, "After hitting back at the aggressors as far as is necessary, our frontier forces will turn to guard strictly the frontier of our motherland."

"We don't want a single inch of Vietnamese soil. What we want is a peaceful and stable frontier," the paper said.

The Vietnam News Agency claimed yesterday that heavy fighting was going on from Quang Ninh province along the coast to Lai Chau province in the west.

Turn to VIETNAM, Page A-20

Carter lauds slain envoy

United Press International

WASHINGTON — President Carter yesterday condemned the slaying of U.S. Ambassador Adolph Dubs as a "despicable act of violence" and then comforted a weeping Mary Ann Dubs with a gentle kiss and words of praise for her husband.

Dubs was "a good man, a courageous man" who died honorably serving his country in Afghanistan, Mr. Carter said after the landing of the presidential jet that carried the slain diplomat's body home.

Mr. Carter stood solemnly throughout the bitterly cold ceremony at Andrews Air Force Base that honored Dubs, who

Turn to DUBS, Page A-20

'Stop before it's too late,' says Kremlin statement as Russians consult with Vietnam

Associated Press

MOSCOW — Warning China to "stop before it is too late," the Soviet Union pledged yesterday to honor a recent treaty with Vietnam calling for consultations and mutual support after an attack.

Immediately after the statement was made public, Soviet Foreign Minister Andrei A. Gromyko received Vietnamese Ambassador Nguyen Huu Khieu, apparently to discuss how far the Kremlin would go to help its ally after Saturday's invasion by China.

The treaty is not a military alliance, and makes no specific provisions for sending troops. The statement said Vietnam "is capable of standing up for itself," indicating that a Soviet troop commitment was unlikely, at least for the moment.

One western analyst here said the Soviet "range of options is across the board" under the treaty. Another said he saw it as "raising the level of warning" to China's relatively new leadership.

The Soviet statement said: "All responsibility for the consequences of continuing the aggression by Peking against the

Turn to SOVIET, Page A-20

Iran's new regime breaks off diplomatic relations with Israel

Journal-Bulletin Wire Reports

TEHRAN — Iran's new revolutionary government broke diplomatic relations with Israel yesterday in a move timed to coincide with the arrival in Tehran of Palestine Liberation Organization leader Yasser Arafat.

"Today Iran, tomorrow Palestine," Arafat said. He predicted Iran would shut off all oil supplies to Israel.

Premier Mehdi Bazargan was reported by Iran radio to have described the break in relations as being "fully in keeping with the policy announced before we came to power of cutting all ties with Israel."

The government said the 22 Israeli diplomats in Iran had been ordered to leave the country and had already done so, and that Iranian diplomats in Israel had been recalled.

A buoyant Yasser Arafat met with Iran's provisional leaders yesterday and said the Iranian revolution has turned the strategic balance in the Middle East "upside down."

Arafat won assurances from Ayatollah Ruhollah Khomeini that Iran will "turn to the issue of victory over Israel," after the nation consolidates its strength, Tehran Radio reported.

The Moslem holy man's secret Islamic court continued rounding up officials of the old regime, and Khomeini aides predicted that more executions would take place.

• • •

TEHRAN RADIO said Khomeini's forces were searching for deposed Prime Minister Shahpour Bakhtiar, whose 38-day-old government was swept aside by Khomeini's forces on Feb. 11. The station denied its previous report that he had been arrested and was awaiting trial.

Iran's official Pars news agency said

Turn to IRAN, Page A-20

6-below reading record for date

We broke another one.

The National Weather Service at Green State Airport in Warwick reported that the thermometer bottomed out at six below zero at 7:30 a.m. yesterday. That broke a record for the date of minus-three degrees, set in 1958.

Bill Tobin, a Weather Service meteorologist, said Rhode Island is in for a dusting of snow early this morning, with flurries continuing into the afternoon.

Tobin said Rhode Island, which has been experiencing record low temperatures for more than a week, may see some relief by Wednesday or Thursday, when the mercury may rise to the mid to upper 30s.

Coast Guard helicopter crashes at sea; 3 dead

By LEE DYKAS
Journal-Bulletin Staff Writer

A Coast Guard helicopter crashed into the sea early yesterday, killing at least three members of its five-man crew while on a rescue mission about 180 miles southeast of Cape Cod.

One of the five, Hospital Corpsman 2nd Class Bruce Kaehler, 27, of Fort Collins, Colo., was still missing last night. Three were known dead: Lt. Cmdr. James Stiles, 33, the pilot; Capt. George Burge, 38, of Fredericton, New Brunswick, the copilot, who was on an exchange program from the Canadian Forces, and Aviation Electronics Technician 2nd Class John Tait, 22, of Silver Spring, Md.

The fifth crewman, Aviation Machinist Mate 2nd Class Mark Torr, 20, of Rochester, N.H., who survived the crash, was picked up by a Japanese fishing vessel and later was transferred by another Coast Guard helicopter to the consolidated air station at Otis Air Force Base. A Coast Guard spokesman in Boston said Torr was "in pretty good shape" last night.

The spokesman said the helicopter initially was sent to the Japanese fishing vessel Kaisei Maru about 9:45 p.m. Saturday to airlift a crewman, Suzuke Masaji, 47, who had suffered a severe head cut, to the Cape Cod Hospital at Hyannis.

The chopper returned to the air base after it was found that an error was made in the initial location given to the pilot.

The helicopter was refueled, and with the same crew left Cape Cod again about 3:15 a.m. It was making its second pass over the fishing vessel, with winds gusting to 30 miles an hour and seas running up to 25 feet, about 5:25 a.m. when "something went wrong and it crashed into the sea," the spokesman said.

The Japanese picked up the survivor and the bodies of the three victims.

• • •

A SECOND HH3F long-range helicopter was dispatched from the air base at

Turn to COPTER, Page A-20

The Providence Journal/

stories, and the third for four or five major news stories.

News briefs ran across the top of the page, pictures were laid out in a rectangular block running from beneath the briefs to the bottom of the page, and news filled the rest of the page.

Palazzo planned inside pages and section covers that grouped similar news and followed the cover format of blocking pictures. Headlines were centered, the first line being longer than the second.

''The new paper is designed for fast reading,'' Palazzo wrote, ''and provides news that is easy to get at and understand.

''The original logotype was retained but enlarged and run across the top of the page instead of being crammed in an ever-decreasing space at the top left of the page. It was also relettered to bring back the esthetic forms of the original letters . . . ''

The objective, Palazzo wrote, was ''to create an exciting new format that's **easy** — easy in makeup and easy in composition.

''An attempt was made to be orderly, simple and consistent in design . . . There is little waste and guidelines are used extensively . . . Pictures are collected throughout when possible for maximum impact and to show them to greatest advantage . . .

''Space devoted to news and information is collected and more organized and, therefore, looks as impressive as it should and is easier to locate.

''Although contemporary and functional in design, the new format has enough of the traditional to give it continuity with the past.''

Orioles pound Red Sox, 10-3
Page B-1

PawSox sweep at Columbus
Page B-3

Lockwood hit by batted ball.

Evonne titlist at Wimbledon
Page B-3

Sykes captures Publinx golf
Page B-2

The New York Mets and Montreal Expos battle at Shea Stadium.

Providence Journal-Bulletin

Saturday, July 5, 1980
Section B

Sports WEEKEND

- Classified/ Page B-8
- Junior Edition/ Page B-15
- Comics/ Page B-16
- People in the news/ Page B-18
- What's going on/ Page B-18

MANUEL ORANTES won at Longwood in '77 and '78.

— AP Photo

— Journal-Bulletin Photos

STAN SMITH, right in photo above, and Bob Lutz won the Miller doubles title last season at Newport Casino, below.

— Journal-Bulletin Photo

BRIAN TEACHER won last year's fog-shrouded final at Newport.

JIMMY CONNORS will be seeded No. 1 at Longwood.

Miller, U.S. Pro events serve up tennis tradition

By MIKE SZOSTAK
Journal-Bulletin Sports Writer

If you have the time, New England has the tennis.

At least for the next two weeks. Tennis fanatics seeking their summer highs will be appeased in two days with the start of play in the $100,000 Miller Hall of Fame Tennis Championship at the Newport Casino.

Then, after seven days of serves and volleys and fruit salads and ice cream cones on the lawns of the 100-year-old Casino, they will be able to turn to the $175,000 U.S. Pro Tennis Championships at the Longwood Cricket Club in Brookline, Mass.

This marks the first year the tournaments are running back to back. Newport has become a homecoming for Americans and the first port of call for foreigners who have played in Italy, France and England during the spring.

* * *

LONGWOOD, WHICH traditionally has been held during the third week in August, will be held July 14-20 this year. The change is one of several the Longwood Cricket Club has made in an attempt to restore the tournament to its previous stature in this country as second in prominence only to the U.S. Open.

This is the fifth year of the Miller tournament, and while the event has never attracted a star-studded draw it always has provided exciting action. And it seems to have settled comfortably into its role as a second-tier attraction in a game where big money flows like the cream over those strawberries at Wimbledon.

Brian Teacher, currently ranked No. 26 in the world, defeated Stan Smith last year for his first major Grand Prix championship at Newport. Rain delayed the start of the match for two hours and fog swirled about the Casino's Stadium Court during the match.

''It was the eeriest feeling playing in this fog,'' Smith said at the time. ''It was like a dream.''

Smith and Teacher will be back next week. Smith, ranked 18th in the world, could very well be the top-seeded player.

* * *

BERNIE MITTON, an unheralded South African, defeated John James, an unheralded Australian, for the $75,000 title in '78. Mitton deserved the championship. He won his first match in a tie-breaker, his second in three sets, his third in straight sets over Arthur Ashe, his semifinal on a Sunday morning and the final that afternoon in a tie-breaker.

Mitton, ranked 51st on the Association of Tennis Professionals computer, will be in Newport next week.

Tim Gullikson, the right-handed partner of the Gullikson brothers (Tom is the lefty), was the 1977 title. He beat Hank Pfister in what was a $50,000 event for his very first Grand Prix tournament championship. Tim and Tom finished second in the doubles that year but came back and won in '78.

Tim, No. 33 in the world now, will return again next week. So will Tom, who is about 70 rungs down the ATP ladder. He has a wild card berth.

Vijay Amritraj of India won the inaugural Miller tournament in 1976, a $35,000 competiton with a draw of 16. Amritraj defeated Teacher, who was in his first year on the tour. He won the final point of the match with an ace. Amritraj, No. 33 on the ATP computer, will try for his second Miller title next week.

* * *

ALSO ON HAND will be the other two wild card entries, John Sadri, explosive in temperment and talent and ranked No.

Turn to DOUBLE TREAT, Page B-5

Newport, Boston tennis facts

EVENT: Miller Hall of Fame Tennis Championships, a Volvo Grand Prix tournament. Men's singles and doubles tournament. Men's singles and doubles. Singles draw of 32.

WHERE: International Tennis Hall of Fame, Newport Casino, 194 Bellevue Ave., Newport.

WHEN: Monday through Sunday.

PRIZE MONEY: $100,000.

TIME: Play will begin at noon Monday through Friday and at 2 p.m. Saturday (semifinals) and Sunday (finals).

TICKETS: Available at the Casino (846-4567) or through Tennis N.U.T.S. (885-1530). Tickets range from $6 to $10.

EVENT: U.S. Pro Tennis Championships, a Volvo Grand Prix tournament. Men's singles and doubles. Singles draw of 64.

WHERE: Longwood Cricket Club, 564 Hammond St., Brookline, Mass., 02167.

WHEN: Monday, July 14, through Sunday, July 20.

PRIZE MONEY: $175,000.

TIME: Afternoon sessions will begin at noon Monday through Friday and at 1 on Saturday and Sunday. Evening sessions will begin at 7:30.

TICKETS: Range from $6 to $12 and are available by mail at the club, through Tennis N.U.T.S., at all Ticketron outlets or by phone charge to American Express, Visa or MasterCharge by calling (617) 731-4500.

The Providence Journal/

Details of the Palazzo design have changed, but the original concept is alive. A change in advertising makeup meant a change for news when the Journal moved to a format of six columns for news on nine columns for ads. Standing heads were changed from Palazzo's open letterform to Poster Bodoni, which could be generated on the Journal's Atex system.

The Bulletin is modular and horizontal, in an effort to look different from the more vertical Palazzo design for the Journal. It can't be too different, though, because some pages are common to both newspapers. Food and Weekend sections, says David Gray, Journal-Bulletin graphics editor, offer each newspaper a chance to find its own identity.

"Some of the best design we do is in those special sections, as well as Sunday business sections and a few others," says Gray. "Most are non-Palazzo."

The Palazzo concept of blocked pictures has been hard for editors to accept, Gray says, because it flouts training and tradition. Gray argues that "there is a terrific impact to be had by blocking pictures on a page" but "also a very valid argument to be made . . . that the reader shouldn't have to read back and forth from pictures to captions to heads to text to get the story."

"Palazzo," says Gray, "has abandoned the idea that pictures can 'lead you into a story' and has tried, I think, to make editors realize that pictures have integrity of their own apart from the story, something I can also agree with."

Like many redesigned newspapers, the Journal considers its design still in a state of flux.

St. Petersburg Times/

Redesign was done by staff members

"We created our new design about five years ago to modernize a look which we thought had outlived its edge," said Robert J. Haiman, executive editor of the St. Petersburg Times.

"It was also created to take into account that we were changing from letterpress to offset and from hot metal to cold type. It also was created at a time we were reducing web-width with the effect of a 10 percent reduction in newshole.

"So the new design had to contain as much news as the old design, in 10 percent less space, **and still look very open and white-spacey.**"

Unlike many newspapers contemplating redesign, the Times did not call in an expert.

"Our design was done completely by staff members," said Haiman. "I firmly believe that the best people to redesign a paper are those who will have to make it a reality every morning thereafter.

"It's not easy to redesign a paper. But it's much harder to keep the design pure and functioning 300 papers, or 3,000 papers later."

Haiman created a redesign committee by selecting the best graphics people from each Times newsdesk and a few artists. Andrew Barnes, then metropolitan editor, was chairman because, said Haiman, "he had a first-class mind, great news judgment. . . and knew nothing whatsoever about typography. Who better to lead the typography freaks who made up the committee?"

Hot

High in lower 90s. Low in the 70s. S-SW winds 10 mph. Rain: 20%. Data 2-A.

St. Petersburg Times

Florida's Best Newspaper

NOTICE
Each Depositor now insured to $100,000.00
FIRST GULF BEACH BANK AND TRUST CO.
Member Federal Deposit Ins. Corp.

VOL. 97 — NO. 3 56 PAGES ST. PETERSBURG, FLORIDA, MONDAY, JULY 28, 1980 20 CENTS A COPY

Shah dies in Cairo; Iran says hostages' fate still uncertain

By CHRISTOPHER S. WREN
© New York Times

CAIRO — The shah of Iran, Mohammed Reza Pahlavi, died Sunday morning at an Egyptian hospital, leaving behind a legacy of tattered dreams of glory and an unsolved crisis to which he was the key. He was 60.

Attending physicians attributed the shah's death to the collapse of his circulatory system, entailing trauma, some hemorrhaging and dwindling blood pressure. His resistance had been virtually wiped out by residual infection from an abdominal abcess and by lymphatic cancer, which had spread to his liver.

The inside stories

- ✓ *Relatives of the hostages react to the news with mixed emotions, 6-A*
- ✓ *Just how villainous was the shah's rule in Iran? 9-A*
- ✓ *The shah's life in words and photos, 10-A*
- ✓ *Police arrested 169 Iranians in Washington as a demonstration in support of Iran's regime erupts into violence, 11-A*
- ✓ *A roundup of other world reaction is on 11-A*

Iran's revolutionaries rejoiced at word of their ex-king's death, but indicated that it would not hasten the release of the 52 captive Americans in Iran.

THE YOUNG Moslem militants holding the hostages said the death would make no difference, that their captives will not be freed until the "stolen" Pahlavi wealth is returned to Iran. And a spokesman for Iranian President Abolhassan Bani-Sadr was quoted as saying the shah's death "will have no effect on the hostage issue."

The country's revolutionary leader, Ayatollah Ruhollah Khomeini, has decreed that the hostages' fate must still be decided by the Iranian parliament.

In Washington, U.S. officials also said privately they doubt the shah's death will speed the release of the hostages. (**See reaction stories at right**).

President Anwar Sadat ordered a state funeral on Tuesday for the deposed Iranian monarch, who will be buried with honors befitting his former status at Cairo's Al Rafai Mosque in a mausoleum where the last of Egypt's royalty lies interred.

Sadat paid tribute to the shah as a "brother of Islam and humanity . . . Let history judge the reign of the shah as a ruler, but we in Islamic Egypt will remain loyal to ethics and faithful to (humane) values."

The shah resigned himself to permanent sanctuary in Egypt last March after a 14-month-long odyssey that took him through five other countries. His swollen spleen was removed in surgery in Cairo on March 28, four days after he arrived weak and ailing from Panama.

HE WAS HOSPITALIZED again for the last month for an infected cyst in his pancreas that had to be drained in operations here on June 30 and July 5. The shah seemed to be improving until he relapsed in shock Saturday evening at the Maadi Military Hospital, six miles south of Cairo.

See SHAH, 11-A

Shah Mohammed Reza Pahlavi: 1919-1980. AP

Iran reaction:

'The bloodsucker of the century has died at last'

Associated Press

Iran's revolutionary leadership rejoiced Sunday in the death of the "bloodsucker" Mohammed Reza Pahlavi but said it would not affect the hostage crisis.

The young Moslem militants holding the American hostages in Iran declared that their captives will not be freed until the deposed shah's "stolen" wealth is returned to Iran, a French radio newsman reported from Tehran.

Since seizing the U.S. Embassy and hostages last Nov. 4, the young radicals have demanded both the return of Pahlavi's money and the extradition of the former shah himself to face trial.

"THE DEATH OF the former shah will have no effect on the hostage issue," the British Broadcasting Corp. (BBC) quoted a spokesman for Iranian President Abolhassan Bani-Sadr as saying. Other Iranian officials reaffirmed that the fate of the 52 hostages, in their 266th day of captivity Sunday, remains in the hands of the Iranian parliament.

The official Iranian news media withheld announcement of Pahlavi's death in Cairo for about two hours after the first reports flashed from Cairo. Foreign reporters said people in Tehran at first reacted with disbelief when they told them the news.

Then, apparently after the Iranian government confirmed the report to its satisfaction, state-run Tehran Radio interrupted its regular programing and proclaimed:

"Mohammed Reza Pahlavi, the bloodsucker of the century, has died at last."

See IRAN, 11-A

U.S. reaction:

Administration issues muted response; Reagan salutes ex-monarch

By GEORGE GEDDA
Associated Press

WASHINGTON — The Carter administration responded with a carefully muted voice Sunday to the death of Shah Mohammed Reza Pahlavi, expressing neither mournfulness at his passing nor tribute for his long alliance with the United States.

The official government reaction contrasted sharply with the statements aired by Republican presidential nominee Ronald Reagan and his running mate, George Bush, both of whom saluted the deposed monarch as a good and loyal friend.

Former President Richard Nixon also praised the shah as a friend and ally of the United States. Nixon informed Egyptian President Anwar Sadat that he would attend the ex-monarch's funeral in Cairo on Tuesday, according to the Middle East News Agency in Egypt. Officials at Trans World Airlines (TWA) in New York said Nixon and his son-in-law, Edward Cox, left New York aboard an overnight TWA flight for Cairo.

Nixon may be one of the few current or former heads of state to attend the funeral because of the possible provocation such a presence could initiate with the revolutionary regime in Iran.

PRIVATELY, U.S. diplomatic officials said they doubted the shah's death would hasten release of the 52 American hostages held in Iran for almost nine months. White House press secretary Jody Powell said it was "almost impossible to predict" the impact upon the hostage crisis.

See U.S., 11-A

Experts are wary on prospects for hostages' release

By BERNARD GWERTZMAN
© New York Times

analysis

WASHINGTON — Once the center of the hostage crisis, the former shah was almost a peripheral figure at the time of his death in Cairo Sunday, rarely mentioned in Tehran, and even less so here.

Although the militants holding the American embassy had always demanded the shah's return as a condition for the release of the hostages, the view here and elsewhere is that because the shah had already faded from world view, his death in itself is unlikely to produce the immediate release of the remaining 52 Americans.

But like so much in the 8½-month Iranian situation, little can be stated with certainty. Experts, who have seen their predictions go awry so often in the past, were wary Sunday afternoon about the future. "I honestly don't know what's going to happen, now that the shah's dead," one senior official said, "and anybody who tells you he does know is kidding you."

PUBLICLY, THERE was an effort to avoid expectations that the shah's death could be translated into freedom for the hostages. But privately, officials said that events in Tehran were again at what one aide called Sunday "a very, very delicate stage."

The death of deposed Shah Mohammed Reza Pahlavi, they said, comes at a crucial time in the Iranian drama and could affect the hostages. The months-long political struggle in Iran seems to be nearing a climax, with the new government close to being completed, and the Iranian parliament likely to take up the hostage question soon thereafter.

"If they want to end the crisis, they could do it and use the shah's death as a partial justification," one official said. "But the question is: Is there political will to do it."

For months, President Abolhassan Bani-Sadr has been engaged in a fight for power with the Islamic Republican Party, whose clerical leaders are more traditionalist and anti-modern than Bani-Sadr's relative moderates. As part of that conflict, the Islamic Republicans chose to oppose Bani-Sadr's efforts last winter to negotiate an end to the hostage crisis.

See IMPACT, 11-A

'Every door I kicked in, I found a body.'

— A firefighter

Fire at N.J. home for handicapped kills 23

By CAROL PHETHEAN
Associated Press

BRADLEY BEACH, N.J. — A roaring fire killed 23 persons in a boarding home for the mentally handicapped, officials said Sunday. Many of those killed locked themselves into their room in the confusion and panic.

The fire touched off smoke alarms at the well-kept boarding home, but some residents returned to their rooms at the Brinley Inn after finding that fire had blocked the only escape route they'd been taught in simplified fire drills, one official said.

"Every door I kicked in, I found a body," said firefighter Jeffrey Ralston, who arrived at the home to find it engulfed in flames in the fire that broke out shortly before midnight Saturday.

"THEY MUST have panicked and bolted themselves into their rooms," he said.

Fourteen people managed to escape from the four-story, wood-frame boarding home. One person was under intensive care at a local hospital on Sunday.

Firefighters said many of the elderly residents were afraid to come down a fire escape.

"People wouldn't come down. We couldn't coax them down," said firefighter Mitch Rosen.

About half the residents were mentally retarded and the rest were outpatients from Marlboro State Psychiatric Hospital, said Jeff Scott, a caseworker for the state Division of Mental Retardation. They ranged in age from the 20s to 70s, but most were elderly.

GENE WILKINS, director of Monmouth County First Aid Squads, said the home routinely conducted two fire drills a month, but residents were only shown how to get out the front door. The fire escape is in the back of the building.

See FIRE, 4-A

Firemen remove one of the bodies from the rooming house. AP

inside

Heat wave 1980 . . .

. . . in the cities and farms of the Southwest, it's threatening a way of life. St. Petersburg Times Staff Writer Peter B. Gallagher reports on the physical and emotional toll in today's Section D.

Ann Landers	3-D
Bridge	9-D
Business	5-B
Classified	9-24-C
Comics	9-D
Crossword	8-D
Directory	2-A
Editorial	10-A
Horoscope	9-D
Jumble	9-D
Letters	11-A
Obituaries	7-B
Outdoors	9-C
Sports	1-10-C
Theaters	6-D
TV-Radio	5-D
Weather	2-A

162

St. Petersburg Times/

The committee wanted the Times to continue to look like the Times, but to be more readable and to carry continuity of design style throughout its sections. Although the process of redesign was spelled out in a lengthy manual, filled with rules that left little question of the typographical way to go, flexibility of approach was encouraged.

The design plan contemplated modular makeup for news and ads, a dominant photo or illustration on each section page, an adjustment in use of white space, smaller but bolder headlines and more units of news on covers.

A new headline type — Univers — was adopted. Roman headline type was the rule, with light and bold used to provide contrast. Page layout people were encouraged to use different measures of type to avoid a possible monotonous look.

"It took them six months to create the design," Haiman said, ". . . and six more to write the manual which was its bible."

"If I had to do it all over again . . . I would do it exactly the same way."

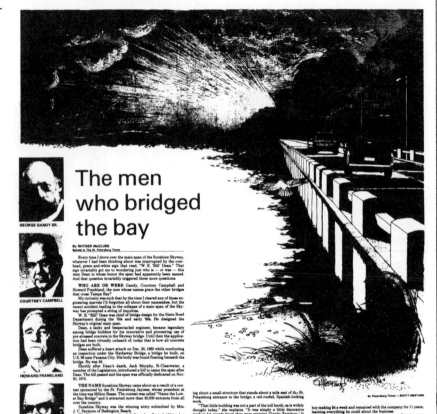

The men who bridged the bay

GEORGE GANDY SR.
COURTNEY CAMPBELL
HOWARD FRANKLAND
WILLIAM DEAN

By RHYDER McCLURE
Special to The St. Petersburg Times

Every time I drove over the main span of the Sunshine Skyway, whatever I had been thinking about was interrupted by the overhead, green-and-white sign that read, "W. E. 'Bill' Dean." That sign invariably got me to wondering just who is — or was — this man Dean in whose honor the span had apparently been named. And that question invariably triggered three more questions:

WHO ARE OR WERE Gandy, Courtney Campbell and Howard Frankland, the men whose names grace the other bridges that cross Tampa Bay?

See BRIDGES, 8-D

Day DIGEST

'Roughnecks' enjoyable alternative to Republican Convention coverage, 4-D

Biological clocks can be reset

By MARY EVERTZ

Success is something special to Doria Karampelas

By JONATHAN GREER
St. Petersburg Times Staff Writer

See SUCCESS, 7-D

San Francisco Examiner/

An evolving design without rigid rules

If the San Francisco Examiner looks a bit like the Minneapolis Tribune, there's good reason. Frank Ariss, who redesigned the Tribune in 1971, started a redesign of the Examiner in 1972.

A prototype was produced but the kidnaping of Patty Hearst interrupted the redesign process, Ariss left the Examiner and Michael Keegan, who had been a designer at the Minneapolis Tribune, carried on the planning. The redesign was introduced in 1976, a section at a time.

A need to tighten up on newsprint brought 8.7 point body type on 9.5 and elimination of space between paragraphs. Like the Tribune, the Examiner uses large pictures, decks on some headlines and extensive maps and charts.

Like designs of other newspapers, the Examiner's is evolving.

"It's a slow, incremental process, with few hard and fast rules," says Ed Orloff, assistant managing editor, as the effort to establish a unified graphics department continues. What has evolved, for one reason or another, is not a rigid style, he says.

Keegan describes design in this way:

"Design is a process and not an end, and it is a process that is continually redefining itself. The task of a newspaper interested in good design is to be able, at any given point, to put a finger on what constitutes new and innovative design and yet retain its own integrity and identity."

Now a design consultant working on

Examiner

San Francisco

1st edition
Evening/15 cents/No 32/109th year

Wednesday 18 July 1973

Led Zeppelin/ Their enormous popularity and bankroll/35

Wild Watergate payoff tales

Examiner News Service
Washington

Former New York detective Anthony T. Ulasewicz makes his second appearance before the Senate Watergate committee, told today of the troubles he had delivering cash to the seven original Watergate defendants.

Ulasewicz, delivery agent for those behind the conspiracy to conceal high-level involvement in the Watergate affair, told the science of those initially arrested in a story conforming to the details of what Herbert W. Kalmbach told the committee Monday and yesterday.

Branching in times on a standup comedian, Ulasewicz gave the committee a breezy, New York-accented account of how he carried money from Kalmbach around in laundry bags and brown paper sacks, passing it in prearranged drops in telephone booths and luggage lockers.

Lawyers of two of the arrested men, Douglas Caddy and Paul O'Brien, initially refused to take the first cash delivery of $75,100, he said.

Finally, lawyer William O. Bittman took delivery of $25,000 in a telephone booth in the lobby of his Washington office building. Ulasewicz said Bittman is the lawyer for Watergate conspirator E. Howard Hunt.

Ulasewicz said he watched as a pick-up man dressed the way Bittman told him he would be dressed, came and took the money.

In another instance, Ulasewicz said he left money for Hunt's wife, Dorothy, in a locker at National Airport just outside Washington. He said he put the key to the locker in an isolated phone booth and watched as she secretly came to pick up the money.

Hunt's wife, who died in an airliner crash in Chicago last December, has been mentioned as a conduit for getting some

Continued/Ex-cop/24

Showdown/Can Cox get evidence he wants from the White House?

Special prosecutor Cox relaxes with his newspaper during early morning walk

By Rowland Evans and Robert Novak
Washington

The showdown between the White House and Special Watergate Prosecutor Archibald Cox may be hastened by the revelation of the Nixon tapes. Even before the taping bombshell, backstage negotiations over Cox's request for White House papers threatened deep trouble for the President.

Now it is the prosecutor who will require the tapes, and may well be refused them

on Mr. Nixon's order, the possibility of a public broke between the White House and Cox is enhanced. Such a rupture could be lethal in seeming to confirm a guilty Mr. Nixon hiding the truth.

Whereas the President denies documents to the Senate on grounds of constitutional separation of powers, Cox's prosecution is part of the Executive branch. On what grounds, then, can the tapes be denied? "We can't have government lawyers rummaging around in Presidential papers," a senior presidential aide told us lamely.

The underlying relationship between the White House and Cox exudes tension. Mr. Nixon agreed to a special Watergate prosecutor only after irresistible congressional pressure. Nor was he pleased when his new Attorney General, Elliot Richardson, selected Cox—Democratic liberal, Harvard, Kennedyite.

The relationship went downhill from there. Presidential aides complained privately, when lawyers first named to Cox's staff were liberal Democrats. Mr. Nixon boiled over when told of a published report, greatly exaggerated, that the prosecutor was studying the financing of the President's San Clemente estate. But such quibbling pales before this basic

question.

Can Cox obtain documentary evidence he wants from the White House?

The prosecutor's office erred originally in asking for material informally over the telephone. The material was not supplied. After that Cox's lawyers were formal and precise in requesting specific papers in contrast to the Ervin Committee's shotgun approach.

The response was a leisurely stall, leading to secret negotiations for release of the papers. Cox, trying to avoid a rupture with the White House, maintained a tight secrecy lid. But White House spokesman Gerald L. Warren revealed last week that talks were underway.

If the tapes are refused Presidential lieutenants believe Cox may resign, so the immense embarrassment of Mr. Nixon. But prior to any resignation, Cox might make matters hot. Refusal of the tapes could be followed by Cox's going public with his confrontation and then going to court to secure the tapes.

If that fails, Cox might, in fact, resign. That would also undermine Atty. Gen. Richardson's continuation in office.

Tony Ulasewicz spills the beans

United Press

Kalmbach thinks he acted illegally

United Press

Pulse

Phase IV today—may jack up food prices

Price and economic controls enter their fourth and final phase today, aiming inflation without plunging the nation into recession—have already come into some. Today the Nixon administration unfurls Phase IV, described as "tough and realistic," details by the President's chief economic adviser, Treasury Secretary George P. Schultz ready to announce details to newsmen at the White House this morning, for a Phase IV should be assure a soft landing for the high-flying economy. Bad news for housewives, with the food industry to be given an early date from the once freeze a temporary boost in food prices is predicted.

The President gets back to work

Tucked in Bethesda Naval Hospital say President Nixon has shaken off the pneumonia that laid him low last Thursday. He'll be released from the hospital Friday or any weekend's rest at Camp David. Yesterday, Nixon resumed a full work schedule (details/8), presiding over meetings on Phase IV, pow-wowing with congressional leaders and chatting with Vice President Agnew.

Violence renewed in Northern Ireland

The past 24 hours have been the most violent for some months, a spokesman for the British Army said yesterday. Belfast Explosions killed three men and wounded at least 18 others, the first North Irish fatalities in a week

extremist pro-visional wing of the Irish Republican Army took credit for planting explosives in a Belfast apartment complex, killing two soldiers, wounding two others. And when a bomb-laden car exploded outside a crowded bar in nearby Aghalee Village, one man died and at least 16 others were wounded. Another bomb destroyed a Londonderry bank, and a sniper injured a soldier in Belfast.

IRA sources told United Press that the day's events signal the start of a new offensive against the presence of British troops in Northern Ireland.

An interview with an IRA priest, who says the conflict is not a religious war/17

Consumer advocate Ralph Nader is indignant (details/Money/39) at the food industry, which—he said yesterday—is so concentrated that it collects $2.65 billion annually in monopoly overcharges. The spectre of monopoly has also aroused the Federal Trade Commission's indignation, in the form of an antitrust complaint (details/4) against the nation's eight leading oil companies.

The season of our indignation

Sen. William Proxmire's indignation (details/8) is directed at generals and admirals who are "providing themselves with unbelievable luxuries and special privileges at public expense," he says. And almost the whole Congress is indignant to learn (details/8) that the Defense Department deliberately concealed hundreds of B-52 bombing missions in Cambodia during 1969

These are indignant times.

BART talks stymied, strike continues

A union official says negotiations to end the 17-day-old Bay Area Rapid Transit strike have broken down (details/4) and no further talks are scheduled.

How our kids get along in school

A survey of 3440 San Francisco elementary school students (details/Scene-25) indicates significant differences in reading levels between different ethnic groups. Anglo-American and Asian-American kids tend to out-achieve others. Which may account for the finding that Latin American and black students worry more about taking tests, not being promoted being asked questions in class.

Pacific Heights wins a high-rise battle

A committee of the Board of Supervisors has agreed (details-6) with the Pacific Heights Association that "The City's finest residential district" should be safeguarded against massive high-rise apartments.

Did voiceprints nab the wrong man?

The other day, one vocal identification expert said tape recordings conclusively linked Stephen C. Chapter with a bomb threat against Pacific Telephone. But yesterday (details/6) two more "voiceprint" experts told a Marin judge it was very unlikely" that Chapter's is the voice in the recordings.

lichman's tape of their conversation—but stuck to his story that he felt payments to Watergate defendants were for humanitarian reasons. Though he never told the President his suspicions about Watergate-related payments, Kalmbach now believes his 1972 activities were illegal. Senators wondered aloud how a sophisticated corporation lawyer such as Kalmbach could place such unquestioning faith in the agents of Watergate.

More Watergate developments/2

Weather coastal fog

Fog persisting near the coast, extending inland night and morning. Low tonight in the 50s. High tomorrow near 60 on the coast to mid or high 70s inland. Westerly winds 10-20 mph. Small craft advisory warning for Suisun Bay. Full report/24

Bay smog index

	Clean	Heavy
North		
Central		
South		

Prototype of Examiner redesigned front page, 1973.

San Francisco Examiner/

the redesign of the Los Angeles Herald Examiner, Keegan's redesign goals aim for typographical and design consistency. Every newspaper, he says, needs a look of its own, its contents should be well organized and its artwork should be of high quality.

The Ariss-Keegan prototype for the San Francisco Examiner, shown on the preceding page, was not accepted, but some of its characteristics are evident in the present appearance of the Examiner.

TGIF

Scene/Page E1

Willie Nelson and six new movies

Pro football forecast

Sports/Page F1

Stocks down 3.84 Page C1

San Francisco Examiner

★★★★

Final edition
Complete stocks

116th Year No. 44   Friday, August 1, 1980   20¢

Billy admits getting cable

Billy Carter, right, chats with friends over breakfast this morning at Americus, Ga., coffee shop

United Press International

But he doesn't remember how he received it

☐ Texts of the cables: Page A2

Associated Press

Billy Carter acknowledged today that someone in the White House gave him a cable concerning his 1978 trip to Libya but said it was only an insignificant memo from a U.S. diplomat thanking him for the goodwill mission.

President Carter's younger brother yesterday denied having any State Department cables in his possession.

"I have State Department copies of nothing," the president's brother said. "Jimmy has not shown me anything."

But at a news conference today in Plains, Ga., Billy Carter said he did receive a copy of a State Department cable in which the U.S. charge d'affaires in Tripoli said "that he appreciated me coming there and that it helped his job."

Asked who gave him the cable, Carter replied, "I assume I got it from someone in the White House."

Asked if the president gave him the cable, he replied, "I won't comment on that directly. It was over a year ago and I don't remember."

Carter said the document since had been released to columnist Jack Anderson under a Freedom of Information Act request and that he doubted it was ever classified.

White House press secretary Jody Powell said, however, that parts of a cable dealing with U.S. views on a Libyan matter were deleted from the documents released to Anderson.

Billy Carter said the cable is now in his lawyer's possession.

Asked why he denied receiving any cables on yesterday, Carter replied, "I didn't realize you were talking about it. The charge d'affaires' memo."

The president's brother also acknowledged depositing $20,000 loaned to him by the Libyans in a bank on Dec. 31, 1978. But, he said, the money was not deposited in the People's Bank of LaGrange, Ga.

Joel Lisker, an investigator for the Justice Department, said earlier this week that he had a copy of a deposit slip showing that Billy Carter made the deposit in the LaGrange Bank.

However, in a subsequent interview with the New York Times, Lisker corrected himself and said the $20,000 actually had been deposited in the Columbus Bank & Trust Co. in Colum

—See Back Page, Col. 1

Today

Topic A

BILLY CARTER, reversing himself, acknowledged that he had been given a State Department cable concerning his Libya trip. But he said the document was an "insignificant" memo. Page A1.

City/State

RACIAL AND sexual quotas for San Francisco's boards and commissions have been rejected in the proposed new city Charter, but "representative" selections will be required. Page A1.

IT WAS the stormiest condominium conversion hearing in a year, but this time tenants were on the landlord's side — and the landlord's sweet deal was rejected by the San Francisco Planning Commission. Page B1.

FEDERAL OFFICIALS are receptive to San Francisco's Redevelopment Agency building a Hunters Point housing project instead of having it done by a controversial joint venture. Page B1.

A 73-YEAR-OLD San Francisco man who leaped from the Bay Bridge and requested his rescuer to "throw me back in" was reported in stable physical condition after his arrival at San Francisco General Hospital. Page B4.

RACIAL AND sexual quotas for San Francisco's boards and commissions have been rejected in the proposed new city Charter, but "representative" selections will be required. Page A1.

A STATE agency has recommended a series of bond sales totaling $25 million to finance completion of the Dumbarton Bridge and to help build a new bus terminal in San Francisco. Page B36.

Nation

UNEMPLOYMENT IN the country rose to 7.8 percent in July, with blacks and other minorities suffering the most. Page A1.

DON'T USE DMSO, the "miracle drug" pain reliever, until the government completes studies to determine its safety, the director of the FDA says. Page A4.

World

MEXICO'S PRESIDENT has warned the U.S. that his country will not stand for any abuse toward China. Page A4.

AN AFGHAN reports that many of his countrymen are being held by the Soviets in Moscow, and detained from emigrating to the West against their will. Page A5.

ISRAEL'S JUSTICE Minister plans to resign because of over-representation of his party in the Knesset. Page A5.

Sports

SEBASTIAN COE of Britain won the 1,500-meter gold medal at the Moscow Games with a closing kick that carried him past Jurgen Straub of East Germany. Englishman Steve Ovett, the favorite, wound up third. Page F1.

FIRST BASEMAN Mike Ivie felt troubled and was excused from playing for the Giants in their hard-fought 6-4 victory over St. Louis at Candlestick Park. Page F1.

PALO ALTO'S Terri Baxier, a surprising 15-year-old, tied leg star Tracy Caulkins for first place in the 200-meter breaststroke, one of the finals in the U.S. Swimming Championships. Page F1.

PATRICK DEPAILLER, French Formula I racing star, was killed in a West German race test run. Page F5.

Business

THERE IS a way to take on American Express. So says an executive of Chicory Services Inc., who was in San Francisco to promote a new high-speed system for purchasing pre-signed travelers checks by phone. Page C1.

UNITED CALIFORNIA Bank is starting a statewide telephone bill-paying service as part of an ambitious plan to bring the electronic revolution in banking into the home. Page C1.

Opinion

THE EXAMINER'S VIEW: Mayor Feinstein appears to have saved the Redevelopment Agency from itself in cracking down on a proposed Hunters Point housing contract. Editorials, Page B2.

Weather

BAY AREA: Fair through tomorrow except for patchy coastal fog nights and mornings and occasional higher clouds. Highs near 70 at the beaches to the upper 70s and 80s inland; lows in the mid-50s to mid-60s. Details, Page B15.

Inside

What Kennedy, Anderson got out of talk

By Carl Irving

With the Democratic National Convention approaching, independent presidential candidate John Anderson and Sen. Edward Kennedy seem to have reached an understanding, its most important part unspoken, that they will help each other in their campaigns against President Carter and Ronald Reagan.

In a surprise 55-minute meeting yesterday in the Capitol in Washington, Anderson said he would reconsider his independent candidacy if anyone but President Carter were to win the Democratic nomination.

But today, the Republican congressman from Illinois said in Philadelphia that he "fully expects" Carter to be renominated and hopes that dissident Democrats, including Kennedy, will join his independent campaign.

"I don't see anyone else who will be in a position to get the majority of Democratic delegates," Anderson said before a fund raising luncheon where he announced that petitions to place his name on the Pennsylvania ballot would be filed Aug. 12.

After yesterday's meeting, Kennedy said he would make sure, if he is the nominee, that Anderson will join in television debates and that the Democratic National Committee will stop undermining his candidacy.

He backed up that assurance with a telephone call to Reagan, who agreed to the three-way debates if Anderson is a viable candidate.

Carter told Anderson last night at a Washington party that he, too, will debate Anderson in the fall.

There's more behind the Anderson-Kennedy meeting, however, according to top officials in both campaigns.

"Kennedy supporters believe that he has received a boost in persuading Carter delegates to abstain from their first choice of being Reagan because it would be a two-man, not a three-man race," a top Kennedy official told The Examiner in a telephone interview from Washington.

"If Carter has the nomination, it's clear from Anderson's statement that it will be a three-man race, and look at the polls," added the official, who asked not to be named.

The polls show Reagan far ahead, with Carter and Anderson or Kennedy and Anderson closely matched.

In San Francisco, Richard Skiar, a Kennedy delegate, said, "Anderson has made the gesture, involving heart and conscience. Maybe it will help persuade Carter to step aside."

Anderson's people don't interpret their candidate's statement in quite the same way. After the meeting, Anderson said, "It would only be prudent to reconsider what my position then would be" if Kennedy were nominated.

William Coyle, Anderson's national deputy campaign manager, said in a phone interview from Washington that the meeting involved

—See Back Page, Col. 1

Jobless rate rises slightly

WASHINGTON (UPI) — Nationwide unemployment rose slightly to 7.8 percent in July but jumped to 14.3 percent for minorities, the Labor Department reported today.

California's unemployment rate was 6.7 percent in July, down from 7.3 percent in June.

The nation's 7.8 percent rate was only one-tenth of a percentage point above June's 7.7 percent mark and was unchanged from May, signaling an apparent leveling off of the recession.

The department's Bureau of Labor Statistics said the jobless rate last month for blacks and other minorities was the highest since August 1977, when it was the same rate. That compared to 13.6 percent for minorities in May.

The rate for teen-age blacks and other young minority workers increased by 2.2 percent during July to a two-year high of 38.6 percent.

Except for August 1977, a bureau spokesman said the minority unemployment rate was the highest since September of 1975.

In defiance of economic predictions, the number of Americans holding jobs in July rose sharply for the first time in five months; 450,000 jobs were added, as measured by a survey of American households.

That gain was wiped out because people entered the labor market at a faster rate than jobs were created.

Some 650,000 people began looking for jobs in July, leaving the number of jobless Americans up by 300,000.

The administration has predicted as recently as last month that the jobless rate might climb to 8.5 percent this year, and some private forecasts that it could go as high as 9 percent.

The prediction, however, was based on the very rapid deterioration in economic activity during the spring, a trend that appears to have slowed significantly in the past month.

But department economists also pointed to a

—See Back Page, Col. 5

Unemployment in the U.S.

Seasonally adjusted
Source: Bureau of Labor Statistics

Examiner graphics

Charter panel rejects quotas

By Len Daniels

The city Charter Commission has rejected racial and sexual quotas for San Francisco's boards and commissions in favor of requiring that those bodies be "representative" of the broader community and that they include members of both sexes.

The substitute motion was approved, 11-3, last night at a special commission meeting. It replaces the wording approved by the commission Monday, which would have required that city boards and commissions "consist of no more than a simple majority of one sex, race or ethnic

A hard look / The nurses: frustration, lib and that burned-out feeling

By Russ Cone

... Why, if there are plenty of trained nurses available, would a hospital offer paid Hawaiian vacations or $125-a-month rent supplements to any nurse willing to go to work there?

The answer, management experts and nurses say, has to do with job dissatisfaction, job burn-out and a late but heavy dose of women's liberation.

Whatever the reason, an extraordinary situation exists in California, where many hospitals are desperate for nurses because of an unusual turnover in nursing jobs — 24,200 statewide last year, according to the California Hospital Association.

The Hawaiian vacation or rent subsidy offer is being made at modern Mills Hospital in San Mateo where there are openings for 25 registered nurses.

"We feel if we can get their attention, they will come to work here," says spokeswoman Daphne Copenhagen. "We have an awfully good hospital, a good benefit package."

The offerred rent subsidy and the four nights in Hawaii, expenses paid, are contingent upon the nurse working one year at Mills where journeymen pay is $1,668 a month.

Getting nurses doesn't seem to be nearly as difficult as keeping them.

At San Francisco General Hospital, 21 registered nurses are needed, said a

Laguna Honda Home, short 50, no bonuses are being offered. But these municipal institutions do offer a $1,857 salary plus city health and pension benefits.

Pacific Medical Center keeps staffing up by continuous advertising. A spokesman noted that "good staffing reinforces itself."

Peter F. Drucker, a management theorist, has told hospital operators that nurses are unhappy and restless because "you don't let them do the work they know most well they are being paid for. I don't think anyone

—See Back Page, Col. 1

San Francisco Examiner /

Scene

Lively arts/34
What's going on/38

Examiner/San Francisco
Wednesday 18
July 1973

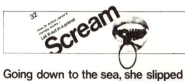

25

Scream

How Dr Arthur Janov's therapy works /
Let it out in a primal

What children think about their schools

And what their teachers think

We

How payola works on whom

Dick's bugs and Joe's bumper stickers

Bootblacks feel the inflation pinch

Del Courtney's amazing recovery

Uncle Sam lets it all hang out

The handwriting on the walls

The price of bow ties question

Going down to the sea, she slipped

Photo: Teresa Zabala

Looking shipshape/Hurrying to first watch, new member of USS Sanctuary crew slips, mussing white gloves

Krazy Kat / By Herriman The Examiner's series of classic comics–Krazy Kat/1933

Mockup of section cover, 1973.

Telegraph Herald/

'Typography adds dimension of meaning'

"I believe typography and design should be functional. It makes a newspaper interesting to read and easily read, and it establishes a tone and rhythm that is in harmony with the material."

James A. Geladas, former managing editor of the Telegraph Herald at Dubuque, Iowa, so describes his design philosophy, which, he says, has shifted once or twice during his thirty years of "playing" with typography.

Geladas is now director of the newspaper's project research and community affairs resources.

The Telegraph Herald's design manual translates the philosophy into fact.

"Good typography," it says, "enhances copy and pictures, forging the mix of words, images and graphics into a cohesive, coherent, purposeful whole. Typography adds a dimension of meaning and interpretation that aids understanding.

"No longer is typography the sprinkles on the cupcake — mere decoration, or the path of least resistance — but it's an important catalyst that makes our product meaningful . . .

"Some good key words in typography are: simplicity, balance, dominance, variety, unity and harmony. Typography should be used to guide the reader's eye around the page so that he doesn't miss anything."

White space, says the manual,

Pack moving beef kill to Illinois

By BOB FREUND
Telegraph Herald Staff Writer

The Dubuque Packing Co. is buying a Joslin, Ill. meatpacking plant and will slaughter beef cattle there instead of at its Dubuque plant.

Dubuque Packing spokesman Clifford Less announced this morning the closing of the beef kill and other allied operations at Dubuque after talks with the union representing its production employes collapsed yesterday.

Less said in a news release that the beef butchering in Dubuque will be halved by the end of September and completely halted on Dec. 12, as announced last month.

Dubuque Packing will move its beef operations to Illinois Beef Packers, Inc., headquarters plant in Joslin about 15 miles east of the Quad Cities and will double that plant's capacity in the near future, said Less. The pay rate at that plant reportedly is below that paid at Dubuque.

The acquisition will not expand Dubuque Packing's share of the livestock market, he said. But it will trim production costs that the company has blamed as the primary reason for shutting down the beef kill, beef break, boning, cooler and hide departments at Dubuque.

The loss of jobs there and in allied areas, such as the stockyards, freezer, offal, rendering and casing departments, will amount to between 350 and 500, according to company announcements.

Since July 3, the company and the Local 150A of the United Food and Commercial Workers Union have conducted three last-ditch bargaining sessions on upping the beef line's production standard from 115.8 head an hour.

Mel Maas, Local 150A president, said in an interview late yesterday that the union has offered to speed up the line at a rate of five animals an hour every week to an agreed limit, but the company has refused to budge from a demand of 165.5 head to begin immediately.

The production standard sets the floor for incentive pay, which Maas says is the real company target.

"They're after the incentive program," he said.

The union still is willing to negotiate, Maas said, but company officials closed the door in a stormy session that ended just before noon yesterday.

Even if production were quickened to the 165.5 demanded by the company, "there would be no assurance this high standard would keep the company from pulling the beef slaughtering operations out of Dubuque," Maas said.

"Evidently, the Dubuque Pack has its mind made up to leave Dubuque," Maas said.

Attempts to contact Illini officials this morning were unsuccessful. All company officers were tied up in meetings all morning, their secretaries said.

Dubuque Packing officials also said they would have no further announcements on their plans today.

Mayor Carolyn Farrell said this morning that the city will continue its efforts to head off further job losses at the Dubuque meatpacking plant.

"The city will continue to look at sewage rates and any other kind of dollar relief we can continue to offer the Pack . . . but we can't do it alone," she said.

There has been speculation that hog-killing operations also are marked for elimination, a move that could end as many as 2,300 jobs, Maas has said.

Last year, the company shifted its veal operation to a small plant near Madison, a move that the union alleged as a contract violation.

Dubuque Packing officials have said that, although their corporation is financially solid, its Dubuque operations are not.

Employes in the beef kill have an average seniority of more than 20 years, Maas said yesterday. The company has said low production and high pay rates have endangered the financial stability of the Dubuque operation.

---

digest

Platteville, Wis., is bigger than neighboring Cuba City down the road. But its hospital is smaller. And both are in Grant County. Yet a proposal to merge the facilities isn't all that clear-cut. Telegraph Herald health reporter Kathy Schwar looks into the merger milieu. **Page 28.**

Two Oelwein, Iowa, people are charged in connection with recent arson fires there. ... **Page 8.**

Dubuque Airport Commissioners reverse themselves and back route changes by Mississippi Valley Airlines. .... **Page 8.**

A man and two boys are held in connection with the beating and robbing of an 85-year-old Dubuque man. .... **Page 8.**

Five Flags Civic Center finishes its first fiscal year $100,000 short of expected income. .... **Page 14.**

A Dubuque delegation to the Iowa Transportation Commission gets two bits of better-than-nothing news concerning funding on highway 561. .... **Page 14.**

Expense accounts filed by 10 of 17 Iowa legislators who attended a five-day convention in New York City earlier this month show it cost state taxpayers an average of $973 to foot the bill for their trip. If the average holds true for the remaining seven lawmakers, the tab could exceed $16,500. .... **Page 12.**

The Soviet Embassy invokes the issue of human rights against the United States, calling the decision to grant political asylum to a 12-year-old boy a "violation of all principles of morality and humanism." .... **Page 24.**

An FBI agent calls the shooting of a former Iranian diplomat at his Bethesda, Md. home "a highly organized and carried out assassination." .... **Page 24.**

Exxon Corp. reports second-quarter profits up 24 per cent over a year ago but well below first quarter earnings, the highest quarterly profits in U.S. corporate history. .... **Page 2.**

The Senate Judiciary Committee meets under the chairmanship of Sen. Edward Kennedy to decide whether to hold hearings into the Justice Department's handling of the Billy Carter case. ... **Page 2.**

At least six people are killed and nearly 100 others injured in a series of bomb explosions in Tehran. .... **Page 22.**

Telegraph Herald

144th Year, No. 175   3 SECTIONS   44 PAGES   DUBUQUE, IOWA, and EAST DUBUQUE, ILLINOIS   WEDNESDAY, JULY 23, 1980   25 cents

Verdict triggers violence

CHATTANOOGA, Tenn. (UPI) — Police restored order today in a black district wracked by firebombings and looting triggered when blacks rebelled at an all-white jury's lenient verdict for three Ku Klux Klansmen.

Four buildings were heavily damaged by fire bombs and rocks and at least one fireman was slightly injured in the violence that flared Tuesday night and early today in Chattanooga's Alton Park district.

At the height of the disturbance, groups of angry blacks roamed the streets shouting obscenities and proclaiming "we want justice."

Order was restored about 7 a.m.

The trouble erupted following the acquittal of two Ku Klux Klansmen and a light sentence for a third klansmen in a shotgun attack on four black women.

Firemen and police were called into the area about midnight to deal with a string of fires apparently set by arsonist. About 50 officers sealed off the area and stood guard while the firemen battled to bring the fires under control. One of the firemen was injured when hit by a rock thrown by one of the demonstrators.

Police said night blacks were arrested on looting charges, including six who were caught inside a store.

Police continued to stand guard over the area during the day.

An all-white jury Tuesday convicted klansman Marshall Thrash, 30, of opening fire and wounding four black women outside a tavern last April 19. He and two of his companions had set fire to two crosses in the black district and, according to testimony in the trial. Thrash went "berserk" and began shooting when none of the blacks seemed to be paying any attention to the burning crosses.

Thrash was convicted on three counts of assault and battery and a third count of simple assault.

Two other members of the klan group, William Church, 23, the Imperial Wizard of the Justice Knights of the KKK, and Larry Payne, 26, were acquitted. Their lawyers claimed they were just along for the ride.

Looking like a mushroom cloud from an atomic blast, a 60,000-foot plume of steam and ash rises above Mt. St. Helens   UPI photo

Volcano erupts with renewed fury

VANCOUVER, Wash. (UPI) — Mount St. Helens ended a month-long lull with renewed fury, blasting out the crater's lava dome, spilling hot gas and rock down its slopes and sending an ash-filled cloud soaring 10 miles high and as far north as Canada.

There are no apparent injuries or new damage from Tuesday's eruptions, which followed a series of rapid tremors. Geologists said three distinct eruptions shook the mountain, which spewed steam and ash into the night.

The appearance of the huge mushroom-shaped cloud clogged evening rush hour traffic in Portland, 50 miles to the south, as office workers stopped to stare at the spectacle. In Seattle, residents gathered at viewpoints on the city's hills to watch and the Space Needle was packed with spectators.

"It was the third major eruption since the Cascade-peak first exploded with cataclysmic force May 18 — a blast that devastated thousands of acres, blanketed a three-state area with tons of ash and left 64 people either dead or missing.

The light gray cloud was visible 100 miles north in Seattle and as far south as Salem, Ore., where Washington Gov. Dixy Lee Ray and Oregon Gov. Vic Atiyeh were meeting to talk over volcano-related problems and other topics.

Prevailing winds spread the cloud over the central and northeast part of Washington state and into Canada, the National Weather Service reported. Very light ash fall was reported in Yakima, Ellensburg, Wenatchee, Quincy and Randle.

Upon these stones he built his faith and family

John McCormick
Circuit writer

BELLEVUE, Iowa — They lived as best they could in Luxembourg, a European grand duchy no bigger than two Iowa counties.

He was Matthias Fritz, a 33-year-old stonemason. She was Maria Forenti Fritz, the young mother of their 11 children.

They wanted America, indeed yearned for it, promised themselves that they would go there as one.

Still, the children were young. Their odds of a safe passage? Little better than a toss-up.

But they would not just go there as one, said Matthias, they would arrive there as one. They would arrive and prosper. And in thanksgiving, he would do what he could. He would build a chapel of stone to the God who delivered them.

They sailed in 1852. Forty-two days by ship across the Atlantic to New Orleans, more days by boat up the Mississippi to St. Louis, still more days by overland trudge to the valley of Spruce Creek.

There Matthias found and farmed a small acreage. Maria bore two more children, their 12th and 13th, and farmed along with him.

They joined the country parish of St. Nicholas. Each year, on the Roman Catholic feast of Corpus Christi, they would walk through the valley of Spruce Creek with their congregation, worshiping in procession at each of four scattered shrines that flanked their small church.

Matthias had helped build that church. But still he owed his God a chapel. One of those four skimpy shrine settings — it was between a hill and a wind in the road — would be the spot.

He laid out 7-foot sides and an 8-foot back. He hewed a frontal arch from a single walnut tree. He crafted an altar, and atop the altar he built a cross, and for the cross he carved a crucified Christ.

One day the chapel was finished. So Matthias went on to other projects. He had a night school of sorts, teaching French to the children of the valley. At home, Maria tutored her brood as well.

One day, at a time when the children were near-grown, Matthias and Maria went to town. As they completed the northwesterly drive back to their farm, the family dog startled their team. The catapulting horses upset Matthias Fritz' light spring wagon. Maria, just 45, died of a broken neck.

She is buried in Bellevue, beneath a tombstone sculpted by her husband. He died later, in 1880, at the age of 80, and he now lies with her. But the tombstone doesn't bear his name. Only hers. It is just as he wanted it to be.

He left little that remains but his chapel, Fritz Chapel, a spot hand-manicured ever since, first by his family, and now by its neighbors.

This Sunday, at 1 p.m., more than 200 descendants Matthias and Maria never knew will gather at Fritz Chapel. They will stand with the cedars and the lilacs, and they will give the spot a dedication ceremony.

When it is done, some of them may linger in the valley of Spruce Creek, the valley of the chapel.

Matthias Fritz' stonework will be there, with the 7-foot walls and the 8-foot back and the walnut frontal arch, with the altar and the cross and the crucified Christ.

It will be just as Matthias Fritz left it for them. And, like the tombstone, just as he wanted it to be.

Carol Ernst, 9, is one of the many neighbors who take care of the chapel northwest of Bellevue, Iowa

Staff photos by John Barry

Telegraph Herald/

provides visual relief, "enlivens a page, reduces clutter, adds appeal." But, the manual adds, if white space is badly used, a page may fall apart. "The rule is: Keep the white space to the outside of typographical elements; don't trap it."

The Telegraph Herald uses boxes around stories or pictures to emphasize and draw readers' attention to them.

The newspaper uses blurbs "to supplement a headline, to grab the reader and get him into the story, to add information about the story, and to break up a gray page."

"Photographs," the manual says, "should be treated with respect as worthy and important communications elements. Words and pictures, of course, can enhance one another. But many times a picture can communicate as much as or more than any number of words."

Horizons

Church and state: A taxing situation

By TERESA BARKER
Telegraph Herald Staff Writer

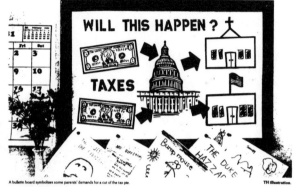

A bulletin board symbolizes some parents' demands for a cut of the tax pie.   TH illustration

CATHOLIC EDUCATION
The tailoring of tradition

Tomorrow: Public and parochial partners.

Money from bingo, bake sales and prayer

Bingo is one source of school finances.   Staff photo by John Berry.

Times-Union/

Where graphic redesign is a constant process

The design of the Times-Union was the work of Paul Back, Newsday design director. The redesign plan was presented in the fall of 1977. In early 1979 the newspaper did a prototype edition and in January, 1980, the official change was made.

Back's original design was modifed, clarified, expanded and changed, said J. Ford Huffman, assistant managing editor of the Times-Union, by Executive Editor Robert H. Giles, then Managing Editor Nancy Woodhull and Huffman.

"In fact," said Huffman, "we're discovering new uses for some of the typographic elements each day we face how to challenge the news . . . We'll never be finished with the graphic redesign, and that's the best part about our new format."

Nearly all the stories in the Times-Union are boxed with hairline rules, Huffman said — "probably the most distinctive thing about our paper.

"That means we can't throw a box around a story to make it special, to make it stand out. We use the boxes to organize content. What's **inside** the boxes is what has to catch Times-Union readers' eyes."

A readership study of the Rochester newspapers in 1977, plus an urge to make changes, led to the redesign. The study indicated that readers saw little difference between the morning Democrat and Chronicle and the evening Times-Union. Editors sprang into action.

Back gave the Times-Union a mockup of the redesign which proposed a change in headline type (from Bodoni

---

ROCHESTER, NEW YORK

TIMES-UNION

Tuesday Evening, May 6, 1980 — Published by Gannett — 25 Cents

GREATER ROCHESTER INSIDE
☐ State Senate overrides Gov Carey's veto of death penalty, issue goes to Assembly — 4A
☐ Bush, Kennedy face tough times in today's primaries — 2A
☐ Golf pro Frank Commisso to retire — 1D

Astrology 19C | Money 5-7D
Bridge 19C | Newswatch 2B
Comics 19C | Sports 1D
Crossword 19C | Television 2, 3C
Deaths 4C | Theaters 20C
Editorial 18A | Want Ads 14C
Food Guide 5C | Word Game 19C

WEATHER
Variably cloudy tonight, low near 40. Cloudy with chance of showers tomorrow, high 60 (Details, page 2A.)

President may order huge airlift

Earlier story, page 5A
United Press International
WASHINGTON — President Carter may order a massive airlift of Cuban refugees to the United States and may decide to admit 250,000 Cubans and 250,000 Haitians to this country, Rep. Richard Kelly, R-Fla., said today.

Kelly and other members of the Florida congressional delegation met with Carter at the White House.
Please turn to back of section

'Gas' price rise slows

Some lowered a few cents, dealers say

By KEVINNE MORAN
Times-Union Money staff

Gasoline prices have increased about 3 percent or less than 4 cents a gallon since late February, a Times-Union survey of 24 stations yesterday indicated.

The rate of price increases is much slower than in surveys taken periodically by the Times-Union over the past two years.

And what yesterday's survey does not track is just how much gasoline prices have gone down in the last few weeks.

Duane Neu, president of the Retail Gasoline Dealers Association of Monroe County, said many dealers have lowered prices from 1 to 4 cents per gallon in the past few weeks.

"Basically, they did it to get rid of their allocations," Neu said.

The dealers are cutting prices to offset the double effect of "conservation by consumers on the one hand and higher allocations of gasoline from the oil companies on the other," Neu said.

"When the supplies were down, the prices were pretty much the same and we could keep pretty good hours. The customers had to go along with our wishes.

"Now it's back to a buyer's market. If you don't cut prices and you're on a corner with three other gas stations, the motorists will just go across the street," Neu said.

Nationally, the trend is the same, mainly because of excess gasoline stocks. But analysts say prices will shoot up again next week with the imposition of President Carter's 10-cent-a-gallon import fee.

Even if prices continue to slip after May, predicts oil industry expert Dan Lundberg, it is doubtful the amount would be sufficient to offset the dime
Please turn to back of section

Blaze set for birds backfires

The Associated Press
MIO, Mich. — A raging brush fire swept through the only nesting area of the rare "Bird of Fire."

It burned out of control today after scorching 30 square miles of forest land and forcing more than 1,000 people from their homes in Huron National Forest.

One firefighter died in the blaze, forest service officials said.

The fire was set intentionally yesterday by the Forest Service to clear timber from the nesting area of the endangered bird, the Kirtland's Warbler, authorities said.
Please turn to back of section

On Page 19A:
☐ British believed failure to act would have cost more lives
☐ The SAS — the force that retook the embassy was designed to strike hard, fast and ruthlessly

'My God, those men are brave'

By NIKKI FINKE
The Associated Press

LONDON — When the bomb went off and the firing started, I thought, 'My God, if anybody comes out unscathed, it will be an absolute miracle,'" said Canadian banker Morley Smith after watching British commandos storm the Iranian Embassy down the block from his home.

"My God, those men are brave," he added, and reported that his knees were shaking and heart was pounding as he kept his binoculars trained on the five-story townhouse just off Hyde Park.

The drama started at 4:39 p.m. when police reported "two or three shots" coming from the direction of the embassy which Arab-Iranian terrorists seized last Wednesday and where they were holding 21 hostages.

Just before 7 p.m., a body was pushed out the embassy front door and dumped on the porch.

British officials were horrified to find one of the Iranian hostages had been murdered — the first death in the six-day-old siege. And the terrorists were threatening to kill one captive every half-hour unless the Iranian government met their demand for the release of 91 other Arab-Iranians they said were imprisoned in Iraq.

"My wife had heard that somebody was killed, so I thought I'd go out and see what was going on," said Smith, a Bank of Nova Scotia official.

"At first, nothing was going on. Then I saw a couple of people appear above the embassy about a block away from me. Then a second, third and fourth person appeared."

They were members of a 30-man team from the Special Air Services Regiment, an elite and highly secretive anti-terrorism squad.

"Within about three or four minutes there were about six or eight black figures on the roof. Shortly after that, three ropes were hanging down the side of the building.

"Six of the men slithered down the rear of the building to the second floor.

"Just as six of the commandos were halfway down the ropes, the roof exploded and smoke started coming out," Smith went on.

"Then an explosion took place in the window
Please turn to page 19A

Smoke and flames pour from Iranian Embassy in London.
United Press International

The Iraqi connection

By YOUSSEF M. IBRAHIM
The New York Times

LONDON — The five-day siege that ended last night in explosions and fires at the Iranian Embassy here is believed by some Arab diplomats here to have had its origins in a growing confrontation between Iran and the Arab neighbor, Iraq.

These diplomats say they believe the embassy takeover was planned in coordination with Iraqi intelligence services, with the actual attack made by disaffected members of the Arab ethnic minority of Iran. Similar charges of Iraqi involvement have been made by Iranian leaders in Tehran.

There are nearly a million and a half people of Arab descent among Iran's population of 35 million, most of them living in the southwestern province of Khuzestan, where all of the country's oil is known to be. Disaffection has been spreading, it is estimated, to tens of thousands, and the number is said to be constantly growing.

The issue include a desire by the ethnic Arab minority for greater autonomy and for a larger share of Iranian oil wealth to be allocated to Khuzestan, one of Iran's poorest provinces. These long-standing grievances, the diplomats
Please turn to page 18A

Journey home for bodies

The Associated Press
The bodies of the American servicemen killed in the futile hostage rescue attempt in Iran arrived in Zurich, Switzerland, today and were transferred to U.S. custody for the journey home.

In a ceremony at a Zurich airport hangar, Greek Catholic Archbishop Hilarion Capudji, who accompanied the coffins on a Swissair flight from Tehran, formally transferred them to Swiss officials who then passed them on to U.S. Ambassador Richard Vine.

A U.S. Air Force C-141 transport plane stood by to fly the remains back to the United States later today.

Confusion persisted over the number of
Please turn to back of section

TURMOIL IN THE MIDEAST

On page 20A:
☐ Our helicopters encountered dust cloud, not sandstorm
☐ Carter tells Vance he rules out force
☐ Col. Beckwith wanted rescue mission in January
☐ Khomeini turns 80

Coffins bearing remains of American rescue team members are blessed by Archbishop Capudji in Zurich today.
United Press International

Driving with a heart

There would be one on 'I Love New York' plates

By RICHARD BENEDETTO
Gannett News Service

ALBANY — A major color change is in store next year for New York state license plates if a bill to inscribe the familiar "I Love New York" slogan on them is approved, as expected, by the State Legislature.

The new plates would probably be white with blue letters instead of the traditional blue and gold, said Edward O'Neill, an associate commissioner of motor vehicles. The "I Love New York" slogan would feature a red heart in place of the word "love," he added.

Assemblyman Paul E. Harenberg, D-Bayport, sponsor of the bill to mandate the slogan on plates, said the change was suggested by a student in his Long Island district who sent him a drawing of a plate bearing the slogan.

"Until then, I never thought about it," said Harenberg. "But I realized that other neighboring states have slogans. It seemed fitting that we should fill the gap.

New Jersey, for example has "Garden State" on its plates and Connecticut has "Constitution State," he said.

He noted that New York dropped the "Empire State" slogan in 1973. And many will recall New York plates promoted the New York World's Fair in 1964-65 with the inscription "World's Fair."

Harenberg said the "I Love New York" inscription fits well with the state's tourism promotion campaign. The new plates, he said, might encourage out-of-staters to travel by the Empire State if they see it on the license plates of visiting New Yorkers.

No major opposition to the bill is seen in the Legislature, and the Department of Motor Vehicles has submitted a memo in support of the measure, O'Neill said. The new plates would be phased in beginning late next year and continuing through 1982, he said.

Times-Union/

to Century Bold), a different body type (Century Schoolbook instead of Aurora), a sig style using Helvetica extra bold condensed, use of Times roman type on section flags and the page one nameplate, a new cutline style, a switch from six to five columns on each open page and use of hairline rules around stories.

The conversion took more than two years, during which elements of the redesign appeared from section to section. The gradual implementation allowed editors to experiment and readers to become accustomed to the changes.

The major move came Jan. 28, 1980, when new body type and headline faces were introduced. Other changes followed and the redesign was completed.

The Times-Union has used Helvetica type more freely than planned — in special display headlines and for street-sale play headline type on page one.

Please turn to page 5C

Festive occasions

Comic energy despite cramped stage

The 'new' Rick Nelson: Crowd loves him

The Washington Star /

'Design is key element in a paper's success'

The story of the redesign of The Washington Star is best told in the words of its design director, Eric Seidman, who joined The Star in May, 1979, after 12 years with The New York Times.

Seidman wrote about the project in the Washington Journalism Review (April 1980). Excerpts from his story are used here.

"I view my job as an expert in communications rather than decorations — not crafting words like a reporter, but creating pages that serve some definite and practical functions for the reader . . ." Seidman wrote.

His job, Seidman said, was to take the headlines, the stories and pictures and put them together for easier and faster reading — and to give the reader more pleasure and more understanding.

Seidman sees the front page as "a very sacred place. In fact, the identity of the paper may rest here."

The redesigned front page, Seidman determined, should look like The Star, but have a cleaner appearance. He added a structural rule to secure the news summary position. He simplified the typography, cutting story count from nine to six or seven, and limiting the headline type style to one face and four sizes.

"It was important," Seidman said, "that with the new design, a new philosophy of story placement and headline sizes emerge as well. This included the use of more space for graphics throughout the editions."

The Washington Star/

The next big step, Seidman said, was redesign of the Friday Calendar section. Out of this came two important decisions: "first, the choice of a masthead style that would be used for the rest of the paper. Second, involvement with the paper's business side became essential."

Seidman decided on a masthead typeface that would be distinctive from the rest of the newspaper's typography, but he discarded the notion of using a set size and fixed location on all section covers. He chose a typeface — Egyptian Bold Condensed — that could be altered in size, position and treatment for each section but still be recognizable as belonging to the same family.

"Everyone had expected to deal solely with a new cover design," Seidman said. "I don't like designing this way. A section should be regarded as an entire package — design integrated with editorial material."

The Star's movie guide was paid advertising and therefore off limits to editorial. But Seidman worked with the advertising department on a redesign for the guide that brought it into harmony with the rest of the section format.

The Star's classified section is another example, Seidman said, of "how service advertising can be enhanced by the designer without interfering with the integrity of the paper."

And so redesign went, and still was proceeding at The Star in early 1980. Until the process is finished, Seidman said, "we'll keep plugging away with the conviction that design is a key element in a newspaper's success or failure.

SECTION E — The Washington Star — NOVEMBER 18, 1979

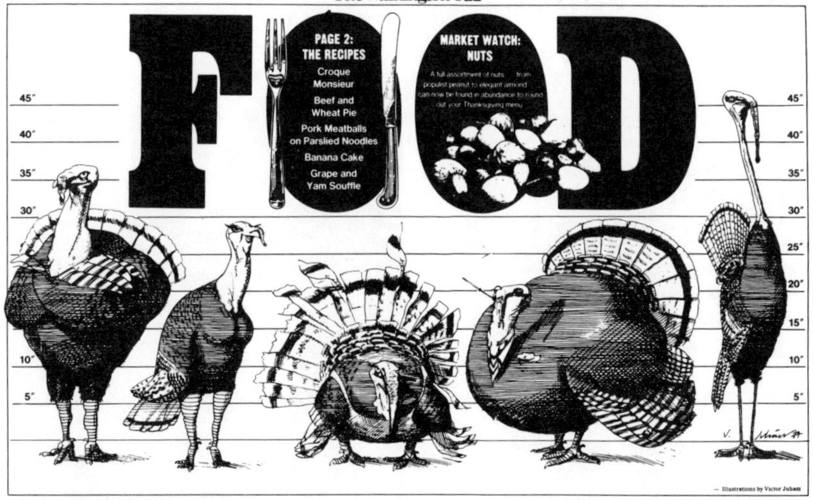
FOOD
PAGE 2:
THE RECIPES
Croque Monsieur
Beef and Wheat Pie
Pork Meatballs on Parslied Noodles
Banana Cake
Grape and Yam Souffle
MARKET WATCH: NUTS
A full assortment of nuts from populist peanut to elegant almond can now be found in abundance to round out your Thanksgiving menu
45″
40″
35″
30″
25″
20″
15″
10″
5″

— Illustrations by Victor Juhasz

THE COOK'S COLUMN By Lee Thompson

History's brazen little tarts

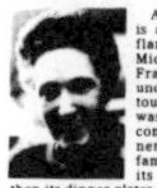

A tart is a tarte is a tourte is a flan. During the Middle Ages in France, the undercrust of the tourte or tarte was the most common of dinner plates. A family first ate its dinner, and then its dinner plates. Pizza is a current analogy.

A tart, sweet or savory, may be a quiche if it comes from Lorraine. A tart may also be called a pie, but not all pies are tarts. An open, one-crust pastry, the crisp buttery tart is served free-standing, unlike a pie which requires the support of its dish. A rich, delicious switch on the traditional Thanksgiving pie, the pastry may be prepared well in advance and frozen in its tart pan; it may be baked and filled the day before the holiday without loss of texture or flavor. And, as an extra advantage for the novice baker, there is little danger of overworking the pastry and making it tough.

Use a tart pan with a removable bottom. The pans are made of metal, are about an inch deep and are usually 8 or 9 inches in diameter. They are reasonable in price.

The sides of the tart shrink during baking. After removing the pan from the oven, place it on a can or pedestal smaller than the tart ring and the ring will drop off leaving the tart on its metal base.

Some things to know before you start: The cooler the ingredients and the environment, the easier to work pastry. Heat causes the fat in the recipe to flow instead of amalgamating smoothly with the flour and other ingredients. Keep all ingredients chilled until the last moment. Use a dough scraper as much as possible; never touch dough with the warm palms of your hands. Marble is a superior working surface because it stays cool; a Formica countertop works very well, too.

For tender pastry, let the dough rest refrigerated at least 12 hours, better yet, 24. Resting relaxes the elasticity which develops during the working of dough and which causes roughness.

When preparing the tart shell, make the sides almost double the thickness of the bottom. Build the sides high to counteract shrinkage.

Chill the dough before pressing it into the tart pan and chill the lined tart pan before baking. Do not grease the tart pan.

Bake filled or unfilled tart shells on a heated cookie sheet on the lowest shelf of the oven. Should the sides of an unfilled tart shell turn too brown during baking, cover the shell loosely with a piece of kitchen parchment paper.

• • • •

These tarts are made of rich, sweet pastry (*pate sucree*) and the fruit is topped with a golden custard mixture of cream and egg. To use this pastry for a savory tart, omit the sugar and the lemon rind or vanilla.

The techniques suggested are simplified and are well within the capacity of an inexperienced cook. The instant flour is easy to blend; the resting period of the dough ensures tender pastry; no rolling is required.

Black Cherry Tart Alsacienne

The pastry:
1¼ cup Wondra or other instant flour
1 stick butter, chilled, cut in ¼-inch cubes
¼ cup granulated sugar
½ teaspoon salt
1 egg yolk
Grated rind of 1 lemon (or ½ teaspoon vanilla extract)
1 to 2 tablespoons ice water

The filling:
2 16-ounce cans black pitted Bing cherries, drained
3 tablespoons kirsch
3½ to 4 ounces almond paste (marzipan)

The topping:
2 egg yolks
3 tablespoons heavy cream or creme fraiche
3 tablespoons superfine sugar

To prepare the pastry by hand (methods for electric mixers and food processors are given below): Put flour on working surface. Make a well in center and add butter, sugar, salt, egg, lemon rind or vanilla and 1 tablespoon of ice water. With fingertips and/or pastry scraper, work the butter with the other ingredients in the well, then draw the flour gradually from the inside of the ring into the well. When all the flour has been incorporated, gather the dough together with a dough scraper. Pinch off a piece of dough; with the heel of your

See TARTS, E-10

The original Thanksgiving cast

By Vicki Ostrolenk
Special to the Washington Star

When the Pilgrims landed on Plymouth Rock, few knew what could be successfully farmed in the New World. Only after Indians shared with them their food, shelter and agricultural knowledge was the new arrivals' survival assured.

The first Thanksgiving gave testimony to this symbiotic yet uneasy relationship. But as the truce between white and Indian nations deteriorated, so did the faith many Native Americans placed in a holiday they viewed as irrelevant to non-white America. Today, most Indians honor the holiday with a Thanksgiving feast similar to the ones held by their ancestors.

According to Maude Paul, who many members of the local Native American community consider to be their best cook, only the meat is different. "Turkey is the white man's meat we now have because we don't go out and hunt," says Paul, a Cherokee. "But I see Thanksgiving as a feast with squirrels, pheasants and wild turkeys which is what we always had on the reservation."

To Paul, "the reservation" is Cherokee, N.C., where relatives and friends still celebrate the holiday with traditional rituals. "Mother will have gone to the mountains to find her 'wish,' a huge mushroom that looks like a cabbage," says Paul. "It's par-boiled and seasoned with bacon grease. Everyone gets a piece."

As for the meal itself, squirrel or pheasant leads the reservation menu. There is also bean bread made from cornmeal and pinto beans and served with warm bacon grease, hominy cooked in oak ashes, ramps (a wild green that's a cross between garlic and onions), sochan, poke salad or fieldcrest (all wild greens), choke cherry jelly made from wild cherries, succotash and pumpkin bread or pie.

"White man's more traditional foods," says Paul, "candied yams, cranberry sauce and green beans — are also on the menu."

Maude Paul first left Cherokee, N.C., to attend Kansas' Haskell Institute, an exclusively-Indian high school which attracts students from all parts of the country. It was at Haskell that she met her husband, Wilber, a Blackfoot from Browning, Mont. On leave from his job on the Indian desk of the Department of Commerce's Economic Development Association, Wilber is currently working toward a masters degree in education at Harvard University.

During their first years of marriage, Wilber's military service and jobs with the Bureau of Indian Affairs took the couple all over the country. They settled in Washington about 10 years ago and have become active in the American Indian Historical Society.

See NATIVE, E-15

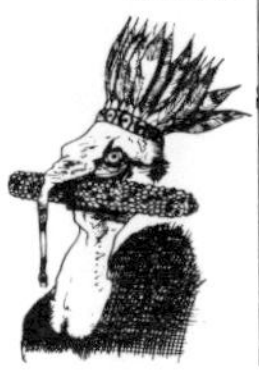

Tradition is the main course at America's favorite holiday feast

By Lisa Yockelson
Special to the Washington Star

"This (Thanksgiving) festival was always kept at Plumfield in the good old-fashioned way, and nothing was allowed to interfere with it. For days beforehand, the little girls helped Asia and Mrs. Jo in storeroom and kitchen, making pies and puddings, sorting fruit, dusting dishes, and being very busy and immensely important. The boys hovered on the outskirts of the forbidden ground, sniffing the savory odors, peeping in at the mysterious performances, and occasionally being permitted to taste some delicacy in the process of preparation."

— From "Little Men," by Louisa May Alcott

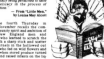

The fourth Thursday in November recalls the community spirit and ambition of New England men and women who learned to scratch the soil with a sharp stick and scatter corn kernels in the hollowed out spaces; who fed on wild flowers and nettles when stored produce turned moldy and raised infants on the liquid from boiled chestnuts and newly pressed corn.

The traditional Thanksgiving meal is a faithful recreation of that which was served by those stalwart colonists. Central to the original feast, of course, was the corpulent turkey, hefty with stuffing and surrounded by myriad accompaniments. But duck pigeon, roasted venison and goose stuffed with chestnuts, bread and spices were also served. On wooden trays came great masses of food, sauces made of cranberries (also known as "bounceberries," for their capacity to ricochet off the ground when ripe), and pies of Sweet Greening apples, nuts or maple-laced pumpkin.

By definition, Thanksgiving means ceremony. Here are some time-honored ways in which that ceremony can recreate the goodness and bounty of early American feasts:

Roast Turkey with Apple Stuffing

1 cup chopped onions
12 tablespoons unsalted sweet butter
1 cup chopped celery
3 large cooking apples, peeled, cored and cubed
Juice of ½ lemon, strained
6 cups bread cubes, from a loaf of day-old, unsweetened bread trimmed of crusts
Salt and freshly ground pepper, to taste
3 tablespoons finely chopped parsley
1 cup unsweetened apple juice, or as needed

Saute onions in 6 tablespoons butter until soft and translucent. Stir in celery; cook with the onions for 4 minutes, stirring often. While the celery cooks, toss the apple cubes in lemon juice, then add to sauteed vegetables. Coat apples thoroughly.

Combine the sauteed mixture with bread cubes, salt, pepper and parsley. Pour in apple juice, moistening the bread cubes and vegetables evenly. Add additional juice if the stuffing seems too dry; the amount that you add depends on the age and absorbency of the bread. Melt remaining butter; drizzle over stuffing.

Cool the stuffing. Fill the cavity of the turkey with the stuffing, sew up opening with heavy duty string and a trussing needle or skewer before roasting according to your favorite method. Yield: Enough to stuff a 12-pound turkey.

Puree of Acorn Squash

6 cups squash puree, made from 4 pounds acorn squash (see below)
7 tablespoons unsalted butter, melted
3 tablespoons very fine granulated sugar or granulated brown sugar
¼ teaspoon freshly ground nutmeg
Salt and freshly ground pepper, to taste
4 tablespoons Madeira
½ cup light cream

To prepare puree, bake acorn squash in a preheated, 375-degree oven for 60 to 75 minutes depending on the size of each vegetable. When the squash is cool enough to handle, remove skin, scoop out seeds and press flesh through a fine-meshed sieve.

Put puree in a deep saucepan and set over moderate heat. Stir in butter, sugar, nutmeg, salt and pepper; heat until very hot. Stir in Madeira and cook over low heat for 3 minutes. Fold in light cream. Adjust seasoning and heat thoroughly before serving. Yield: 8 servings.

See THANKSGIVING, E-15

Turkey roasting times

No matter what method you use to cook your Thanksgiving turkey — in a foil-tent at a low temperature, fully wrapped at a high temperature or in an oven cooking bag — several variables affect roasting times.

Uneven oven temperature, the shape of the bird and the degree of thawing are among these variables; it is important, therefore, to check the turkey for doneness 30 minutes to one hour before the end of its recommended roasting time. Turkey is done when a meat thermometer registers between 180 and 185 degrees, when the thick part of a drumstick feels soft when pressed with the thumb or forefinger or when the drumstick moves easily. After removing your turkey from the oven, let it stand at room temperature for 15 to 20 minutes to facilitate easier carving.

The stuffing within the turkey should reach 165 degrees to be sufficiently cooked. And remember, always remove stuffing from the bird as soon as it comes from the oven. Dense, moist stuffing that remains packed in a cooling turkey will often retain enough heat to breed bacteria.

The following are approximate cooking times for each of the most common turkey-roasting methods:

Approximate Roasting Times for Foil-Tent Turkey

Temperatures	Weight	Unstuffed	Stuffed
Non-preheated oven	8 to 12 lbs.	3 to 4 hrs.	4 to 5 hrs.
temp.: 325°F	12 to 16 lbs.	3½ to 5 hrs.	4½ to 6 hrs.
Internal temp.: 180-185°F	16 to 20 lbs.	4½ to 6 hrs.	5½ to 7 hrs.
Stuffing temp.: 165°F	20 to 24 lbs.	5½ to 6½ hrs.	6½ to 7½ hrs.

Approximate Times for Fully-Wrapped Turkey

Temperatures	Weight	Unstuffed	Stuffed
Non-preheated oven	8 to 12 lbs.	1¾ to 2 hrs.	2 to 2½ hrs.
temp.: 450°F	10 to 12 lbs.	2 to 2¼ hrs.	2½ to 2¾ hrs.
Internal temp.: 180-185°F	12 to 16 lbs.	2¼ to 3 hrs.	2¾ to 3½ hrs.
Stuffing temp.: 165°F	16 to 20 lbs.	3 to 3½ hrs.	3½ to 4 hrs.
	20 to 24 lbs.	3½ to 4½ hrs.	4 to 4¾ hrs.

Approximate Times for Oven-Cooking Bag Method

Temperatures	Weight	Unstuffed	Stuffed
Preheated oven	8 to 12 lbs.	2 to 2½ hrs.	2½ to 3 hrs.
temp.: 350°F	12 to 15 lbs.	2½ to 3 hrs.	3 to 3½ hrs.
Internal temp.: 180-185°F	15 to 20 lbs.	3 to 3½ hrs.	3½ to 4 hrs.
Stuffing temp.: 165°F	20 to 24 lbs.	3½ to 4 hrs.	4 to 4½ hrs.

The Washington Star/

"In much the same way that newspapers have to concentrate more on local news and community services, I believe they must adopt a slick 'less is more' presentation. Specifically, this means fewer words per story, more summaries, fewer jumps and better indexing . . . For diehard newspaper people this is a tough nut to swallow.

"Indeed, one of the reasons papers are dying in this country is because management at these papers don't pay the kind of attention to design and graphic presentation which they should — attention that will be vital to them if they wish to survive."

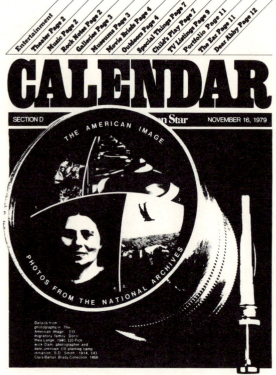

Entertainment Page 2. / Theater Page 2. / Music Page 2. / Rock Notes Page 2. / Galleries Page 3. / Museums Page 3. / Movie Briefs Page 4. / Outdoors Page 4. / Special Things Page 7. / Child's Play Page 7. / TV Listings Page 9. / Portfolio Page 11. / The Ear Page 11. / Dear Abby Page 12.

CALENDAR

SECTION D   Washington Star   NOVEMBER 16, 1979

THE AMERICAN IMAGE

PHOTOS FROM THE NATIONAL ARCHIVES

Details from photographs in "The American Image." (1) migratory family, Dorothea Lange, 1940. (2) Pickwick Dam, photographer and date unknown. (3) planting camp meeting, S.D. Smith, 1914. (4) Clara Barton, Brady Collection, 1866.

Through the lens, a century of American life

By James Cassell

In a time when the photograph has achieved the status of a valued aesthetic object, it's useful to consider its historically predominant function — documentation and visual evidence.

As the repository of all material that has affected or borne witness to the development of the American nation, the National Archives holds about 5 million photographs that served in some practical way the needs of a government agency and then were passed into the public realm. Of these 5 million and from the period 1860 to 1960, 191 are now on display in an exhibition titled "The American Image," which will run through the fall of 1980.

It's no small task to distill 191 photographs from such an immense number. The main guidelines were to choose images that were both visually arresting and historically interesting. After the staff at the Archives had whittled the number to a thousand, the final selection was made.

The services of Will Stapp, curator of photography at the National Portrait Gallery, and photography collector Samuel Wagstaff Jr. were included. Caryl Marsh, curator of exhibitions and research at the National Archives, was exhibition director, assisted by coordinator Christina Rady. Most of the photographs that are not vintage (original) were meticulously printed and toned by Gerd Sander of the Sander Gallery here.

It's important to note, as Alan Trachtenberg discusses at length in the accompanying book for this show ("The American Image," Pantheon, $10), the Archives' procedure for acquiring photographs. They are not, as one might guess, gathered according to subject or, in the case of an art museum, by photographer. Instead they are placed in the "record group" that corresponds to a particular government activity. It's not the job of the archivist to be concerned with the aesthetic content or the importance of the photographer. This is left to the student of photography, to the curator or aesthetician.

But an essential characteristic of the photograph is its tendency to age well, and with age, it frequently loses its sense of function and becomes an object of visual curiosity and delight.

For example, if the West was to be settled and crossed by railroads, it was necessary to know what it looked like. So the Jacksons and O'Sullivans put their cumbersome equipment onto wagons and mules and went out to survey the land. But their photographs have survived and been claimed by museums and collectors, the only reminder of their original purpose in the occasional number or title etched carefully into a corner of the plate. They have all been matted and framed and they are revered as important works of art.

Other photographs, as can be seen in this show, indicate milestones and idealize American progress: the panoramic view of a newly constructed dam, Truckee-Carson project in Nevada (1905); a formation of American bombers over the nation's capital (1931). Still others only hint at events and situations in our history that many of us would sooner forget: the cruelties of the Civil War portrayed so extensively by Mathew Brady; the impact of the Great Depression, especially for those who had only known poverty; the incarceration of Americans of Japanese descent during World War II.

As one views the parade of imagery from this hundred-year period, it's important to distinguish an evocation of the past from an understanding of it. While the

See IMAGES, D-3

A fine film dilutes fact with fiction

By Tom Dowling

"Northern Lights," winner of the Golden Camera Award for best first film at the Cannes festival this year, was originally intended to be a historical documentary of the rise of the Nonpartisan League to North Dakota political power in 1915.

The film's co-directors and co-producers, John Hanson and Rob Nilsson, had the sort of family roots that made the quest for North Dakota's dim agrarian-reform past accessible. Hanson's grandfather was a farmer and early member of the Nonpartisan League, which — with its program to drive out the Eastern moneylenders — controlled the North Dakota legislature from 1916 to 1922 and founded state-owned banks and grain elevators for the benefit of small homesteaders. Nilsson's grandfather was a filmmaker in North Dakota during the World War I era and left behind a treasure trove of period footage. Together, Hanson and Nilsson had at their disposal the oral and visual stuff of documentary history.

But somewhere along the line Hanson and Nilsson determined to make "Northern Lights," which

Susan Lynch in "Northern Lights"

opens today at the Inner Circle, into a feature film. And that is the rub. It's not that the material implicit in the Nonpartisan League's political history is undramatic, or even unsuitable for feature-film treatment. It's that the original notion of a documentary treatment keeps getting in the way.

People are the stuff of features, just as political movements are the stuff of documentaries. And when it comes to the structural crunch, "Northern Lights" abandons the story of its fictional characters in order to pursue the factual story of the Nonpartisan League movement.

See NORTHERN, D-6

A garden of botanic delights

By Marcia Schnedler

Trees that proudly sported fall finery in bright shades of red, yellow and orange a few weeks ago now look like they're headed for Skid Row.

If you want one last look at fall plants still elegantly attired, though, you can head for the annual chrysanthemum show at the U.S. Botanic Garden, now through Nov. 27

And once you've accepted the fact that drab winter days are here to stay, you'll still be able to add some color to your life at the Botanic Garden's annual Christmas greens exhibition, Dec. 4-9. You can savor a year-end spot of brightness, too, at the

In and out of town

garden's Poinsettia Show, running from mid-December through New Year's Day.

The charming glass conservatory of the U.S. Botanic Garden, constructed in 1934, sits at First Street and Maryland Avenue S.W., at the foot of Capitol Hill. It is open every day of the year except Christmas.

See GARDEN, D-12

The Washington Star/

SECTION D ••• The Washington Star Comics

washington life

TUESDAY NOVEMBER 27, 1979

TV TONIGHT

By Bernie Harrison

Movies and Government

Whatever it is that's wrong with systems of government, in theory or practice, there's never been any lack of entertainment eager to spell it out for us, or even sing it out.

Go out to the movies, for example, and you'll find Al Pacino singlehandedly confronting the legal system in "And Justice for All." Need we add "Apocalypse Now"?

Stay home, and you've got David Birney, as a blue collar worker, taking on the police and a coverup in **"High Midnight"** (WDVM-9 at 9), after his wife and a child are killed in a mistaken no-knock drug raid.

Stay home, and you've got the doomsaying of Bertold Brecht set to the music of Kurt Weill in "The Rise and Fall of the City of Mahogonny," **"Live From the Met"** (on public TV at 8).

Television Time, D-6

There was plenty to be gloomy about in Germany 50 years ago when they collaborated on this opera about a mythical lawless community in America, founded by three fugitives, and their overriding dramatic device was the threat of an annihilating hurricane. Brecht's outlook: sheer anarchy. Whether or not we're now in the "eye" of that hurricane is something to think about as you ponder Brecht's vision, which accommodates the colorful aberrations of a society.

New York critics gave the production — bound to rile opera traditionalists as it always has — very good marks and the cast, with music director James Levine, is outstanding: Teresa Stratas, Astrid Varnay, Richard Cassilly, Ragner Ulfung, Cornell MacNeil, Paul Plishka and others. It's sung in English, of course, and the Met's Francis Robinson hosts.

Speaking of hedonistic reflections in a mottled eye, we remind you of the conclusion of the glittering soaper, **"Beggarman, Thief"** (WRC-4 at 9) at the Cannes Film Festival. The German terrorists plan to kidnap Festival winners as hostages for their imprisoned comrades and the Jordaches, of course, are in the middle, where else? Stuck with the script: Jean Simmons (Gretchen), Glenn Ford as her lover (Donnelly), Andrew Stevens (Billy), Tovah Feldshuh (Monica), Lynn Redgrave (Kate) and others. We've been there before; so has the unlucky Ford.

Children's Viewing

The **"Bugs Bunny Looney Christmas Tale"** (WDVM-9 at 8) with Bugs concocting a scheme to enlighten Scrooge (Yosemite Sam), and an unlikely Santa Claus in the person of the Tasmanian Devil, may numb unwary grownups. Perfectly cast: Tweetie Bird as Tiny Tim. . . . **"The Fat Albert Christmas Special"** (WDVM-9 at 8:30) is the charmer, a rerun in which the Cosby kids help a family in distress, and learn that the mean old Tyrone, who plans to destroy their clubhouse, is only mean to mask his grief and loneliness. That's Cosby's voice as young Bill.

Movies

"High Midnight" (WDVM-9 at 9). This one is classic in its confrontation, the little guy, (David Birney), whose family is tragically brutalized by a mistaken no-knock narcotics raid, during a birthday party, no less, against the bad guy — a paranoid officer (Mike Connors) who swears his men to secrecy, and destroys the records. And that's the rub. Birney's rage is as real as the turns of the onesided plot are predictable, including the destruction of the home by fire, thereby destroying evidence of the raid and placing him under police suspicion. The vital clue as he undertakes his battle is the officer's overwhelming ego and zeal, and for a temporizing note, not all of the cops are ready to play it his way. A climacting

See TV TONIGHT, D-5

Astrid Varnay at the Met

This City Has Nothing To Offer in Architecture

Washington does not, in fact, exist. Washington is a figment of the imagination.

This article is adapted from an address given by Peter Blake, chairman of the department of architecture and planning at Catholic University of America, at a two-day Department of the Interior conference on Washington planning and architecture earlier this month at Dumbarton Oaks.

By Peter Blake

I'd like to put Washington into perspective. I have lived in New York most of my life, and in Boston part of my life, and I have spent a little time in every state except Alaska.

The view of Washington that outsiders like myself have is best described by that famous New Yorker cover by Saul Steinberg — a bird's-eye view of America from Midtown Manhattan, looking due west. That panoramic view shows 10th Avenue in the foreground, then 11th Avenue, then the West Side Highway, then the Hudson River, then New Jersey (with Chicago in the distance on the right), then Los Angeles, slightly to the left, behind South Dakota, then the Pacific Ocean, then Japan, then China — and that's it! (Newark may be in the left foreground.)

There is, of course, no sign of Washington at all. Washington does not, in fact, exist. Washington is a figment of the imagination.

The most baffling experience that Visitors from the Real World get when they first come to Washington is this enormous sense of importance that Washingtonians have of themselves — people in this city actually think that what happens here is *important*, and *significant*, and *newsworthy!* People in this city actually think that people in the Real World have their eyes riveted on Washington and care desperately about what happens here.

I don't know who or what gave Washingtonians that peculiar idea: For the fact, as my friend Saul Steinberg observed so clearly, is that Washington doesn't exist at all! It is a figment of your imagination.

Let me explain why:

The only thing I am an expert on, other than Washington, is architecture. In America, which is a country on the other side of the Potomac, architecture has been alive and well for the past hundred years or more; in my own favorite cities, New York and Boston, there are wonderful buildings by people like Frank Lloyd Wright and Louis Sullivan and H. H. Richardson and Raymond Hood, and Le Corbusier and Walter Gropius and Alvar Aalto and, more recently, by people like Robert Venturi — all of them major figures in American and/or World Architecture.

No buildings by any of these people stand in what is jokingly refered to as the Nation's Capital. This is as if London had no buildings by Sir

See Washington, D-3

THE EAR

STUDIO 54, WHERE ARE YOU? . . . You know, darlings, how the whole Andy Warhol tribe tramped into town to Push His Book the other day. It included Bob Colacello, editor of Andy's drop-dead trendy *Interview* maggie. Bob, natch, demanded to be whisked around the chic Club Scene here. Proper Protocol assistant Patrick Daly obliged. Now, Ear hears, Bob's rating of Washington Clubs is being bandied all over the Ap: Elan got two spoons; Pisces, one; and the Polo Club, half a spoon. Ear, of course, does not understand.

HAVEN'T WE MET BEFORE? . . . That was the Honorable Viron Vaky, assistant secretary of state for Inter-American Affairs 'til the other day, and *maybe* our next Ambassador to Brazil: He was stiffly suited in line with the Jeaned Ones, outside a showing of "10" . . . That was Bert Lance, perched in the Waldorf's Peacock Alley restaurant in the Ap, chatting up a Mid-Easterner on investments in Atlanta. He's tickled, he said with his "the best news in two years," recently in the Atlanta papers, and the way things are shaping up for Great Trial January 14 . . .

In faraway San Francisco, that was former Star sportsman and now Chicago Trib columnist David Israel asking pals: *Should* he chuck his Newspaper Career? Should he take that job he's been offered, with Teddy K's campaign in Washington? It was Dave Burgin, now editor of the Times Trib out there, who cried: "Look: If you work for Teddy there's only gonna be one star. And it ain't gonna be you." Ear likes to think this all took place in a hot tub, and that David just held his nose, and sunk under, and bobbled bubbles.

PEACE IN OUR TIME AND STYLE NOTE DU JOUR . . . Come, O.P., Ear's been flung out of the *very* finest spots. But *never* out of John Coleman's Warhol soiree. John acted just a tad odder than usual and Ear had a hot date with the Wisk. As for a feud, good gravy. Ear would not even crack wise about his appearance in the new *Harper's Bazaar* as a Desirable Bachelor, except in the privacy of its hot tub. On top of *that*, please note: This is The Star. Then, there is The Other Paper. This is Correct Usage, as it was, is now, and ever shall be.

Tomorrow: Smoke gets in your Ear.

Linda Gray Sexton: 'We had high-powered expectations'

Washington Star Photographer Robert Greiser

A New Women's Call to Compromise

By Judith Weinraub
Washington Star Staff Writer

Their mothers were converted by "The Feminine Mystique." Their boyfriends supported the ERA. Now they were to be the New Women — the first generation who had come of age on the crest of the Women's Movement. They were to be living proof that you could have it all — a career, a liberated marriage and children. Life would treat them differently than it had their mothers.

Now listen to Linda Gray Sexton, Radcliffe '75, a onetime self-described "rabid feminist" and the author of "Between Two Worlds, Young Women in Crisis" (William Morrow, $9.95):

"We had high-powered expectations that were simply not in keeping with reality. We were led to believe a career would just sort of happen without any planning. Most of all, we thought it would be easy. We needed to believe it, because if we realized how hard it really is, we would have given up in total defeat. There are a lot of very angry women out there."

Linda Sexton almost became one of them. That she didn't is a testament to her willingness to face herself honestly — and to her determination to find out if other young women were encountering similar confusions about their own lives.

Her dilemna presented itself soon after she graduated from college. Like most of her friends, she had taken a liberal-arts major and hadn't given very much thought to a career, except that she would have one. And she was living with a man who certainly didn't want a traditional wife, or at that point any wife.

At first she was kept busy as literary executor of the estate of her mother, the Pulitzer Prize-winning poet, Anne Sexton. But then she had to face the reality that she was not equipped for any profession. She had to decide what to do with her own life.

"I was really scared," Sexton says. 'Despite my ritzy degree, I had no more qualifications for a job than my mother had after a year at a junior college. Then I started having these unanticipated urges to be married and a mother. I wanted that commitment and companionship. I suddenly wasn't sure I wanted a career, and I was ashamed of it. I knew I shouldn't be feeling that way."

For a woman who thought of herself as a feminist, and for whom wearing a bra or shaving her legs was a political issue, her questions about her own identity came as a surprise. "We were so insecure we had to stand with absolutes," she says of her earlier, more strident years. "We had no sense of humor about anything. I even felt I had to hide in the bathroom to blow-dry my hair. And what difference did shaving your legs make if you were preparing for a career, but few of us really were."

As she talked to the young women she knew, Sexton found that many of them also felt conflicted and ambivalent. She wanted to see if other women were experiencing the same conflicts, and with encouragement from her now-husband, John Preund, she set out to write a book about what women of her generation were experiencing. She limited her study to women born between 1945 and 1955, the women who were 18 or younger when Betty Friedan's groundbreaking "The Feminine Mystique" was published in 1973.

She originally planned to interview 100 women; but she stopped after 30 and selected 15 profiles that she has presented not as generalizations for an entire group of women, but rather as a kaleidoscope of feelings. Her sampling, which crosses all economic strata, ranges from

See SEXTON, D-4

MUSIC

By Roger Glass
Special to The Washington Star

Old Jazz And New Musicians

The beak of his cap tugged down over his eyes, saxophonist Antione Roney is winding up his solo on John Coltrane's "Naima" as his brother Wallace slips in behind him. A spittin' image of a young Miles Davis, Wallace picks up where his brother left off, spouting off a series of notes like the famed Davis.

Minutes later Antione Roney rejoins his brother for a duet, capping off the Coltrane classic.

All of this would be of little news value if it were not for the fact that Wallace Roney, who is only 19-years-old and his brother, Antione, 16, are playing music made popular long before they were born. They are among a handful of young D.C. musicians who have elected to play jazz while many of their peers have opted for pop, funk or disco.

Together the Roneys make up two-fifths of the Wallace Roney Quintet which appeared last night at Blues Alley.

The quintet, whose average age is 21-years-old, jump feet first into the creative waters of jazz. The foot-tapping, straight-ahead kind.

Currently woodshedding with Horace Silver and Dollar Brand, the older Roney has listened to plenty of Miles Davis. He has also paid close attention to what Lee Morgan has had to say. Davis' smoothness and Morgan's imagination was present in his trumpet work.

On Richie Powell's "Gertrude's Bounce," Wallace Roney exchanged musical licks with his brother, both eager to get their point across. The trumpet player responding to his brother's prodding sax with a determined voice of his own.

The common nuances that the Roneys possess made for some frequently brillant trade-offs, as Charles Seay's steadying bass laid the foundation from whence they sprung.

Wallace Roney can be a bit to structured though, seemingly reluctant to overstep established boundaries. His individuality suffers as a result.

Antione, on the other hand, shows signs of being a little more adventurous. While his playing dragged on some of the ballads, his lyricism was sharp, and his playing simply lethal at times. On

See YOUNG, D-5

—Washington Star Photographer Walter Oates

Clarence Sea on bass, Wallace Roney on trumpet, and Antoine Roney on sax.

Chapter

9/

Design/

Handling
the news on
a big day

Introduction /

How newspapers used design on a big news day

What happens to design when there's a big news day? It's not disregarded, by any means — or shouldn't be. If anything, design makes the job easier for editors racing to get the news onto the page.

Such a big news day was Jan. 20, 1981, when two major events took place at virtually the same time. In Iran, the 52 American hostages were freed. In Washington, Ronald Reagan was inaugurated as president.

Newspapers represented in the previous chapter were asked to furnish for this book the front pages announcing the two events. In no case is design abandoned.

In the interest of design — and of history — the pages are reproduced here.

The Courier-Journal/

METRO EDITION — Louisville, Ky., Wednesday morning, January 21, 1981 — 25¢

54 Pages
Vol. 252, No. 21
****

The Courier-Journal

Home delivery
85¢ week

Copyright © 1981, The Courier-Journal

American hostages' flight to freedom adds to drama of Reagan inaugural

Freedom for hostages heralds a day of joy, thanks

By GAYLORD SHAW and OSWALD JOHNSTON
© The Los Angeles Times

WASHINGTON — Free at last, the 52 American hostages who endured so much for so long began their journey home yesterday to a nation that never forgot them during 444 agonizing days.

The end of the crisis came 33 minutes after Ronald Reagan assumed the presidency at noon from Jimmy Carter, whose last hours in office turned national humiliation into what he called "this day of joy and thanksgiving."

All across a thankful land, with silent prayers, the pealing of church bells and a cacophony of sirens and horns, Americans joined in spontaneous celebration.

"They're Free! They're Free!" flashed a huge sign in New York's Times Square.

The torch atop the Statue of Liberty was lit. So was the National Christmas Tree in Washington, symbolically dark during two trying holiday seasons in which the Americans were held captive.

The long-awaited flight to freedom carried the 50 men and 2 women — diplomats, soldiers, administrators and teachers — to Algeria, the north African nation that acted as middleman in negotiating the agreement exchanging frozen Iranian gold and bank deposits for the hostages' release.

Americans got their first glimpse, via Algerian television, of all the hostages when they left the Algerian jetliner last night that carried them from Iran. The jet landed at Houari Boumedienne Airport in Algiers about 7:30 p.m. EST.

Two hours later, the hostages boarded two U.S. military DC-9s for a flight to Frankfurt, West Germany. They arrived in Frankfurt shortly at 12:45 a.m. EST today and were to be transferred to a military hospital at Wiesbaden for a period of rest before a triumphant return to heroes' welcomes in their homeland.

Carter, whose crushing loss of the presidency stemmed in part from the hostage humiliation, was ready to fly to Germany early today to represent the United States — at Reagan's invitation — in officially welcoming the hostages to freedom.

The outgoing chief executive had labored through the final hours of his presidency to bring the hostages home, but it fell to his successor to announce that they had been freed. Reagan did so with a mixture of prayer, a Hollywood-style reference and a toast.

Standing before congressional leaders at an inaugural luncheon, Reagan lifted his glass of California wine and said, "with thanks to Almighty God . . . I have been given a tagline, the get-off line that everyone wants for the end

See U.S.
Back page, col. 1, this section

- The families of the hostages cheered and wept at the news that their loved ones had finally been released. Page A 2.
- The hostage negotiations were as unpredictable as the crisis itself. Page A 3.
- When the bells of a Louisville church rang out to mark the release of the 52 hostages, worshippers gathered at a Mass of thanksgiving. There were exactly 52 of them. Page B 2.

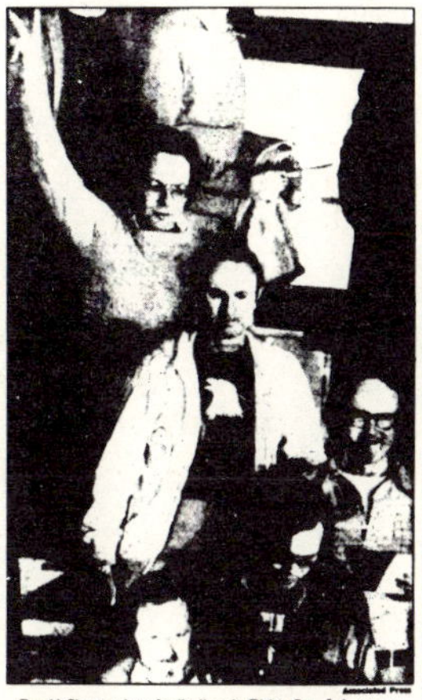

Associated Press

Donald Sharer, whose family lives in Rising Sun, Ind., gave a victory wave after the plane that flew the hostages to freedom stopped in Algiers yesterday. (Related story, Page A 2.) Below, Barbara Timm, mother of Kevin Hermening, the youngest of the hostages, reacted to the news with her husband, Kenneth.

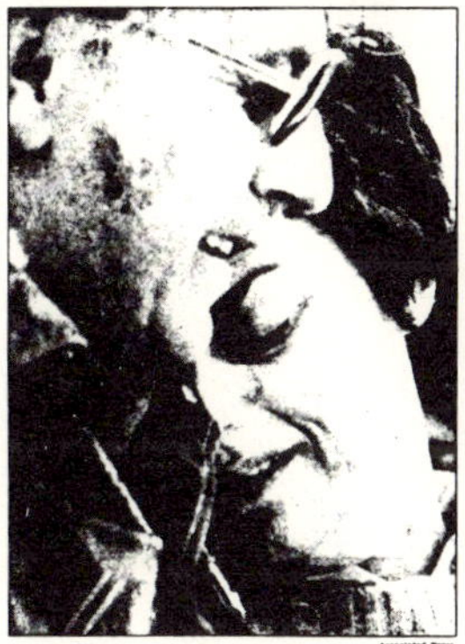

Associated Press

First flight takes freed Americans to Germany

By LOUIS B. FLEMING
© The Los Angeles Times

ALGIERS, Algeria — The 52 American hostages arrived here safely from Tehran early today, seemingly in good health and clearly overjoyed to have their 14½ months of captivity behind them.

In Algiers, they boarded an U.S. Air Force plane for West Germany, where they landed at Rhein-Main Air Base at Frankfurt at 6:45 a.m. German time today (12:45 a.m. EST).

Their Algerian jetliner landed in light rain at 12:37 a.m. (7:37 p.m. EST yesterday) and taxied slowly to the VIP lounge at Boumedienne Airport, about five miles from the Algerian Foreign Ministry where the agreements that led to their freedom had been signed early Monday.

U.S. and Algerian officials, led by the Algerian foreign minister, Mohammed Seddik Benyahia, and former Deputy Secretary of State Warren M. Christopher were at the bottom of the ramp to greet the hostages.

The freed Americans walked down the line of greeters, shaking hands and exchanging kisses. A few of them looked pensive and tired, but most wore broad smiles.

The two women among the hostages, Kathryn L. Koob of Fairfax, Va., and Elizabeth Ann Swift of Washington, were first off the Air Algeria 727. They wore yellow ribbons — the symbol of the hostage crisis and a nation's hope for a successful return — in their hair.

Inside the VIP lounge, the hostages were given refreshments and chatted informally among themselves and with the American and Algerian officials.

Christopher, expressing America's thanks, declared that without the assistance of the Algerian government, "today's events would not be taking place.

"We're deeply indebted to you," he told Algerian officials. "This event answers our prayers." He paid tribute to Benyahia and others "for having performed this humanitarian role with such high skill . . . .

"During the last week I believe that the foreign minister has devoted on many days 20 hours a day to the problem and I know there have been several nights in a row leading up to today when he has not slept," Christopher said.

The former hostages, rising to their feet, applauded loudly and L. Bruce Laingen, the ranking American diplomat among them, went up to the Algerian foreign minister and told him, "Thank you for the flight to freedom and the hospitality of your government."

Then Benyahia and Christopher each spoke briefly, Christopher thanking the Algerians for their role as middle-men during the past two months, accepting responsibility for the former hostages and welcoming them "home."

Then the freed Americans lined up and walked past the two diplomats, shaking hands and exchanging a few words.

Next stop for the 52 Americans, after the brief stop in Algiers, was Rhein-Main Air Base near Frankfurt, West Germany. They were taken from there to the U.S. Air Force hospital at Wiesbaden, 25 miles west of Frankfurt, for a period of rest, medical and psychological testing and debriefing.

On their arrival in Germany, they were greeted by a throng of Americans gathered at the base, including Cyrus Vance, who was secretary of state at the time of their capture.

They had begun their long flight,

See AMERICANS
Back page, col. 1, this section

Staff Photo by Bill Luster

President and Mrs. Reagan waved to the crowd from the inaugural platform after Reagan's inauguration speech yesterday.

New president calls for 'national renewal,' pledges to reduce taxes

By JACK NELSON
© The Los Angeles Times

WASHINGTON — Ronald Reagan assumed office as the nation's 40th president yesterday with a passionate call for an "era of national renewal" and a pledge not to compromise on his promises to cut taxes and reduce the size of the federal government.

In his first official act as president, less than an hour after being sworn in, the former California governor signed an order imposing a federal hiring freeze that he said "will eventually lead to a sizable reduction in the federal work force."

"It is time for us to realize that we are too great a nation to limit ourselves to small dreams," Reagan declared in his inaugural address. He had charged during the 1980 campaign that President Carter had too limited a view of the nation's potential.

"We're not, as some would have us believe, doomed to an inevitable decline," he said. "I do not believe in a fate that will fall on us no matter what we do. I do believe in a fate that will fall on us if we do nothing. So with all the creative energy at our command, let us begin an era of national renewal."

Inaugurated as the American hostages were being freed in Iran, Reagan also had a warning for international terrorists. He declared that no weapon against them is so formidable as one employed by Americans — "the will and moral courage of free men and women."

"Let that be understood by those who practice terrorism and prey upon their neighbors."

Reagan made no direct reference to the hostages in his forcefully delivered, 19-minute inaugural address. But the high drama of their release dominated the conversations of many of the thousands who turned out to watch the inaugural ceremonies and parade under cloudy skies and in almost spring-like weather.

The planes carrying the hostages to freedom took off from Tehran just a

See REAGAN
PAGE 5, col. 4, this section

- Text of President Reagan's inauguration address. Page A 13.
- It was a festive and exciting day for Kentuckians attending the inauguration in Washington. Page C 1.
- For television, the inauguration and hostage release combined for an extraordinary double-feature — a thriller and a pageant. Page A 4.

Breaking a gray

National Weather Service

LOUISVILLE area — Cloudy with rain ending today. Clearing and colder tonight, partly sunny tomorrow. Highs today and tomorrow, low 40s. Low tonight, upper 20s.

KENTUCKY — Cloudy with rain ending from West today. Clearing tomorrow. Highs today and tomorrow, 40s. Lows tonight, low to mid-30s.

INDIANA — Clearing and cool today. Mostly sunny tomorrow. Highs today low-30s to low 40s, tomorrow mid-30s to mid-40s. Lows tonight, 20s.

High yesterday: 46, low: 34
Year ago yesterday: High, 39, low, 30
Sun: Rises 7:56 EST, sets 5:53
Moon: Rises 7:31 p.m., sets 8:50 a.m.

Weather map and details, Page B 12

Commandments must go, opinion says

By RICHARD WILSON
Courier-Journal Staff Writer

FRANKFORT, Ky. — The state's public schools must remove all copies of the Ten Commandments from their classrooms, Attorney General Steven Beshear said in an opinion yesterday.

Beshear's advisory opinion was delivered to the state Board of Education, which recommended that local school districts comply with it.

However, the opinion may not end the nearly three-year legal battle provoked by a 1978 state law requiring the commandments to be posted in every public-school classroom.

Two supporters of the law said last night that they question whether local school districts will abide by Beshear's opinion.

The Rev. Tom Riner and his wife, Claudia, a state representative from Louisville, said they believe some school officials feel so strongly about the issue that they may continue to post the commandments.

The law was challenged in a suit filed by four Jefferson County residents who were represented by an attorney for the Kentucky Civil Liberties Union.

They took their case to the U.S. Supreme Court after Kentucky's Supreme Court upheld the law last April.

The U.S. high court ruled 5-4 last November that the law violated the freedom-of-religion clause in the First Amendment to the U.S. Constitution.

Shortly after the ruling was issued, state Superintendent of Public Instruction Raymond Barber asked Beshear if the thousands of copies of the Ten Commandments already posted in classrooms had to be removed.

Beshear and other state officials then asked the Supreme Court to clarify its opinion.

But when the court refused to issue a clarification last week, the issue was back in Beshear's lap.

Yesterday's opinion was delivered to a meeting of the state board by Deputy Attorney General Robert Chenoweth. Chenoweth recommended that the board advise each of the state's 181 school districts to follow the opinion, which does not have the force of law.

Barber said later, after the board recommended that Chenoweth's advice be followed, that he will send copies of the opinion to local school districts in the next few days.

In the opinion Beshear noted that local school officials who do not comply with the Supreme Court ruling may be subject to lawsuits that might seek compensatory or punitive damages.

"Therefore, each local school board is encouraged to carefully consider the legal ramifications of their actions

See COMMANDMENTS
Back page, col. 1, this section

INSIDE

Many parts of the country will be unable to meet the health and environmental standards of the Clean Air Act on schedule and some will never be able to achieve them without economic disruption, a National Commission on Air Quality report says — A 6

The Emporia Gazette/

THE·EMPORIA·GAZETTE

91st Year, No. 169 — Tuesday, the Twentieth Day of January, MCMLXXXI — Twenty-four Pages

FREEDOM FLAG — A large 48-star American flag, which has been in storage for more than 20 years at Emporia State University, was hung today from the flagpoles in the Sunken Garden on campus. John Greene, director of the physical plant at E.S.U., said he just thought it was appropriate to hang the flag to celebrate the release of the U.S. hostages by Iran. (Photograph by Sam Van Leeuwen)

Aircraft Carrying U.S. Hostages Leaves Tehran; Release Coincides With End of Carter Presidency

* * *

Assets Are Deposited Into Iranian Account

By the Associated Press

The 52 American hostages flew to freedom today after 444 days of captivity in Iran, the official Iranian news agency Pars announced.

Their departure coincided with the inauguration of President Ronald Reagan who replaced Jimmy Carter as president.

Departure of the hostages was marked by the same confusion and uncertainty that characterized the hostage crisis and the long give and take of negotiations leading to their release.

Pars said the hostages boarded the plane to shouts by Iranians of "down with America, down with Reagan."

President Reagan confirmed in Washington that the aircraft had taken off from Tehran.

Departure was arranged after negotiations finally wrapped up agreement to exchange the hostages for Iranian assets frozen by the United States.

The 3,000-mile flight to Algiers would take 6¾ hours or more, depending on the route and whether refueling stops were made. It was expected that the hostages would go on to a U.S. Air Force hospital in Wiesbaden, West Germany, a 1,000-mile flight from Algiers that normally takes 2¾ to 3 hours.

There were reports from Western sources monitoring the hostage situation in Ankara that flight plans filed by the Algerian aircraft included a refueling stop in Ankara or Damascus, Syria, Rome, or Athens.

President Carter had tried to complete an agreement with Iran on Monday, but as the hours slipped away, he was deprived of a chance to greet the hostages before he left office.

The hostages were seized Nov. 4, 1979 by young Moslem militants who stormed the U.S. Embassy in Tehran. They said the hostages would be released if the United States handed over Shah Mohammad Reza Pahlavi, then undergoing medical treatment in the United States. The shah found refuge in Egypt and died in Cairo on July 27, 1980.

Release of the hostages would end 14½ months of negotiations. American economic and diplomatic pressure and the failed attempt last April to send American commando teams to Tehran to free the hostages by military action.

The 52 Americans were the remaining hostages from among 66 seized by the Moslem revolutionaries nine months after the Islamic revolution in Iran.

The hostages include diplomats, Marine guards, communications specialists, teachers and a businessman. They range in age from 30 to 64. About 30 are servicemen.

The final push toward a settlement came in weeks of intense negotiations with Algerian diplomats acting as intermediaries.

On Dec. 19, the Iranians demanded that the United States deposit $24 billion in cash and gold in Algeria as a "guarantee" that Iran's financial demands would be met, including its demand for the late Shah Mohammad Reza Pahlavi's wealth.

The E.P.A. said it filed the complaint in U.S. District Court in Topeka.

Ottawa City Manager Robert Mills said a tentative agreement, calling for a fine of $2,500, has been reached by the city and the E.P.A. to resolve the complaint. The agreement requires approval of the city commission.

However, Terry Watt, chief of the legal branch in the E.P.A. Enforcement Division in Kansas City, said she couldn't confirm an agreement had been reached. "We have been in negotiation," she said. "No formal agreement has been reached. We're waiting for the city to get back to us on a couple of points."

The United States rejected this, and on Jan. 2 offered a counter-proposal: only the approximately $10 billion in Iranian government assets frozen by the United States would be returned. The remaining hostages linked to arrangements for resolving claims and counter-claims by the two sides.

On Jan. 7, Iranian negotiator Behzad Nabavi said Tehran "generally" accepted the latest proposal, and the next day Deputy Secretary of State Warren Christopher flew to Algiers to establish closer contact through the Algerian go-betweens.

* * *

Good Evening

We have a great idea for all of those vivid yellow ribbons. How about tying them, really tight, around Khomeini's neck?

☆ ☆ ☆

Emporia Weather

1 P.M.	41 degrees
High Monday	39 degrees
Low last night	33 degrees
Barometer	29.35 steady
Humidity	82 percent
Wind	N 12

☆ ☆ ☆

Topeka:

Death Penalty Bill Reviewed

Carlin Vetoed Similar Legislation Last Year

TOPEKA, Kan. (AP) — A bill to reinstate the death penalty was reviewed by a Kansas Senate committee Monday, but a decision whether to introduce it into the upper chamber was put off until later in the week.

The Senate Federal and State Affairs Committee discussed the proposal, which is similar to a capital punishment bill vetoed last year by Gov. John Carlin. Although no action was taken, debate centered on whether the committee should introduce the measure.

As drafted, the bill calls for a death penalty or mandatory life sentence as a choice for a jury after murder convictions in three categories — premeditated, murder in commission of a kidnapping, and in commission of rape or sodomy.

Also included in the measure is a provision for automatic review by the Kansas Supreme Court of any death sentence.

Method of execution will depend upon constitutional tests. But the committee's draft called for death by injection as the first choice. If the courts strike that down, death by hanging would be used. And electrocution was listed in the draft as a final alternative.

Because of Governor Carlin's vetoes of death penalty bills in the past two sessions, Senator James Francisco, D-Wichita, told the committee he thought they were wasting time by considering the issue, and should address matters such as a proposed severance tax or classification of property.

"We've known that the governor spoke loud and clear for the last two years. He spoke specifically to this bill. This governor is no different than any other governor in the history of this state. He's going to be consistent, I'm sure," said Senator Francisco.

The Senate has narrowly approved death penalty bills during the past two years, and such a measure is expected to meet less resistance this session because changes in the makeup of the upper chamber. However, the main obstacle to enactment is whether the 160 Legislators can muster a two-thirds majority to override a veto by Carlin.

In the Senate Ways and Means Committee meeting, the state's Unified Judicial Department asked for reinstatement of about $1.96 million cut from its budget request by Governor Carlin.

* * *

Reagan To Lead Nation

WASHINGTON (AP) — Ronald Reagan was inaugurated 40th President of the United States today, summoning Americans to "an era of national renewal" amid bells and cannon, music and pageantry that became a celebration, too, for 52 American hostages reported freed at last from Iranian bondage.

At the stroke of noon, power passed from James Earl Carter Jr., Democrat, to Ronald Wilson Reagan, Republican, conservative, veteran of Hollywood, governor of California, overwhelming choice of his countrymen.

Denied a second term, Carter watched as Reagan raised his right hand, put his left on a family Bible and swore the simple 35-word oath of office. A 21-gun salute boomed out over the Capitol and the marble monuments of American government.

Moments before, George Bush had taken the almost identical oath of vice presidential office.

With all the creative energy at our command let us begin an era of national renewal. President Reagan said in his inaugural address. Let us renew our determination our courage and our strength. Let us renew our faith and our hope. We have every right to dream heroic dreams.

President Reagan asked Americans are entitled for they are themselves heroes. you the citizens of this blessed land.

Your dreams your hopes your goals are going to be the dreams the hopes and goals of this administration. so help me God.

President Reagan's invocation to his new administration began with a pledge to confront and handle an economic affliction of the worst proportions. We must act today in order to preserve tomorrow. And let there be no misunderstanding — we are going to act beginning today.

The new president said the nation's economic ills will not go away in days weeks or months but they will go away.

In this present crisis government is not the solution it is the problem. President Reagan said a line sounded the day after campaign day in the quest that won him the White House by a landslide last Nov. 5.

Harold Durst, dean of the School of Graduate and Professional Studies, expects the graduate enrollment to equal or exceed last year's 1,070 total.

(E-State News Release)

Americans' Average Personal Income, Consumer Prices Up

WASHINGTON (AP) — Americans' average personal income climbed 1.1 percent last year, but the increase was more than gobbled up by higher consumer prices, according to new government figures.

The nation's inflation rate, as measured by the government's consumer price index, was running at an annual rate of 11.5 percent for the first 11 months of 1980 with December's CPI figure due Friday.

After personal income increased 1.3 percent in October and 1.1 percent in November, Commerce Department figures released Monday showed a December rise of only 0.9 percent. That placed the yearly total at 11.1 percent.

Inflation rose just over 11 percent in 1979, while personal income increased 12.8 percent, according to previously adjusted government figures.

The Commerce Department also reported Monday that housing starts were down slightly in December for the first time since May and that building permits for future construction were down substantially.

A Commerce Department economist called the housing statistics "remarkably steady"

in light of high interest rates. But an industry spokesman said they indicated big declines coming up in a "very very slow" first half of 1981.

In another economic development Monday, the government's Chrysler Loan Guarantee Board approved a plan under which creditors and workers at the financially troubled No. 3 automaker would make big financial concessions and the government would grant $400 million in new federal loan guarantees. A final board vote is scheduled for two weeks from now.

In disposing of their income in December, the Commerce Department said, Americans increased personal-consumption spending by just 0.3 percent after recent increases of better than 1 percent per month.

At the same time, income channeled into savings grew at an annual rate of nearly 10 percent last month, in contrast to declines in October and November. the department said. At year-end, the department estimated the nation's savings rate — the percentage of disposable income that people save — at 5.1 percent, the same as in 1979.

German Seeks 17th District's Seat In Kansas House

TOPEKA, Kan. (AP) — The publisher of the Burlington Daily Republican Monday became the first person to file with the Kansas secretary of state as a candidate for nomination in the August 1982 primary election.

Putting his name on the line nearly 17 months in advance of the election, the newspaperman, Glenn R. German, officially became a candidate for Republican nomination to the Kansas House in the 17th district. Mr. German resides in New Strawn, Kan.

The district is represented now by Anita Niles, Lebo Democrat, who is in her fourth term.

Task Force Predicts Rapid Rise in World Coal Market

WASHINGTON (AP) — Forecasting a rosy future for U.S. coal exports, a government task force predicts the United States will be supplying 38 percent of total world demand by the end of the century.

The Interagency Coal Export Task Force appointed by President Carter said this rapid increase is possible with very little federal aid.

The United States supplied about 6 percent of the 78.5 million tons of coal sold on the world market in 1979, the task force said in a report Monday.

It forecast that would triple to 18 percent in 1985, increase to 26 percent in 1990 and hit the 38 percent figure by the year 2000.

Meanwhile, the report also forecast a rapid rise in total coal sales as more countries looked for an alternative to expensive and unreliable supplies of oil.

The report estimated the world coal market excluding Communist and developing

countries would increase to between 471 million and 565 million tons by 2000.

The problem of clogged port facilities which added an average of 40 days waiting time for ships seeking U.S. coal in 1979 and 1979 sessions. Study Representative James Lowther, an Emporia Republican who is chairman of the House Education Committee, said Saturday that he expects to see the earlier measure re-introduced this year.

Approximately 35 million tons of new coal loading capacity are usually is already being built at the nation's ports and there are plans for another 180 million tons, according to the report.

The development of new piers and associated coal loading equipment is not the responsibility of the federal government, but rather that of private industry, the states and local governments," the report concluded. "Their response now appears to be entirely adequate."

Lowther Plans Own Bill. . . .

Anita Niles Proposes Teacher Tests

By Lynn Bonney

The question of testing the competency of Kansas teachers and the desirability of a competency test for professional education and general subjects, junior high and high school teachers would also be tested on their field of specialization.

Mrs. Niles, a former teacher, said Saturday the measure was a logical step to follow statewide competency-testing of students, a program still in the planning stages.

"If we are asking students to pass proficiency tests, it only follows that teachers should also be tested," she said. "I feel that teachers are professionals, and most professions require a person to pass a proficiency exam to practice in a field."

Mrs. Niles, who has been working on the measure since last summer, said she was pleased that Gov. John Carlin had endorsed the idea in his "State of the State" speech earlier this month.

"It was good to see that the Governor seemed to be pushing that way in his speech," she said.

Testing teachers' competency has come before the Legislature on two previous occasions, in the certificates were issued, renewed or reinstated. However, Mr. Lowther said Mr. Watt would probably change the manner to require only one test, to be given before a teacher is first licensed in the state.

Mr. Lowther said he supported the one-time test because of teacher shortages in some fields.

"We've got enough of a problem hiring teachers for certain areas, like vocational subjects, that I don't think we should discourage students who may be planning teaching careers in those fields," he said. "Low salaries are already making it hard to attract teachers, and also *(See Tests, page 2)*

Ottawa Is Cited For Violating Clean-Air Act

KANSAS CITY, Mo. (AP) — The U.S. Environmental Protection Agency has filed a complaint against Ottawa, claiming the northeast Kansas town violated clean air standards by constructing a power plant addition without federal approval.

The E.P.A. said it filed the complaint in U.S. District Court in Topeka.

Ottawa City Manager Robert Mills said a tentative agreement, calling for a fine of $2,500, has been reached by the city and the E.P.A. to resolve the complaint.

Trent to Become Deputy Secretary Of Transportation

WASHINGTON (AP) — Darrell Trent, a 42-year-old Pittsburg, Kan., native won quick approval from a U.S. Senate committee Monday to become President-elect Ronald Reagan's deputy secretary of transportation.

The action by the Commerce Committee, on the eve of Reagan's inauguration, is expected to assure the former Kansan of easy confirmation by the full Senate, preferably shortly after Reagan is sworn in.

Mr. Trent, a 1956 graduate of Pittsburg High School, served five years as domestic affairs aide to former president Richard Nixon until 1974, when he became a senior research fellow at Stanford University's Hoover Institute.

☆ ☆ ☆

Emporia State:

Gain Reported In Enrollment

Increase in Students Already Is Over 200

Spring enrollment at Emporia State University is up over a year ago at this time, according to Clint Webber, registrar. After the third day of classes Friday, Emporia State had enrolled 238 more students than for the same period in 1980.

The official day for counting enrollment totals is the 20th day of classes (Feb. 10). Based on figures universities then have 10 days in which to prepare and submit the final enrollment report.

Spring 1980 enrollment was 5,758. Mr. Webber predicts the final spring 1981 count will reach 5,960. The total for the third-day report was 4,506 compared with 4,288 for the same period in 1980.

The largest increases thus far have come in unclassified students, 211, compared with 147 a year ago, and graduates, 668, compared with 586 in 1980. After the third day of classes, Emporia State had increases in sophomores, juniors, and seniors. Freshmen were down three, from 1,075 to 1,072.

"We had an outstanding community enrollment this spring," Mr. Webber said. "We enrolled 206 people. That's a new record, about 100 more than we normally have for community enrollment."

"We've also had a significant number of transfer students enroll this spring. So far we've had 104 transfers enroll, compared with 73 we had for all of last spring."

The Kansas City Star/

The Reagan era dawns with gift of freedom

By the Associated Press

Washington—Ronald Reagan today became the 40th president of the United States, summoning Americans to "an era of national renewal" amid bells and cannon fire, music and pageantry that also became a celebration for 52 American hostages reported freed from Iranian bondage.

At the stroke of noon, power passed from James Earl Carter Jr., Democrat, to Ronald Wilson Reagan, Republican, conservative, veteran of Hollywood, former governor of California, overwhelming choice of his countrymen.

As one presidency yielded to another, an Algerian plane carrying the hostages took off from Iran, beginning a journey home that ended 444 days of captivity.

Denied a second term, Carter watched as Reagan raised his right hand, put his left hand on a family Bible and took the oath of office. A 21-gun salute boomed over the Capitol and the marble monuments of American government.

Moments before, George Bush had taken the nearly identical oath of vice presidential office.

"With all the creative energy at our command, let us begin an era of national renewal," Reagan said in his inaugural address. "Let us renew our determination, our courage and our strength. Let us renew our faith and our hope. We have every right to dream heroic dreams."

Reagan said Americans are entitled to dream, for they are heroes. "You, the citizens of this blessed land.

"Your dreams, your hopes, your goals are going to be the dreams, the hopes and goals of this administration, so help me God."

Reagan's invocation to his new administration began with a pledge to confront and handle "an economic affliction of the worst proportions. We must act today in order to preserve tomorrow. And let there be no misunderstanding—we are going to act beginning today."

The new president said the nation's economic ills "will not go away in days, weeks, or months, but they will go away . . . .

"In this present crisis, government is not the solution, it is the problem," Reagan said.

Reagan said he intended to curb the size and influence of the government he now heads. He said he would make government "work with us, not over us . . . . stand by our side, not ride on our back."

He promised to ease the tax burden, restore the balance among various levels of government and promote American enterprise.

"These will be our first priorities and on these principles, there will be no compromise," he said.

In an era of renewal at home, Reagan said, the nation will stand abroad as "the exemplar of freedom and a beacon of hope for those who do not now have freedom."

He promised the United States would be a faithful ally to friends, and told potential adversaries that peace was America's highest aspiration. "We will negotiate for it, sacrifice for it; we will not surrender for it—now or ever."

Reagan said forbearance should never be interpreted as a failure of will. "When action is required to preserve

See Oath, pg. 2A, col. 1

THE KANSAS CITY STAR.

C Tuesday evening, January 20, 1981, Main Edition, 38 pages 25c

They're free — at last!

By the Associated Press

Two Algerian 727 jetliners carrying the 52 American hostages took off today from Tehran's Mehrabad Airport, the Iranian news agency Pars reported.

President Ronald Reagan later confirmed that the Americans were airborne. He did not make the announcement until the planes cleared Iranian airspace, about an hour after takeoff. The time of departure was reported to be 11:33 a.m. (Kansas City time).

"They are airborne," Reagan said after his succession to the White House. He said he had been informed "moments ago" that the first plane was airborne at 11:33, and the second left minutes later.

Pars said the Americans boarded the planes to the jeers of Iranians shouting, "Down with America, down with Reagan."

The Pars announcement came after a tense six hours of waiting for Americans, which followed an announcement by Carter administration officials early today that the United States had complied with all the terms of the settlement with Iran.

The national yearning to have the hostages on the way home was fed by half a dozen reports beginning about 10:15 a.m. that the Algerian aircraft had taken off.

The departure came after long negotiations to wrap up final agreement—a trade of the hostages for Iran's frozen assets.

The 3,000-mile flight to Algiers, if that was the destination, would take 6 to 10 hours, depending on whether refueling stops were made. It was expected that the hostages would go on to a U.S. Air Force hospital in Wiesbaden, West Germany.

Asked at the podium of Reagan's inaugural stand if the hostages were free, President Carter said, "Can't say yet." Carter's spokesman, Jody Powell, said Carter would have no further comment until after he returned to Plains, Ga., later today.

But Edmund S. Muskie, outgoing secretary of state, said Carter would leave for Wiesbaden tonight, where he will welcome the hostages to freedom. Muskie will go with him.

In his inaugural address, which concluded at 11:20 a.m., Reagan did not mention the hostages.

Darkness at the Tehran airport caused a delay in the hostages' departure, due to blackout conditions imposed as a result of Iran's war with Iraq. But the runway lights were turned on for the take-off.

The release of the hostages came after Carter, pressing for an end to the ordeal at the dawn of Reagan's presidency, settled one last account with Iran early today.

Carter worked overnight in the Oval Office with his vice president and two intimate friends. He bartered the final contract terms and then ordered the re-

See Hostages, pg. 5A, col. 1

Iran's most wishful thinking can't erase history's scorn

By C.W. Gusewelle
associate editor

News comment

There is an odd turn of Middle Eastern thought which frequently allows leaders to claim, with utter conviction, a shining triumph—even as their routed armies stumble shrieking and shoeless out of the dunes.

Wish is confused with fact. There seems somehow to be a belief that, if wished fervently enough, it may indeed *become* fact.

But no amount of wishing by the Tehran regime can snatch a victory out of the ashes of Iran's failure in the crisis just ended. The United States, say the Iranian authorities, has been humbled—the Great Satan brought to its knees.

But what actually has happened?

In exchange for the release of its captives, the Khomeini regime has gotten back some, but by no means yet all—and possibly *never* all—of the financial assets it lost when the hostages were taken in the first place. And that, evidently, is the whole of this poor "triumph."

No fortune of the fallen royalty. No spectacle of public abasement by the United States. Not the $24 billion Tehran ludicrously first demanded, nor the $14 billion it later said it would accept. Not even, immediately, the full $8 billion in assets which the U.S. concedes is due, but only a part of that—the rest to be held against Iranian debts in this country.

The imagined victory, then, is a sorry spectacle of weakness. Bankrupted by war and fearful of the future of American policy under a new president, Iran has settled on the best terms it could get, which is to say the only terms that ever were really available.

There have been times in the past when, caught up in rage at some monstrous wrong in the world and impatient with diplomacy's slow grindings, I have yearned—as no doubt you have—to hold

See Scorn, pg. 5A, col. 1

Tears of joy overwhelm family of freed hostage

By Robert J. Pessek
staff writer

More stories about the American hostages are on pages 8A and 9A.

Krakow, Mo.—Rocky Sickmann is coming home.

At 11:51 a.m. the Virgil Sickmanns were telephoned by the U.S. Department of State that the 52 Americans being held hostage for 444 days in Iran were airborne from Tehran, that country's capital city. On that plane is Marine Sgt. Rodney V. "Rocky" Sickmann, their 23-year-old son.

Unabashed tears and quavering voices, along with nearly disbelieving smiles were major elements at the press conference held by the Sickmann family about 12:30 p.m. today in the Krakow town hall.

"I don't even know if I can talk, I'm so overjoyed," Mrs. Toni Sickmann, Rocky's mother said. "God has been so good to us to give us back the hostages."

The Sickmanns were gathered in their yellow frame house, as they have been the last few days while the hostage crisis seemed to be nearing a conclusion.

Their first news that the hostages were coming home was based on unconfirmed

See Tears, pg. 5A, col. 4

Having spoken the oath of his predecessors, the nation's 40th president, Ronald Reagan, kissed his wife, Nancy. The passing of power in Washington coincided with a report that the 52 American hostages had been freed from Iran. Reagan was updated on the captives' status after taking the oath. (**Associated Press**)

The Carter years: Successes and failures

By James Gerstenzang
Associated Press writer

Washington—On Jan. 19, 1977, the day before Jimmy Carter became the 39th president of the United States, his senior aides gathered in the dark-paneled White House mess.

They were the luncheon guests of Gerald R. Ford's chief of staff.

"There was a can-do attitude, a feeling of never having a defeat, never having to compromise," recalled one participant. "There was a real excitement."

Now, after four years, came the final day. Reality set in long ago; the excitement dissipated, compromises were many, so were defeats. The most distinct defeat—the election-day avalanche—culminated in Ronald Reagan's succession to the presidency today.

As Carter left the White House, his aides were dispersing, unanimously professing the belief that history will treat the Carter administration with greater kindness than did the nation's voters.

In a series of interviews, Washington figures in and out of government reviewed the Carter years, enumerating the president's greatest successes and assessing what went wrong. They count themselves among the president's political, if not personal, friends. Most sought anonymity.

Their words, guarded before Election Day, seemed to tumble out at the finale. Their comments draw a portrait of the Carter White House that was a study in contrasts:

- Carter's relationship with Congress was a series of running skirmishes, yet a high percentage of his legislative proposals were enacted.
- Energy prices skyrocketed, sparking a steep recession, but the nation's energy production increased and its dependence on imported oil dropped. The president offered, to use one of his favored words, a "comprehensive" energy program, but it was comprehensively revised by the Congress.

See Carter, pg. 2A, col. 1

Mother urges stiff penalties at hearing on marijuana bill

By Rick Alm
The Star's Jefferson City correspondent

Jefferson City—The mother of a drug-dependent teen-ager told a Missouri House committee Monday that her daughter would have been better off "busted" at age 13 for smoking marijuana.

Testifying before the Civil and Criminal Justice Committee against a bill that would reduce the penalities for marijuana use, Mrs. Linda Nelson of Jefferson City said her daughter's arrest might have meant help at a time when she needed it.

"Before you vote on this bill, come and spend two days with me where I work," said Mrs. Nelson, a hospital drug and alcohol abuse counselor. "Give first-time offenders some help, but give them the maximum (penalty).

"It (drug use) destroys whole families," she said. "I've seen kid after kid after kid lose his right to an education. He may be on parole. He may have damaged his brain."

Sponsored by Rep. David Christian, D-Kansas City, the bill would decriminalize possession and sale of small amounts of both marijuana and hashish, a drug made from the resin of marijuana plants.

The hearing Monday drew critical testimony from the Missouri Police Chiefs

See Bill, pg. 5A, col. 4

Inside

Vol. 101, No. 107

Weather

Partial clearing late tonight with the low in the upper 20s is the National Weather Service forecast for the Kansas City area.

	Station D	R	K		Station D	R	K
Midnight	[illegible]	[illegible]	[illegible]	7 a.m.	37	[illegible]	[illegible]
1 a.m.	[illegible]	[illegible]	[illegible]	8 a.m.	37	37	[illegible]
2 a.m.	[illegible]	[illegible]	[illegible]	9 a.m.	[illegible]	37	[illegible]
3 a.m.	37	37	[illegible]	10 a.m.	[illegible]	[illegible]	37
4 a.m.	37	37	[illegible]	11 a.m.	[illegible]	[illegible]	[illegible]
5 a.m.	37	37	[illegible]	Noon	41	[illegible]	[illegible]
6 a.m.	37	[illegible]	[illegible]	1 p.m.	41	[illegible]	[illegible]

Starbeam

As the day began, only one hostage was certain to be released today — the one in the White House.

The Area

Firefighters maintain a "holding pattern" on a wrecked rail tanker that is slowly burning off its flammable contents. **Page 3A.**

The Army Corps of Engineers is talking about restoring wildlife habitat destroyed by its work but farmers say the the corps has done enough. **Page 3A.**

Star Style

When you remarry, your wedding dress can be as high-fashion or as simple as you like. **Page 1B.**

Newscaster Jessica Savich is reaching for the top. **Page 1B.**

Star Sports

Spies are everywhere in pro football. **Page 1D.**

Where to Call

Star City Desk (816) 234-4300
Star Business/Financial News 234-4370
Classified Advertising, (816) 234-4000
Circulation, (816) 234-4545
Sports Scores, (816) 234-4350
Other Departments, (816) 234-4141

Minneapolis Tribune /

Minneapolis **Tribune**

Wednesday
January 21, 1981
Volume CXIV
Number 197
M   0

1A   Final

3 Sections

25¢ Single Copy

Copyright 1981 Minneapolis Star and Tribune Company

Day 1 of a new life

In the end, there was yet another small delay as the plane sat on the tarmac in Algiers.

The television cameras showed the open door, with cabin attendants and Algerian airline officials moving to and fro. Suddenly, L. Bruce Laingen, the Minnesota native who was charge d'affairs in Teheran, emerged with the two broadly smiling women pictured at left: Elizabeth Ann Swift and Kathryn Koob. After 444 days of captivity in Iran, Laingen, Swift, Koob and 49 other Americans were safe on the ground in Algeria.

In a joyous welcome witnessed by millions on television, they were officially transferred to U.S. government control. Ninety minutes later they were on their way to an American military base in Wiesbaden, West Germany, for several days of physical and mental evaluation.

The ribbons in Swift's and Koob's hair were yellow, like the thousands of ribbons that appeared all over the United States during the long wait. The ribbons usually were tied around trees, but also showed up in such unlikely places as the 27th floor of the Foshay Tower in Minneapolis.

The hostages were finally free.

Hostage release details:
2A, 3A, 4A, 1B, 6B, 7B

Day 1 for a new leader

Minutes before the hostages' plane left Teheran, Ronald Reagan was sworn in as President of the United States.

After taking the oath of office as the 40th president, Reagan and his wife Nancy turned from the lectern to wave to onlookers, left, on the west front of the Capitol building.

In his inaugural address, the new president called for "an era of national renewal . . . It is time," he said, "to reawaken this industrial giant, to get government back within its means, and to lighten our punitive tax burden. These will be our first priorities, and on these principles, there will be no compromise."

Less than an hour later, Reagan signified the seriousness of his intent by ordering a freeze on the hiring of all federal civilian employees.

Former President Jimmy Carter, who had been without sleep for two nights, went home to Plains, Ga., after the ceremony for a brief rest before leaving today for Wiesbaden, where he will be Reagan's envoy to greet the hostages.

Inauguration articles:
6A, 7A, 8A and 10A

▼ **Almanac**

Wednesday, Jan. 21 1981
21st day; 344 to go this year
Sunrise: 7:44. Sunset: 5:05.

Today's weather
Balmy

A high in the low 40s is likely today in the Twin Cities area.

Arts	5B	Obituaries	8C
Business	15-18A	Sports	1-6C
Comics	4B	Theaters	7C
Corrections	4A	TV, Radio	7B
Editorial	14A	Weather	5B

Tribune telephones
372-4141 News General
372-4242 Classified
372-4343 Circulation

The Morning Call/

AMERICA HELD HOSTAGE — A 16-PAGE PULLOUT

Index

THE MORNING CALL

Weather

Mostly cloudy today through tomorrow; high in upper 30s today, near 40 tomorrow. Chance of rain 20 percent today, tonight. For details, see **Page B2**

NO. 28,992 (USPS 363-060)
LEHIGH VALLEY'S GREATEST NEWSPAPER
ALLENTOWN, PA. 18105, WEDNESDAY, JANUARY 21, 1981
25¢

ALIVE, WELL, FREE

66 I'm so happy to have my boy returning to America and be a free man . . . I really can't believe it. 99

Mrs. Theresa Lodeski, mother of Bruce German

66 . . . we are . . . delighted to accept the responsibility of seeing to it that you return to your homes and your families. 99

Deputy Secretary of State Warren Christopher

Relatives of hostages weep, rejoice

The Pennsylvania relatives of the U.S. hostages who were held in Iran wept and rejoiced yesterday after the State Department confirmed that America's 52 captives had embarked on their long journey home.

"I feel terrific, wonderful, happy," Harry Metrinko cried, embracing his weeping wife, Alice. Their son, Michael Metrinko, was among those who were being flown to freedom.

The news came at 12:54 p.m., in a call from Henry Precht, a member of the special State Department section on Iran.

As Metrinko handed the phone to his wife, she asked, "Henry, where are they? They're in the air? And this is it?"   Can we tell the newsmen that the planes are in the air?"

Then she turned, and in an almost inaudible voice said, "It's official."

Across the state, champagne corks were popping, sirens blaring and relatives celebrating.

"I'm so happy to have my boy returning to America and be a free man," said Theresa Lodeski, the mother of hostage Bruce German of Rockville, Md. "I really can't believe it. Last night I was so set back — they were at the airport, in the plane, not in the plane. I didn't know what to think. But today, they are on their way to Algeria."

Outside her Edwardsville home, near Wilkes-Barre, Mrs. Lodeski rang out the message of freedom.

"I rang the cowbell. I've been out

Please See FAMILIES Page A5►

A group of unidentified American hostages wave victory signs as they arrive at the airport in Algiers.

Associated Press

FLIGHT TO FREEDOM

1 Hostages board an Algerian jet at Tehran's Mehrabad Airport. They depart at 12:26 p.m. EST.

2 Plane carrying hostages arrives in Athens, Greece, at 4:03 p.m. EST to refuel. Leave for Algiers at 8:25 p.m. EST

3 Hostages arrive in Algiers 8:10 p.m.

4 Aboard two U.S. Medevac planes, hostages leave Algiers at 9:46 p.m. EST, arrive at Air Force hospital in Wiesbaden, W. Germany, at 12:46 a.m. EST.

Morning Call Map by KEN RANERE

W. Germany welcomes hostages

From Call news services

FRANKFURT, West Germany — The 52 former hostages arrived to the cheers of hundreds of fellow Americans here early today on their way home to freedom. They immediately boarded buses for the 20-mile drive to a U.S. Air Force hospital.

A huge cheer arose from hundreds of military and civilian personnel gathered along the tarmac in frigid pre-dawn temperatures to greet the former captives as they arrived on two medevac planes from Algiers, where they were flown after release from Tehran.

Former Secretary of State Cyrus Vance and other U.S. officials greeted the freed Americans as they came down the steps from the plane, wearing parkas against the cold.

A crowd stood in front of the control tower, which was bedecked with yellow ribbons and banners welcoming the former hostages. Members of the crowd waved small American flags wildly as the aircraft taxied toward them.

"USA — USA — USA," chanted members of the crowd as the hostages got off the plane.

"We've Got a Full Deck Now — 52," read one of a series of signs carried by those gathered to greet the former captives.

"We Couldn't Forget," "You're Half-Way Home," "Welcome Back, Gold bless America" and "U.S. Students Welcome You Back," said other signs and banners.

One family had camped out at the

Please See HOSTAGES Page A27►

Ronald Reagan takes oath as wife Nancy looks on.

Associated Press

Reagan becomes 40th President

Inaugural promise: Era of national renewal at home, restraint abroad

By WALTER R. MEARS
Of The Associated Press

WASHINGTON — Ronald Reagan became President of the United States yesterday, promising "an era of national renewal" at home and restraint but never surrender abroad, his inauguration blending the passage of power with a passage to freedom for 52 American hostages.

"They are now free of Iran," said Reagan, little more than two hours after his inauguration.

Later, at his new desk in the Oval Office, the President said release of the hostages "just makes the whole day perfect.

"They're on the way home."

At the noon inauguration, the promise of freedom had not become the fact of freedom, and Reagan did not mention the hostages in the 20-minute address he directed to "this breed called Americans," countrymen he described as the heroes of the land.

But the liberation of the captive Americans was the focus of his last briefings by Carter, and his first hours as 40th President.

And so the announcement the nation awaited came in his toast to congressional leaders at a traditional Capitol luncheon.

"And now to conclude the toast, with thanks to almighty God, I have been given a tag line, the get-off line that everyone wants for the end of a toast or a speech or anything else.

"Some 30 minutes ago, the planes bearing our prisoners left Iranian airspace and they are now free of Iran. So we can all drink to this one — to all of us together, doing what we all know we can do, to make this country what it should be, what it can be, what it always has been.

It was the announcement Carter had waited so long to make himself, but it came too late for him. So President Reagan made it, while citizen Carter flew home to Georgia.

At the stroke of noon, presidential power passed from James Earl Carter Jr. of Georgia to Ronald Wilson Reagan of California, 69, oldest man ever to take office, former movie actor.

Please See RENEWAL Page A27►

The New York Times/

"All the News That's Fit to Print"

The New York Times

Weather: Midwest, partly cloudy, some snow. Spotti, cloudy with rain or scattered showers. West and Southwest, mostly sunny with rain in the north. Details are on page 47.

VOL.CXXX....No. 44,835   Copyright © 1981 The New York Times   NEW YORK, WEDNESDAY, JANUARY 21, 1981   50 CENTS

REAGAN TAKES OATH AS 40TH PRESIDENT; PROMISES AN 'ERA OF NATIONAL RENEWAL'

MINUTES LATER, 52 U.S. HOSTAGES IN IRAN FLY TO FREEDOM AFTER 444-DAY ORDEAL

'ALIVE, WELL AND FREE'

Captives Taken to Algiers on Way to Germany — Final Pact Complex

By BERNARD GWERTZMAN
Special to The New York Times

WASHINGTON, Jan. 20 — The 52 Americans who were held hostage by Iran for 444 days were flown to freedom today. Jimmy Carter, a few hours after giving up the Presidency, said that everyone "was alive, was well and free."

The flight ended the national ordeal that had frustrated Mr. Carter for most of his last 14 months in office, and it allowed Ronald Reagan to begin his term free of the burdens of the Iran crisis.

The Americans were escorted out of Iran by Algerian diplomats, aboard an Algerian airliner, underscoring Algeria's role in achieving the accord that allowed the hostages to return home.

Plane Stops in Athens

The Algerian plane, carrying the former hostages, stopped first in Athens to refuel. It then landed in Algiers, where the 52 were seen outside Iran for the first time. They were to be transferred to United States Air Force hospital planes that will take them to Wiesbaden, West Germany where they will stay at an American military hospital and where they will be visited by Mr. Carter, as President Reagan's representative, tomorrow. They will stay there for a week or less to "decompress," as one official described it.

The 52 Americans were freed as part of a complex agreement that was not completed until early this morning, after the last snags holding up their release were removed by Mr. Carter and his aides, in the final diplomatic action of their Administration.

Under the terms of the accord, the Algerian plane left Iranian air space, nearly $1 billion of Iranian assets that had been frozen by the United States were returned to Iran, and many more billions

Continued on Page 5, Column 5

Anxious Families and Towns Erupt Into Long-Postponed Celebrations

By JOSEPH B. TREASTER

Saying his final farewells at Andrews Air Force Base yesterday, Jimmy Carter spotted Anita Schaefer, the wife of one of the hostages, and exuberantly embraced her.

"Tom is in the air," Mr. Carter said, speaking of her husband, Col. Thomas E. Schaefer of the Air Force, who was the senior military officer at the United States Embassy in Teheran.

"Really, truly, Mr. President," she whispered.

"Really, truly — at long last," he said, "Tom is safe. I'll be with him tomorrow morning in Germany."

"Oh, thank God, Mr. President."

Then they both cried. And they embraced again.

The News Is Shouted

Penne Laingen, the wife of Bruce L. Laingen, the embassy's chargé d'affaires, heard the news shouted by a military policeman as she sat in reserved seats at the inauguration of President Reagan.

Some had gotten the word from radio and television broadcasts, and still others, like Marjorie Moore, the wife of Bert C. Moore, the administrative consul, received phone calls from the State Department.

Most of the homes of the hostages' families, torn by doubt, fear and anger for so long, exploded with joy. They cried and cheered, praised God and hugged each other. Champagne flowed. Neighbors brought in red, white and blue cakes, baked hams and cold cuts.

The joy contagiously swept the nation. Everywhere, in small towns and big cities, men and women ran up American flags, rang church bells, honked car horns and sounded fire alarms.

The excitement seemed greatest in small towns, like Olyphant, Pa., that were home to some of the former captives. Michael Metrinko, a 34-year-old

Continued on Page 1, Column 1

Anita Schaefer, wife of a hostage, embraced Mr. Carter at airport.

Black Star / John Troha for The New York Times

Teheran Captors Call Out Insults As the 52 Leave

By JOHN KIFNER
Special to The New York Times

TEHERAN, Iran, Jan. 20 — The 52 American hostages began to roll down the runway to freedom today minutes after President Reagan finished his inaugural address.

As the Algerian 727 lifted off from Mehrabad Airport, ending 444 days of captivity for the Americans, they could see, most of them probably for the last time, a full moon picking out the sharp white peaks of the Elborz Mountains to the north. The time was 8:55 P.M. (12:25 P.M., New York time.)

"God is great! Death to America!" cried the young Islamic militants who seized the embassy on Nov. 4, 1979. They kept custody of the hostages to the last minute, hustling them to the stairs of the airplane.

They Seen Are 'Former Hostages'

The American diplomats, Marine guards and the other hostages emerged one at a time from a bus, whose windows were covered with checked curtains, into a clear cold night. As they touched the tarmac, two young militants, the hoods of their parkas up against the chill, took them just above the elbows and propelled them through the shouting crowd toward the Algerian plane with its red stylized bird emblazoned on the tail.

Looking dazed, some with long hair and beards that contrasted with the neat trims of their official days, they stumbled into the first-class section of the plane. Now they were what a bulletin on Pars, the state press agency, would describe later as "former hostages."

"They seem stunned, as if they cannot believe they are going free," Ahmad Azizi, the Government's director of foreign affairs remarked to an Iranian state television crew covering the departure.

Three Planes Fly Away

At 8:30, the doors were sealed, Pars reported, and the engines began to whine. A small band of militants, revolutionary

Continued on Page 8, Column 1

11:57 A.M.: Ronald Reagan being sworn in as 40th President by Chief Justice Warren E. Burger. Nancy Reagan held the Bible and Senator Mark O. Hatfield witnessed the ceremony.

The New York Times

12:25 P.M.: Sgt. Joseph Subic Jr. being seized by militants and hustled to plane in Teheran.

Pars via Associated Press

A Hopeful Prologue, a Pledge of Action

By HEDRICK SMITH
Special to The New York Times

WASHINGTON, Jan. 20 — For a President who has promised Americans a new beginning, an era of national renewal at home and restored strength and stature abroad, the release of the American hostages in Iran was exquisitely timed.

The extraordinary deadline diplomacy that put the 52 captured Americans into the air over Iran minutes after the inauguration witnesses thundered a new leader into office provided a graceful unit for Jimmy Carter, a hopeful prologue for Ronald Reagan and relief for a nation weary from 14 months of humiliation and seeing impotence.

Almost unavoidably the human drama

News Analysis

in Iran overshadowed an inaugural address that was less an inspirational call to national greatness than a plain-spoken charter of Mr. Reagan's conservative creed, less a sermon than a stump speech, less a rallying cry than a ringing denunciation of overgrown government and a practical pledge to get down to the business of trimming it at once.

For all the new President's vaunted

reputation as one of the nation's most polished political orators, his inaugural address offered surprisingly few rhetorical flourishes beyond the popular tribute to ordinary Americans that "those who say that we are in a time when there are no heroes, they just don't know where to look."

Although Mr. Reagan made no direct mention of the hostages, their release was as everyone's lips. Moments before Mr. Reagan took his oath of office, word that the hostages were about to be flown out of Iran swept through the crowd stretched out before the Capitol, and though that news was premature, it provided the perfect symbolic backdrop for

Continued on Page 18, Column 1

FREEZE SET ON HIRING

Californian Stresses Need to Restrict Government and Buoy Economy

By STEVEN R. WEISMAN
Special to The New York Times

WASHINGTON, Jan. 20 — Ronald Wilson Reagan of California, promising "an era of national renewal," became the 40th President of the United States today as 52 Americans held hostage in Iran were heading toward freedom.

The hostages, whose 14 months of captivity had been a central focus of the Presidential contest last year, took off from Teheran in two Boeing 727 airplanes at 12:33 P.M., Eastern standard time, the very moment that Mr. Reagan was concluding his solemn Inaugural Address at the United States Capitol.

The new President's speech, however, made no reference at all to the long-awaited release of the hostages, emphasizing instead the need to limit the powers of the Federal Government, and to bring an end to unemployment and inflation.

'Government Is the Problem'

Promising to begin immediately to deal with "an economic affliction of great proportions," Mr. Reagan declared: "In this present crisis, government is not the solution to our problem; government is the problem." And in keeping with this statement, the President issued orders for a hiring "freeze" as his first official act. [Page 15.]

Wearing a charcoal gray club coat, striped trousers and dove gray vest and tie, Mr. Reagan took his oath of office at 11:57 A.M. in the first inaugural ceremony ever enacted on the western front of the United States Capitol. The site was chosen to stress the symbolism of Mr. Reagan's addressing his words to the West, the region that served as his base in his three Presidential campaigns in 1968, 1976 and 1980.

The ceremony today, filled with patriotic music, the firing of cannons and the pealing of bells, marked the transfer of the Presidency back to the Republicans after the four-year term of Jimmy Carter, a Democrat, as well as the culmination of the remarkable career of a conservative former two-term Governor of California who had started out as a baseball announcer and motion picture star.

Oldest to Assume Presidency

At the age of 69, Mr. Reagan also became the oldest man to assume the Presidency, and in five months he will become the oldest man to serve in the office.

Mr. Carter, flocking haggard and worn after spending two largely sleepless nights trying to resolve the hostage crisis

Continued on Page 28, Column 2

More News And Pictures

The Inauguration

The Providence Journal/

The Providence Journal

Published in Providence, R.I. — Wednesday, January 21, 1981 — Seven Sections/80 Pages — 25 Cents; $1.30 per week by carrier

EAST BAY EDITION

Hostages are flown to freedom; Reagan becomes 40th President

Promises to launch an era of renewal

The New York Times

WASHINGTON — Ronald Wilson Reagan, promising to launch "an era of national renewal," became the 40th President of the United States yesterday. Minutes after he took the oath of office 52 Americans held hostage in Iran dramatically gained their freedom.

The hostages, whose 14 months of captivity were a central focus of the presidential campaign last year, took off from Tehran in two Boeing 727s at the very moment Mr. Reagan was concluding his inaugural address at the Capitol.

The President's speech made no reference to the long-awaited release of the hostages 8,800 miles away, emphasizing instead the need to limit the powers of the federal government, and to bring an end to unemployment and inflation.

Promising to begin immediately to deal with "an economic affliction of great proportions," Mr. Reagan declared: "In this present crisis, government is not the solution to our problem. Government is the problem."

And in keeping with this statement, the President issued orders for a federal hiring freeze as his first official act.

* * *

THE CEREMONY yesterday — filled with patriotic music, the firing of cannon and the pealing of bells — marked the transfer of the presidency back to the Republicans after the four-year term of Jimmy Carter, as well as the culmination of the remarkable career of a conservative former two-term governor of California who had started out as a sports announcer and motion picture star.

At the age of 69, Mr. Reagan also became the oldest man to assume the presidency, and in five months he will become the oldest man to serve in the office.

Carter, looking haggard after spending two largely sleepless nights trying to resolve the hostage crisis as the final chapter of his presidency, flew from

Turn to INAUGURATION, Page A-12

The Inaugural

The speech

Text of Reagan's inaugural address. Page A-8.

R.I. delegation has a lukewarm reaction. Page A-8.

The celebration

Thousands line Pennsylvania Avenue for colorful parade. Page A-4.

Portsmouth High band performs with style. Page A-4.

Rhode Islanders celebrate at Chateau de Ville. Page A-4.

Going home

Carter gets warm welcome on return to his hometown of Plains, Ga. Page A-9.

Freedom smiles

Elizabeth Ann Swift, left, and Kathryn Koob join hands as they leave an aircraft in Algiers early this morning. The women and the other 50 hostages stepped into freedom after being held captive in Iran for 444 days.

—AP Photo

40th President

Ronald Reagan recites the oath of office on the West Porch of the Capitol in Washington yesterday. His wife Nancy holds a Bible as he is sworn in.

—AP Photo

Sun heralded the day of Reagan's dream

Knight-Ridder Newspapers

WASHINGTON — When he arose, the Capitol was bathed in pink sunrise.

While his family shuffled in nearby rooms of Blair House, he packed his two suitcases and glanced over 19 carefully lettered index cards that carried his speech.

So began the day that finally brought Ronald Wilson Reagan to the presidency he had sought for 12 years.

It was a day that saw triumphs and...

Joyous welcome greets Americans in West Germany; Carter to meet 52 former captives in Wiesbaden

Associated Press

Fifty-two Americans, so long hostage to a distant revolution, flew from their Iranian nightmare to their dream of freedom, arriving early today in Frankfurt, Germany.

Their first stop was Algiers where, after a joyous welcome, they boarded two U.S. medical evacuation jetliners for the last leg of their "freedom flight" and the planes left Algiers for the U.S. military base in Wiesbaden, West Germany, near Frankfurt.

There was a day and a half of confusion over when they would leave Iran, and the captives finally were flown out of Tehran's airport aboard an Algerian jet minutes after the presidency passed from Jimmy Carter to Ronald Reagan at noon yesterday.

"God Bless America," one of the hostages shouted as he boarded one of the military planes for the flight to Germany, which will close the final chapter in a 14½-month hostage-holding without precedent in modern diplomatic history.

A U.S. Army spokesman said earlier that the hostages would be served a Thanksgiving dinner of roast turkey during the 2-hour, 35-minute flight to the Rhein-Main Air Base near Wiesbaden, where they were to be admitted to a U.S. Air Force hospital for a period of "decompression."

Former Secretary of State Cyrus Vance arrived at the German air base early today to prepare to welcome the Americans. He headed the State Department when they were taken captive.

And Jimmy Carter, his hope of being able to announce freedom for the hostages before leaving office denied him, flew home to Plains, Ga., yesterday as a private citizen — but with one final official mission for the U.S. government ahead of him.

As a personal representative of newly inaugurated President Reagan, Carter and former Vice President Walter F. Mondale were to leave for Wiesbaden, West Germany, to head the group welcoming the U.S. captives back to freedom.

After a brief stopover at Plains for a welcoming celebration from the homefolk, the former president was to return to Washington last night, pick up Mon-

Turn to HOSTAGES, Page A-12

Free at last

The people

Waves of relief wash over families of freed hostages. Page A-5.

Transition to normal life difficult. Queen warns. Page A-5.

State Department urges public support. Page A-5.

Wiesbaden ready to give all possible help. Page A-6.

Finances

How the final logjam was broken. Page A-7.

Work begins on setting up panel to adjudicate Iran's claims. Page A-7.

The last day

Rhode Islanders offer prayers of thanksgiving. Page A-6.

Chronology of the final day. Page A-5.

Iran task force is disbanded. Page A-6.

Hostages doubted reality of freedom at long last as they prepared to leave

Associated Press

In the minutes before the 52 American hostages left Tehran on their Air Algerie flight to freedom, they were laughing, crying and hugging one another, a Swiss diplomat said yesterday.

Erik Lang, the Swiss ambassador, who has represented U.S. interests in Tehran, witnessed the departure and said some of the hostages were seeing each other for the first time in 14 months. He said many expressed disbelief that they were finally making their way to freedom.

All appeared to be in good health, except that two seemed to have difficulty walking, he said. He said the older hostages, especially, appeared to have aged from their 14½-month experience as captives.

There were a few strained smiles, but most of the hostages shown in a 20-minute film broadcast on Iranian television wore the pale, empty expressions of resigned prisoners.

They looked shocked, like someone in a daze, said Ahmad Azizi, one of the negotiators in the hostage crisis, as the Americans of at...

commentary in the Iranian television studio as the film was being broadcast.

* * *

THE HOSTAGES were taken one by one from a bus parked a few yards from the the plane as a small crowd of revolutionary guards pressed around, some waving their fists, chanting "Death to America" and "God is great."

The routine was for two revolutionary guards to escort each hostage — one guard on each arm — through the demonstrators, who were well behaved despite the exuberance.

At the foot of the plane's boarding ramp, the hostage was released and the guards would go back for the next one.

The windows of the bus were curtained and most of the hostages squinted into the television light as they took their first steps toward freedom.

Many were wearing army jackets and camouflage uniforms — attire that is commonplace in Iran since the revolution two years ago.

But by the time the jetliner carrying the 52 American hostages landed at

Turn to SCENE, Page A-12

White House for a quiet, slow motorcade to the swearing-in ceremony at the Capitol.

* * *

CARTER LEARNED in his limousine that the airplanes carrying the hostages were about to lift off, and Mr. Reagan was told only minutes before taking the podium outside the Capitol.

Later, as a grim former President was on his way to Georgia and members of Congress gathered in the Capitol's Statuary Hall, lifting their glasses to honor the new President, Mr. Reagan turned to give a...

State

THE PROMOTER of the horse track proposed for Johnston makes a nonrefundable down payment on a Plainfield Pike site. Page B-8.

THE STATE'S key witness in the murder trial of Andre O. Maltais testifies that he saw Maltais hold a rock over the head of Barbara Raposa. Page A-3.

A BILL that would strengthen the state's campaign finance law is filed in the House. There are indications it faces trouble in the Senate. Page A-3.

EAST PROVIDENCE RULES and practice in naming special police officers is contrary to state law, which bans sale of handguns to persons under 21. Page C-1.

What's news this morning

World/National

AT LEAST 39 are killed in El Salvador, and fighting between government troops and guerrillas leaves 35 towns without telephone communications. Page B-5.

FIVE SOUTHERN CALIFORNIA Mafia bosses are sentenced to federal prison terms of up to five years for racketeering and extortion. Page B-6.

THE GOVERNMENT agrees to replace its basic employment test as part of a settlement of a suit by minorities charging discrimination. Page B-6.

Sports

KEVIN COMPTON, a freshman, sinks a pair of free throws with one second left, giving the University of Rhode Island a 62-60 victory over Pitt. Page B-1.

ERNIE DeWITT and Paul Berio combine for 45 points, leading Bryant to a 68-63 triumph over the University of Lowell. Page B-1.

THE DETROIT PISTONS score the final 12 points of the game and shock the Philadelphia 76ers, 83-75. Page B-5.

Weather

SUNNY today. High in the mid-30s. Increasing cloudiness tonight. Low 20 to 25. Cloudy with a chance of rain or snow tomorrow. High about 40. Winds light northerly today, becoming light and variable tonight. Page A-2.

St. Petersburg Times/

Breezy
Low, upper 40s;
High, low 60s.
Westerly winds at 15.
Map, data, 2-A.

St. Petersburg Times
Florida's Best Newspaper

VOL. 97 — NO. 180   66 PAGES   •   ST. PETERSBURG, FLORIDA, WEDNESDAY, JANUARY 21, 1981   20 CENTS A COPY

Hostages: Day 1 of freedom
Reagan's call: Heroic dreams

Ceremony marks new political era

By CHARLES STAFFORD
St. Petersburg Times Washington Correspondent

WASHINGTON — Ronald Wilson Reagan, a player of parts, began his new role as President of the United States Tuesday with a challenge to the American people to "dream heroic dreams" as he leads them into "an era of national renewal."

As he spoke — with a disappointed Jimmy Carter seated nearby — an American embarrassment came to an end. Shortly after 11:57 a.m., the moment when the presidential torch passed from Carter to Reagan, the first of two Algerian airliners bringing 52 Americans out of bondage lifted away from the soil of Iran.

This Inauguration Day was real-life drama. There was no movie-script finish for Jimmy Carter, no last moment rush to the podium to announce that the hostages were free. The moment came 36 minutes too late.

In Tehran, well before Washington's noontime, an airport policeman said the hostages had departed. But as Carter walked to the inaugural stand to give up the presidency, as *Hail to the Chief* was played in his honor for the last time, he told a questioner, "Not yet."

REAGAN DID not mention the hostages in his 18-minute Inaugural Address. But a bit less than one hour into his presidency, waiting at the Capitol to begin the journey down Pennsylvania Avenue to the White House, Reagan told reporters: "They are airborne." It would take about an hour for the planes to clear Iran's borders, he said, "and that's when you really feel safe."

And Carter? Yes, he was airborne, too, en route by helicopter to Andrews Air Force Base for a quick trip home to Plains, Ga. He said he would fly to West Germany early today to meet the hostages as Reagan's personal envoy.

This was a day of drama. The swearing in of the 69-year-old Californian — sportscaster, movie actor, governor — marked the beginning of a new era of conservatism in American government, the coming to power of the West, the joy of Republican victory, the agony of Democratic defeat.

You could tell a Republican congressman. They were the ones in Reagan's prescribed dress of grey morning coat and striped pants. Most Democrats defied the Reagan request of formal attire. Texas Rep. Jack Brooks showing up in a tan cowboy hat and blue suit. But that old Florida liberal, Rep. Claude Pepper, was not only natty in morning coat and striped pants, he also wore a top hat.

YOU COULD TELL a Republican congressional office. They were the ones with early-morning crowds loading up on coffee and Danish. Democratic offices were mostly quiet, except that of Rep. Sam Gibbons of Tampa. There folks were celebrating the congressman's 61st birthday.

Out on the Capitol's west lawn, it was warm for January. In another climatic oddity, the sky divided above the freshly-painted dome of the Capitol — bright blue to the north, grey and overcast to the south.

The ceremony began at 11:30 a.m.

See REAGAN, 22-A

inside

'This event answers our prayers'

BULLETIN
The two U.S. Air Force planes bringing the 52 freed Americans to West Germany from Algiers landed at the Rhein-Main Air Base at 6:45 a.m. (12:45 a.m. EST) today.

Compiled from Los Angeles Times, AP wires

ALGIERS, Algeria — The 52 American hostages arrived here safely from Tehran early today, seemingly in good health and clearly overjoyed to have their 14½ months of captivity behind them.

Their Algerian jetliner landed in light rain at 12:37 a.m. (7:37 p.m. EST Tuesday) and taxied slowly to the VIP lounge at Boumedienne Airport, about 5 miles from the Algerian Foreign Ministry where the agreements that led to their freedom had been signed early Monday.

After a joyous welcome here, they boarded two U.S. medical evacuation jetliners for the last leg of their "freedom flight" and the planes left Algiers for West Germany.

With the last of the hostages finally freed, one of those who had been in the first group released within weeks after the seizure of the U.S. Embassy revealed Tuesday in a television interview that Iranian militants had played "Russian roulette" with two of the female hostages, tied others to a table and waved guns "in our faces" during the early days of the seizure.

But Lloyd Rollins, 40, of Columbus, Ohio, said the scare tactics stopped within days after the Nov. 4, 1979 takeover "when they got to know us."

"GOD BLESS America!" one of the hostages shouted as he boarded one of the military planes in Algiers Tuesday night. A U.S. Army spokesman said the hostages would be served a Thanksgiving dinner of roast turkey during the 2½-hour flight to West Germany.

There had been a day and half of confusion on when the hostages would leave Iran, and the captives finally were flown out of Tehran's airport minutes after the U.S. presidency passed from Jimmy Carter to Ronald Reagan at noon Tuesday.

And although the final delay cheated Carter of the satisfaction of bringing the crisis to a close "on his watch," it was announced that he will fly to West Germany today to greet the hostages.

U.S. and Algerian officials, led by the Algerian foreign minister, Mohammed Seddik Benyahia, and former Deputy Secretary of State Warren M. Christopher were at the bottom of the ramp to greet the hostages here.

The freed Americans walked down the line of greeters, shaking hands and exchanging kisses. A few of them looked pensive and tired, but most wore broad smiles.

The two women among the hostages, Kathryn L. Koob of Fairfax, Va., and Elisabeth Ann Swift of Washington, were first off the Air Algeria 727. They wore yellow ribbons — the symbol of the hostage

See HOSTAGES, 9-A

... and an ecstatic Donald Sharer gives a victory wave as he walks down the ramp to freedom after 444 days in captivity.

Elizabeth Ann Swift, left, and Kathryn Koob, their hair tied with yellow ribbons, step off the plane in Algiers.

Ronald Reagan, decked out in morning coat, and his wife Nancy, resplendent in a red wool coat and matching toque, wave to the crowds after he is sworn in as the 40th president of the United States. To the upper left in the photo is Sen. Strom Thurmond, who is partially hiding Senate Minority Leader Robert Byrd. The man with the camera to the right of Thurmond is Senate Majority Leader Howard Baker. The white-haired man is Speaker of the House Thomas "Tip" O'Neill, who is standing in front of Rep. John Rhodes. Clapping, to the right, is Vice President George Bush.

St. Petersburg Times — RICARDO FERRO

More on Iran, inauguration

Page 8-A: Around the world, the news of the hostages' release brought reactions of joy and relief. A wrapup of the reaction from the hostages' families, foreign leaders and people around the nation. Also, a report on how U.S. officials hope for better relations with Algeria.

Page 9-A: Photos of the hostages arriving in Algiers.

Page 10-A: For the Carters, a bittersweet day in Plains, and the Reagans step out to the evening galas.

Page 11-A: Analysis of Reagan's speech. Roundup of Floridians' day in Washington. Also the latest on Reagan's Cabinet nominees.

Page 12-A: Text of inaugural speech and foreign reaction.

Page 22-A: A page of color photos of the inauguration.

San Francisco Examiner /

FREE AT LAST

Hostages are coming home!

Stocks down 20.31
Page C1

San Francisco Examiner

★★★★
Final edition
Complete stocks

116th Year No. 191   Tuesday, January 20, 1981   20¢

First photos

The Reagan Inauguration
A special section starts on Page B1

RONALD REAGAN TAKES THE OATH
A beaming Mrs. Reagan held the Bible

Reagan vows era of renewal

By W. E. Barnes
Examiner Political Writer

WASHINGTON — Ronald Reagan, blending patriotism and humble heroes into a new mosaic of America, called for a new era of national renewal as he became the 40th president of the United States today.

His inauguration was marked both by the traditional 21-gun salute and by the freeing of 52 American hostages, held for 444 days in Iran. The actions seemed to give him joy at the beginning of a four-year term in which he started with a pledge of fiscal austerity and a decision to freeze federal hiring for the indefinite future.

Reagan's day seemed complete when he was able

Stock market slumps

The stock market reacted to the inaugural and the release of the hostages with an unexpected slump today. The Dow Jones industrials were down 20.31 to 950.68. Analysts said the dip represents investor concern for the future in the wake of President Reagan's call for an "era of national renewal."

Full report/Business, Page C1.

to announce — just an hour into his presidency — that "they are airborne" in Tehran.

If his was complete, it was a somber day for President Jimmy Carter, who sat on the inaugural platform, unable to announce the freeing of the hostages as his last act. Carter listened with closed eyes to much of the Reagan speech, seemingly depressed by the ill-timing of the hostage flight.

Reagan appeared to blink tears when he talked of a World War I soldier who had expressed his patriotism. The new president also appeared emotional as he issued his summons.

With all the creative energy at our command, let us begin an era of national renewal. Let us renew our determination, our courage and our strength. Let us

—See Back Page, Col. 4

Inside

Because of special coverage of the inauguration and the hostages, some news sections have been rearranged in today's editions.

American hostage Joseph Subic Jr. of Redford Township, Mich, led to plane by taunting guards at Tehran airport

Billions transferred to Iran

Examiner News Services

NEW YORK — Billions of dollars in frozen Iranian assets flowed from the United States to an Algerian escrow account at the Bank of England early today, the White House and the British central bank said.

The assets transfer was the last step need to win release of the 52 Americans held in Iran since November 1979. The liberated captives flew out of Tehran some five hours after confirmation of the transfer.

The announcements came after an all-night wait by bankers across the country who had been poised to begin the transfer of more than $8 billion in Iranian gold and bank deposits seized by the United States in 1979.

"At 6:47 this morning, the president was notified by Deputy Secretary of State Warren Christopher that the frozen Iranian assets had been transferred to the escrow account of the Algerian Central Bank at the Bank of England," White House press secretary Jody Powell said in Washington.

The step completely fulfills all steps agreed to by the United States prior to the release of the hostages, he said, adding that Algerian intermediaries informed Iran of the move at 8:17 a.m. EST.

President Carter's press secretary and the Bank of England did not disclose the amount of money the United States had transferred, and spokesmen for several commercial banks and for the Federal Reserve Bank of New York had no immediate comment on the move.

Preparations for the Iranian asset transfer began last week, and an agreement signed by Christopher and United States vowed to give back to Algiers yesterday cleared the way for the switchover to begin.

Under the agreement, the transfer could not be completed until the Algerian Central Bank certified that the 52 Americans held in Iran since Nov. 4 1979 had safely departed. The assets were seized shortly after the hostages were taken.

Powell told reporters early today that the latest hitch in the negotiations was resolved with the receipt of an acceptable transfer authority instruction, a set of instructions on establishing an escrow account for the Iranians.

Under terms of the agreement signed by Christopher Iran agreed to return the 52 Americans and the United States vowed to give back immediately about $5.2 billion of the $8 billion to $9 billion in Iranian assets

—See Back Page, Col. 1

HOSTAGE DONALD COOKE OF MEMPHIS, TENN.
Iranians jeered 'Down with America' as captives left

Iranians jeer as they leave

Examiner News Services

Laughing, crying and hugging each other, the 52 American hostages flew out of Iran to freedom today after 444 days of captivity.

With shouts of "down with America" ringing in their ears, the United States transferred about $8 billion in frozen Iranian assets to a London account for Iran and as Jimmy Carter's presidency ended.

The Americans left Tehran's Mehrabad Airport just after nightfall aboard an Algerian 727 jet, and their plane landed in Athens, Greece, 3½ hours later for refueling. The hostages were bound for Algiers, where they were to change planes for a flight to a U.S. military hospital in Wiesbaden, West Germany.

On hand to greet the Americans in Athens were U.S. Ambassador to Greece Robert McCloskey and other embassy officials. They would be the first U.S. officials to have seen all 52 since they were taken as hostage by Iranian militants Nov. 4, 1979.

U.S. Embassy officials reported a U.S. military doctor had flown in from Wiesbaden and was expected to fly with the hostages to Algiers.

Reporters and photographers were barred from the area where the Algerian

—See Back Page, Col. 1

Telegraph Herald/

Iran finally lets our people go

By United Press International

Iran freed the 52 American hostages today on the 444th day of captivity in exchange for return of its $8 billion in frozen assets, giving Jimmy Carter a dramatic victory in the closing minutes of his presidency.

The liberated captives flew from the Moslem nation just after nightfall aboard two Algerian 727 aircraft.

Word of the release came at 10:35 a.m. CST by telephone to London from Tehran airport officials at the end of day of non-stop negotiations in four capitals involving bankers and government officials in the largest financial transaction in history.

The U.S. Treasury confirmed the $8 billion was transferred to an Algerian account in London to be turned over to Iran.

Algerian officials said the hostages, including Col. Leland Holland of Scales Mound, Ill., and Kathryn Koob of Jesup, Iowa, were expected to arrive in Algiers at approximately midnight local time (6 p.m. CST). The Air Algerie aircraft carrying the hostages and their baggage were expected to land at Ankara airport in Turkey for refueling.

Their fredom came just minutes before the engineer of the triumph, Jimmy Carter, surrendered his presidency to Ronald Reagan.

Carter's hopes to greet the returning Americans while he was still chief of state were dashed by last-minute hitches that extended over Sunday and Monday. But President Reagan graciously invited Carter to go to Wiesbaden, West Germany, and greet the Americans as Reagan's personal representative after the inauguration. Carter accepted.

The liberated Americans included diplomats, 20 military guards, communications specialists and a businessman. About 20 are servicemen.

Lights burned in government offices in Tehran, Algiers, Washington and London throughout the early morning as officials worked toward the final mechanism to deposit the assets in an Algerian account in London for transfer to Iran — the "go" signal for the long-awaited release.

The assets were frozen by Carter Nov. 14, 10 days after the hostages were seized by 450 militants who stormed the U.S. Embassy to protest the hospitalization in New York of the exiled shah. For months, until the shah's death of cancer in July in Cairo, the militants demanded the fallen monarch's return as the price for freedom for the hostages.

More than 90 people initially were taken hostage. Sixty-six were Americans. Thirteen American hostages — women and blacks — were released Nov. 19 and Nov. 20, with Ayatollah Ruhollah Khomeini calling it a victory for oppressed minorities. A 14th hostage, Richard Queen, 23, of New York, who was suffering from multiple sclerosis, was freed July 11 as a "humanitarian gesture" by Khomeini.

Koob Holland

On planes headed for Algeria

The release on inauguration day ended 14½ months of frustration and feelings of helplessness. The hostage seizure inflamed Americans. Iranian students were attacked early in the crisis by enraged Americans and cries for the students' deportation resounded through the country.

Diplomatically, the impasse paralyzed much of U.S. foreign policy and contributed to an image of U.S. impotence. Throughout the drawn-out dilemma, America never got its European allies to go along with complete sanctions against Iran.

The blocking of the assets was one of the earliest steps taken to force a solution. It was followed by U.S-backed condemnation of the hostage-taking at the United Nations and the successful pursuit of a suit at the World Court in the Hague, the Netherlands. The court ruled the Iranian government's backing of the hostage seizure illegal.

But the most dramatic attempt to force a solution was an April 25 military rescue raid that ended in a debacle in the Iranian desert, killing eight American servicemen — burned to death when a helicopter collided with an aircraft. Ironically, the two craft collided as the American commando group was trying to pull out after the mission was called off due to mechanical failure.

The rescue attempt angered the militants who promptly announced they were dispersing the Americans from the Embassy to different sites around Iran. And their wherabouts following the April mission were unknown.

All Monday night, messages flew back between Carter and Deputy Secretary of State Warren Christopher in the go-between capital of Algiers. White House Press Secretary Jody Powell came out to speak to the press five times on the hour-by-hour progress as the clocked ticked away on the Carter presidency.

The crisis, the longest holding of diplomats in modern history, resulted in the largest financial transaction and brought about the only loss of American lives in military action since the Vietnam War. It also caused the first resignation of a U.S. secretary of state, Cyrus Vance, since 1915.

The freed hostages can be expected to be bitter. Richard Queen, the first American hostage to come home from Tehran, has nothing but contempt for many of his captors.

"I never sympathized with their cause, their goals, and I sure as hell will not do that now," Queen said in an exclusive interview with UPI. "I will not be unhappy when that religious government falls to pieces."

The release was won in 10 days of non-stop negotiations conducted through Algeria with Christopher leading the U.S. team and a 30-year-old Moslem revolutionary, Bezhad Nabavi, working on the Iranian side in Tehran.

But the impasse was broken in November by the man who observers long said held the key — Khomeini. He proposed a four-point plan calling for return of the shah's wealth and Iran's frozen assets, a pledge of non-interference in Iran and dropping of claims against Iran resulting from the hostages' seizure.

Analysts say that the Iraq attack on Iran Sept. 22 and the start of the Persian Gulf war forced Iran to settle the crisis. Other observers said the last-minute warning by Carter that they would have to start all over with Reagan turned the tide.

Related stories: Page 11

Telegraph Herald

145th Year, No. 17 | 5 SECTIONS | 36 PAGES | DUBUQUE, IOWA, and EAST DUBUQUE, ILLINOIS | TUESDAY, JANUARY 20, 1981 | 25 cents

weather

PARTLY CLOUDY ...... **Page 11.**

index

digest

POLITICIAN SHOT — Price Daniel Jr., a former Texas House speaker and the son of a former governor, was shot to death at his home Monday night. Police said they believe the 40-year-old politician — a direct descendent of Sam Houston — was "shot more than once" with a .22-caliber rifle. Police said today they would question his wife, who may have witnessed the attack.

Dubuque's KDUB-TV might respond differently the next time authorities come wanting news tapes in light of yesterday's setback in court. .... **Page 5.**

The Dubuque City Council sends back for reworking an ordinance designed to control fencing of stolen property. .... **Page 5.**

The Dubuque school district and its teachers continue arguing their sides before an outside mediator. .... **Page 5.**

The Oelwein, Iowa, hospital is for sale at the same time that plans are made for a major renovation. .... **Page 6.**

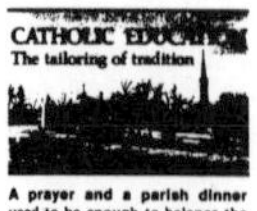

A prayer and a parish dinner used to be enough to balance the budget at small parish schools. But times have changed and so have efforts to raise money for Catholic schools. The third in a five-day series of articles explores the fiscal future of parochial education. .... **Page 9.**

Reagan calls for a 'national renewal'

WASHINGTON (UPI) — President Ronald Reagan, calling for "an era of national renewal," vows to begin trying to solve America's mounting foreign and domestic crises immediately.

"We must act today in order to preserve tomorrow," Reagan said after being inaugurated as the 40th U.S. president. "And let th be no misunderstanding — we are going to act beginning today."

Reagan was inaugurated just before 11 a.m., after George Bush had taken the oath as vice president.

Reagan solemnly intoned the 35-word oath as his left hand rested on the Bible of his mother Nellie. With those words, Reagan, the actor-turned-politician, ended a 13-year quest for the presidency during which he became the national spokesman for a flood of new conservatism.

Within minutes of taking the oath of office "to preserve, protect and defend the Constitution," Reagan took his first action as president, clamping a hiring freeze on federal employment as a first step in his battle to control the inflation that confounded his predecessor.

Reagan and his wife Nancy rode with President Carter up Pennsylvania Avenue from the White House after getting his last briefing as a private citizen on the national nightmare known as "the hostage crisis" — the 444-day-old captivity of 52 Americans released today in Iran.

Thousands lined the parade route as their motorcade passed. Security was tight with police fanning out to the Capitol, the White House and along the "Avenue of Presidents" in between.

Temperatures inched toward the unseasonably warm and spring-like 60-degree mark as the inauguration ceremonies got under way. A crowd estimated at 100,000 looked on, and millions more viewed the ceremony on television.

Justice Warren Burger swears in Ronald Reagan as the 40th president as Nancy Reagan, Sen. Mark Hatfield and former President Carter look on UPI photo

Reagan took pains to thank Carter for "his gracious cooperation in the transition process" and for his help "in maintaining the continuity which is the hallmark of our Republic."

The new president warned his audience the country faces "an economic affliction of great proportions," that "threatens to shatter the lives of millions of our people."

The address had echoes of Reagan on the campaign stump. He blamed big government for most of the country's problems. "We are a nation that has a government — not the other way around," he said.

"It is time to check and reverse the growth of government which shows signs of having grown beyond the consent of the governed," he said, adding that he wants to make the vast, monolithic bureaucracy "work with us, not over us.

"So, with all the creative energy at our command, let us begin an era of national renewal," Reagan said. "Let us renew our determination, our courage, and our strength. Let us renew our faith and our hope.

"We have every right to dream heroic dreams."

The new president also touched a campaign theme in rejecting national pessimism: "We are too great a nation to limit ourseves to small dreams. We are not, as some would have us believe, doomed to an inevitable decline."

Related stories: Page 12

Getting across is their only point

Staff photo by Max Winter

Charlie Mason of McGregor, Iowa, cranks up his scratcher-boat to run Mr. and Mrs. Russ Bernhard to their Prairie du Chien, Wis., bakery.

By Telegraph Herald Staff Writers

The point of all this fuss over a closed Mississippi River bridge hit home this morning when two men almost drowned because they couldn't cross the span from Marquette, Iowa, to Prairie du Chien, Wis.

Authorities feel that people on both sides of the river have done a pretty fair job of coping with the broken connection. But there is fear that amateurish solutions to the problem could take lives before a safe way of getting across the river can be arranged.

The most likely alternative to the bridge appears to be a 51-passenger ferry boat that would ply a narrow channel cut through the ice north or south of the disabled span.

Late this morning, officials from the Wisconsin and Iowa transportation departments and the city of Prairie du Chien were out on the ice, examining the possibility of ferry service from Marquette to a causeway that connects the closed bridge with Prairie du Chien.

Earlier today, Kenneth Galloway, 31, of Fennimore, Wis., and Robert Boss, 27, of Prairie du Chien found themselves inadvertently operating their own ferry service, and it nearly cost them their lives.

About 2 a.m., Galloway and Boss attempted to cross the river ice to Wisconsin from a point near Waukon Junction, Iowa, about 8 miles north of Marquette. They were riding in Galloway's 1972 Volkswagen.

"We was going along pretty good, then we saw open water," Galloway said later. "I couldn't stop. And a few feet before we got to the edge, the ice broke off. That car went right in. There were a few bubbles, and that was it."

Galloway and Boss lunged from the car into the water, grabbed chunks of ice and drifted downstream to an island. "We huddled in the swamp grass and weeds and tried to get warm," Boss said. "I guess we were there about a half-hour." That's when Galloway set out to get help for Boss, who wears an artificial leg.

> ★ ★ ★
> ***Consultant is sought to design bridge fix***
> Story: Page 6

Galloway set out for the Wisconsin shore, but was so disoriented that he walked to the Iowa shore by mistake. Authorities then came to his assistance.

Two rescuers then walked back to the island, each man clutching a blanket so he could pull the other out of the water if the ice broke. They found Boss, built a fire to warm him, and waited for an airboat from Prairie du Chien to pick them up. Galloway and Boss declined offers of medical treatment, authorities said.

The business of crossing the Mississippi went more easily for scores of area residents Monday and today. Many travelers, though, continued to make the trip via a 67-mile detour north across a bridge from Lansing, Iowa, to a point north of Ferryville, Wis.

"It wasn't so bad this morning because it was a beautiful morning," Donna Cipra, a secretary who lives in Wisconsin but works in Marquette, said Monday. "But if I have to drive it every day, I won't like it. Economically, you can't afford to."

Other immediate alternatives included riding atop the ice in airboats, or in flatboats equipped with "scratchers" that chew their way across the surface.

Some people walked, but most dragged small boats behind them with ropes. "I won't let 'em cross if they don't have a boat," Marquette police officer Don Hackett said. "If they don't have something to

Other ways across.
Continued on page 6.

Times-Union/

ROCHESTER, NEW YORK

TIMES-UNION

Tuesday Evening, January 20, 1981   Published by Gannett   25 Cents

2 FULL PAGES INSIDE

They're free!

Reagan says two planes left about 12:30 p.m.

INSIDE

On page 2A:
- ☐ Hostages served Iran's purposes
- ☐ Iranian says his country still wants nothing to do with U.S.
- ☐ Fear eases for Iranians in U.S.
- ☐ Congressional hearings due on protecting American diplomats

On page 3A:
- ☐ For families, worrying to the end
- ☐ Decompression: The pros and cons
- ☐ For ex-hostage, an end to "a special kind of hell"

On page 22A:
- ☐ America ready with parades, prayers
- ☐ Terms of what some describe as the biggest financial transfer in history

THE OATH Ronald Reagan is sworn in as 40th president of the United States today. His wife Nancy held Bible.

The Associated Press

Times-Union wire services

Iran today freed the 52 American hostages on the 444th day of their captivity.

President Reagan told reporters that two Algerian Boeing 727 jetliners took off apparently about a half hour after he was sworn in at noon. He said he was told the first plane left at 12:33 p.m. EST (9:30 p.m. Tehran time) and the second 10 minutes later.

The Iranian news agency Pars also reported the planes were in the air.

In his final briefing as press secretary to President Carter, Jody Powell said said it would take about an hour after the hostages were airborne for the aircraft to clear Iranian territory. He and Reagan spokesman Larry Speakes both said no official announcement would come until that had taken place.

The Americans took off for Algiers on the first

Please turn to back of section

Reagan vows 'national renewal'

By WALTER R. MEARS
The Associated Press

WASHINGTON — Ronald Reagan was inaugurated the 40th president of the United States today, summoning Americans to "an era of national renewal."

At the stroke of noon, power passed from James Earl Carter Jr., Democrat, to Ronald Wilson Reagan, Republican, conservative, veteran of Hollywood, governor of California, overwhelming choice of his countrymen.

Denied a second term, Carter watched as Reagan raised his right hand, put his left on a family Bible and swore the simple, 35-word oath of office. A 21-gun salute boomed out over the Capitol and the marble monuments of American government.

Momenta before, George Bush had taken the almost identical oath of vice presidential office.

"With all the creative energy at our command, let us begin an era of national renewal," Reagan said in his inaugural address. "Let us renew our determination, our courage and our strength. Let us renew our faith and our hope.

We have every right to dream heroic dreams."

Reagan said Americans are entitled, for they are themselves heroes, "you, the citizens of this blessed land.

"Your dreams, your hopes, your goals are going to be the dreams, the hopes and goals of this administration, so help me God."

Reagan's invocation to his new administration began with a pledge to confront and handle "an economic affliction of the worst proportions. We must act today in order to preserve tomorrow. And let there be no misunderstanding — we are going to act beginning today."

The new president said the nation's economic ills "will not go away in days, weeks, or months, but they will go away.

"In this present crisis, government is not the solution; it is the problem," Reagan said, a line sounded day after campaign day in the quest that won him the White House by landslide last Nov. 4.

Reagan said he means to curb the size and influence of the government he now heads. He said he will make government "work with us,

Text of Reagan's speech is on page 12A.

not over us . . . stand by our side, not ride on our back."

He promised to ease the tax burden, restore the balance between various levels of government, promote American enterprise.

"These will be our first priorities and on these principles, there will be no compromise," he said.

And in an era" of renewal at home, Reagan said, the nation will stand abroad as "the exemplar of freedom and a beacon of hope for those who do not now have freedom."

He promised the United States will be a faithful ally to friends, and told potential adversaries that peace is America's highest aspiration. "We will negotiate for it, sacrifice for it; we will not surrender for it — now or ever."

Reagan and forbearance should never be misread as a failure of will. "When action is required to preserve our national security, we will act," he said. "We will maintain sufficient

strength to prevail if need be, knowing that if we do so we have the best chance of not having to use that strength."

For Carter, the path led home, to the political obscurity of Plains, Ga., after a single term and a re-election bid hampered by futile efforts to free the hostages.

For Reagan, it led along the ceremonial route of presidents, from the Capitol 16 blocks down Pennsylvania Avenue to the White House.

On the steps of the Capitol, the monuments to George Washington and Abraham Lincoln before him, Reagan was speaking the simple oath of all his predecessors:

"I do solemnly swear that I will faithfully execute the office of President of the United States, and will, to the best of my ability, preserve, protect and defend the Constitution of the United States."

Chief Justice Warren Burger was to administer the oath, as Reagan placed his left hand on a family Bible that once belonged to his mother, Nelle.

It was open to a verse of Chronicles:

"If my people, which are called by my name, shall humble themselves, and pray, and seek my face, and turn from their wicked ways; then will I hear from heaven, and will forgive their sin, and heal the land."

Justice Potter Stewart was administering the almost identical vice presidential oath to George Bush, once a classmate at Yale University.

By Constitution, presidential power passed from the defeated Carter to the victorious Reagan at the stroke of noon.

A 21-gun salute heralded the Reagan era. Then it was for the new president to speak his goals in a brief inaugural address, delivered from index cards like those that were his trademark as a campaigner.

Reagan wrote it in longhand, on nine pages, much of it as he flew from Washington to Los Angeles on Jan. 8. "The plane landed too soon," Reagan said then. He finished it two days later.

Please turn to back of section

GREATER ROCHESTER

INSIDE

Astrology	15C	Money	4-6D
Bridge	15C	Newswatch	2B
Comics	15C	Sports	1D
Crossword	15C	Television	2, 3C
Deaths	15C	Theaters	6C
Editorial	20A	Want Ads	12C
Food Guide	1C	Word Game	15C

THE WEATHER

Fair tonight, low in the teens. Partly cloudy tomorrow, high 26 to 30. Scattered showers or flurries Thursday through Saturday. (Details on page 4A.)

City property taxes out of whack, T-U finds

FOR WHAT IT'S WORTH
PROPERTY ASSESSMENT

This is the first in a series examining assessment processes in Rochester.

By DOUG MANDELARO and GREG VICTOR
Times-Union

The house at 1117 Park Ave. sold last year for $75,000. The new owner's taxes will be $1,032.

The house at 80 Hamilton St. sold last year for $12,000. The tax on this property also is $1,032.

Why the same tax on property six times the value of another?

The city's tax assessments are up to 50 years old. As a result, hundreds of city property owners pay too much in taxes. And hundreds

of others pay too little.

A month-long *Times-Union* study of city assessment practices showed homes in some of Rochester's poorest neighborhoods, and many in middle income areas, often are assessed at much higher percentages of their property's real worth than homes five or 10 times their purchase price. All houses were purchased within the past 18 months.

FOR INSTANCE, a house at 27 Atkinson St. in the revitalized Corn Hill area sold for about $65,800. At that price, records show, it is assessed at 8 percent of its full value. The annual tax bill is about $930, excluding charges for city refuse collection, water and street clean-

ing and snow removal.

But a $9,000 house at 74 Avenue D, in the Clifford Avenue-Avenue D "conservation district," is assessed at about 47 percent of its full value. That homeowner will pay about $723 in taxes.

How much you pay isn't necessarily a true indicator of whether it's your fair share of the tax burden. The way to compare property assessments is to measure them against the state equalization rate. That's the state's estimate of the difference between the city's average assessed value and the full, or current

Please turn to page 18A

The Washington Star/

A REPORT IN TWO SECTIONS

THE INAUGURATION SPECIAL

1981 SOUVENIR EDITION

Weather
Chance of Rain or Snow Tonight
Cloudy Tomorrow
Low Tonight 31
High Tomorrow 44
See C-2

The Washington Star EXTRA

129th Year No. 20 — The Washington Star Co. Copyright 1981 — WASHINGTON, D.C., TUESDAY, JANUARY 20, 1981 — Phone (202) 484-5000 Classified 484-5000 Circulation 484-3000 — 20 Cents

Inaugural News

TO OUR READERS
The first two sections of today's newspaper are devoted to news relating to the inauguration. Other news can be found beginning in Section AA, the third section.

Hostage News

Reagan Takes Office
Hostages Now Free

Ronald Reagan takes the oath of office as the 40th president of the United States. Chief Justice Warren Burger (right) administers the oath.
The Washington Star Ken Heinen

'Dream Heroic Dreams,' President Urges

Reagan Says The 52 Now 'Free of Iran'

By Walter Taylor and David Wood
Washington Star Staff Writers

President Ronald Reagan announced today that the 52 American hostages were free after 14 months of captivity in Iran.

Reagan's announcement that the hostages "are now free of Iran" came during the inaugural festivities at the Capitol, two hours and 20 minutes after he took the oath as America's 40th president.

At 2:20 p.m. the new president said he had been advised the hostages were now out of Iranian air space on their flight to freedom after 444 days in captivity.

He made the formal announcement at the end of a luncheon celebrating his inauguration on the West Front of the Capitol. It was the "tag line" all have been waiting to hear, the smiling president said as he concluded his luncheon appearance.

Earlier, the Pars news agency in Iran had reported that the two Algerian airliners had taken off at 12:25, but no formal announcement was forthcoming from the new administration until they had cleared Iranian air space. But that time, former President Jimmy Carter had left Washington for Plains, and President Reagan was able to report the happy news.

The official Iranian news agency, Pars, carried an announcement of the departure and said all the hostages were on board.

The planes were to fly to Algiers, but were expected to make a refueling stop en route, probably in Athens, Greece.

Release of the hostages apparently had been timed by the Iranians to
See HOSTAGES, AA-8

Reagan Singles Out 'Economic Affliction'

By Lisa Myers
Washington Star Staff Writer

Pointing to monuments to patriots past, President Reagan today urged Americans to "dream heroic dreams" and summon forth the creative energy needed to restore this country to its true place as the "exemplar of freedom and a beacon of hope."

In a 15-minute speech immediately after he was sworn in as the 40th president of the United States, the former California governor warned that the nation faces "an economic affliction of great proportions" that threatens to "shatter" the lives of millions.

To continue this trend of progress past inflation, unemployment, high taxes and runaway government "is to guarantee tremendous social, cultural, political and economic upheavals," he said.

Yet the president stopped short of declaring a national emergency. He quoted the words of Dr. Joseph Warren, a Massachusetts patriot who gave his life on Beacon Hill: "Our country is in danger, but not to be despaired of. . . . On you depend the fortunes of America."

And paraphrasing Winston Churchill, Reagan added, "I did not take the oath I have just taken with the intention of presiding over the dissolution of the world's strongest economy."

The priority placed on economic matters was reflected in their dominance of the speech, which Reagan wrote largely himself. Only four paragraphs of the five-page text concerned international affairs. And, even then, America's position in the world was tied to domestic prosperity.

"As we renew ourselves here in our own land, we will be seen as having greater strength throughout the world," Reagan said. "We will again be the exemplar of freedom and a beacon of hope for those who do not now have freedom."

While declaring peace the highest aspiration of the nation, the president cautioned that "our reluctance for conflict should not be misjudged as a failure of will."

To return America to its rightful place economically and internationally, Reagan called for an "era of national renewal" — a renewal of determination, courage, strength, faith and hope. "We are too great a nation to limit ourselves to small dreams," he said. "We have every right to dream heroic dreams."

Just as he challenged the notion that America is doomed to an inevitable decline, Reagan scolded those who mourn the absence of modern-day heroes. The heroes, he said, are "you, the citizens of this blessed land."

"Your dreams, your hopes, your goals are going to be the dreams, the hopes and goals of this administration," he vowed, "so help me God." Reagan also vowed to do his part by carrying out the campaign promises on which he was elected. "It is no coincidence that our present
See DREAM, A-22

Text of speech, A-6

He Freezes Hiring as First Act

By Lyle Denniston and Phil Gailey
Washington Star Staff Writers

Symbolically facing West and the shrines to the nation's giants, Ronald Wilson Reagan became the nation's 40th president today — three minutes early.

Promising, in a solemn but not stern inaugural address, to "act today in order to preserve tomorrow," Reagan urged Americans to "dream heroic dreams."

True to his vow to start acting immediately, he went into the Capitol after the ceremony and signed an order putting a freeze on any new hiring for government jobs.

The transfer of power took place on the West Front of the Capitol, a break with tradition that illustrated Reagan's call for "an era of national renewal" and symbolized the political shift that had brought a landslide victory for the conservative Californian and favorite son of the Sun Belt.

Even as Reagan walked onto the podium, reports circulated that the American hostages in Iran had at last begun their long journey to freedom.

Reagan, who said later he was informed of their departure from Tehran just after the inaugural ceremony was over, announced the hostages' freedom at a congressional luncheon inside the Capitol.

The new president, given his oath by Chief Justice Warren E. Burger at 11:57 a.m., did not mention the hostages in his 20-minute speech. He did vow, however, to marshal the nation's "moral courage" against "those who practice terrorism and prey upon their neighbors."

Reagan's moment of triumphal en-
See INAUGURAL, A-22

Cheers Greet New President At Swearing-In

By Marc Kaufman
Washington Star Staff Writer

To the call of 14 Marine Corps Band trumpets and the cheers of the assembled thousands, Ronald Reagan marched smiling today onto his inaugural platform.

The joyous crowd — heady with delight over his assumption of the presidency and the almost simultaneous release of the hostages — could hardly contain its enthusiasm.

Even outgoing President Jimmy Carter, elegant in his formal wear, appeared to have an easiness to his manner.

The day was warm, the guests were glittering in their affluence and formality, the vista from the Capitol's West Front was spectacular, and most seemed to believe — as Reagan had long promised — that America was about to start on "a new beginning."

And so when Ronald Reagan was finally sworn in at noon, with his hand on his mother Nellie's old Bible, a wild cheer rang out from the dignified crowd.

A most unlikely spokesman, pop artist Andy Warhol, seemed to sum up the feeling by saying, "Gee, this is the most beautiful day in the world."

Happy thoughts also came from the likes of the Rev. Jerry Falwell.
See GOP, A-22

The President and Mrs. Reagan embrace at the end of inaugural ceremonies.
The Washington Star Ken Heinen

INDEX

Ear	B 1
Editorials	AA 5
Features	C 12
Garmond & Wetcover	AA 3
Horoscope	B 11
Local News	C 1
OLIPHANT ON AA 7	
Movies	C 11
Bridge	C 13
Obituaries	C 11
Business	D 5
Sports	D 1
Classified	B 12
Today's People	A 4
TV	C 1
Column	C 12
Washington	
Comics	C 12
Calendar	AA 4
Crossword	C 12
Life	C 1
Dear Abby	B 10
Weather	C 2

Lottery Number on D-4
Pr UZZLE $500 — B-16

Chapter 10/

Notes/

Notes/

Notes/

Notes/

Notes/

The design of this book follows
Minneapolis Tribune style in most
basic details. Helvetica type is used,
as on Tribune special section covers.
Type is set 12.5 picas, the normal
Tribune column width. Type size is 9
point on 9.5, conforming to Tribune
style and reflecting the Tribune grid.
The flush-left principle is followed.
Graphics illustrating Tribune design
style are shown full size or reduced
50 percent.